AF333499

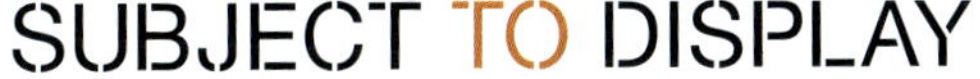
SUBJECT TO DISPLAY

THE MIT PRESS   CAMBRIDGE, MASSACHUSETTS   LONDON, ENGLAND

SUBJECT TO DISPLAY

Reframing Race in Contemporary Installation Art

JENNIFER A. GONZÁLEZ

MIT Press books may be purchased at special quantity discounts for business or sales promotional use. For information, please email special_sales@mitpress.mit.edu or write to Special Sales Department, The MIT Press, 55 Hayward Street, Cambridge, MA 02142.

This book was set in Chaparral by The MIT Press. Printed and bound in Spain.

Publication of this book has been aided by a grant from the Wyeth Foundation for American Art Publication Fund of the College Art Association.

Library of Congress Cataloging-in-Publication Data

González, Jennifer A.
Subject to display : reframing race in contemporary installation art / Jennifer A. González.
    p. cm.
Includes bibliographical references and index.
ISBN 978-0-262-07286-1 (hardcover : alk. paper)
1. Installations (Art)—United States. 2. Art, American—20th century. 3. Art, American—21st century. 4. Minority artists—United States. 5. Race in art. I. Title.

N6512.5.I56G66 2007
709.73'09049—dc22   2006036344

10 9 8 7 6 5 4 3 2 1

FOR WARREN

CONTENTS

ILLUSTRATIONS

I started pursuing the ideas in this book nearly a decade ago, and the final product has been supported by individuals too numerous to mention comprehensively. Some colleagues were instrumental in the beginning; others contributed important insights near the end. I am grateful to Jon Beller, Maurice Berger, Lisa Bloom, Victor Burgin, Kathleen Caruso, Kathy Checkovitch, Ron Clark, Jim Clifford, Roger Conover, Karen Mary Davalos, Teresa De Lauretis, Angela Davis, Coco Fusco, Kirsten González, Anne Harley, Amelie Hastie, Loie Hayes, Stephen Heath, Ellen Fernandez-Sacco, Esther Kaplan, Mary Kelly, Grant Kester, Pamela Lee, Sarah Lookofsky, David Marriot, Kobena Mercer, Naomi Mezey, Chon Noriega, Kate Ramsey, Lisa Rofel, Tere Romo, Warren Sack, Vivian Sobchack, Bernice Steinbaum, Neferti Tadiar, Anna Tsing, Hayden White, Brian Wolf, and Tomás Ybarra-Frausto, who offered a range of intellectual, editorial, or moral support and important critical observations along the way. I would also like to thank my research assistants Robert Martinez, Krista Lynes, and Raissa Burns, who were extremely helpful.

Grants in support of research for the book include the University of California President's Fellowship in the Humanities, the American Council of Learned Societies Junior Fellowship, and several annual grants from the UCSC Senate Committee on Research, and the UCSC Arts Division Committee on Research. I would also like to thank the History of Art and Visual Culture Department and the Institute for Advanced Feminist Research at UCSC for additional research assistance. The Joanne Cassullo fellowship at the Whitney Museum Independent Study Program provided the valuable opportunity for research time in New York. Substantial publication grants from the Andrew Wyeth Foundation for American Art and the UCSC Arts Research Institute provided the funds necessary to include full color reproductions, for which I am especially grateful.

I am indebted to the artists and their assistants who were generous with their time, resources, and critical engagement. Thanks are also due to the museums and galleries for supplying images and additional archival information.

I want to express my deep gratitude to the members of my extended family, who have been patient, supportive, and encouraging with warmth and good humor: Kirsten and Crispin González, Consuelo González, Richard Middleton, Karl Crispin Dyer, Ronald and Margaret Sack, and Leslie Sack. Finally, I owe a great debt to my life partner, Warren Sack, for his extraordinary, loving support and my son, Felix, who graciously shared his first two years with the preparation of this book.

INTRODUCTION
SUBJECT TO DISPLAY

ACKNOWLEDGMENTS

IN 1992 THE INSTALLATION artist Fred Wilson staged
a rare, satirical performance for a group of docents at
the Whitney Museum of American Art in New York.
After greeting his small audience, he arranged to meet
them in an upstairs gallery where he was ostensibly to
give them a tour of the ongoing exhibition. The artist
then disappeared, quickly changed into a uniform worn
by the museum security guards, quietly took up a post
in the appointed gallery, and remained silent when his
audience arrived. The docents wandered the galleries
looking for the artist they had met only moments earlier, but he was no longer visible to them, no longer part
of their world. He had become an anonymous man, an
invisible man, a black man like many of the other guards
working the museum floor. When Wilson revealed himself to the docents, they responded with surprise and
a little embarrassment that they had walked past him
more than once without recognizing him.[1] *My Life As
a Dog,* as the performance was titled, demonstrated to
both the docents and the artist the race-specific framing
effect of the museum where "black" bodies are visible if
they appear in works of art, or in the midst of a generally
"white" museum-going public, but are effectively invisible as part of the staff. The performance embodied Wilson's critical insight into the numerous ways museums
create visual regimes that support cultural, racial, and
class hierarchies, even at the most banal levels, and was
no doubt inspired by the years the artist spent as a staff
member and educator at art institutions in and around
New York City including the Metropolitan Museum of
Art and the Museum of Natural History. Through daily
encounters within the space of public museums, Wilson
observed the forms of decision making that comprise

curatorial practice and became acutely aware of the ideological structures that inform the institutional displays of art, artifacts, and people that are consequently rendered both visible and invisible.

Over the past two decades, artists working in the United States have addressed the social, historical, and even aesthetic frameworks through which subject formation transpires in relation to race discourse, extending methods inherited from conceptual art to produce innovations in installation art. Their works have drawn attention to the fact that the collection and display of bodies, images, and artifacts is a primary means by which a nation tells the story of its past and locates the cultures of its citizens in the present. James Luna, Fred Wilson, Amalia Mesa-Bains, Pepón Osorio, and Renée Green have each offered a critical articulation of the history and persistence of race as a form of visual hegemony. Although each artist relies upon individual exhibition methods, and each addresses a unique set of cultural concerns, important parallels exist among them. Formally, they share materialist display techniques, building room-sized installations and public art projects structured around the twin logics of the artifact and the archive. Conceptually, their works are committed to unearthing the complex social relations that have defined membership in communities, rights to citizenship, and the material conditions of subject formation in the United States and across its borders.

I have chosen to focus on U.S. artists, not because I wish to limit my analysis to an artificially narrow concept of the nation, but because together these artists reveal a breadth of concerns that pertain to the history of race in the United States. Brought together here, the artworks echo and reinforce a critical approach to the landscape of cultural difference that defines Latino, African American, and Native American subjects at the turn of the twenty-first century as part of a broader interest in the intersection of historical colonialism, race dominance, and visual culture. Moreover, these works have had a transformative impact on contemporary "American" art, changing the framework for understanding what that category comprises. All five artists are of U.S. territorial origin and produce works largely pertaining to the United States, but they have also worked internationally, examining the social and political inequities that are shared by diverse immigrant, colonial, and postcolonial cultures. This transnational aspect is made explicit in many of the artworks and effectively comes to serve as evidence that the United States, as a nation, a concept, an ideology, has always been defined by permeability and heterogeneity around its borders and across the body of its population. Indeed, the work of these artists reveals the fact that the "nation" is not a stable concept with a stable location or a clearly defined subject-citizen. In this respect, that is, in its destabilizing efforts, the work is an important form of antifoundational U.S.-specific art practice.[2]

Race Discourse and the Logic of Display: "Epidermalization" and the Object

What is *race discourse*? For the purposes of this book, it can be understood as the intricate intersection of philosophies, regimes of representation, and systems of enforcement that work in concert to define human beings as racial types. I take my conception of race as a discursive formation from the thinking of Stuart Hall, who has argued that race is best understood as a discourse constructed by thought and language that responds to concrete conditions of cultural difference.[3] It is that long history of pseudoscience, eugenics, and image production that invents categories and hierarchies of people based on physical and cultural attributes. It is both the invention of the concept of "race" and its popular perpetuation. Michael Omi and Howard Winant suggest that the idea of racial *formation* offers a way to understand this social phenomenon.[4] Racial formation is the process by which designations of race are created and manipulated historically. Racial formation can be found in both small moments (microlevels) of racist encounter and in systemic (macro-level) epistemological approaches to both cultural and ontological understandings of human beings. It is that which underlies conceptions of cultural difference understood as absolute Otherness. It is that pattern of social reasoning that both formed and followed from the practices of enslavement and the economic pursuits of colonialism. Race as a discursive formation is that which is currently used—particularly through the denial of its existence—to perpetuate forms of social dominance and material disenfranchisement.

Arguing that race is a discursive formation, rather than an essential, biological, or ontological category, entails recognizing that the concept necessarily changes with the shifting currents of culture and language, techniques and methods of representation, and scientific imperatives. Recognizing that race is a social construct rather than a biological fact does not imply, however, that the stakes in the contest over its meaning have decreased. For the most part, the meaning of race has left the realm of science behind (despite recent efforts to revive genetic typologies) but has continued as an intensified struggle, familiar in the arts, over the politics of representation. Race discourse *is* the politics of representation (in museums, art, literature, popular culture, music, film, journalism, and other media) that insists on presenting people as "racialized" subjects. Race discourse can thus be understood as the process or experience of *subjection* through which people are transformed into signs of culturally preconstituted subject positions. Judith Butler offers a useful summary of Michel Foucault's concept of subjection, which is "literally, the making of a subject, the principles of regulation according to which a subject is formulated or produced. This notion of subjection is a kind of power that not only unilaterally *acts on* a given individual as a form of domination, but also *activates* or forms the subject."[5] Race discourse *produces* the subject it supposedly describes.

This is also Paul Gilroy's complaint in *Against Race,* where he argues for a rejection of the concept of race as an organizing principle altogether, for either cultural or political forms of emancipation. The persistence of the concept of race, according to Gilroy, signals a regressive, colonialist taxonomy that masquerades as a progressive multiculturalism. For Gilroy, race as a framework of social understanding maps biopolitics onto an essentialized body "of color" and is used to support either "clockwork" forms of racial solidarity or marketing strategies for advanced capitalism.[6] I find Gilroy's criticisms of the term *race* and its current uses convincing. My goal here is not to perpetuate a simple use of race as an organizing device, but rather to demonstrate how the artists find ways to undermine race discourse and its colonialist logic, its systems of power, its discourse of visibility. In other words, I see the work of the artists here joining with Gilroy by participating in a parallel critique of the idea of race and its inherent flaws.

Many histories of race provide compelling accounts of its discursive origins, its modes of enforcement, its currency at the contemporary moment, and the necessity for its rethinking.[7] A number of publications have also specifically addressed the visual culture of race discourse, whether in the form of histories of photography that trace the origins of its role in the perpetuation of the science of eugenics or in studies of much earlier forms of racial typologies such as those found in the eighteenth-century *casta* paintings of New Spain.[8] Books such as Coco Fusco's *English Is Broken Here,* bell hooks's *Black Looks: Race and Representation,* Darby English's *How to See a Work of Art in Total Darkness,* and the anthologies *Unthinking Eurocentrism: Multiculturalism and the Media, Race-ing Art History,* and *Shades of Black: Assembling Black Arts in 1980s Britain,* among many others, have argued persuasively for the significance of visual culture and the visual arts in the production, perpetuation, and critique of race discourse.[9] It is not my purpose to rehearse these arguments here. Nevertheless, I want to draw attention to fact that most of the analyses focus on images of human bodies and their deployment in different media from painting to photography to performance. The body is the site where race discourse is seen to play out because it is where race is presumed to reside. As an artifact of cultural framing, the human body is the object that must always display its signs. There is no escape from the fact of its "epidermalized" status; the materiality of the body is understood to offer a continuous surface of legible information. The "raced" body, as generations of theorists have argued, is a reified body, a body that has become an object in the process of becoming a subject.[10] As Stuart Hall points out, in the epidermalization of the racial look described by Franz Fanon, "exclusion and abjection are imprinted on the body through the functioning of these signifiers as an objective taxonomy—a 'taxidermy'—of radicalized difference; a specular matrix of intelligibility."[11]

The concept and lived experience of race are thus entwined in a discourse of visibility that enables subsequent forms of hierarchy or oppression to become naturalized, that enables membership in communities to be established, and that facilitates the process by which categorical distinctions become unwritten laws. One might say that race discourse is what emerges when a particular kind of visual attraction or visual revulsion meets a particular kind of body and the desire to see that body as black or white or brown overwhelms other elements of vision. In *Against Race* Paul Gilroy notes that the "cognition of 'race' was never an exclusively linguistic process and involved from its inception a distinctive visual and optical imaginary. The sheer plenitude of racialized images and icons communicates something about the forms of difference these discourses summoned into being."[12] Race discourse, in all is historical complexity, is not reducible to visuality; visual representation is merely one of the most powerful techniques by which it operates and is maintained as evident and *self-evident*. Subjected to these techniques, the human body becomes itself a form of material evidence of social and historical events.

The visual discourse of race involves a conceptual and categorical slippage between the body as object and the body as subject. A parallel slippage occurs when the material culture of everyday life, such as artifacts collected in museums of art and anthropology or forms of commodity production and consumption, participate in the construction of race discourse by supporting processes of subjection. Objects come to stand in for subjects not merely in the form of the commodity fetish, but as part of a larger system of material and image culture that circulates as a prosthesis of race discourse through practices of collection, exchange, and exhibition. Annie E. Coombes, in her book *Reinventing Africa: Museums, Material Culture and Popular Imagination,* examines the role of museums in creating the "spectacle of empire" in Britain, demonstrating the ideological parallels between exhibition taxonomies and racial taxonomies. She writes, "Because of the concentration on the relation of physical 'evidence' to mental and inherited characteristics, the association of the body of the African with displays of material culture did much to encourage the popular conflation of living Africans with inert 'specimens.'"[13]

Just as living humans can be conflated with material culture, so material culture can acquire the racial status of humans. Objects, in other words, can become *epidermalized.* The process of epidermalization is one in which the object is positioned in history, in a collection, in the marketplace, or in a museum display as racially defined. This process can be observed in obvious examples, such as mass produced caricatures (black Sambos or mammies) that are designed to perpetuate a visual culture of race hierarchy, and in less obvious examples, such as pre-Columbian clay sculptures or African masks that are exhibited differently from European material culture in fine art museums. Scholars in material culture studies have begun to explore this concern, and a wealth of material culture analysis concerning how *things* mean has emerged since the late 1980s in museum studies, archeology and art history.[14] The artists discussed here bring their audiences into a novel relationship with material culture to suggest the role it plays in the construction and maintenance of race discourse via institutional systems of production and circulation. The resulting installations become spaces of historical and cultural analysis that rely upon the social legibility of the artifacts that the artist chooses to exhibit as well as their rhetorical placement within a discourse of display.

In this context, it is possible to see how race discourse produces an economy of visibility—and simultaneous invisibility—by which group members are subject to a disciplinary gaze that operates to fix their position within a given social or political landscape through techniques of exhibition (in museums, on the street, on the screen, etc.). For Coombes and the artists discussed here, however, the human body is only one of many signs that work to guarantee the status of the subject—other artifacts and display strategies work in concert to produce this subject as a raced subject. Scholar Beth Coleman has suggested that race be conceived of as a set of techniques or a technology.[15] Following her insight, I would argue that elements of race discourse can be best understood as a *visual* technology comprising a complex web of intertextual mechanisms that tie the present to the past through familiar representational tropes. If the body is the site of disgust or affect because of its phenotype or color, this is also only because it is part of a broad iconographic history that serves as a reservoir of circulating signs for this purpose.

This intertextuality guarantees that race discourse is never just about race; it is also always about gender, class, and geography. Race is written on the bodies of men and women differently and has varied consequences for working-class and bourgeois subjects. When bodies and subjects are caught in the web of race discourse, they are also physically regulated by it, whether through architectural forms of segregation such as those developed in the "separate but equal" apartheid era in the United States of "colored" and "white" restaurants, hotels, and schools, or through less explicit forms of voluntary and involuntary ghettoizing in cities and suburbs, shopping malls and museums. Race discourse and its logics of display create rules of inclusion and exclusion, where being black or white can also mean being out of *place*. In her book *Terra Infirma: Geography's Visual Culture*, Irit Rogoff follows Rosalyn Deutsche in arguing that feminist artists "facilitate a recognition—through spatialization, geographization, and location—of the constitutive dimensions of disavowed difference. Such a recognition subsequently permits difference to be re-positioned in the world via a manipulation of an ocular/spectatorial regime."[16] Rogoff suggests that this artistic manipulation actively *genders* public space through its linguistic confrontations and unexpected demands on viewers. The same can be said for artists working to articulate the spatial and ocular regimes of racial difference and their necessary intersection. Those who have experienced racism recognize just how much the situation, scene, or visual and material topography determines the racial legibility of bodies. To stand out in a crowd can be dangerous; to cross into hostile territory can be lethal. Race discourse thus contributes to intricate visual/spatial imaginaries that have real-life consequences. By turning to installation art, the artists considered here take up this visual/spatial imaginary directly in order to map—and to remap—its topography.

Situating the Subject of Installation Art

The term *installation art* has been used increasingly since the 1960s to denote temporary, site-specific art works designed to surround or interact with the spectator and/or extant architecture in a given exhibition space.[17] Formal and conceptual precedents are most often traced to Dadaist or surrealist exhibitions of the early twentieth century or to the environments and happenings of the late 1950s and early 1960s when artists in Latin America, Japan, Western Europe, and the United States sought to redefine the role and function of the work of art, rejecting the formalist paradigms and market-oriented production governing more traditional media, such as easel painting, to embrace the possibilities that ephemeral materials and staged performances could offer.[18] The resulting installations followed at least two different, although not necessarily mutually exclusive, trajectories in their conception of space and spatial practice: one that explored the idea of space as a set of formal conditions to be manipulated by the artist and another that addressed space as a social construct.

For example, Jennifer Licht's catalog essay from the Museum of Modern Art exhibition *Spaces* of 1969 suggests that installation art, or what was then still called "environment art," redefines the spatial condition of art's reception. "In effect," Licht writes, "one now enters the interior space of the work of art . . . and is presented with a set of conditions rather than a finite object. Working within the almost unlimited potential of these enlarged, more spatially complex circumstances, the artist is now free to influence and determine, even govern, the sensations of the viewer. The human presence and perception of the spatial context have become materials of art."[19] Licht's view emphasized the phenomenological focus of much early environment art that sought to engage the viewer with the physicality of the exhibition space, in which, as she suggests, human presence becomes an active ingredient in the work of art. Her observations parallel those of Allan Kaprow, who saw environment art as indebted to the heritage of painting in its concern for color, space, surface, and the disruption or questioning of the "field" of representation. For Kaprow, visitors to his environments and happenings were more than spectators; they were also to be seen as dynamic formal elements in the work itself, as colored shapes in motion that could add to the overall composition.[20] Both Licht and Kaprow understood the art audience to provide essential material for the artwork—whether in the form of perceptions or bodies—and both saw exhibition space primarily as a system of formal constraints within which an artist might produce new forms of sensory experience. It is possible to see how these two views might have developed directly out of the logic of abstraction—in both painting and sculpture—that had dominated art practice of the 1940s and 1950s.

For others exploring the possibilities of installation art, the space of art's production was to be understood primarily as constrained by a set of social conditions. A significant inspiration for this new approach to art making were the social movements—student protests, civil rights and feminist movements—that sought to overturn the political and artistic institutions of the time. Emphasizing or reproducing the field of art's signification in the work itself, environments (and later installations) disrupted the traditional semiotic and somatic boundaries assumed to exist among the audience, the work of art, the site of exhibition, and the world beyond. As early as 1958, the Situationist International redefined art practice as the creation of a situation, a moment of life concretely and deliberately constructed, or in some cases, a psycho-geographical study of the effects of the social and political environment on the behavior of individual subjects.[21] An analog of this approach can be found in Victor Burgin's 1969 essay "Situational Aesthetics," which argues for a new way of reading the concerns of conceptual, temporary, and site-specific or event-specific works of art.[22] By recognizing art production as an intervention in a continuous perceptual field, the artist may be less inclined to create new material forms, Burgin suggests, than to coordinate or reorganize existing forms.[23] The term "situational aesthetics" appears again— more narrowly defined—in the writings of Michael Asher, who uses the concept to describe an aesthetic system that reorganizes predetermined elements found within an institutional framework (such as a museum or library). Such signs or elements are extracted from a familiar discourse— recognizable and identifiable by the public because they are drawn from the local context itself—and placed in a new arrangement.[24]

The art installations considered here take part in a situational aesthetics to the degree that they recontextualize existing social institutions and de-emphasize production of new objects in favor of sampling and reorganizing found elements. Following this logic, such works also decenter the eye, or the "I," of the spectator who is no longer located in the transcendental role of solitary contemplation vis-à-vis the work of art, but is rather positioned as a culturally situated subject who both constitutes, and is constituted by, the work of art.

In her book *Installation Art: A Critical History,* Claire Bishop argues that each form of installation art has been designed to produce different experiences, and moreover that each modality of experience implies a different model of the viewing subject.[25] Bishop offers four examples of this viewing subject and the kind of installation art designed for each: the psychoanalytic subject (who is plunged into dreamlike environments), the phenomenological subject (who experiences space through the body's perceptions), the disintegrated or disoriented subject (who is engulfed or overwhelmed by the installation), and the political subject (who is imagined as an actor in a political social sphere).[26] Her approach emphasizes European and U.S. installation art produced primarily between 1965 and 1975, but she also mentions more recent works including Fred Wilson's *Mining the Museum* of 1992. At the same time, Bishop carefully defines the scope of her project within clear cultural parameters. As a kind of disclaimer she writes, "In order to keep this book focused on one aspect of installation, its viewing subject, there is no discussion of the work of those non-western artists whose desire to immerse or activate the viewer springs from different traditions."[27]

Certain parallels are evident in our approach, since Bishop and I are both interested in examining how viewing subjects are engaged by installation art. Because I am writing about U.S. artists who are trained in a Western (European) tradition in art schools, but who sometimes choose to include cultural traditions and references that extend beyond this training, it is not possible to limit my analytical framework with categorical distinctions such as "Western" or "non-Western." Indeed, these terms lose their salience altogether. Moreover, I am interested in how the process of *subjection* itself becomes the focus for installation art. Many of the installations I examine here take the political subject as a given, yet also offer dreamlike or disorienting environments in order to invite the viewer to identify (or disidentify) with a specific subject position.

The activity of the artists discussed here can be understood to employ a radical or critical situational aesthetics concerned with exploring how public and private spaces are imbedded with the history of race discourse and related forms of subjection. They do so by recreating or infiltrating public spaces such as museums, prisons, libraries, and barbershops, or intimate spaces such as bedrooms, living rooms, and boudoirs, in order to articulate those signs and spaces that play a central role in the process of subjection—both in constraining the social definition of the subject and the constitutive forms of its possibility. In this respect, the art installations are effectively environmental microcosms, three-dimensional representations that have a metonymic relation to the social spaces they mimic and critique. The work of a previous generation of installation artists including Edward Keinholz and Marcel Broodthaers employed a pseudorealist aesthetic to create artificial environments in order to comment on real-world spaces. The artists discussed here extend this tradition by attending to the historical materiality of the objects they present in their displays; in other words, they care about where the objects came from, who created them, who owned them, who bought or sold them, how they were stored, how they were collected, how they were marketed, how they were (or are) used in different cultural traditions, and how they were (or are) part of a given cultural hegemony. When human bodies appear in the installations, they do so through a mediating frame that recalls the forms of carefully choreographed display found in the theater, the cinema, the museum, or spaces of commerce. More commonly there is no body on display in these installations, but rather the objects that attest to its presence: the rooms it occupies, the furniture it inhabits, the trinkets that adorn it, the photographs that mirror it, the clothing left behind. We are invited to imagine the missing body that is overdetermined by the objects used to signify its absence, or we are occasionally invited to take up the position of the missing body ourselves. The objects in the installations therefore function not only as metaphorical signs but also as indexical links to a larger social history of people and things. In turn, this social history of things is shown to "situate" human subjects, to contribute to the processes of their subject formation and/or subjection. Installation art offers the frame to examine these processes and sometimes becomes the site for their critical restaging.

Paradoxically, but not surprisingly, racial stereotypes and reactionary conceptions of ethnicity recur as a focus of the artworks. Reflecting on the ways in which language socially positions individual subjects Judith Butler writes, "It is not a question of an opposition between a reactionary and progressive usage; it is rather a function of the progressive usage requiring and repeating the reactionary in order to effect a subversive reterritorialization."[28] In other words, it is necessary to acknowledge and articulate the position in which one is already fixed by systems of power before one can resist and oppose its terms. Legacies of colonialism, uneven power relations, the politics of gender, and the opacity of history are all primary themes explored in these works that touch on Puerto Rican, Chicano, African American, and indigenous American cultures. The effort to revisit, to revise, and to critique race discourse, whether directly or indirectly, also means that the artists frequently engage the very images and stereotypes they wish to transform. By staging what might be called *spaces of subjection* with material artifacts, the artists here enact a deterritorialization and reterritorialization of the signs that guarantee the limits and contours, the narratives and histories, of race discourse.

Neither "Identity" nor "Ethnography"

One goal of this book is to demonstrate that the artwork presented here is better understood without recourse to the loaded concepts of *identity* or *ethnography*. In contemporary criticism and scholarship, to say that a work of art is about "identity" frequently implies that its primary purpose is to "represent" a specific cultural, racial, or gender identity, or that it is the artist's own identity that is in question or under analysis. Many recent textbooks and anthologies on modern and contemporary art contain a chapter or section about "identity" that serves as a convenient category for work by women artists, queer artists, and artists of color. While some contemporary artists have consciously made "identity" a focus of their work, most who are subsumed by this category actually focus on other topics such as colonialism, patriarchy, racism, or homophobia. By focusing on the notion of identity as a valorizing representation of the "self," many scholars ignore the possibility that the artworks in question might be intended to *dismantle* categories of identity, to reject essentialist notions of ethnicity, to destabilize typologies of containment. In fact works by the artists discussed here interrogate precisely the conditions under which monolithic categories of identity—such as "primitive," "black," or "Latino"—have been created and sustained.

Of course, as with any concept, there have been productive uses of the term *identity* as well.[29] Especially noteworthy are the writings of Stuart Hall who has perhaps done the most to successfully articulate the progressive possibilities and pitfalls of the concept of identity and the complex histories of identification that work through it. He recognizes the importance of the politically necessary (but narrowly essential and homogenizing) first wave of antiracist celebrations of cultural difference and identity that began in the post–civil rights era.[30] In contrast to this early phase, Hall articulates the emergence in the late twentieth century of what he calls "new ethnicities" that "are composed of multiple social identities, not of one."[31] Kobena Mercer echoes these sentiments in his essay "Black Art and the Burden of Representation," which examines the stakes for artists whose work deals with questions of subjectivity and race. In it he critiques the way race and class are conceived in reductive ways, and the hegemony of "ethnic absolutism" by which complex subjectivities are reduced to essentialist identities on both the political right and left.[32]

It is possible to imagine how mainstream art criticism, when faced with new and unfamiliar forms of cultural difference in contemporary art, became trapped by an inherited essentialist identity politics, despite the fact that the artists who were subject to this kind of reading had long since abandoned these narrow categorical frameworks. Craig Owens saw the danger in this situation, arguing that it is precisely in being represented by the dominant culture that marginalized groups have been "rendered absences" within it. He suggests that artists who take up a critical position in opposition to these representations do not seek the fallacy of the "positive" image; rather, "these artists challenge the activity of representation itself which, by denying them speech, consciousness, the ability to represent themselves, stands indicted as the primary agent of their domination."[33] All of these writers saw the potential merits and inherent dangers of working with concepts of "identity" in relation to social domination and representation in the early 1990s.

In his 1996 essay "The Artist as Ethnographer," Hal Foster took an equally cautionary turn away from simple concepts of identity, to suggest that new site-specific art concerned with questions of cultural specificity be read as a kind of ethnographic practice. Although his essay like those mentioned previously was published more than a decade ago, its terms are still in circulation and therefore deserve to be revisited. Foster began by noting conceptual and methodological parallels shared by anthropology and the fine arts.[34] As his essay rightly points out, this liaison is not new to twentieth-century art; the activities of ethnographers have been closely linked with modern artists in a "primitivist" tradition for decades. The narrative that Foster constructs for contemporary art is more problematic. He claims that anthropologists and ethnographers have been led by a kind of artist-envy to turn to literary modes of analysis, and that artists have been inspired by a parallel ethnographer-envy to adopt a culturally specific, self-critical, contextualizing analysis as a model for artistic production.[35] Unlike previous primitivist and anthropological tendencies (Foster cites surrealism, art brut, abstract expressionism, earthworks, and even conceptual examples), this newer kind of artistic ethnographer-envy is seen to utilize incompatible modes of analysis and representation, resulting ultimately in a realist misrepresentation and distancing of the cultural Other *as other*. In short, Foster's essay forms a dialectic around the problem of cultural difference that first warns against naïve and romantic fantasies about "the Other" projected onto subaltern populations, then warns against an equally naïve essentialist celebration of cultural difference from within those subaltern populations, and then concludes with a safely ambivalent admonition against over-identification with, or disidentification with, cultural Others.[36]

There is a definite merit to this dialectic, but it is important to ask not only who identifies *with* the Other but also who counts as Other, who is allowed to make representations of this Other, and who has the authority to enforce these representations. Ludmilla Jordonova has written, "Because self and other are mutually constitutive, identification and objectification go hand in hand. Otherness is as much about the construction of oneself, as it is about creating distance. Indeed the sense of distance is generally made, manufactured, and then treated as if found, discovered, as if in other words, it was a natural object rather than a social construction."[37]

Foster locates a broad spectrum of art practice under the rubric of *eth-nography*. Works by artists James Luna and Jimmie Durham are seen to challenge stereotypes through self-conscious parody.[38] Fred Wilson and Renée Green are also cited for their innovative works, but Foster warns that the *"quasi-anthropological role set up for the artist can promote a pre-suming as much as a questioning of ethnographic authority, an evasion as often as an extension of institutional critique"* (italics in original).[39] Foster's essay is helpful to the degree that it cautions against simplistic realisms or fantasies of "authentic Otherness," but it also reduces a wide variety of complex art practices to the limits of ethnography, subtly evacuating the political dimension of the work. This conceptual frame becomes problem-atic when an explicit *critique* of colonial ethnographic and anthropologi-cal discourse is central to much of the artwork, as we will see.[40] The artists discussed here certainly do not claim to be ethnographers, nor do they pretend to represent entire ethnic communities. Part of their working process may involve conversations and interviews, but their work is not a form of fieldwork, nor are they engaged in primarily documentary proj-ects. Instead, each artist explores ethnicity and race as a shifting cultural construct that operates through material and visual culture to define and delimit subjectivity.

When viewed as a representation of identity or as a form of ethnographic realism, the artwork is generally reduced to the status of an *additive* rather than *critical* intervention. In other words, both readings tend to disregard the possibility that the artwork serves as a metadiscursive critique of systems of representation, emphasizing instead the ways in which the art offers views of an Other culture or Other perspective, not commonly seen in the white mainstream art world. The difficulty experi-enced by those scholars and critics who encounter cultural difference only *through* a work of art is evident in the concluding section of Foster's essay when he writes that artists using an ethnographic method "work *horizon-tally,* in a synchronic movement from social issue to issue, from political debate to debate, more than *vertically,* in a diachronic engagement with the disciplinary forms of a given genre or medium. . . . This horizontal way of working demands that artists and critics be familiar not only with the structure of each culture well enough to map it, but also with its history well enough to narrate it. . . . To coordinate both axes of several such dis-courses is an enormous burden."[41] Why an enormous *burden*? The artists discussed in Foster's essay are certainly able to produce works that are politically astute and richly referential (working both "horizontally" and "vertically"). If they shoulder any burden, it is the burden of representa-tion articulated by Mercer; the critics and the public are those who pre-sume the artist speaks for (or is trying to speak authoritatively about) a specific ethnic community. The real burden in Foster's analysis seems to fall on the art critic, who might be required to delve into unfamiliar, or perhaps uncomfortable, cultural terrain to grasp the semiotic complexity of the work. While "The Artist as Ethnographer" is among the more intelligent critical responses to this art practice in the mid-1990s, it is also symptomatic of a general ambivalence toward an influx of new paradigms, cultural differences, and aesthetic vocabularies.

Rather than resorting to identity or ethnography as framing concepts that function to place artists in a category of Otherness, I have tried to show how these artists work both within a vernacular tradition and in relation to artistic precedents, both historically and with attention to the politics of the moment.

Abolitionist Voices

If race discourse is "summoned into being," at least in part, by the production of a specific image culture, then it is possible to argue that it is also in and through image culture that it must be radically critiqued. The artists discussed here explore this web of visual tropes, pointing to their social and political effects. Recognizing that the discourse of race is a discourse of visual and material representation and a discourse of display, they produce artworks to interrogate this logic. By turning to installation art, the artists directly reference traditions of display by restaging or reframing their spatial and cultural forms. Their works examine how not only the visual arts and museum exhibitions, but also religious architecture, mass media, commercial commodities, government agencies, and material culture, in the past and the present, have fixed the social landscape of raced subjects. At the same time, their works produce a new visual technology of race discourse by participating in its progressive disruption and revision. I want to emphasize from the outset, however, that "race" is not the only, or nor in every instance the primary, focus of each artwork. Rather, race discourse is the logic that structures the underlying set of social conditions—such as cultural or economic oppression—within which and against which the artists work. For the most part, their works examine the historical *effects* of race discourse and its residue in contemporary systems of power and representation.

I begin my analysis with the works of James Luna (chapter 1), whose staged performance of *The Artifact Piece* (1987) was a generative moment in contemporary installation art. Combining the endurance tactics of 1970s body art with a demystifying critique of representation, the artist installed his own body and personal belongings as "artifacts" in the section devoted to the Kumeyaay Indians at the San Diego Museum of Man. Lying in a display case, covered with a deerskin loincloth as if frozen in time, Luna enacted the ideological effect museums have upon living populations when they present indigenous peoples (such as his own Luiseño tribe) as already extinct. As both performance and installation, *The Artifact Piece* articulated new boundary conditions between artist and museum, art and artifact, performer and spectator. Directly and indirectly, the artwork inspired a number of artists to examine the relation between living subjects and the museum's colonial gaze.

Luna's work emphasizes the politics of "Indian" subjection and the historical condition of cultural and geographical displacement. Using humor and exaggeration, the artist performs multiple subject positions for his viewers, working playfully with performance personas, self-portraits, and customized props that present a mix of cultural references. Luna's concerted effort to offer two views of indigenous American life—the mythological view produced by mainstream popular culture and a less glamorous view from inside the reservation—places viewers from both communities at a critical distance from stereotypes inherited from the past.

Fred Wilson (chapter 2) produces a critical, materialist investigation of museums and the social politics of the circulation of artifacts they contain that shares many concerns with Luna's *The Artifact Piece*. Following in the tradition of a situational aesthetics, many of Wilson's installations have offered a conceptual interrogation of the categorical logic and rhetorical staging of systems of display that are part of museum culture. By taking on the role of visiting curator, Wilson has temporarily reinstalled numerous permanent collections—from the Maryland Historical Society to the Seattle Art Museum—producing provocative juxtapositions of objects that make reference to the history of slavery, the logic of race discourse, the legacy of collecting practices, and the visual mechanisms used by large cultural institutions to announce their power and authority. When a subject is constituted—at least in part—as a subject of history by the history of things, then those things tend to be carefully guarded to prevent their loss. Modern museums are instituted with such preservation as their stated goal, but it is more often a preservation of interpretive frames than a preservation of objects that is at stake.

Taking museums of fine art and anthropology as his primary focus, Wilson investigates the framing taxonomies inherited from academic disciplines that function to separate art from artifact. Every detail of museum exhibition practices, from labels to lighting, comes under scrutiny in Wilson's reinstallations. One of his primary objectives is to encourage a visual attentiveness on the part of museum visitors so that they, too, become aware of the process by which they "read" art and artifacts as such. While Wilson's work interrogates systems of representation that delimit and constrain readings of material culture, it also presents its own alternative readings. He examines objects that perpetuate race discourse across the spectrum of fine arts, decorative arts, and commercial production. Working archeologically to unearth hidden stories or forgotten archives that represent the lives of Africans, African Americans, and Native Americans, Wilson not only points to gaps in historical representation but also reveals the logic behind a condition of continued invisibility.

Like Fred Wilson, Amalia Mesa-Bains (chapter 3) is interested in the spatial politics of representation supported by institutions, but chooses to examine social institutions (such as the family or the church) for their role in subjection at a more intimate level. Reproducing interiors that refer to boudoirs, gardens, harems, cabinets, or libraries, the artist investigates the politics of display that attends such representational spaces and the place of women within them. Her installations are frequently modeled on Catholic iconography central to the everyday lives of many Mexican Americans. In particular, the home altar serves the artist as a framework for the investigation of the institutional power of religion, gender roles, and the history of colonialism in the Americas. One of the primary threads that runs through all her work is the paradoxical position of the Chicana in contemporary U.S. culture, situated between religious and secular traditions, between a Mexican and an American cultural identity, between English and Spanish languages, between traditional feminine roles and a new feminist consciousness. Chicanas (and Chicanos) commonly rely upon expressive forms that work across and through these apparent oppositions. For Mesa-Bains, this means producing innovations in art practice through the reclamation of cultural traditions. Some of her works reference the history of Spanish conquest or the current state of U.S.-Mexico border relations, but the majority of her installations engage with the discourse of gender as it intersects that of race. Developing a definition of a culturally specific feminist practice she calls *domesticana,* Mesa-Bains interrogates the power of cultural archetypes to shape feminine subjectivity.

Pepón Osorio (chapter 4) also works within or across two cultural and linguistic traditions. Drawing upon his experience as an immigrant to New York from Puerto Rico, the artist actively investigates what might be called the *spatial imaginary* of dislocation; his public art projects and installations create transitional places where otherwise divided populations intersect. By spatial imaginary I mean a mental repertoire of inhabited spaces that form discrete arenas for social action. Osorio creates condensed or distilled versions of both commonplace spaces (the bedroom, the living room, the barbershop) and uncommon spaces (the prison cell, the courtroom) in order to render explicit their ideological structure. A number of his works explore the site of home as a domain of culture contact and social conflict, where opposing ideologies and systems of power meet. In addition to exploring the distinctive qualities of everyday life for many working-class immigrants, Osorio exposes the workings of masculinity in the perpetuation of social hierarchies and in the policing of local geographies. In this way Osorio's works produce a kind of *institutional displacement,* disrupting a familiar spatial imaginary in order to offer the possibilities of a new limit politics for social interaction.

Historical discourse, its intersections and flows, its unconscious and deliberate omissions, and its residue in the present are the focus of the work of Renée Green (chapter 5). Returning to the formal and theoretical heritage of conceptual art, both implicitly and explicitly, Green maps histories of culture contact from the period of European colonial expansion to the global networks of communication today. She takes a self-critical, genealogical approach to the questions: How is history recorded? How is memory constructed? How is power consolidated? How is cross-cultural communication possible? Who has the right to decide? Green's aesthetic is minimalist, almost clinical. Her reference points are scientific museums, anthropological texts, and the logic of the gaze of power. Green's early works address histories and economies of slavery, ideologies of color and power in the United States. Many of her more recent works assess the contemporary residue of colonial histories in countries such as Portugal, Spain, France, and the Netherlands. These works draw attention to the fact that the histories of cultural contact and the economic legacy of this past are deeply embedded, even today, in the everyday construction of race discourse. At a time when European countries are facing a crisis in national identity—an identity that can no longer be easily equated with ethnicity—Green's work reminds her audience to take the long view of the past, to see how it is always already reflected in current practices and inequalities. More self-referential and text-based than that of the other artists, Green's work includes self-authored books and catalogs to accompany many of her installations. Especially in her later works, film, video, and sound come to dominate Green's interrogation of private and public memory, understood as necessarily mediated through these forms.

By focusing in detail on the work of a few artists, rather than producing an overview of a broad range of contemporary work, this book hopes to avoid using artworks as illustrations of general concepts, and to offer, instead, an account of contemporary art practice as itself a theoretical and critical endeavor that develops a series of intersecting and internal arguments. To this end, the chapters delineate the conceptual trajectories of each artist, suggesting how each produces a critical apparatus for the interrogation of race discourse.

My methodological approach is historical and dialogic. In trying to articulate how each artist produces a critical response to the intersection of race discourse and spatial discourse, I have chosen to read their works as parallel but distinct interventions that are part of a historical moment in u.s. art history. When this project began, the available literature on the artists' work was relatively scarce. Interviews with the artists became a crucial primary source for my research; in fact, some of the artists were interviewed more than once over a number of years. In many cases, my own interpretations of the works are interleaved with observations, comments, and arguments made by the artists themselves. My citations of our interviews should not be read as an attempt to provide an authoritative interpretation of the work, much less an ethnographic account. My own views often diverge from the stated aims of the artists, but I nevertheless find that their comments provide a richer sense of the political context, conceptual framework, or challenges faced in the working process. I also try to situate the art practice in relation to its artistic antecedents.

Separate chapters are organized around the work of each artist because each has developed unique responses to race discourse that can be best revealed by exploring a larger body of work over time. Although this does not necessitate a chronological approach, and not every chapter is strictly chronological, the thematic concerns linking individual works often emerge during the same historical period in the artist's practice. It is my intention to demonstrate how the artists' works develop unique conceptual frameworks with distinct but parallel insights.

The primary focus is on works produced during the 1990s, which was a fertile period for innovations in installation art and a time when artists working on critical engagements with race discourse were increasingly welcomed by both museums and art galleries in comparison with previous decades.[42] Any number of artists might have been included in a book on race discourse and contemporary installation art in the United States.[43] These have been selected for their emphasis on a materialist approach to the history of subjection. Installation art serves as an appropriate form for their critical practice because it allows the artists to stage objects in architectural settings that often mimic the very spaces and display mechanisms that they wish to critique. Overall, the analysis of the artworks is intentionally documentary and descriptive, in part because this book is intended for general readers who have little or no knowledge of the artworks, and in part because the work demands this kind of close reading in order to be properly understood. Much of what is presented here will be familiar to specialists in contemporary installation art, but they should also find one or two new observations. Because the artists share conceptual concerns and employ similar materials or display tactics, rather than attempting to address them all in this introduction I emphasize specific theoretical issues within each chapter. For example, I address the question of hybridity and histories of photography in chapter 1, theories of institutional critique and museum display in chapter 2, the relation of gender to spatial frameworks in chapters 3 and 4, and the concepts of the archive, genealogy, and historical citation in chapter 5. It will hopefully be evident, however, that these theoretical concerns extend beyond the individual chapters and are frequently applicable to works of the other artists.

Each chapter also includes recurrent themes or critical approaches that are shared by the artists. For example, they all produce at least one auto-biographical work that relies on the collection and display of personal mementos that I have called an *autotopography*.[44] The production of an autotopography is a spatial practice, but also a semantic practice that produces a grammar of juxtaposition that follows its own narrative logic. Existing as a collaborative prosthesis or skeletal armature to a life story, it has in common with public museums the imperatives of archiving and preservation. Unlike museum displays, however, autotopographies gen-erally do not produce rational taxonomies or categorical frameworks. Like an autobiography, an autotopography can be uneven, ambivalent, and by equal measures confessional or dissimulating, but it is also always a practice of claiming ontological rights through the preservation and display of personal objects: the right to exist, the right to a story, and the right to a territory, whether imaginary or actual, where the psyche of the subject dwells and leaves behind a physical trace.

Additionally, a conceptual and formal attention to color, including its racial connotations, symbolic valences, historical references, and taxo-nomic orderings appears in several works by each artist. Skin color is the logic upon which race discourse has historically been built and is obvi-ously one concern, but the artists also explore the meanings inherent in paint colors, in sacred or religious colors, in the colors traditionally used on the walls of museum displays, in colors that reference the design sensibility of a historical era, etc. At a time when the exhibition standard for contemporary art spaces is still the white cube, the artists' sometimes serious and sometimes spirited engagement with color can also be seen as a chromatically inflected critique of this historical default.

Finally, it is significant that all five artists engage in extensive historical research and share an interest in the overlapping or layering of temporal-ity in their works. In many cases, their installations contain signs whose references are hetero-chronic, producing resonances of multiple pasts in the present. This transhistorical approach should not be confused with a conservative form of postmodernism that takes borrowed signs from the past purely for the sake of stylistic pastiche. These artists use historical references in their contemporary works with specific, critical narratives in mind. A materialist historian, according to Walter Benjamin, must act as "one who digs," to pull signs from the past into a new confrontation with the present. "To write history," Benjamin asserts, "therefore means to *quote* history. But the concept of quotation implies that any given histori-cal object must be ripped out of its context."[45] Just as historical discourse partakes in this modest violence, so do the artworks discussed here.

In a catalog essay published in 2001, I borrowed Walter Benjamin's defi-nition of historical materialism in order to argue that the work of Fred

Wilson might be conceived as a kind of "conceptual materialism," implying a conjunction of the institutional and epistemological investigations of conceptual art with a profoundly materialist attention to the history of artifacts and their concrete role in the production and reproduction of ideologies.[46] While this observation may be apt, this pairing of terms has since emerged as a generic description applied by other writers to a variety of art practices, unrelated to my own usage.[47] For this reason I have chosen not to apply the label systematically to the artworks considered here, despite the fact that I see them operating within and between these conceptual and materialist registers.

Moreover, I have begun to rethink the general academic desire to label a given art movement, to frame the limits of its interpretation, to make pronouncements about its final meaning. While there is something appealing to scholars, myself included, about the prospect of being able to encapsulate a significant transformation in art practice with new terms such as "conceptual materialism," "autotopography," "institutional displacement," and so forth, and while these reformulations occasionally do important conceptual and descriptive work, it seems much more important to reveal the key social and political struggles that underlie the semantic richness of this transformation. If I develop several neologisms, such as the preceding ones, to assist in my own critical analysis of various works, I make no claims that a general rubric should be applied to all.

Here I agree with Mercer when he writes, "If the 'responsibility of the artist' lies in the quality of his or her response to what calls for thinking, criticism contributes to the conversation not by imposing the closure of is own conceptual system but by entering into a critical, dialogic, inquiry into the voices that do the calling."[48] These artists share a critical approach to material and visual culture that examines, and ultimately attempts to undermine, racist, colonialist, and sexist discourses in a long tradition of *abolitionism*.[49] The goal of this book is to engage these voices through a form of critical inquiry that will allow the complexity of their enunciations to emerge.

JAMES LUNA

ARTIFACTS AND FICTIONS

I don't want to be an Indian any more
I don't want to be an Indian for historical reasons
I don't want to be an Indian for commercial reasons
I don't want to be an Indian for 'Sentimental Reasons'
I don't want to…

JAMES LUNA

It is a peculiar sensation, this double-consciousness,
this sense of always looking at one's self through the
eyes of others, of measuring one's soul by the tape of
a world that looks on in amused contempt and pity.

W. E. B. DUBOIS

IN A 1992 PERFORMANCE at the Centro Cultural de la Raza in San Diego,[1] James Luna expressed his desire not to be an "Indian" anymore, not to be the classic villain to the cowboy hero, not to be the lonely romantic figure at the end of the trail, not to be named for a European misinterpretation of a geographical mistake.[2] Not wanting to be an Indian was of course no guarantee that Luna might fully escape the pervasive and oppressive forms of myth and legend that ensnare Native Americans to this day. Luna's art practice responds to these persistent myths of the Indian that have become codified in mass culture yet invade the living soul, a condition that produces a state of mind W. E. B. DuBois called "double-consciousness" a century ago. Although DuBois was addressing the specific condition of African Americans in his book *The Souls of Black Folk*, all ethnic minorities living in the United States have long experienced this condition of double-consciousness, of being forced to look at the self through the eyes of others.

DuBois's observation speaks to the double valence or double vision of James Luna's art that parodies stereotypes of the Indian in order to ultimately demystify them. Intimate portraits of the everyday lives of Native American friends and neighbors from the La Jolla Reservation near San Diego, California, serve as salutary antidotes to the narrowly conceived typologies of spiritual shamans, stoic warriors, and defeated tribes that circulate in popular culture and the fine arts. In a single work, audiences may be exposed to both visions, and thereby invited to imagine the gulf that divides fantasy from fact. Luna is careful, however, to demonstrate how inseparable the "raced" subject is from the conditions of its formation. To be or not to be an Indian in the

United States is not a choice, but rather a constant struggle against the contempt and pity, desires and fantasies, of others.

Combining performance, installation, and photography, Luna exposes the networks of human artifacts and mythologies that produce the idea of the Indian. Sometimes his installation art serves as a stage for a live performance to be viewed by gallery audiences later when the artist is no longer present, effectively extending the impact of the live performance with strategies of display incorporating creatively designed props that become sculptural objects in their own right. Sometimes the building of the installation is integrated directly into the artist's performance, and sometimes the installations serve as experimental environments that operate independently from performance altogether. Because Luna borrows from Native American forms of ceremony, ritual, and dance—both ironically and respectfully—he has commented that the non-traditional versatility of installation and performance art allows for the flexible mix of media and formats needed to best articulate his ideas.[3] Taking his own body as a primary medium of expression, Luna offers viewers the opportunity to encounter a tangible human presence as an alternative to pervasive cultural fictions. His approach is often full of humor and campy theatricality, producing an irreverent yet poignant portrait of Native American life. At the same time, Luna addresses very serious subjects that are of central concern in many tribal communities, including alcoholism, poverty, racism, and the loss of a homeland.

Red Is a Color

One of Luna's early installations, *Two Worlds/Two Rooms* (1989) mapped the conditions of DuBois's double-consciousness by creating a spatial intersection of traditional ritual practices with contemporary consumer culture. In the first version of the installation, a white female mannequin in a red suit, high heels, and pearls casually held an unlit cigarette in her right hand and the leather strap of a dog leash in her left. At end of the leash, a disembodied face floated above the ground, that of a red-skinned Indian in a brightly colored headdress (figure 1.1). A pair of strategically placed moccasin-style loafers and work gloves were positioned below, as if their wearer were crouched on his hands and knees like an animal, a pet.[4] Within a scene of racial dominance, the artificially posed mannequin gazing down on the disembodied Indian staged a strangely comical cross between a surrealist exhibition and a low-budget commercial window display. Nearby, wall text above a simple wooden bench described a drunk driving accident that resulted in a fatality; on the bench a single wingtip shoe remained as evidence of the accident victim. Several beer bottles were strewn on the floor beside what looked like the remains of a makeshift fire. In this world of stark economic disparity and senseless death, the Indian is found in a profoundly abject position, as either the

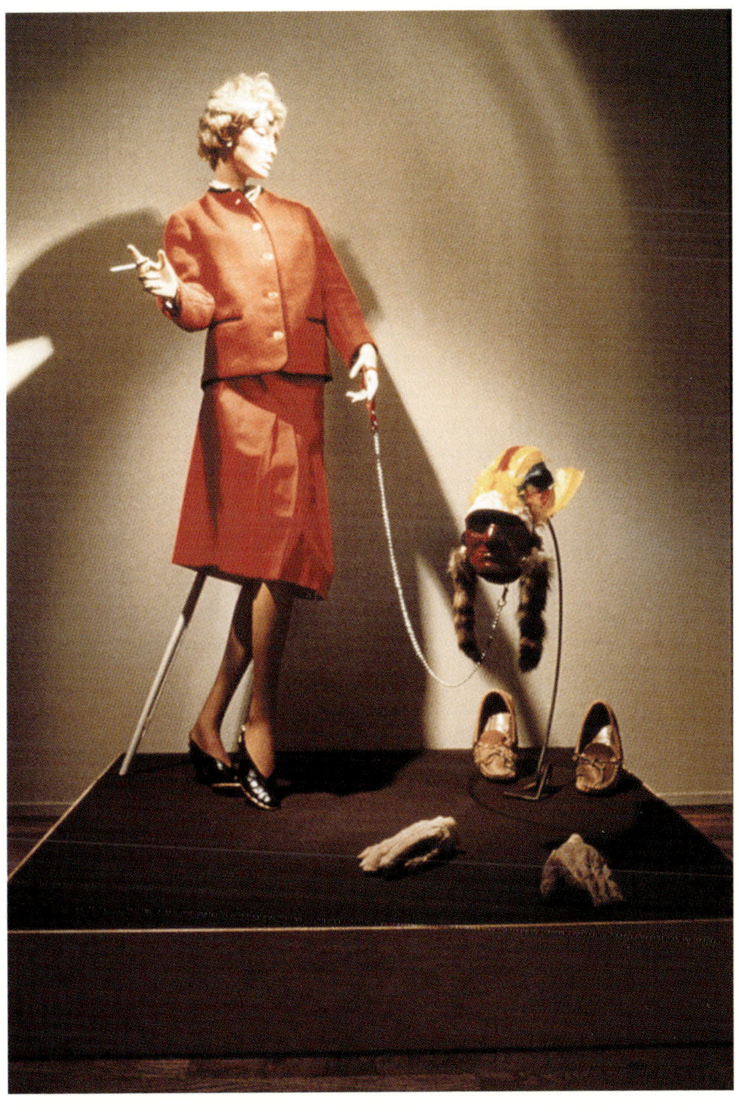

1.1 James Luna, *Two Worlds/Two Rooms*, 1989. Installation view of outer room. Photo courtesy of the artist.

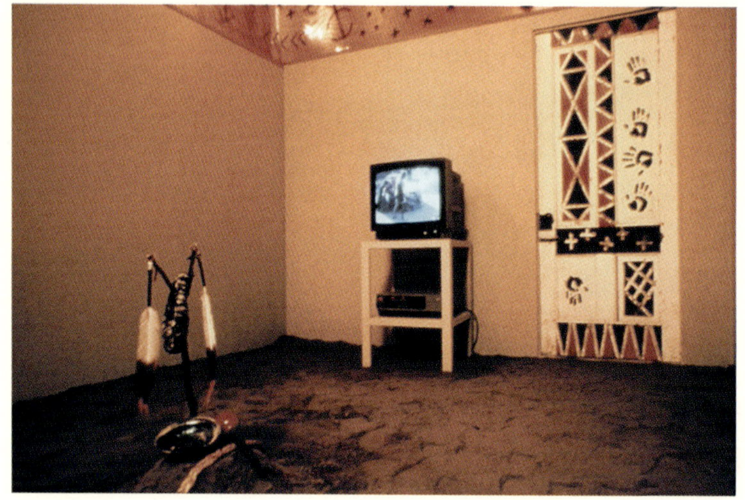

1.2 James Luna, *Two Worlds/Two Rooms,* 1989. Installation view of inner room. Photo courtesy of the artist.

plaything of the rich white establishment or the victim of poverty and neglect. Except for his red face and feathered headdress, the Indian of this world is effectively an immaterial ghost.

Behind a green door in the gallery wall that served as a transitional threshold, another world could be glimpsed, a minimalist sanctuary with an earthen floor. The back of the door was marked with five hand-prints, painted diamonds, and crosses in red and black. In the center of the room, on a mound of earth, a number of ritual objects were carefully placed: an abalone shell with burned incense, two feathers hanging from a stick, a rattle, and a woven sweet grass braid, lending a sense of quiet reverence to the space. A video on a television monitor introduced the traditional sweat lodge as a place of spiritual purification and detoxification that allows participants to regain a sense of balance. Rather than abject Indian stereotypes, viewers saw only themselves reflected in a mirror placed on the ground (figure 1.2).

A year later, in a reprise of the installation titled 2 *Worlds* (1990), Luna imagined a futurology of objects by elaborating further on the sweat lodge, which became "high-tech," furnished with a bright red nylon tent and a white microwave oven—instead of a fire—for warming stones (figure 1.3). Two pot holders and a pair of red plastic salad tongs completed the scene (figure 1.4). Around the room were a number of other sculptural assemblages mixing traditional cultural motifs with consumer objects. Against one wall, a table was set with red napkins, a can of Diet Coke, and a traditional grindstone or *metate* in the place of a dinner plate. Titled "Stoneware," the ensemble offered a comic rendition of the commercial and traditional diets consumed by contemporary Native Americans (figure 1.5). On a nearby pedestal, a shiny chrome fan and rattle were decorated with black, red, yellow, and white streamers, beads, feathers, and a carefully painted step-pyramid pattern (figure 1.6). On another pedestal, a white high-top tennis shoe mounted on bedsprings, titled "War Dance Technology," was similarly adorned with bells, beads, two feathers like rabbit ears or wings, painted pyramid patterns, and an elaborate nine-point star medallion (figure 1.7).

These were not merely decorative details; each element also referenced a long tradition of adornment that has specific historical and cultural significance. For many Native Americans, particularly in the western United States, black, red, yellow, and white represent four sacred colors that indicate the four cardinal directions.[5] Variations of this pattern exist, and different meanings are assigned to the colors by different tribes. In creation myths of some tribes, the four colors signify the four human races and the four elements.[6] Blue and green are also used occasionally to represent the living earth, water, and sky. Because of these variations, Luna's use of color should not be interpreted within a strict or fixed rubric. (The artist

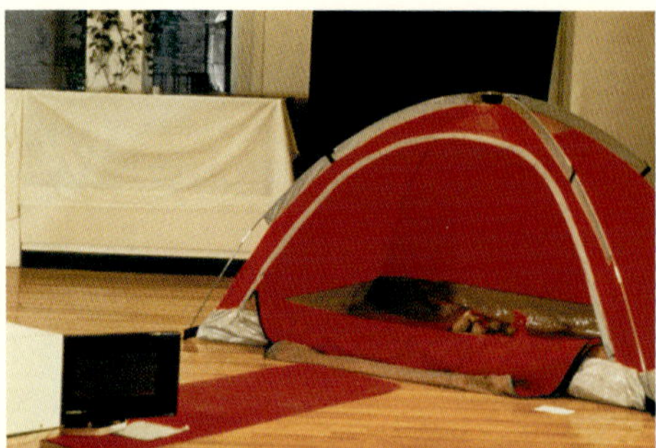

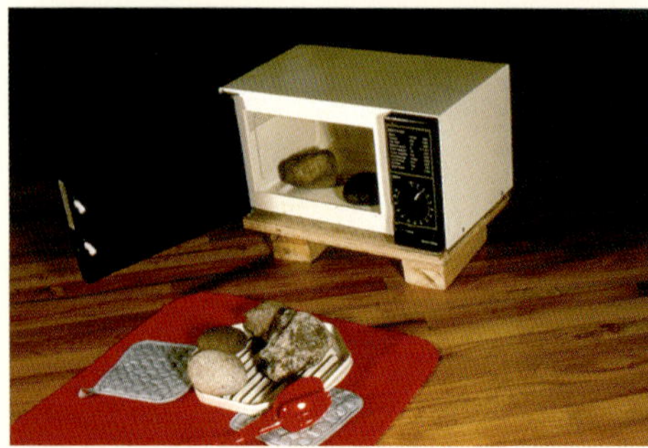

1.3, 1.4 James Luna, *2 worlds,* 1990. Detail of "High-Tech Sweat Lodge." Photos courtesy of the artist.

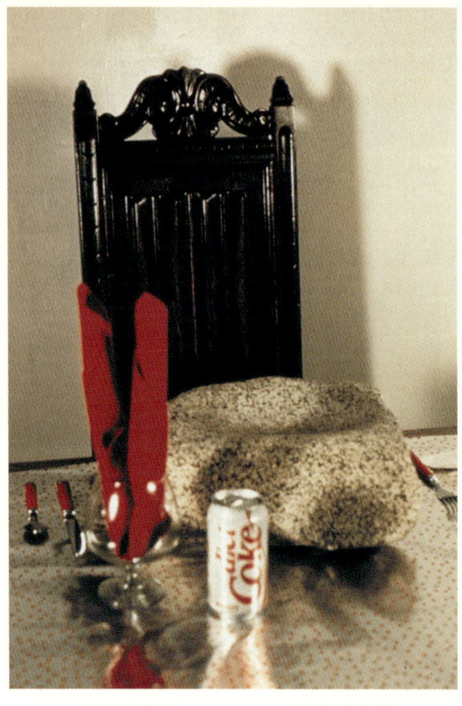

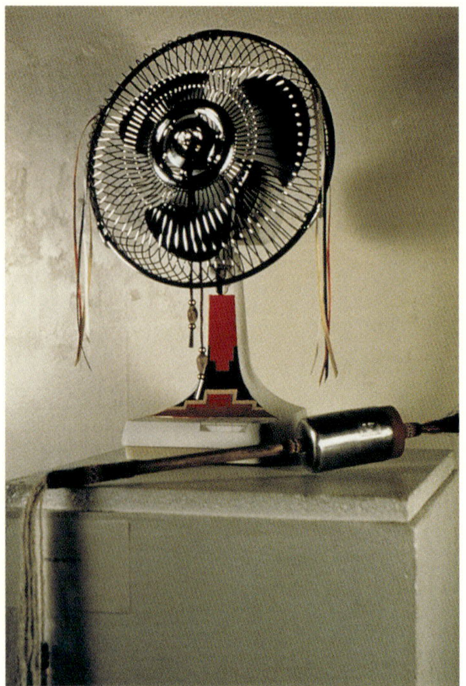

1.5, 1.6 James Luna, *2 worlds,* 1990. Detail of "Stoneware" and of fan and rattle. Photos courtesy of the artist.

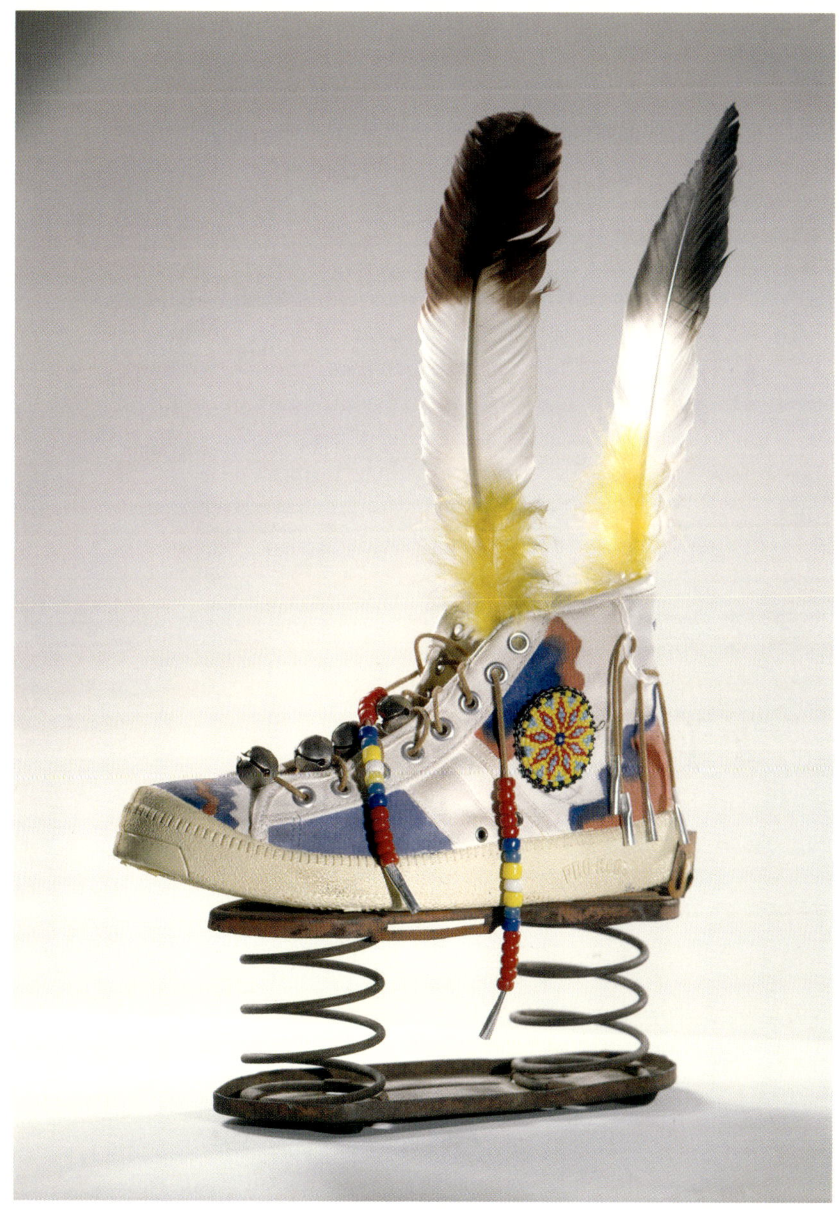

1.7 James Luna, *2 worlds,* 1990. Detail of "War Dance Technology." Photo courtesy of the artist.

claims that the four colors reference indigenous religious traditions, but he does not specify the symbolism of each in his own work.)[7] This color palette occurs with enough regularity in his installations and performances, however, that it is worth some attention. The palette of the *Two Worlds/ Two Rooms* exhibit, for example, is predominantly red and black, colors that frequently symbolize East and West, birth and death. The shoestring hanging from the high-top tennis shoe is embellished with a symmetrical stacking of red, black, yellow, and white beads; the feathers on top of the shoe are yellow, white, and black. While offering a humorous allusion to the winged feet of Hermes, god of war, Luna's "War Dance Technology" also employs color and beadwork to produce a parallel set of legible signs regarding a balance of power to a Native American audience. Luna has remarked, "There are aspects of my work that will be understood only by those who know the Indian traditions, but the same can be said of the way I bring the world of contemporary art to Indians. The art audience perceives my work differently than the Indian audience."[8] Situated within and between several worlds, Luna's work draws our attention to the incommensurability of critical vocabularies that might be used to define it, such as postmodern, or ethnographic. His two-world installations reveal not simply the clichéd stereotypes of cultural duality, but also the commodified and uneven forms of interpretation that take place between hegemonic and subaltern communities. For this reason, and because of its mix of material signs from indigenous and white mainstream sources, it is tempting to define Luna's practice in terms of hybridity.

Theorist Homi Bhabha has defined hybridity as "a problematic of colonial representation and individuation that reverses the effects of the colonialist disavowal, so that the other 'denied' knowledges enter upon the dominant discourse and estrange the basis of its authority—its rules of recognition."[9] Although Bhabha is specifically addressing literary production, one can see how Luna estranges the rules of recognition that inform mainstream art criticism by introducing unfamiliar signs or denied knowledges—such as the four sacred colors—that remain undecipherable for some viewers, thereby shifting the balance of interpretive power to a generally disenfranchised population. In this way, Luna treats exhibition space as an in-between site where semantic networks can be remapped (not simply rejected or reversed). Bhabha's concept of hybridity has relevance to the artwork considered in this book more generally (e.g., he applies the term to the work of Pepón Osorio explicitly).[10] To the degree that each of the artists works *across* rather than *within* commonly established cultural paradigms, it is certainly possible to read their work collectively as "hybrid."

To simply argue, however, that an artwork or written text demonstrates the qualities of cultural hybridity, or counterhegemonic mixing, is not particularly revealing. Cross-cultural forms of semiotic blending have been part of the visual arts since long before the advent of colonialism—or postcolonialism. Rasheed Araeen argues that Bhabha's theory of hybridity is limited to a very narrow conception of this cultural exchange. Rather than addressing "the reality of the historical encounter between the people of non-Western cultures and Western culture," Araeen claims that Bhabha's theory accounts only for the moment when a non-Western culture *enters* Western culture while maintaining its identity as one of *difference*.[11] The Western paradigm, in other words, still maintains its cultural dominance.

In fact, the critical art establishment has shown itself to be only too ready to produce a place (and a market niche) for cultural others as long as they agree to maintain their position of cultural difference. In the past two decades, artists who wished to criticize or simply *estrange* race discourse, particularly in the United States, have been placed in a double bind. When emphasizing racial and ethnic difference, they and their artworks are labeled other by a white critical audience. When references to race and ethnicity are omitted by the artists, their artworks might be accepted by (or, in many cases, ignored by) the mainstream gallery system, but are generally emptied of social critique. (The for-profit art world enforces assimilationist practices that are nearly as insidious, though perhaps not as violent, as the apparatus of the state.) Nevertheless, many artists, including those discussed here, have tried to work around this double bind, choosing to mix dominant and subaltern discourses of representation to draw our attention to the *sites of their intersection,* not as a simple celebration of cultural fusion, but rather as a carefully considered analysis of unequal power relations and the history of their effects. Indeed, these artworks may sometimes enact or represent the very historical encounters Araeen claims are missing from Bhabha's analysis. What is at stake for the artists is the rare possibility of enunciation (having one's story heard) and the necessity of producing this story for an audience that extends beyond the mainstream. The artworks may offer biting critiques of dominant culture or colonial histories, but they are not produced merely for this purpose. They are also engaged in a tactical reinscription and transformation of dominant signs into a subaltern vernacular to be read by a local or culturally specific audience. In short, if they "change the rules of recognition," they do so not only to disrupt the dominant paradigm but also to communicate beyond it. The result is an art practice that is multimodal and categorically elusive, conforming neither to a narrowly conceived multiculturalism that imposes the exotic label of difference, nor to a mainstream imperative to assimilate.

Luna's *The Sacred Colors* (1992–1994) employs this multimodality to reflect on the relation between indigenous traditions and the contemporary limits of race discourse. Focusing again on the question of color, the artist photographed himself and three friends wearing the color typically ascribed to their racial type. A Caucasian woman wore a long white bridal dress, an

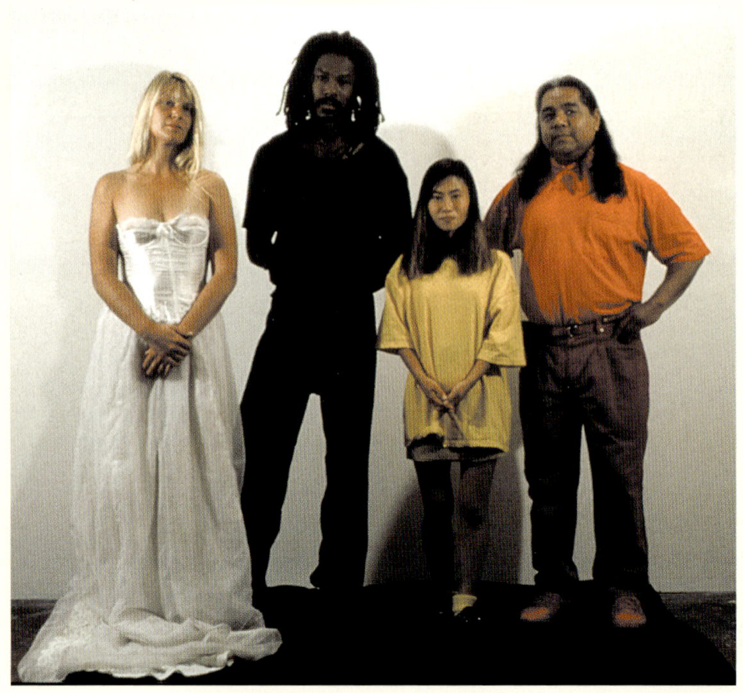

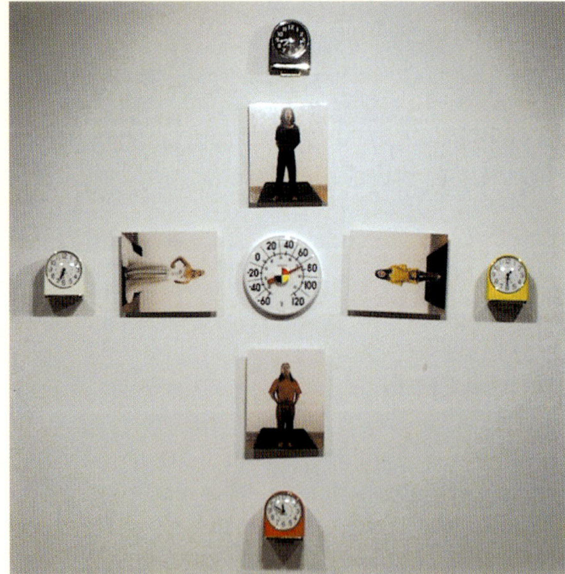

1.8 James Luna,
The Sacred Colors, 1992–
1994. Detail of portraits.
Photo courtesy of the
artist and TRIBE.

1.9 James Luna,
Chapel of the Sacred Colors.
2000. Detail of portraits.
Photo courtesy of the
artist and TRIBE.

Asian woman wore a large yellow T-shirt and socks, an African American man in dreadlocks wore black, and Luna was dressed in bright red with matching shoes (figure 1.8). In 1992 Luna's audience would have been quite familiar with the United Colors of Benetton advertising campaign that pictured people with dramatically different skin color, sometimes dressed in ethnically specific costumes or bright Benetton clothing, joined together in an artificial multicultural embrace. Luna's *Sacred Colors* might be read as responding critically to this advertising campaign while simultaneously recuperating the traditional sacred colors in Native American culture. He has commented, "Like the four directions, we use the colors to distinguish and balance our world. When I began to work on this piece I thought of Indian humor used as a form of knowledge. I thought of presenting something that would make people look at something simple in a different light."[12] His visual rendition of the creation myth that links four races, four sacred colors, and four cardinal points enacted the artificiality of these categories by demonstrating the absurdity of equating skin color with chromatic abstractions such as white, black, yellow, and red. None of the models had skin colors matching the color of the clothing they wore, but the staged approximations made the case more vividly. In this respect, the work was pointedly antiracist, deconstructing historical labels applied to racial types ("yellow peril," "redskin," etc.). By installing the photographs in a traditional ritual pattern indicating the cardinal directions, Luna also referenced the Native American metaphors of interdependence and harmonious balance among people. Like many of Luna's works, *The Sacred Colors* suggested first- and second-order readings, using the same signs in several registers as a critique of racial stereotypes centered on skin color, as a parallel commentary on the commodification of skin color as a clothing accessory in the Benetton campaign, and as a recuperation of indigenous theories of racial difference, harmony, and balance.

Luna returned to this theme in a more recent installation *Chapel of the Sacred Colors* (2000), where floor-to-ceiling curtains in diaphanous red, yellow and black transformed an otherwise unadorned gallery. Furnished with several rows of plastic chairs, an altarlike table, and six display cases that contained handmade artifacts from several of the artist's previous performances, the "chapel" was both a museum and reliquary. Above the "altar," smaller versions of the original four *Sacred Colors* portraits were placed in the shape of a cross next to four clocks of matching colors, each set to a different time of day (figure 1.9). Reminiscent of Felix Gonzalez-Torres's *Untitled (Perfect Lovers)* (1987–1990), which consisted of two commercial clocks set to the exact same time hung side by side, Luna's clocks suggested individual subjects, each operating in a unique time frame, separate from each other, yet linked.

Ritual objects for not-so-traditional rituals were also on display, taking the form of material and visual puns, while mocking the viewer's desire

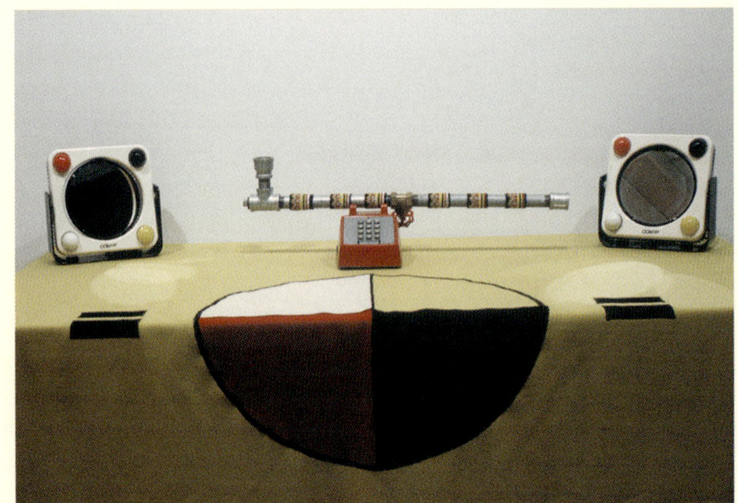

1.10 James Luna, *Chapel of the Sacred Colors,* 2000. Detail of "High-Tech Peace Pipe." Photo courtesy of the artist and TRIBE.

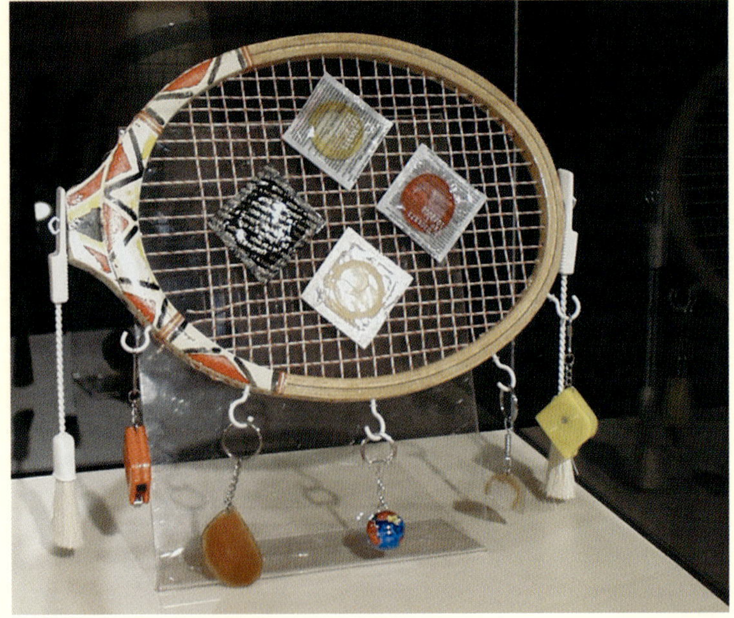

1.11 James Luna, *Chapel of the Sacred Colors,* 2000. Detail of "Wet Dream Catcher." Photo courtesy of the artist and TRIBE.

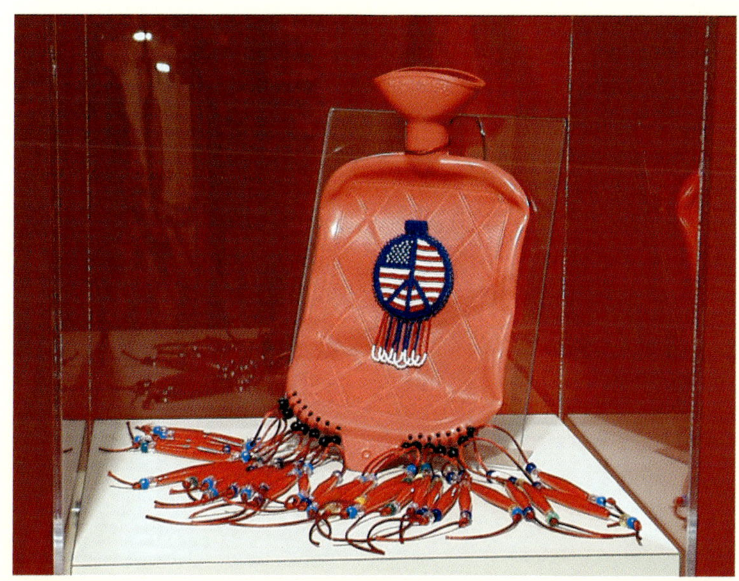

1.12 James Luna, *Chapel of the Sacred Colors*, 2000. Detail of "Hot Medicine Bag." Photo courtesy of the artist and TRIBE.

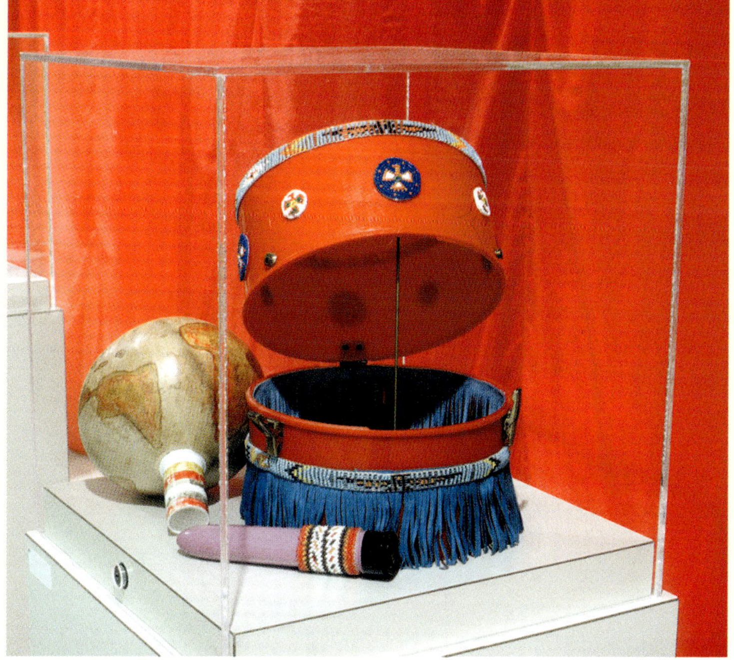

1.13 James Luna, *Chapel of the Sacred Colors*, 2000. Detail of "Electric Rattle." Photo courtesy of the artist and TRIBE.

for contact with "authentic" Indian artifacts. Centrally positioned on the altar was Luna's "High-Tech Peace Pipe," an industrial metal pipe with decorative beads, bolted fittings, and carved peace signs that sat in the place of the receiver atop a red telephone (figure 1.10). Roger Boyce recounts its use in a performance at the Institute for Contemporary Art, Boston, in 1999: "Luna picks up a plastic tool box, kneels, opens it and from its interior retrieves assorted metal pipe fittings. Luna narrates a post-apocalyptic tale of survival as he assembles a Rube Goldberg-like 'sacred pipe' complete with garden faucet. His tale is an inverted origin myth, where 'Indians survive because they know how to make do,' to use what is at hand. To transform profane objects into sacred instruments."[13]

The reverse also takes place when objects that once served traditional ritual practices are appropriated by a mainstream public, eager to share—or steal—their "sacred" significance. Luna's installation includes several artifacts that satirically foreground the acquisitive and even erotic desires that drive this fascination with cultural difference. "Wet Dream Catcher," made from the top of a tennis racket, festooned with lucky rabbit feet and four condoms in the four sacred colors, was one prop among many (including, e.g., a box of Lucky Charms breakfast cereal and Arrowhead water) that the artist has used in his many *Shame-man* (1993–present) performances, parodying the misuse and disrespectful sale of indigenous spiritual ways and objects (figure 1.11).[14] Here, placed in a glass case, the object took on the strange status of a ritual apparatus, along with the "Hot Medicine Bag" adorned with a beaded peace sign (figure 1.12), and the ceremonial "Electric Rattle" showing a rudimentary map of the globe, with its own automatic pink vibrator and decorative carrying case (figure 1.13). For all their campy humor, each artifact also signified a confrontation or contact between the materialism of contemporary mass culture and Native American traditions, between a colonizing culture and colonized culture that have different stakes in the appropriation and transformation of material signs.

One way to think about Luna's resignifying practice is as an exaggeration of already present, though more subtle, resignifying practices that have been performed by indigenous cultures in contact with colonizing populations for centuries. Contested notions of ownership or authenticity are at the heart of Luna's critique. While he addresses the problematic appropriation of indigenous traditions by market capitalism and entrepreneurial whites, he simultaneously demonstrates the indigenous propensity to transform, manipulate, or appropriate mass culture signs themselves. His work suggests that the white mainstream fascination with Indian authenticity underlies any number of abusive misinterpretations of indigenous cultures. At the same time, he shows how notions of authenticity are problematic in general, also within indigenous communities. The apparent contradiction of these efforts can be resolved when relations of power are taken into consideration. Borrowing and appropriation have a different political valence depending on *who* is engaged in the act. When large corporations mass-produce dream catchers for a tourist market, it is not the same political or economic act of appropriation as Luna's placement of a Diet Coke can in his art installation. It is the difference between these two parallel acts, the gulf that divides them, that is the focus of much of the artist's work.

Luna's recombinatory gestures can be understood as part of a larger, continuous process of deterritorialization and reterritorialization of circulating signs. In 1980 Gilles Deleuze and Félix Guattari introduced the notions of *deterritorialization* and *reterritorialization* in their book *A Thousand Plateaus,* and the terms have been employed and redefined by any number of theorists and scholars since that time—most commonly within the field of anthropology, but also by contemporary art theorists to address concerns ranging from creolization and immigration to the redefinition of public space.[15] These concepts have proven to be particularly useful for understanding the complex *spatial* and *representational* practices that arise when different, parallel systems (cultural, hierarchical, bureaucratic) come into contact in such a way that one makes use of the other—through domination or resistance, through strategic or chance encounters—for its own ends.[16] James Luna might be said to deterritorialize objects from mainstream popular culture, in order to reterritorialize them in his installations, forming a circuit of relays, a circulation of signs that are parallel to, but distinct from, that mainstream. Similarly, the mainstream appropriation of Native American traditions for its own ends becomes an act of deterritorializtion and reterritorialization that perpetuates even older forms of colonial conquest.

The Body as Artifact and Fiction

> *My body practices being dead.*
>
> —Bas Jan Ader

Luna received a degree in art in 1976 at the University of California, Irvine, where he studied with the Dutch conceptual artist Bas Jan Ader and the feminist artist Eleanor Antin, among others.[17] Ader's experimental performances, many of long duration and involving the body in some form of physical transformation, influenced Luna's own form of endurance performance art, while Antin, known for creating and posing as female (and male) personas, probably had an effect on Luna's approach to inventing and staging Indian characters. In many of his works, Luna uses his own body as a flexible sign, pliable enough to accommodate a broad spectrum of projected myths. Yet he seems keenly aware of the limits of corporeal legibility, of the way that physiognomy and skin color can suture a person to a racist caricature or a historical archetype. This suturing moment can be understood as a small death for the living subject, and it is this moment that Luna both enacts and critiques.

For *The Artifact Piece* (1987–1990), which is probably the artist's best-known work, Luna created an installation in which his own body and personal belongings became artifacts on display in the section devoted to the Kumeyaay Indians at the San Diego Museum of Man (figure 1.14). The Kumeyaay exhibition is permanently installed on the second floor of the museum, offering a historical view of the Southern California indigenous groups colonized by the Spanish missionaries in the late eighteenth century; Kumeyaay food, dress, pottery, and baskets are displayed as well as a history of games, an overview of ceremonies, and a replica of a traditional Kumeyaay house. While colonial contact is presented as part of the exhibition, the emphasis is clearly on the preservation of artifacts that date before the arrival of the Spanish, ignoring the interesting and inevitable transformation of indigenous daily life during and after colonization.

In the live performance tradition of artists such as Chris Burden (*Bed*, 1972) or Marina Abramovic (*Rhythm 2*, 1974), James Luna engaged in body art endurance tactics by lying, partially sedated, on a sand-covered table, wearing only a loincloth, several hours a day during the run of the exhibit. He was so still and quiet that some visitors did not realize he was alive until they were standing beside him. Placed next to his body were museum labels that identified Luna as a member of the Luiseño tribe, along with other explanatory labels that offered descriptive information regarding various marks and scars on his body, as might be found next to an archeological specimen.[18] One label offered a glimpse into the artist's personal life that contrasted sharply with the romantic image of the noble savage maintained elsewhere by the museum: "Drunk beyond the point of being able to defend himself, he was jumped by people from another reservation. After being knocked down, he was kicked in the face and upper body. Saved by an old man, he awoke with a swollen face covered with dried blood. Thereafter, he makes it a point not to be as trusting among relatives and other Indians."[19] The violence of Luna's story and the unappealing quality of its characters, almost all of whom were either drunk or brutal, undermined the potential for voyeuristic pleasure as visitors stood over the artist's silent, breathing body. Luna consciously leveraged the rhetorical strategies of museum display labels to counteract the comfortably distant gaze employed when most visitors walk through an exhibit. Luna's performance became not only a metaphor for the long history of violence that led Europeans to place Indian bodies on display, but also uncensored evidence of violence in Native American life today.[20] The one redeeming element in the narrative—being "saved by an old man"—illuminated the contradictions of life on the reservation as a mix of abjection and compassion.

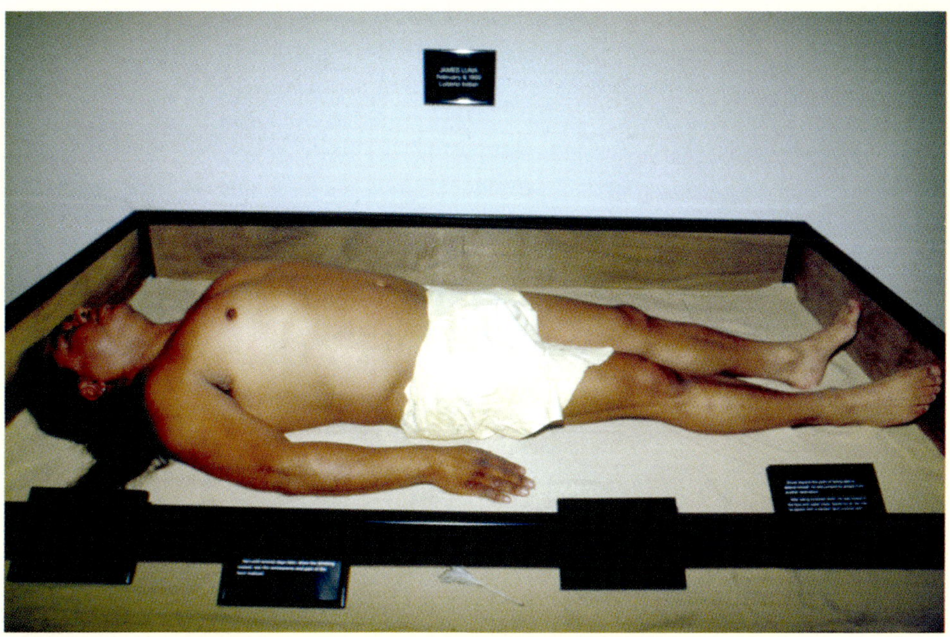

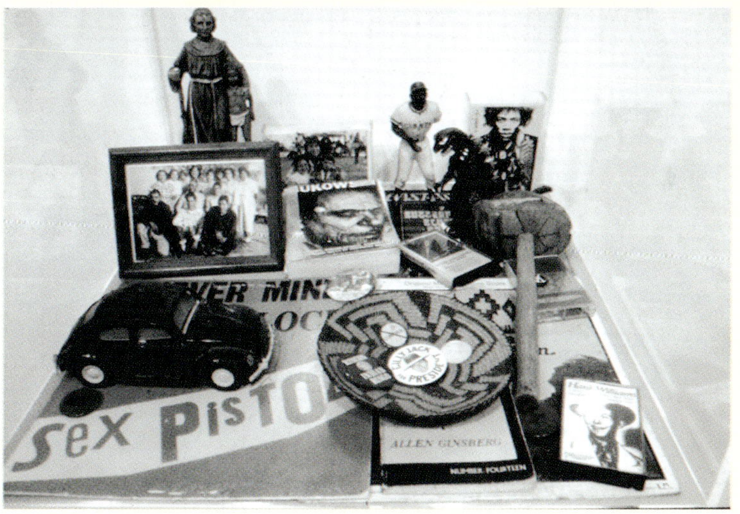

1.14 James Luna, *The Artifact Piece*, 1987–1990. Installation view of artist. Photo courtesy of the artist and the Heard Museum.

1.15 James Luna, *The Artifact Piece*, 1987–1990. Installation view with display case. Photo courtesy of the artist and the Heard Museum.

Other contradictions were to be found in three museum vitrines placed near the artist's body. One contained traditional artifacts and "medicine" objects used in rituals that might be found in other natural history exhibitions of indigenous cultures of the Americas. Another contained a strange assortment of shoes, each customized by the artist to look Indian, and each suggesting a missing presence, a missing subject. The third display case contained Luna's personal belongings and mementos: a current driver's license, a diploma, tapes and records by contemporary musicians such as Miles Davis, the Rolling Stones, and Jimi Hendrix, political buttons for Students for a Democratic Society and the United Farm Workers of America, comic books and writings by Allen Ginsberg and Charles Bukowski, small sports figurines, paper toys, pictures of children, a plastic Godzilla and a statuette of a Franciscan monk with his arm around a small Native American child (figure 1.15).[21] By bringing these private belongings into the museum and by identifying the Indian as one who consumes popular culture, Luna counteracts the perspective of cultural institutions and museums that represent indigenous peoples of the United States as already extinct.

As both living and "dead," Luna produces the conditions for an existential and epistemological disruption of the typical conditions of museum spectatorship. Scholar Jean Fisher observes of *The Artifact Piece,* "There is a diabolical humor in this parody of the 'Indian' in the realm of the 'undead'.... If the purpose of the undead Indian of colonialism is to secure the self-identity of the onlooker, the shock of his real presence and the possibility that he may indeed be watching and listening disarms the voyeuristic gaze and denies it its structuring power."[22] In a parallel argument, Miwon Kwon writes that *The Artifact Piece* "is not an overt insistence on the inclusion of excluded or repressed 'real' histories of particular 'minor' constituencies within official narrative of the dominant culture. Instead, the self-sacrificial gesture of offering his own body and personal effects as gifts to the museum, becoming the "vanquished Indian"—in other words, 'killing' himself—is a strategy of opposition and resistance of a different order.... Even as Luna enacts a personal erasure in order to make visible a social one, *The Artifact Piece* claims life and survival."[23] Luna's performing body, lying in a liminal state of stasis, paradoxically becomes the mummified artifact that refuses to die.

Museum displays, particularly of a colonial kind that permit dominant cultures to display the artifacts and cultures of the vanquished, are structured around a carefully calibrated form of temporal fetishism in which objects operate both as signs of oppression or dominance, and of its disavowal. This fetishism works through a process of denial and substitution. In order to disavow the history of exploration and violence that produced the relations of dominance and control that led to the collection or theft of cultural artifacts, museums create pleasurable environments of contemplation carefully designed to minimize historical references to political and social contact or conflict between cultures. Artifacts are displayed as rare and unique aesthetic objects to be admired for their remarkable craftsmanship, or as utilitarian tools to be examined and understood in the context of their use. Colonial museum displays thus regularly substitute the material object for the historical narrative of its provenance, while providing pleasure in good fetishistic fashion precisely because this substitution allows visitors to see what they desire (aesthetic beauty, other ways of life, their own glorious past) without seeing what they fear (the real history of violence that underlies colonial contact and cultural imperialism, the resentments of racism, the contemporary reality of economic inequality). As Barbara Kirshenblatt-Gimblet observes, "Documentation and exhibition are implicated in the disappearance of what they show."[24] Thorough, thoughtful, tasteful, and often carefully researched exhibitions can unwittingly contribute to this disavowal, denial, or distraction by seeming to provide all the information a visitor could possibly want. *The Artifact Piece* works as a rhetorical foil to this kind of fetishism. It provides information (about contemporary life, violence, alcoholism) the visitor does not want to see, thereby revealing the unconscious habits of display that romanticize and historicize the Indian as part of the vanishing past, existing in a pristine precolonial state. It also reminds viewers that race and ethnicity may be taxonomies whose boundaries are patrolled by exhibitions, but that these taxonomies are also *lived* by human beings.

In *The Predicament of Culture,* James Clifford offers a useful analysis of the art-culture system's production of what he calls machines for "making authenticity." Museums are the most potent of such machines because they function to mark the boundary between the "authentic" realms of art (connoisseurship, the art museum, the art market) or culture (history, folklore, ethnographic artifacts, material culture) and the "inauthentic" realms of fakes, tourist art, and ready-mades.[25] *The Artifact Piece* crosses these traditional divides by presenting an artist as an "artifact" and by placing mass culture objects beside traditional ritual objects. Moreover, Luna's work also shows how museums produce isolated or suspended symbolic orders that mark two kinds of imagined subjects: those who are identified as bearers of an institutional gaze, and those who are identified as objects of that gaze. The imagined subject who sees with the eyes of the institution is the subject for whom the museum is an ideological home—what might be called the *speaking subject* of the museum—whose boundaries of comfort are defined by the limits of the collection and its display. The imagined subject who becomes the object of (or becomes objectified by) the institutional gaze can be thought of as the *spoken subject* of the institution. In Luna's installation, the artist takes advantage of the rare opportunity to perform as both the *speaking* and the *spoken* subject, the one who creates the display and who serves as its object.

The Artifact Piece is not an ethnographic representation. It is a fiction, based on historical fact: an autofiction. In their essay "Autofictions, or Elective Identities," Olivier Asselin and Johanne Lamoureux address the construction of artificial or "elective" identities as a recurrent theme in art practice throughout the twentieth century, observing that artists have developed new ways to represent subjectivity, "through the invention of pseudonyms, alter egos and imaginary lives; through the construction of new images of the self and new accounts of one's life; through fictitious self-portraits, autobiographies and personal mythologies."[26] *The Artifact Piece* also worked as an evidence-laden material self-portrait, what I called an autotopography in the introduction. Like French artist Christian Boltanski's *Vitrine de Référence* (1972), in which the artist displayed photographs of himself, a scrap of a pullover sweater worn in 1949, a ball of hair, family photographs, letters, handmade "tools," and sundry found objects all carefully labeled, Luna's work is a reliquary of a personal past, a mythology of existence that rests on the fragile evidence of fragments. Unlike Boltanksi's work, however, Luna's piece details the cultural paradox of living two contradictory lives, an indigenous traditional life of ritual and ceremony and an assimilated life that participates in mainstream popular culture and political struggles of the moment.

For this reason, Luna's work may also be akin to an autoethnography as defined by Mary Louise Pratt in her book *Imperial Eyes*.[27] There she offers a subtle vision of "autoethnographic expression" that refers "to instances in which colonized subjects undertake to represent themselves in ways that engage with the colonizer's own terms. If ethnographic texts are a means by which Europeans represent to themselves their (usually subjugated) others, autoethnographic texts are those the others construct in response to or in dialogue with those metropolitan representations."[28] Pratt argues that "authoethnography involves partial collaboration with and appropriation of the idioms of the conqueror."[29] Employing devices of museum display that have traditionally formed the means of representing (or erasing) the history of Native Americans, Luna engages with the "colonizer's own terms" to offer a critical response to historical representations of race. If museums have been one of the primary means by which those in power "represent to themselves their (usually subjugated) others," Luna is able to usurp the form through a transformation of style and content. Pratt argues that "autoethnographic texts are typically heterogeneous on the reception end as well, usually addressed both to metropolitan readers and to literate sectors of the speaker's own social group, and bound to be received very differently by each."[30] Rather than reading *The Artifact Piece* as simply a representation of the artist's *identity,* it is possible to see how Luna strategically employs autobiographical elements to produce an ambiguous autofiction, a bicultural autotopography, and a critical autoethnography.

As an artist who interrogates the image of the Indian, Luna has also produced a significant body of photographic works that serve as ambivalent self-portraits. The photographic self-portraits discussed below are carefully staged genre parodies that work to unmask the phantom Indians haunting the popular visual imaginary of the United States, reminding us that the discourse of portraiture always functions within a larger ecology of portrayal. Not only is a portrait an image of someone, but it is also always a representation of the process of looking. To represent the history of a subject for whom ethnic stereotyping is a common obstacle, it may be necessary to take into account the problem of an institutional gaze that forms the contours of an imagined subject. Here the process of looking that underlies the reading of the portrait may be constrained by culturally sanctioned, institutionally supported categories of race and ethnicity.

As a recording device, the medium of photography has always been allied with truth claims: as evidence in courts of law, as the necessary supplement to historical narratives, as the existential proof for the passing of time, or as the unquestioned paradigm for visual documentary. Historians and theorists have engaged critically with this "truth effect" of photography for over a century, assessing the cultural investment in the indexical quality of the image and the connotations of naturalism that it implies.[31] Because of their long association, it is possible to draw a parallel between the truth effect of photography and what might be called the "truth effect" of racial discourse.[32] Both naturalize ideological systems by making them visible and apparently self-evident. As with photography, the visual or visible elements of race function to produce "truth effects" that appear natural.

Perhaps for this reason, the history of photography is inseparable from the history of racial discourse. Particularly in the late nineteenth century, photography was used to support the creation of eugenics, a false science that claimed to determine human character based on the study of phenotype. Because differences in body type (i.e., low-brow, high-brow) were said to reflect moral and intellectual qualities, race became one of the primary objects of the camera's differentiating gaze. Epidermalization became codified through photography, shaping public consciousness in the United States both before the civil war and after, with images of former slaves or colonized natives depicted as little more than zoological specimens.[33] This effect was produced by placing partially clothed or entirely unclothed subjects against a gridded backdrop in order to better measure their physical attributes using the supposedly "scientific" apparatus of the mechanical lens. Anthropometry, as this practice of bodily measurement was called, not only became a dehumanizing tool of pseudoanthropologists, but also was the origin of the criminal mug shot developed by Alphonse Bertillon in France in the 1880s.[34] Anthropometry of African Americans, Native Americans, Native Australians, and Native Canadians was practiced until at least the late 1930s.[35]

It is also the case that well-meaning social scientists and cultural enthusiasts found photography to be the best tool to document what was considered at the time to be the vanishing civilizations of the American Indian.[36] A romantic urge to preserve and protect Native Americans in their authentic state often led to fantastical depictions of native life as divorced from the realities of colonial encroachment. Alan Trachtenberg observes that a major shift in photographic practice can be traced from the 1870s, when a typical image of an Indian consisted of a before-and-after sequence depicting "wild-looking" youth transformed into docile boarding school students, to the 1890s when unassimilated Indians were depicted as objects of desire and fascination. This transition took place, of course, at the very moment that Indians were no longer considered a military or territorial threat.[37]

Edward S. Curtis shot stunning and seductive portraits of many different Indian tribes between 1906 and 1927, but he was also known to carefully pose his sitters, manipulate costumes, or retouch negatives to remove signs of modern life so that the portraits would appear more "authentic."[38] His sitters were paid to perform their roles as Indians before the lens.[39] With titles such as *Kalispel Type* (1911) or *Hopi Man* (1921), actual names, ages, social positions, family connections, and life narratives disappeared into the smoky soft focus of Curtis's pictorialist gaze. Both pseudoscientific and romantic photographic depictions of Native Americans have circulated in American popular culture and consciousness for over one hundred years, creating a pervasive and persistent "truth effect" of innate "Indian-ness" that has become part of the underlying visual sediment upon which more extreme forms of racial stereotyping are built.

Luna's choice of medium for his series of self-portraits appears to derive from a knowing critique of this tradition, both in the history of photography and the history of fine art. One of the first versions of this exploration can be found in the installation *AA Meeting/Art History* (1991). In a room containing four metal folding chairs gathered around a video monitor and an ashtray full of cigarette butts, several photographic self-portraits depict the artist in classic poses from the history of Western European and American art. Wearing a black T-shirt and pants, the artist posed as Rodin's *Thinker,* as a reclining odalisque, and as a slouching figure hunched over a sawhorse with a bottle of beer hanging from his hand; this last was a reprise of James Earl Fraser's *End of the Trail.* The strangely ludicrous and pathetic comparison between these canonical figures of art history and Alcoholics Anonymous participants also figures the cultural abyss that separates them. Indigenous corporeality becomes unmoored from the racial "type" as viewers familiar with the historical references to Rodin or Fraser are able to compare the abjectness—and grace—of Luna's body with the classic images through which, and against which, it signifies. Teresa Harlan writes, "Creating a visual history—and its representations—from Native memories or from Western myths; this is the question before Native image-makers and photographers today. The contest remains over who will image—and own—this history."[40]

By 1890, most Native Americans were confined to reservations and had suffered so profoundly from extermination, disease, and starvation that the overall population reached a historical low (the numbers have increased since then). It was no coincidence that in 1894, when he was seventeen, Fraser produced the first version of his now classic and much reproduced *End of the Trail,* which depicts a defeated Indian warrior, his head bowed in resignation or exhaustion, his braids blown by the wind, his spear hanging dejectedly in his hand.[41] Fraser's father was involved in railroad expansion, but it appears that the young Fraser sympathized with the Indians, who certainly seemed to be vanishing at the time, pushed further and further west by the unstoppable machine of industrialization. A large plaster version of the statue won a gold medal at the Panama Pacific International Exposition in San Francisco in 1915 and quickly became one of the most popular images of the time, appearing on postcards, on calendars, on posters, and in miniature form.[42] Today one can easily find replicas for sale on the internet, and museums across the country have copies in their permanent collections or on display.[43] The original sculpture was recently refurbished and is now housed in the National Cowboy and Western Heritage Museum in Oklahoma City.

Luna's restaging of Fraser's image turns on the calamity of alcoholism in Native American communities. Although the figure appears equally defeated in Luna's depiction, an underlying sense of tenacity or persistence exists. Luna's image returns in a later work superimposed over a color painting of Fraser's original, retitled *End of the Frail* (1991) (figure 1.16).

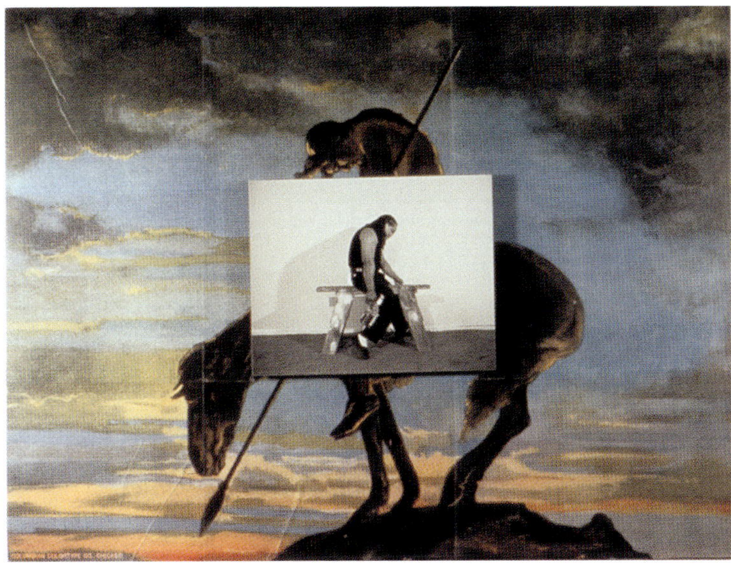

1.16 James Luna, *End of the Frail,* 1991. Black-and-white photo by Richard Lou. Courtesy of the artist.

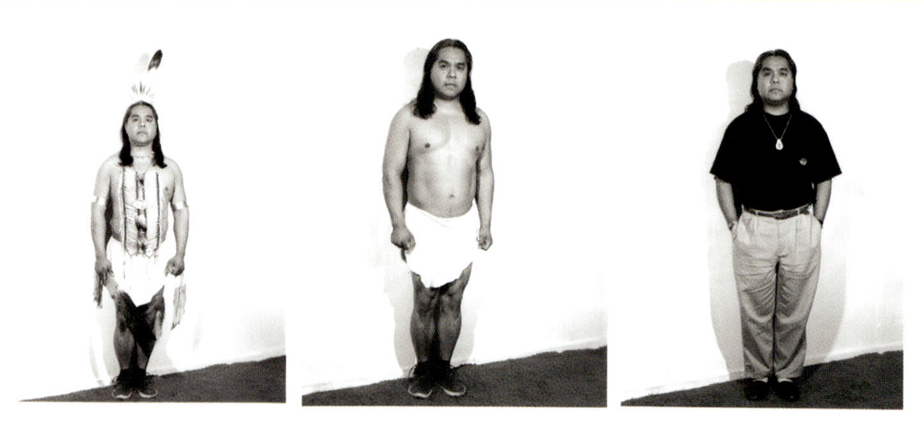

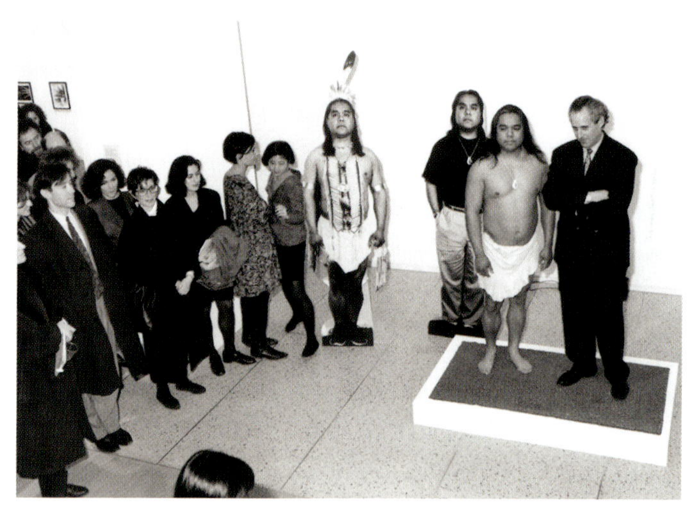

1.17, 1.18 James Luna, *Take a Picture with a Real Indian*, 1991. Photos courtesy of the artist and the Whitney Museum Independent Study Program.

In the photograph, Luna faces in the opposite direction as Fraser's Indian, and the wordplay of the title invites viewers to reassess the presumed frailty of the indigenous population, its purported defeat and demise. Luna's work is also in conversation with that of other contemporary Native American artists who have worked with photography as a cultural trope, directly referencing or deconstructing its anthropological gaze. For example, Marcus Amerman has produced a series of portraits that reconstruct the formal views of Edward S. Curtis's photographs, substituting indigenous men and women unromantically posing in contemporary clothing.[44] Amerman's images suggest that the photographic past infringes on the present as a discourse that can be reimagined though its rehabitation.

While some may assume that the idealization and commercialization of the image of the Indian lies in a past era, and that Luna's work is primarily a historical critique, ample evidence points to the reality that the display of Indian bodies and practices across the United States is still a lucrative commercial business today.[45] Reenacting the objectification of the Indian body as a tourist curiosity, the artist combined live performance with a photo shoot in *Take a Picture with a Real Indian,* staged both by the Whitney Museum Independent Study Program, in an exhibition entitled *Site-Seeing: Travel and Tourism in Contemporary Art* (1991), and later at the Salina Art Center in Kansas (2001). In both performances, Luna stood on a low platform covered in artificial turf with three life-sized photographic self-portraits flanking him on either side, their two-dimensional presence echoing the lifeless "cigar store" Indians that still populate parts of rural America as well as the cardboard cutouts—called "stand-ups"—designed for tourism and advertising. One of Luna's stand-ups wears simple street clothes, another shows the artist in an elaborate warrior costume with feathered headdress and decorative breastplate and in the last Luna wears only a leather loincloth and moccasins (figure 1.17). Audience members had the option of being photographed with the artist who appeared at the performance in each costume in succession (figure 1.18).

The power of the performance lay in the careful dynamics of staging the pose. In the Salina Art Center performance, Luna invited audience members up to the front of the room to "take a picture with a real Indian here tonight, free." Although he did not charge audience members, he emphasized the commercial transaction that normally attends such actions. "You get to take two, you take one home, and you leave one. Take a picture with a real Indian here in the middle of America. America likes to say *her* Indians. Come on," Luna gestured with the rattle in his hand, "take a picture with a *real* Indian."[46] Placing emphasis on the word "real" Luna repeated the phrase several times, challenging the audience to make a decision about what might constitute a real Indian. One of the first groups to come up on stage was a white family with two children.

Fully clothed and posed around Luna, who was wearing only his leather loincloth, their light skin contrasted with his exposed, tan body. Not one of the family members looked at Luna, or talked to him as they stared expectantly at the camera. Luna stood impassively and stoically for all of the shots. His neutrality in the pose and seriousness of expression, not to mention his general silence, invited a similar response from the audience. No communication took place between artist and audience members during the photographic act, which seemed almost pornographic in its live objectification of the artist-as-image. Photography as a mediating procedure became the conceptual focus of the work; as a medium inviting social "contact" through the artificial act of the pose, it also guaranteed that no substantive interchange would transpire. The fact that most participants chose to be photographed with Luna in his traditional rather than contemporary dress suggested that their notion of a "real Indian" depended on familiar stereotypes, not a contemporary artist in khakis and a T-shirt. One white woman who was photographed with the artist commented, "Well it was so disconcerting to stand by him. He was so inert and so unreal in lots of ways...statuesque. But I could smell the leather. Don't you think that's the way real Indians smell...with leather? What did you think?"[47]

It is instructive to compare the 1992 performance-installation *Two Undiscovered Amerindians...*, by Coco Fusco and Guillermo Gomez-Peña who posed as two caged "savages" in a parody of the displays of indigenous populations by colonizing countries that began as early as the fifteenth century and continued well into the twentieth century. Dark-skinned bodies of colonized peoples from Africa or South America, for example, were on display for the enjoyment and curiosity of white audiences at venues as various as world's fairs, nightclubs, circuses, zoos, and natural history museums in Europe and the United States.[48] Although Fusco and Gomez-Peña dressed in faux grass skirts and Converse tennis shoes, leopard skin wrestling masks and sunglasses, some viewers were still convinced that the performance was real and that the two performance artists were members of an indigenous tribe put on display in a cage (the work was exhibited in museums and art galleries in major cities including New York, London, Washington, DC, Madrid, and Sydney). Fusco and Gomez-Peña also offered to pose for photographs with museum and gallery visitors for a fee. In her essay about the performance experience, Fusco writes that "the public investment in [cultural and racial stereotypes] does not simply wither away through rationalization. The constant concern about our 'realness' revealed a need for reassurance that a 'true primitive' *did* exist, whether we fit the bill or not, and that she or he was visually identifiable."[49]

The discourse of the real, the fantasy of the authentic, and the desire for proximity to cultural or racial alterity appears to be nearly as strong in the contemporary art audience as it was for Curtis one hundred years ago. This pervasive fantasy and desire fuels a lucrative market of tourism in the United States where both native and nonnative entrepreneurs live off its perpetuation. In an interview about *Take a Picture with a Real Indian,* Luna remarked, "I saw some Indian selling his red ass to sell jewelry, and I was ashamed but knew what he was doing—he was working, I've worked too. When this opportunity came to do a statement on tourism, I thought of the Navajo and how as Indians we have all been on the tourist line."[50] After posing with numerous audience members, the artist continued his monologue: "America likes to name cars and trucks after our tribes. America likes to name film festivals after our sacred dances. America doesn't like us wealthy.… Americans like romance more than they like the truth. Take a picture with a real Indian in Pine Ridge, South Dakota.… Take a picture on skid row in Oklahoma City. Come to the Indian hospital in Washington State. Come to the res', come to the city, we are all over, we are all over, take a picture with a real Indian."[51]

Concern with "realness" haunts the lives of many Native Americans, and it is a trope that recurs in Luna's work. As suggested earlier, the artist examines the conditions or events that suture actual persons to mythic fantasies; he also demonstrates how these fantasies, in turn, produce the living conditions and racial environment that actual people have to navigate. For Luna both "fantasy" and "real" are suspect categories whose boundaries are permeable. Scholar Ann Marie Acklam argues that Luna's work can be understood not in terms of mimesis but in terms of *mimetic excess* insofar as it engages the performed body as both subject and object in order to "de-mask the artifice of reality."[52] In *Take a Picture with a Real Indian,* Luna debunks the notion that a "real Indian" exists, but he also draws our attention to very concrete conditions of everyday life for Native Americans today.

The artist has commented, "And there's the issue of what's an Indian? Who's an Indian? If you're part Indian, What's the other part? How does that influence you? Does it make you less? Does it make you more? I don't have an answer for that but that's part of my work, questioning that."[53] *Half Indian/Half Mexican* (1990) took up this issue directly in the form of a black-and-white photographic triptych showing the artist posed in a frontal and two profile views. A parody of the traditional mug shot, with its connotations of anthropometric science from the nineteenth century, Luna's somber self-portraits managed to debunk the notion that photography can reveal the truth of the subject (figure 1.19). One profile shows a clean-shaven Luna with long hair and an earring, while the other profile shows the artist with short-cropped hair and a thick mustache. It is the frontal view that is satirical, showing the artist with long hair draped over one shoulder and only half a mustache. Funny, but strangely unsettling, the central image also raises the question of racial and ethnic affiliation as a matter of choice or style—in this case, a shave and hair-cut. Conceptually and formally, Luna's work echoes Adrian Piper's *Political Self-Portrait #2* (1978), which recounts the fraught lived condition of the mixed-race subject. A black-and-white image of Piper is divided in half vertically so that her face appears to have white skin on one side and black skin on the other, like the negative/positive exposures of a photograph. Below the image, the word "paleface" appears in large block letters, and over the image is a poignant typewritten account of life lived as a light-skinned "colored" child that includes descriptions of abuse from both blacks and whites, revealing how living between two racial paradigms can be particularly brutal. Luna's *Half Indian/Half Mexican* is both more lighthearted and more celebratory of mixed cultural heritage than Piper's self-portrait, but it raises a set of parallel concerns about living as a racially split subject: concerns about belonging to a community, about being misread by the public, about rejection and assimilation.

Luna's portrait triptych was originally shown as part of an installation titled *Before Columbus/After Columbus* that included a circle of objects placed on the ground, half Native American (a traditional grindstone, basket with acorns, leather moccasins, flute, and family photographs on a bed of sand) and half Mexican (traditional Mexican *metate,* a can of refried beans in a cast-iron pan, leather boots, votive candles, and family photographs, on bright linoleum tiles). *Half Indian/Half Mexican* is distinctly autotopographical, and in some respects it functions as a risky confession for the artist, who quite possibly gains more support as an Indian artist than he might (particularly in the United States) as a Mexican American artist. In mainstream popular culture Indians, as we have seen, are often viewed as noble, mysterious, and wise, whereas Mexican Americans are often depicted as criminal, poor, and ignorant, despite the fact that genetic heritage and cultural traditions might well be shared by both, as the installation's material artifacts suggest. This is particularly true along the U.S.-Mexico border.

In the same way that *Take a Picture with a Real Indian* replicated the conditions of a roadside attraction in which the Indian's body is valued for its cardboard cutout resemblance to a stereotype, *Petroglyphs in Motion,* which was performed for SITE Santa Fe in 2001, replicated a high fashion runway. Audience members were seated in rows along two sides of a narrow aisle. Strategically placed floodlights along the floor in the darkened room mimicked stage lighting and also cast large, shadowy silhouettes of Luna against the white walls of the gallery space. The artist did not speak, but he was accompanied by a trap drum set played by Apache drummer Darren Virgil Gray. Using the quick change tactics of runway models, the artist appeared in a series of costumes and personas, the first a reference to German conceptual artist Joseph Beuys's ironic performance *I Like America and America Likes Me* (1974). During his first visit to the United

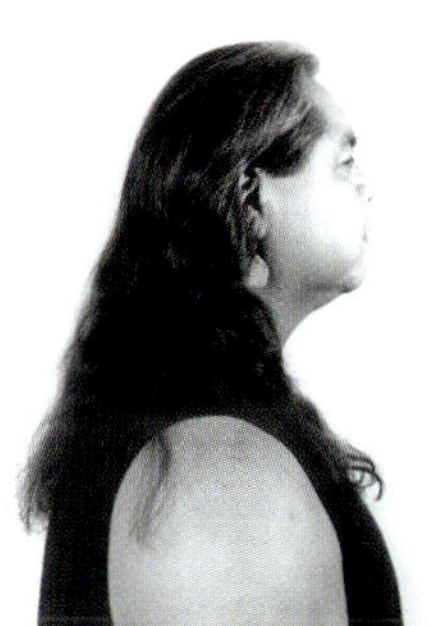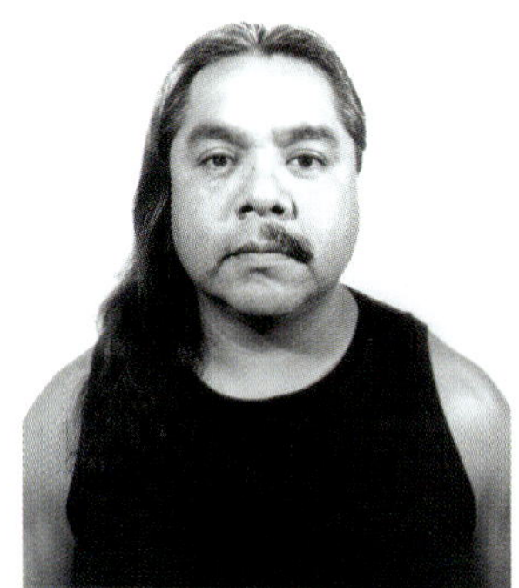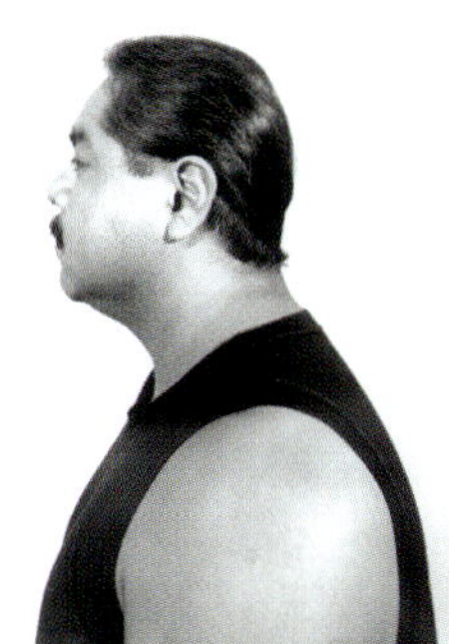

1.19 James Luna, *Half Indian/Half Mexican*, 1990. Photos courtesy of the artist.

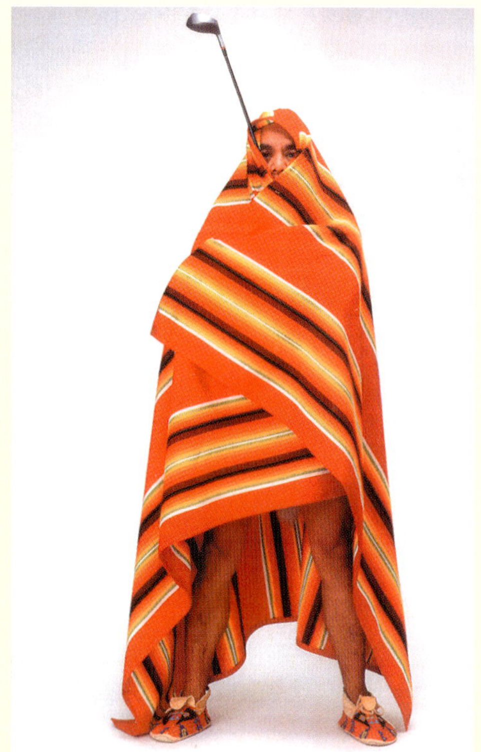
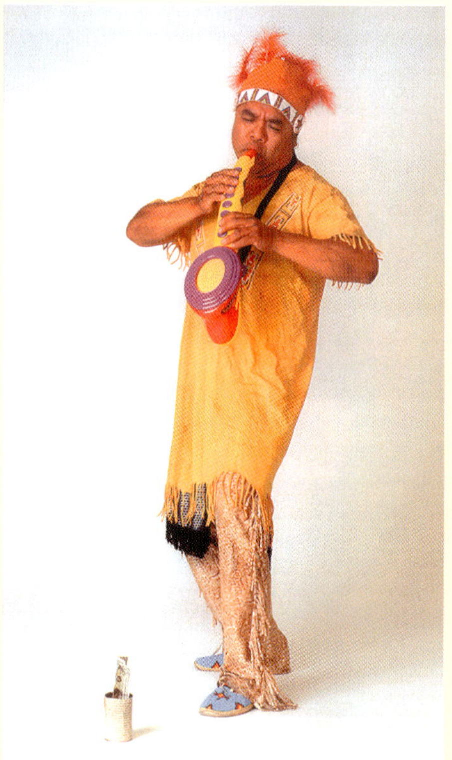

1.20, 1.21 James Luna, *Petroglyphs in Motion,* 2001. Detail of shaman and of playing saxophone. Photos courtesy of the artist.

States Beuys performed a three-day art action at the René Block gallery in New York, isolated with a captive wild coyote. His motive seems to have been a desire to be in the presence of something truly native to the Americas (although he also used the opportunity to protest U.S. foreign policies in Vietnam and critique the capitalistic impulse behind them). In a much-reproduced image of the performance, Beuys appears wrapped in a blanket of felt with a curved walking stick protruding slightly above his head, as if protecting himself from the animal across the room. In Luna's first runway pass, he wrapped himself from head to toe in a patterned 'Indian' blanket with a protruding walking stick (in later versions a golf club) (figure 1.20). For those familiar with Beuys's earlier work, Luna's reference was immediately apparent, and it also brought to mind the fact that Beuys occasionally likened himself to a shaman, freely appropriating and romanticizing the traditional practices of indigenous cultures.[54] Luna's performance is perhaps both homage and critique, for it also echoes the ironic sentiment of Beuys's title: *I Like America and America Likes Me*. After all, the Indian is an idealized cultural icon of the United States, as well as its most abject, defeated subject.

The rest of the performance might be understood to explore this range of contradictory connotations. Luna's subsequent personas included a runner in briefs, who then returned dancing with a rattle, and then returned with a telephone receiver, dialing numbers and gesturing as if in conversation. The audience laughed at this unexpected transformation of the mythological to the modern-day Indian. Luna then returned as a theatrical Indian wearing a commercial costume fringed in bright yellow and red, playing a toy saxophone (figure 1.21). When he proceeded to hold out a paper cup for donations, the audience played along with the joke. But the laughter died down when he returned in dark sunglasses, a *cholo* plaid flannel shirt, and red bandanna, drinking from a beer can and staggering as if drunk. Holding out the same paper cup to the audience for spare change, he got fewer donations, and some audience members looked away uncomfortably when approached. Each persona offered a view into the contemporary lives of Native Americans who suffer from the ailments of modernity (unemployment, alcoholism) or who survive in the face of it. Moving through several more characters, including a foxlike trickster figure, a slick salesman, and a stately elder in a wheelchair, the artist offered the audience a compendium of cultural projections. Although Luna recycled familiar stereotypes as the starting point of his silent petroglyphs (the shaman, the drunk, the trickster), he created nuanced and surprisingly sympathetic revisions of each by emphasizing their subtle, human qualities. *Petroglyphs in Motion* revived a tableau vivant tradition in the guise of a contemporary fashion show. Luna took on the role of the runway model, by definition an object of display, and presented his characters as the reanimation of petrified archetypes. Because of the silhouette effect on the walls, and the way in which the artist posed at each end of the runway, the work paralleled the artist's photographic practice more than his spoken performances. Visibility and invisibility were again at stake in Luna's effort to demonstrate how a fascination with the past, in this case with New Mexico's ancient petroglyphs, can obscure the lives of Native Americans in the present.

Overall, Luna's images are more *iconotropic* than iconoclastic, creating a conscious misinterpretation or reinterpretation of cultural icons to challenge their ideological power. They produce a visual articulation of the way the history of images, particularly photographic, comes to be imbedded in a lived corporeality for the subjects it defines. To live as an icon is to live artificially in relation to a public imaginary. This comes through in *Lunasteen* (2001) a black-and-white photograph of the artist leaping forward, with the neck of an electric guitar in one hand, pasted over an image of rock star Bruce Springsteen who is also leaping in the air, guitar in hand, in front of an American flag (figure 1.22). Formally echoing *End of the Frail* in its revision of an American icon, *Lunasteen* also serves to demonstrate the race politics underlying the public imaginary of national identity. As scholar Ellen Fernandez-Sacco observes, "The work wryly comments on how racial difference—both apparent and real—and iconicity reinforce whiteness in our sense of national identity and reaffirm constructions of white masculinity."[55] Luna's self-portrait is dwarfed by the Springsteen image. His intervention is only a small gesture against the vast apparatus of the U.S. culture industry, and the image demonstrates this fact as a question of scale. By superimposing his body on Springsteen's, the artist also claims the right to an American identity, yet demonstrates precisely how that right is denied, how American icons are usually white, how his own body signifies as racially unsuitable for this iconic role. Luna appears to be waving to someone, and his eyes are open. Perhaps the artist is hailing the future.

Racial Politics of Dislocation

It is a truism that Native Americans are rooted to the land of their ancestors, bound to a geography of the past that sustains a deep heritage tied to local customs. What is less commonly acknowledged but equally well known is the historical fact that most Native Americans over the course of the past two centuries have been displaced, uprooted, and transferred to schools, institutions, reservations, and cities on a systematic basis by the U.S. government. This dislocation, with its attendant cultural politics of deterritorialization and reterritorialization, is one of the most important experiences that Native Americans have in common. To deterritorialize is not only the activity of the subaltern in relation to a system of power but also the activity of those in power in order to maintain control over distributed, shifting ground. Such a politics is made concrete when

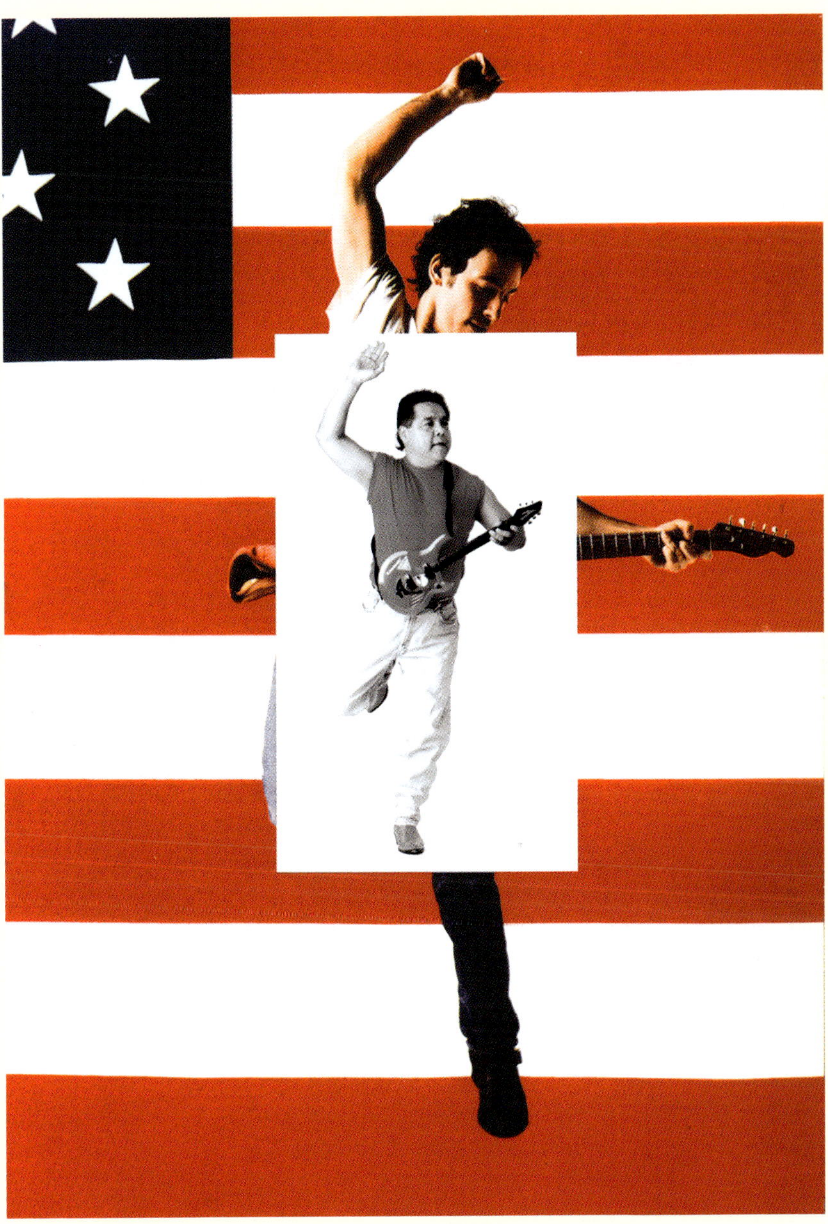

1.22 James Luna, *Lunasteen*, 2001. Photo courtesy of the artist.

people are removed from their native lands and are subsequently confined on artificially constructed (reterritorialized) reservations that are,
in turn, put under siege for their natural resources or tourist amenities.
*The Creation and Destruction of an American Indian Reservation: An Ameri-
can Dilemma 1875–1990* (1990) (figure 1.23) was Luna's effort to articulate
the history of this activity by creating an installation, live, in the space
of the art gallery.[56] I have found limited documentation of this work, and
therefore rely on the detailed description of Andrea Liss who writes,

> The piece opens with Luna appearing as an Indian dressed
> only in a breechcloth and holding a divining feather. Sounds of
> birds and water accompany the Indian's sure, graceful running
> motions around miniaturized simulations of land and trees.
> With each circular running pattern, Luna uncovers and gently
> upturns rocks that become *metates*, grinding utensils. In the
> next scenario, Luna appears as a contemporary Indian dressed
> in Americanized clothing. He unrolls barbed wire and meticu-
> lously begins to create ominous obstructions around the min-
> iaturized set-ups. In the next part, a government construction
> worker nonchalantly unrolls a highway, deposits mail boxes on
> the new road and, in perhaps the most cruel of these ludicrous
> acts, sets up a sign warning of cows along the road where ani-
> mals (not to mention people) once knew no boundaries.[57]

Not only does Luna's performance enact the transformation of land to
property, it also demonstrates the method of engaging territorial space
through the signs that limit its meaning and function. While a conceptual parallel can be drawn between the installation of the artwork and
the imposition of a bureaucratic infrastructure—as forms of reterri-

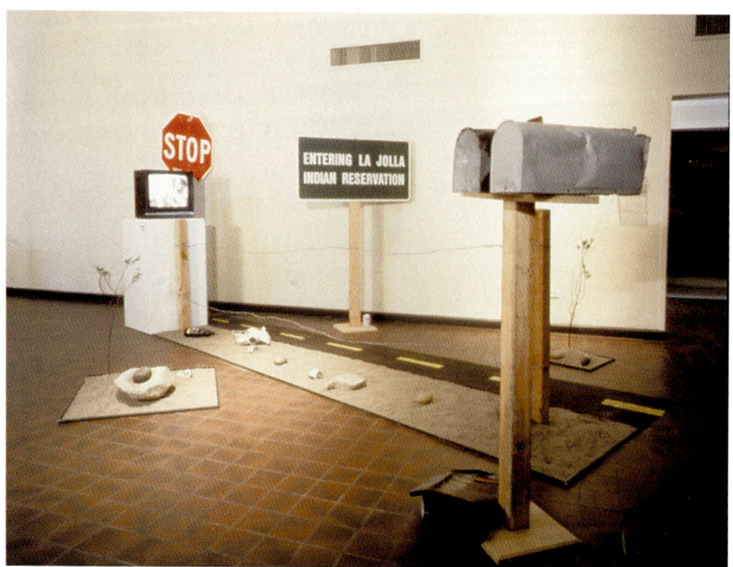

1.23 James Luna, *The Creation and Destruction of an American Indian Reservation: An American Dilemma 1875–1990*, 1990. Installation view. Photo courtesy of the artist.

torialization—the cluttered residue of sculptural elements left behind offers a more tangible, metonymic testament to the barren indifference of state hegemony.

Enforced movement and enforced stasis underlie several of Luna's installation projects, informed by the Indian Removal Act of 1830 that led to the famous Cherokee Trail of Tears in 1838 and to more recent efforts such as the 1954 Bureau of Indian Affairs Termination and Relocation phase of the Reorganization Act of 1934. The termination phase of the act removed government recognition of 61 tribes, leaving hundreds of thousands of Native Americans unqualified for government assistance, and the relocation phase of the act transferred a large number of inhabitants from largely rural reservations to urban areas with the thought that they might be more likely to find work there. For many, the consequences were dire, leaving thousands deprived of rural community traditions and isolated in public housing without a means of subsistence.

Luna's *Relocation Stories* (1993), shown at Pro Arts in Oakland, California, takes as its subject the personal stories of those who felt the effects of Termination and Relocation. Oakland was one of the original sites chosen for relocation, and today the Bay Area has one of the largest Native American populations in the nation.[58] Luna's audience may have identified directly with his narrative accounts, particularly as the artist included projected images of local urban landscapes and low-income housing that suggested the raw anonymity of city life. The work combined a live performance by the artist, recorded sound interviews, and a large-scale installation. In the live performance, the artist took on the personas of John, Montana Woman, and Betty, each with their own experience of dislocation and survival in the city. John tells the story of working in a canning factory, and becoming first an alcoholic and then a Christian; Montana Woman recounts her experience of working as a motel manager, eventually quitting to become a social worker; Betty raises five children and manages to send them all to college, ultimately finding self-fulfillment despite the challenges of transitioning to the city and divorcing her husband.

The artist's installation was divided into four sites that might have been inhabited by these displaced figures: a spare domestic interior with motel furniture; an empty bar animated by the flickering light of a television; a miniature baseball diamond made of artificial turf, bordered on two sides by chain-link fences; and a plot of earth with landscape photographs and the sound of birdsong (figure 1.24). Suggesting life at the economic margins of the mainstream, the domestic interior was furnished with a wellworn sofa and coffee table, an empty bottle of beer and ashtray, cans of food, a narrow cot draped with an army blanket against one wall, a faded and yellowed window shade, a few plaid work shirts unceremoniously hung on nails by the door, and another flickering television set playing

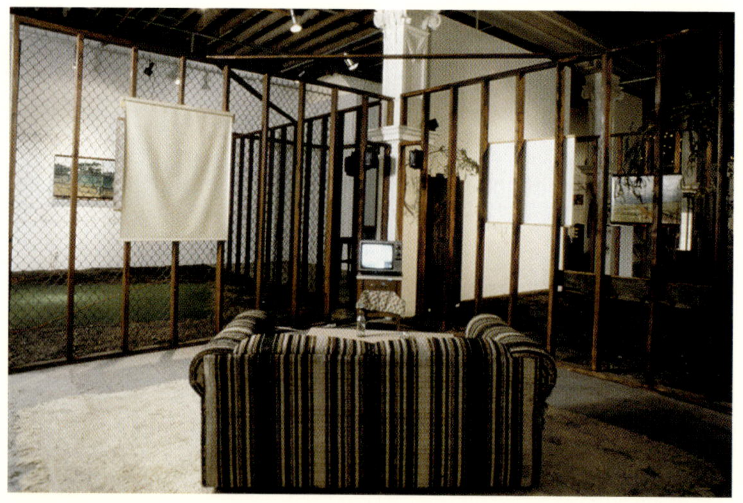

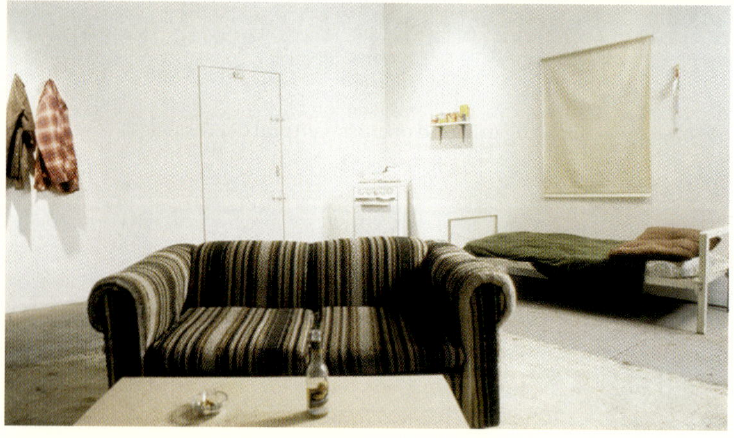

1.24, 1.25 James Luna, *Relocation Stories,* 1993. Installation view and installation view of domestic interior. Photos courtesy of the artist.

a video about the 1950s and the process of relocation (figure 1.25). Each of the spaces had a sound element drawn from the artist's interviews with those who had participated in the relocation program. As in Luna's performance, some of the stories reflected the pain of enforced change, of agoraphobia in the city, of depression and loss. Others recounted survival stories including one woman who had worked with colleagues to institute an annual Native American arts festival. Because the installation spaces were divided primarily by simple skeleton walls of wooden studs, it was possible to see from one to the other and to imagine the passage or slippage between one site, one story, and another.

For this project, installation art provided the ideal vehicle for articulating the effects of dislocation, precisely because it allowed for the construction of spatial environments that could be experienced as a temporary habitation for the visitor, who was invited to imagine what it might mean to occupy these spare and drab rooms or outdoor sanctuaries. It is also precisely the reason why this kind of installation might fail in some respects. The contemporary art audience might have found the spaces simply alienating in their drabness or, alternatively, the audience might have imagined they were participating in a kind of cross-cultural or cross-class voyeurism. Details such as the worn furniture, or the lonely bar, might have appeared as clichés. While recognizing the potential for this kind of interpretation, it is crucial to acknowledge that Luna's multimodal address looks beyond a contemporary art audience, to precisely those working-class Native Americans displaced from the reservation who might respond to his piece with a sense of recognition, with a sense of belonging, with a sense that their stories were not only told but also heard.

History always forgets the remarkable lives of individuals who struggle against the sometimes subtle and sometimes tragic errors of communication and blindness that shape cross-cultural contact. When Luna was asked to represent the National Museum of the American Indian at the Venice Biennale in 2005, he chose to examine the history of contact between Native Americans and Italians, and by extension the history of colonial encounter. Luna's installation *Emendatio* (Emendation) offers a corrective to such historical amnesia by recounting the story of Pablo Tac, a young Luiseño Indian who traveled from the Mission San Luis Rey in Southern California to the Vatican in 1834 to train as a missionary. The life of Tac, who died in Rome at the age of nineteen, became the narrative thread linking several photo and video works, live performances, and a full-scale installation of a chapel in the Fondazione Querini-Stampalia. Each component of Luna's multipart work addressed the possible—and impossible— relations between people across a great religious and cultural divide.

"Chapel for Pablo Tac" was furnished with traditional wooden pews and walls draped with a white cloth painted with a simple pattern of crosses and diamonds reminiscent of the painted interiors of the Spanish adobe missions in California. This pattern is taken from the Pala Mission, which is another twenty miles inland from Mission San Luis Rey, founded in 1816. Somewhat typical of Indian painted murals in other missions, the shapes are a mix of Indian and Catholic symbolism. The square cross, for example, appears in a number of Luna's works, such as 2 *Worlds*, and probably represents a revision of the Catholic icon into a symbol for the four cardinal directions. Objects on the altar were arranged with a modest symmetry; an altar cloth of white linen supported two candles, a woven basket with feather shapes in a cruciform, a chalice such as those used in Holy Communion, a leather medicine bag, an abalone shell for burning incense, and two sacred feathers (figure 1.26). The objects marked an intersection of traditional native spiritual practices and the Catholicism imposed by the Spanish, and by extension the Vatican in Italy. On a woven tapestry hanging behind the altar was an excerpt from the writings of Tac that are preserved in the Mezzofanti collection at the Biblioteca del'Archiginnasio di Bologna under the general heading "Californian Language." The text (translated from the original Spanish) reads: "Each Indian People has its dances, different from other dances. In Europe, they dance for joy, for a feast, for any fortunate news. But the Indians of California dance not only for a feast but also before starting a war, for grief, because they have lost the victory, and in memory of grandparents, aunts and uncles, parents already dead. Now that we are Christians, we dance for ceremony."[59]

Imbedded centrally on the front of the altar, a screen played a looping ten-minute video suggesting the journey of Tac. The rushing sound of the sea and a view of the swirling tide is followed by a ringing bell; church organ music begins to play and sepia toned photographs of Native American men and women from the turn of the century fade in over interior views of adobe missions and a map of Spanish settlements along the California coast. After a fade to black, with church music swelling, the majestic interior of St. Peter's Cathedral in Rome comes into view, followed by an exterior image of the Vatican at Christmas with brightly colored lights shining. We are invited to imagine the profound impression this architectural splendor would have made on Tac after his long voyage from rural California to Italy in the nineteenth century.

If the video had ended there, it would have offered little more than a romantic view of a historical encounter, but Luna's approach is always more irreverent. A strange light emanating from the dome of the cathedral, looking at first like a golden halo or beacon, was in fact footage of a drive along the Las Vegas strip, with brightly lit casinos and car headlights flashing by. Eventually the scene shifted to a contemporary shot of the Venice casino in Las Vegas, with elaborate fountains and faux-finish architecture, then jumped back to the Vatican with its pillared

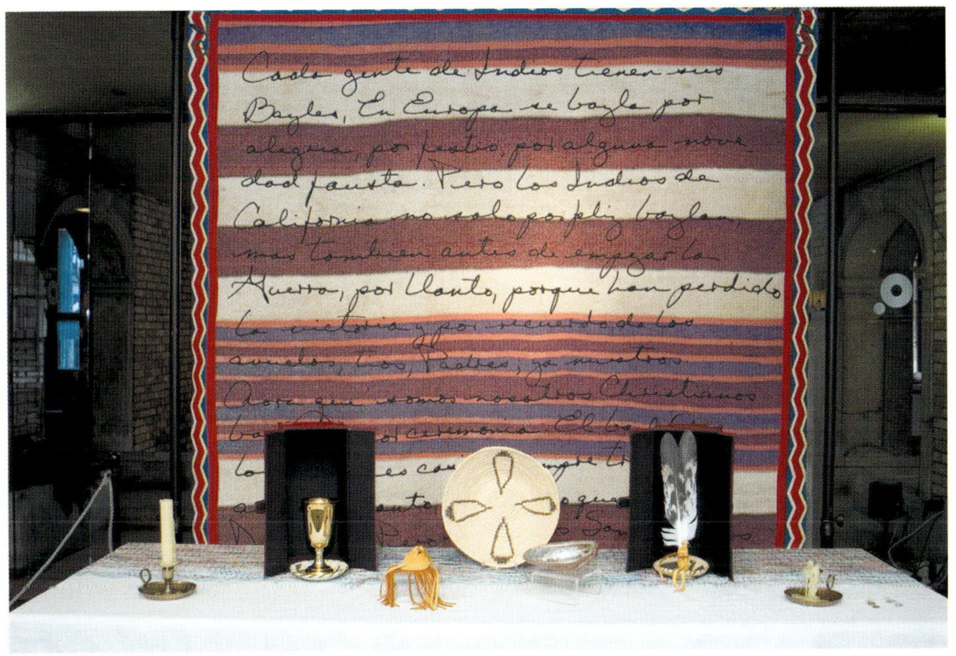

1.26 James Luna, "Chapel for Pablo Tac," one of two installations for *Emendatio*, at the 2005 Venice Biennale or 51st International Art Exhibition. Photo by Katherine Fogden. Courtesy of the artist and the Smithsonian/ National Museum of the American Indian.

piazza and glittering interiors. A number of readings are possible: that the power and visual spectacle belonging to the Vatican in past centuries can also be found in the bright lights of Las Vegas; that Catholicism has always been tied to the accumulation of wealth; that Native American tribes have turned increasingly to building casinos to find some kind of salvation; that money has become a new religion; or that the real and the simulacrum, the past and the present are not so different. Luna choreographed several live performances for *Emendatio,* each staged as a ritual dance. As with *Petroglyphs in Motion,* he enacted and intervened in stereotypes still operative in the European imaginary. Like a present-day Pablo Tac, Luna made the transatlantic voyage to Italy from the Luiseño reservation in Southern California, and was invited to reflect on his cultural heritage there. Luna, like Tac, was a curiosity who performed his difference for an audience.

For Luna, race discourse sets up the conditions for a command performance in which subjects are required to play characters whose roles are often fixed a priori. His installations become the theatrical stage for this performance as in *The Artifact Piece,* or alternative sites of encounter, as in *Relocation Stories.* Although they make reference to history and are frequently satirical or ironic, Luna's installations are designed to be inhabited in the present, to be engaged as environments in their own right—as a museum display, as a high-tech sweat lodge, as a contemplative chapel—but they are not replicas of real places. Rather, if one can imagine a space taking on the qualities of a persona, then Luna's installations are more easily grasped as character studies, such as those he develops in performances and photography. They are excessive, elaborate, and *emending,* with the salutary result of disturbing the complacency of audiences who encounter them.

FRED WILSON

MATERIAL MUSEOLOGY

 engaged in the historical and theoretical analysis of the visibility and invisibility of race and racially marked bodies in museums for nearly two decades. His artworks interrogate relations of power, and their fictions, through an examination of the politics of display and an ongoing reevaluation of the role of the museum as a social institution in which curators, administrators, and audiences participate. In 1987 he installed *Rooms with a View: The Struggle Between Culture, Content and the Context of Art*. It was his first effort to examine the architectural and aesthetic forms of museum display and their parallel interpretive frameworks. Opening at the Longwood Arts Project in the Bronx, the show consisted of contemporary artworks by more than twenty artists curated by Wilson in three distinct exhibition styles.[1] One room took the form of a modernist white cube, with the attendant minimalist aesthetic of bare floors and walls, open space, and sparsely hung works of art, primarily paintings; the décor of the second gallery suggested a late-nineteenth-century salon or richly furnished domestic interior that included a sculpted mantelpiece, potted plants, and hung tapestries; the third gallery took the form of an ethnographic museum display with walls painted in warm sepia tones, glass vitrines, and cordoned off display spaces showing what looked like functional objects made of natural materials. Each gallery presented the contemporary works differently: as fine art, as decorative art, or as anthropological artifact. In an interview with Leslie King-Hammond, the artist commented, "Depending on the room, the art looked and felt either cold and calculated, or authoritative and valuable, or exotic and foreign."[2] The artist's goal was to highlight the fiction of display styles in order to expose the visual and spatial characteristics that formed an interpretive frame for each of the works.

A conceptually foundational project for the artist, *Rooms with a View* appeared at a moment when critical museum studies had emerged in the academy and when many museum curators were trying their own hand at innovative exhibition techniques in the public sphere. In the same year that Wilson exhibited *Rooms with a View*, curator Susan Vogel opened the Art/Artifact exhibit at the Center for African Arts in New York. In her essay "Always True to the Object, in Our Fashion," she notes that the Art/Artifact exhibition "approached the question of perception through individual objects and through installation styles. Recognizing that the physical setting of an object is part of what makes it identifiable as art, the installation showed art objects and non-art objects in such a way as to raise the question in the viewer's mind and to make the trickery of the installation evident."[3] Like Wilson, Vogel produced an exhibit with thematic rooms in which artifacts were displayed as works of art in a minimalist fine arts environment, as "curiosities" displayed in cases and cabinets, and as props in an ethnographic diorama. Vogel hoped to make evident the fact that "these different styles reflected differences in attitude and interpretation, and that the viewer was manipulated by all of them."[4]

The confluence of circumstances that led to both exhibitions can be attributed to a development, simultaneous in the fine arts and in museum studies, of a critical analysis of the museum as an ideological institution that produces and sustains political and social formations. In *Objects and Others: Essays on Museums and Material Culture,* George Stocking argues that in the world of ethnography and anthropology, the emergence of a "new national consciousness in the aftermath of the colonial era, during a period of heightened domestic radicalism in the centers of Euro-American power, called into question the traditional relationship of objects and others in the museum environment."[5] Ownership of cultural artifacts, and the right to interpret their meanings, to assign them a place in the history of art or in the museum archive, became contested and debated among multiple constituencies with conflicting interests. Museums worked to guarantee the meaning of cultural patrimony and, in many cases, colonial privilege for imperial nations. To change the museum and its forms of display was to question not only the validity of the power relations of the past but also the meaning of that past for those living in the present.

Contemporary artists in the 1970s and 1980s played a critical, activist role in drawing attention to museums as institutions that produce ideologies of cultural containment, cultural hierarchy, and cultural legitimacy. Hans Haacke and Louise Lawler, two of Wilson's immediate predecessors, share his critical approach to the social, economic, and ideological function of the museum of art. Haacke's groundbreaking installations such as

On Social Grease (1975) or *Metro Mobiltan* (1985) addressed the complex social and political systems underlying the funding and management of major museums of art.[6] With deadpan wit, Haacke demonstrated how museums participate in a larger culture industry that works to manage public consciousness. Lawler's approach is equally documentary, using photography rather than installation to record the visual logic of museum display spaces and the material conditions of works of art that are hung, stored, and transported in and through them. Her work explores the value of art in the public sphere, in private collections, and in the limbo of packing cases and storage. Early work such as *Figures and Guard* (1983) show a museum interior with sculptures in darkened bronze that seem to dwarf a museum guard in the background. Some of the poignancy found in Wilson's *My Life as a Dog* (see introduction) can also be found in this image that illustrates the uneven value placed on works of art and the anonymous lives of those who are hired to protect it.[7] Andrea Fraser, an artist who is a contemporary of Wilson's, has also used the art gallery and museum as the site and subject of carefully conceived, scripted performance art. Fraser offers critical reflection on gallery representatives who sell the idea of art to gallery patrons in *May I Help You?* (1991); on the way in which artists are invited or required to provide services for art institutions in *How to Provide an Artistic Service: An Introduction* (1994); and on art museums, such as the Guggenheim, Bilbao, that create nearly erotic mythologies about the prowess of their architects and sensuousness of their architecture in *Little Frank and His Carp* (2001).

Douglas Crimp's 1993 essay "On the Museum's Ruins" claimed that practices of "postmodern" art undermined the modernist principles on which museums and their taxonomic structures had originally been based.[8] The delegitimation of absolute authenticity, originality, and aesthetic authority found in institutionalized presentations of "truth," "history," and "beauty" allowed for a new discourse of museum practice and a new domain of art practice to emerge.[9] The metadiscursive activities of artists such as Haacke, Lawler, Fraser, and Wilson have commonly been described as "institutional critique," a useful term that indicates the detailed analyses of networks of power and systems of representation the artists perform in order to reveal the cultural mechanisms at play in museums and other social institutions that market or display art. At the same time, it is not simply an anti-authoritarian, generic critique of the institution qua institution that is operative in this work, but more important, a specific commentary on how the power and pervasiveness of market capitalism, patriarchy, patrimony, or race discourse operates through social institutions, especially art institutions. Recently, the concept of institutional critique has itself come under scrutiny by artists and scholars who seek to better define its origins and its limits.[10] Andrea Fraser writes, "The institution of art is not only 'institutionalized' in organizations like museums and objectified in art objects. It is also internalized, embodied, and performed by people. It is internalized in the competencies, conceptual models and modes of perception that allow us to produce, write about and understand art, or simply to recognize art as art, whether as artists, critics, curators, art historians, dealers, collectors or museum visitors."[11] Fraser argues for a nuanced understanding of institutional critique, recognizing that artists and their works are always already imbedded in systems of display and circulation that are ultimately inescapable. Artist Renée Green observes that the limits of institutional critique as a conceptual description lie in its inability to encompass other parallel efforts by artists including what she calls "abolitionism," "anthropophagia," "diaspora," and "infrasensorial" practices. Green writes, "If we examine the ramifications of these and related ideas, they might change the ways we think about and construct our relations to institutions, and allow us to venture beyond representations of the voice of administrative power linked to the founding notions of Western thought. It might be possible, instead, to investigate in the interstices, where these structures of authority unravel, and locate other subjectivities."[12]

Wilson's critical assessments of art institutions, practices of display, and race discourses can be read as precisely this unraveling of authoritative frameworks, and as a method for locating "other" subjectivities. Never claiming to occupy a position outside the art world apparatus, Wilson nevertheless manages to offer a poignant portrait of the internalized assumptions and racial hierarchies that are at play within it. Recognizing that many museums have historically been structured around the fact of colonial and imperial relations, Wilson decided to take seriously the notion that one might produce a different vision of museum discourse, a view from the "Other" side. The genre innovations of installation art that complemented the curatorial skills he had already developed became the means for responding to the popular critical discourse about cultural "Otherness" that circulated in the early 1990s.[13] Wilson's *The Other Museum* (1990), which showed at White Columns in New York, thus served as a rearticulation of both the concept of Otherness and the history of ethnographic display. With glass cabinets, curatorial text, identifying labels, and "primitive" objects, the gallery installation employed the visual tropes and taxonomic schema of the natural history and anthropology museums it sought to parody and critique. *The Other Museum* was not intended to replicate ethnographic practice, but rather to present a critical and historical view of anthropological and ethnographic discourse and their attendant museum displays. The word *other* in the title invoked both the Otherness of cultural or racial difference (i.e., the colonized Other) and the Otherness of a new ideological perspective.

At the entrance to the exhibition a map of the world was hung upside down, reminding viewers that geography is itself a result of arbitrary domination and uneven distributions of power. Wall labels were written from the viewpoint of the vanquished, presenting a subaltern perspective on colonial conquest and the subsequent international trade in material goods, aesthetic artifacts, and people. Objects were identified neither as the "gift" of a particular donor nor as having been anonymously "acquired" by the museum, but rather as "stolen from" a particular community or sacred burial site. Exposing acts of cultural plunder in non-euphemistic terms, Wilson unmasked the deeply acquisitive nature of colonialism along with the often complicit role of the anthropologist as collector and the museum as repository. "In general," the artist writes, "the designed environment of museums is a formalist system of display rooted in the socio-cultural eras of the past; as such these spaces embody the politics, the pain, the suffering, and the separateness characteristic of the time when the collections were formed."[14]

In one corner of the gallery stood a glass vitrine containing two nineteenth-century engravings from *Harpers Weekly* of 1874 depicting British military confrontations with the Zulu and the Asante peoples of Africa (figure 2.1). One image depicted a battle scene (with a caption that reads "The 'Black Watch' in action—fighting in the forest of Ashantee"), and the other was of a circle of covered wagons, similar to those which have become synonymous with Western expansion in the United States and the elimination of American Indian populations. The glass case also contained a grouping of delicate butterflies and other insects, each neatly boxed and labeled with the name of an African people. Identified as "The French and British Collection 1914," this mock-scientific display signaled the European urge to "collect" colonies and to produce rigid classifications of colonized peoples who were often treated as exotic specimens.

Wilson's installation also suggested how the loot from war could be transformed, via the mechanism of the museum, into cultural treasures. In an anthropomorphizing gesture, the artist installed a row of six wooden masks of African origin, each gagged or blindfolded with a colonial flag (figure 2.2). The group, titled *Spoils,* served as a metaphoric and metonymic sign for the bodily effects of colonialism: starvation, blinding, execution, silencing. On one mask Wilson projected the image of a woman's face (actress Alva Rogers), whose eyes and lips moved, while behind the mask a recorded female voice was heard pleading: "Don't just look at me; listen to me. Don't just own me; understand me. Don't just talk about me; talk to me. I am still alive." The words challenged the complicity of the audience in maintaining a comfortable distance between the art object and the culture from which it was removed.

Sound recording is a frequent device Wilson employs to disrupt the authoritative, familiar, yet repressive sound of silence maintained in galleries and museums. The polite murmur of shuffling feet and quiet contemplation

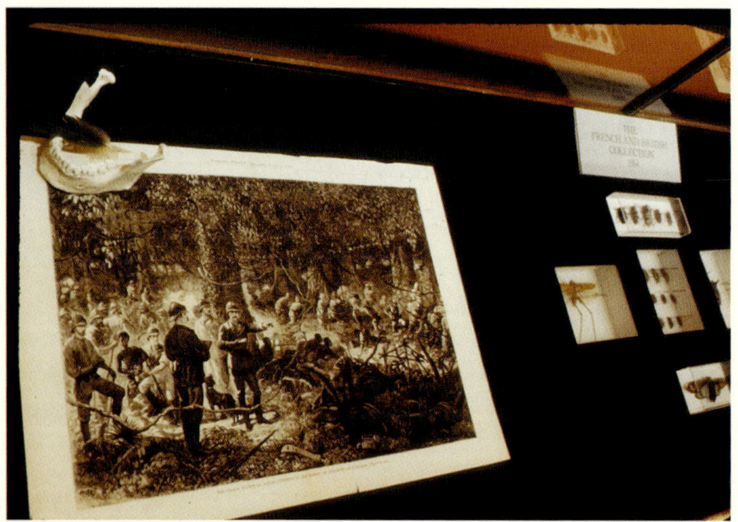

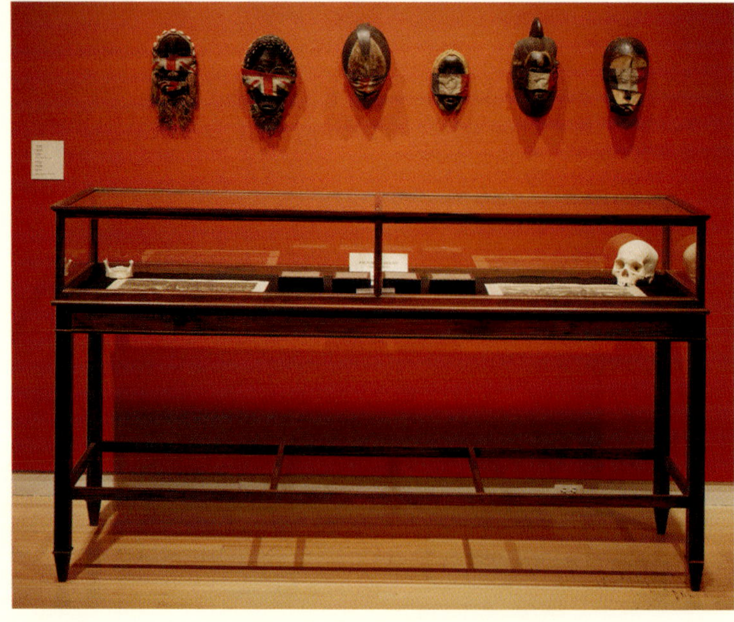

2.1, 2.2 Fred Wilson, "Colonial Collection" in *The Other Museum*, 1990. White Columns, New York. Courtesy of the artist.

that is the instituted norm is irreverently infiltrated by unlikely sounds of violence, narrative, and talking back. The slightly uncanny, unanticipated emergence of sound from otherwise mute objects produces a strategic, ghosting effect that simultaneously functions as a return of the repressed. By giving voice to the object, the artist also invites the visitor into a pseudodialogue while simultaneously constructing a subject position with which, or against which, the visitor is asked to identify.

Wilson's reference to ownership ("Don't just own me") can be read as both a critique of the way African masks become consumer objects stripped of history or cultural context and a metonymic sign for the historical enslavement of Africans. Each of the admonitions also addresses the social and institutional position of the *Spoils* themselves. The equation Wilson constructs between the human subject and the art object as commodities in contemporary metropolitan and industrial contexts enlarges the possible connotations of ownership that colonialism entails. The aesthetic transformation of such *Spoils* into collectible art objects marks a shift in the way objects are perceived by the museum elite: what was once a debased sign of a "primitive" culture becomes an object of desire. Yet this transformation does not necessarily change the balance of power between the colonizer and the colonized or its representation in the museum.[15]

bell hooks observes, "When race and ethnicity become commodified as resources for pleasure, the culture of specific groups, as well as the bodies of individuals, can be seen as constituting an alternative playground where members of dominating races, genders, sexual practices affirm their power-over in intimate relations with the Other."[16] To what degree, Wilson's installation asks, have museums provided a playground for their audiences to explore and affirm their cultural difference from, and cultural superiority over, others? Homi Bhabha suggests, "In fact the sign of the 'cultured' or the 'civilized' attitude is the ability to appreciate cultures in a kind of *musée imaginaire*; as though one should be able to collect and appreciate them. Western connoisseurship is the capacity to understand and locate cultures in a universal timeframe that acknowledges their various historical and social contexts only eventually to transcend them and render them transparent.... A transparent norm is constituted, a norm given by the host society or dominant culture, which says that 'these other cultures are fine, but we must be able to locate them within our own grid.' This is what I mean by a *creation* of cultural diversity and a *containment* of cultural difference."[17] In *The Other Museum,* those "transparent" norms that rule the rhetoric of display constitute the necessary conditions of Wilson's own critical *musée imaginaire*.

On the walls, a series of black-and-white photographs depicting nineteenth-century eugenicist attempts to measure the physiognomic differences among the races—images of naked Africans, Native Americans, and Brazilians placed in front of either scientific or "natural" back-drops—were located alongside other images from the same period showing well-dressed, prosperous Africans and Native Americans. Set side by side in vertical rows, the two sets of photographs were labeled "Early Ethnographers and Other Photographers of European Descent" and "Early Black and Native American Photographers," or "Photographed by Others" and "Photographed by Ourselves." The clear contrast—stylistic and ideological—between the images was its own form of rhetorical argument, revealing the contradictory systems of representation operating at the same historical moment.

While photography is often perceived as a documentary or indexical sign that reveals the truth of that which it pictures, Wilson deftly shows how it reveals primarily and above all the imaginary and ideological position of the photographer.[18] Rather than interrogating the truth of historical images, Wilson offers an analysis of what has been called the "truth effect" of photography.[19] The labels, highlighting the racist implications of photographs taken by Europeans of non-Europeans, reiterated the relations of categorization and control imaged in the photographs, while also drawing attention to the act of labeling itself as a method for circumscribing meaning. In the photographs taken by Europeans, the subjects remained nameless—"Mojave Indians of the Lower Colorado, Western Arizona Region" or "The Sons of Cannibals Contemplating the Passion of the Redeemer"—while those taken by African and Native American photographers were labeled "Mrs. Frank (Jenny) Johnston and Kitty Walker" or "John Thom's Father, Kokla, with Grizzly Bear." The label becomes the sign that confers the rights of subjectivity. Citing Michael Baxandall, James Clifford observes that "labels are not, properly speaking, descriptions of the objects to which they refer. Rather, they are interpretations that serve to open a meaningful space between the object's maker, its exhibitor, and its viewer, with the latter given the task of intentionally, actively building cultural translations and critical meanings."[20]

Wilson thus demonstrated how museums actively participate in shaping what Bhabha has called a "fixed reality" for their viewers. Bhabha writes, "Colonial power produces the colonized as a fixed reality which is at once an 'other' and yet entirely knowable and visible. It resembles a form of narrative in which the productivity and circulation of subjects and signs are bound in a reformed and recognizable totality."[21] Combining material, visual, and linguistic registers, museum displays also bind subjects and signs into re-formed and recognizable "totalities" that are sometimes given the names "culture," "race," "art," or "artifact."[22]

These "totalities" create what must be understood as the conditions of *subjection* for museum audiences, offering narratives that make explicit the historical, geographical, or aesthetic ties between viewing subjects and the objects they encounter.[23] Because such "totalities" are always only partial narratives, they often substitute for and repress other possible stories. Museums thereby establish the conditions not only for identification but also for disidentification: between the colonizer and the colonized, between the collector and the collected, and among different communities of visitors. José Muñoz, in his book *Disidentifications: Queers of Color and the Performance of Politics,* suggests that an important aspect of contemporary performance art is the activity of rejecting hegemonic categories of identity and identification. Insofar as subjectivity and identity are arguably performative, Muñoz claims that "minoritarian" performance artists have found a way to disidentify with the categories that frame them, thereby actively constructing alternative personas to escape limiting stereotypes. Muñoz argues that the dissemination of such performances to a mass audience "allows for the *possibility of counterpublics*—communities and relational chains of resistance that contest the dominant public sphere."[24] If it can be said that museums always construct their audiences as specific interpretative communities, then the emergence of a "counterpublic" or at least the necessary conditions for the act of disidentification may be one outcome of Wilson's work.[25]

The Other Museum became the model for several of Wilson's subsequent gallery installations. In works such as *Primitivism High and Low* (1991) and *Panta Rei: A Gallery of Ancient Classical Art* (1992), Wilson transformed gallery spaces into pseudomuseum environments, staging critical views of the ways material objects (paintings, sculptures, masks, costumes) have been framed historically by racial and cultural hierarchies. *Primitivism High and Low* at Metro Pictures in New York was a wry response to two controversial exhibitions that had been held in previous years at New York's Museum of Modern Art: *"Primitivism" in Twentieth Century Art: Affinity of the Tribal and Modern* (1984) and *High and Low: Modern Art, Popular Culture* (1990).[26] Both exhibitions received some public criticism for their limited conceptions of "the primitive" and of the relations of class that establish such categories as "high" and "low" or "popular culture" in relation to modern art. In his essay "Histories of the Tribal and Modern," James Clifford offers his own critique of the 1984 exhibition, pointing to the euphemistic and promiscuous quality of the concept of "affinity" (which might be better understood, he suggests, as appropriation) and the narrow historical interpretation of the "intercultural encounter" between the tribal and the modern—an encounter in which the primitive object is seen to be redeemed through its incarnation as modern art.[27] Clifford's article also draws attention to the aesthetic and the anthropological interpretation of objects, which, despite their differences, also share an investment in preservation. He writes, "The aesthetic-anthropological opposition is systematic, presupposing an underlying set of attitudes toward the 'tribal.' Both discourses assume a primitive world in need of preservation, redemption, and representation. The concrete, inventive existence of tribal cultures and artists is suppressed in the process of either constituting authentic 'traditional' worlds or appreciating their products in the timeless category of 'art.'"[28]

In Wilson's *Primitivism High and Low,* museums of ethnography and museums of art are shown to produce two different but parallel forms of primitivizing discourse, staging the scene where cultural difference is made into the notion of the "primitive" through the lens of the aesthetic and ethnographic. As in *Rooms with a View,* the artist used conventions of display found in ethnographic and art museums, but a new emphasis was placed on the hierarchical relationship between them. The gallery space at Metro Pictures was divided into two separate rooms, one painted a deep blue-green, the other a pristine white. Attention to the color of the environment and its staging of the "colored" body was in keeping with a long history of museum display. In her book *The Power of Display: A History of Exhibition Installations at the Museum of Modern Art,* Mary Ann Staniszewski traces this intersection of ethnographic display and color schemes in midcentury exhibitions at the museum, writing, "Contextualization of the objects was attempted by painting the gallery walls, display structures and ceilings in hues of eleven different colors that were intended to be representative of each area—for example the 'dark green of the jungle…the sand color and red rock of the Australian desertland.' The galleries were also lit with different types of light to evoke, for instance 'the white light of the coral islands' and 'a dim jungle light.'"[29]

Taking center stage in Wilson's blue-green room a somewhat awkwardly posed, dark-skinned mannequin wearing traditional Nigerian dress stood alone, both regal and forlorn (figure 2.3). Recorded voices in French, German, and English could be heard emanating from his body, along with confused sounds of battle and hand-to-hand combat. One side of the room displayed four glass cases containing human skeletons labeled "Someone's Mother," "Someone's Sister," "Someone's Father," and "Someone's Brother."[30] Their anonymity attested to the general indifference of those who supposedly exhumed them, and signaled the uneven power relations that led to the possibility of one culture's exhibition of another culture's dead ancestors. Along another wall, several miniature dioramas were presented as "American Colonies." Resembling displays commonly found in museums of natural history, each diorama was placed in the wall and carefully lit, and each was labeled with a general geographic area, or in some cases the name of a specific country. For example, "Asia" was represented by a diorama of "The Philippines," whereas "Latin America" remained a general category. Wilson's use of labels and installation techniques invited the viewer to focus on the absurdity of taxonomies that subsume whole populations under geographical regions and at the same time drew attention to the purpose such taxonomies have served for U.S.

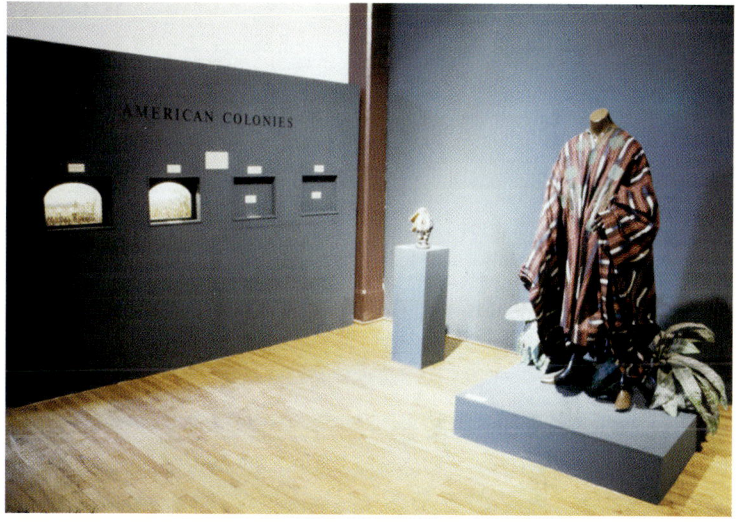

2.3 Fred Wilson, "Friendly Native" in *Primitivism High and Low,* 1991. Metro Pictures, New York. Courtesy of the artist.

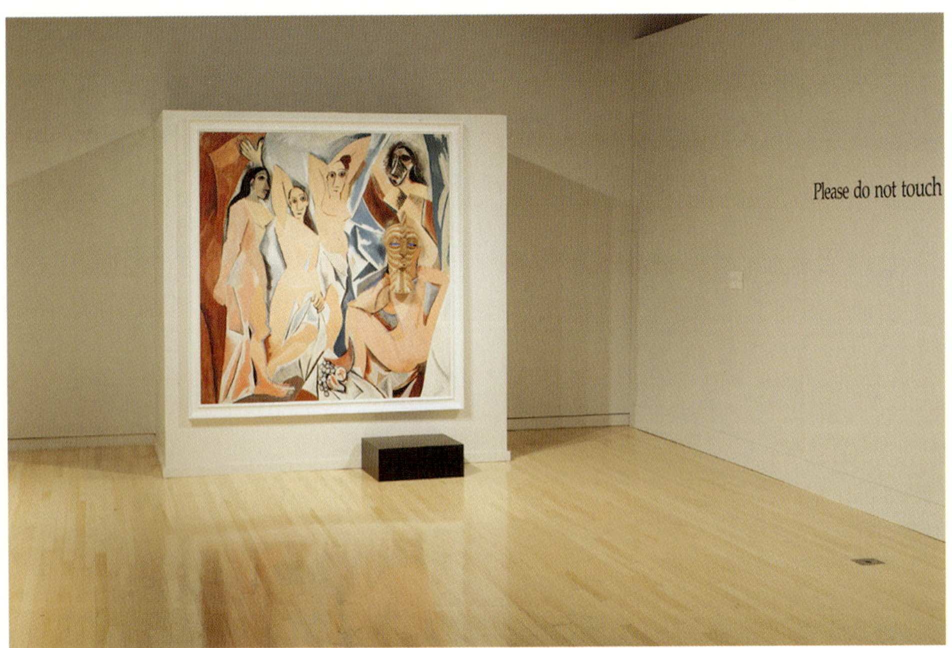

2.4 Fred Wilson, "Picasso: Whose Rules?" in *Primitivism High and Low,* 1991. Metro Pictures, New York. Photo by Dan Meyers. Courtesy of the photographer.

imperialism. The dioramas themselves were found castoffs, constructed before midcentury, depicting quaint and rural scenes of everyday life complete with thatched roofs and barefoot natives. The panoptical effect of the diorama, which derives from the seductive miniaturizing techniques of architectural modeling to produce a bird's-eye view, effectively mimics the act of not only military control but also cultural surveillance from the center of empire.[31]

In Wilson's installation the racialized human body is shown to exist only through the distorting lens of its ex post facto display. Each figure is caught in the bind of a desubjectifying visual apparatus that produces a historical act of silencing: the mannequin is headless, the skeletons are anonymous, the miniature bodies in the colonies are no more than children's toys. In short, any *subjectivity* of the subject is actively repressed by the discourses of "low" primitivism that rely on techniques of display to articulate the developmental inferiority of the colonized body. Even the recorded sounds reveal a colonizing moment of cultural assimilation and dominance.

In sharp contrast, the other half of the installation functioned as a typical white cube exhibition space containing a life-size reproduction of Pablo Picasso's *Les Demoiselles d'Avignon* (figure 2.4) and four museum guards. A paradigmatic moment of the merging of so-called primitive aesthetics with modern art, Picasso's painting depicts five women, two with faces inspired by the pattern and geometry of traditional African masks. Anna C. Chave assesses the historical reception of the painting by art scholars and critics and the ideological mix of fascination and revulsion the work elicits from those who have made it an icon of hyperbole.[32] Female bodies with African-inflected identities suggest both the threat and the allure of cross-cultural contact in modern France. The social and sexual implications of this visual merging, and the fact that the women depicted are ostensibly prostitutes, signals a modernist interest in the racial or cultural Other that is more than stylistic. Ironically, the power of Picasso's vision is not only his innovations in postcubist abstraction, but the painting's ability to effectively mask the actual colonial legacy that led to the conditions of the painting's historical emergence. The object, like a sexual fetish, is used to mask a hidden fear (cultural difference, contamination by sexually transmitted diseases), but it is also used to enable fantasies of inaccessible, or at least inappropriate and dangerous, cross-racial desire. Wilson's reproduction had an added element: a wooden Kifwebe mask was placed over the face of the seated figure in the image. Attached directly to the surface of the painting, the mask stood out in sharp profile, a blue light glowing from behind its eyes. If one stepped up on a platform to peer into the eyes of the mask, one saw Wilson and two Senegalese friends staring back from a video screen. In three different languages, the talking heads asked, "Whose rules decide what is great?"

and "If your modern art is our traditional art, does that make our contemporary art your cliché?" Other questions addressed the role of the work of art in the museum and the standards by which it is judged.

Olu Oguibe has observed that within colonial discourse, art and aesthetic sensibility were crucial signifiers of the civilized state and constituted the unbridgeable distance between savagery and culture.[33] Wilson's installation staged this gulf between the culture of high art and the history of traditional African art as an inferior form, ripe for appropriation. At one end of the room were the words "Please do not touch the works of art," and near the painting another text read, "Can you see anything?" "Yes, wonderful things."[34] Directly across from the painting, Wilson posed four dark-skinned mannequins wearing the security guard uniforms of four metropolitan museums in New York City. Keeping watch over the installation, the "guards" appeared nameless and headless, like their counterpart in African dress. "Guarded View," as the ensemble was called, economically illustrated the relations of race and privilege in fine art museums (figure 2.5). Who belongs to the audience that can look at *Les Demoiselles d'Avignon* in an unguarded fashion? Who is paid to protect it?[35]

Wilson's work might be read as complementary to the feminist analysis produced by Carol Duncan in her now classic book *Civilizing Rituals: Inside Public Art Museums* where she reads Picasso's *Les Desmoiselles D'Avignon* as forcefully asserting "to both men and women the privileged status of male viewers," commenting further that "the use of African art constitutes not an homage to 'the primitive' but a means of framing woman as 'other,' one whose savage, animalistic inner self stands opposed to the civilized, reflective male's."[36] Wilson's reinstallation of the painting, in which the body part that becomes fetishized is the face/race of the subject, foregrounds the fascination with cultural difference as itself a *ritual* activity. It also raises the question of *whose* desire is addressed by the painting, and may operate in dialogue with Lorna Simpson's earlier photographic work *Guarded Conditions* (1989), which depicts, in a row of full-length portraits, a black woman with her back turned to us and the alternating phrases "sex attacks/skin attacks" written below. In both the Wilson and the Simpson works, the black body/black subject is simultaneously anonymous and on display, simultaneously sexualized and desexualized, vulnerable to an exterior gaze yet ultimately hidden and unknowable.

Bhabha has suggested how a fetishistic impulse is at the origin of colonial, racial, and ethnic stereotypes; Wilson reveals that it is also at work in canonical Western works of art and in the very act of canonization itself.[37] In strategically choosing the Picasso, Wilson reveals its function as a "screen object" that serves, like Freud's screen memory, as both an overdetermined site of projection and a site of active forgetting. The iconic status of the painting literally effaces the social relations of colo-

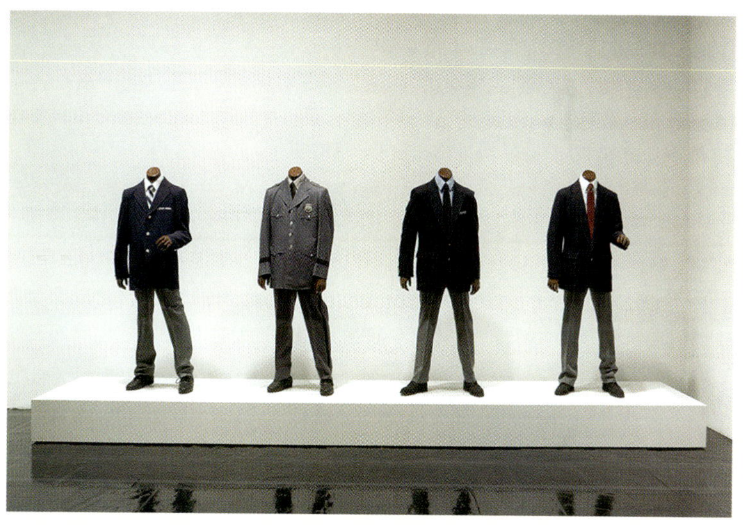

2.5 Fred Wilson, "Guarded View" in *Primitivism High and Low,* 1991. Metro Pictures, New York. Courtesy of the artist.

nialism that led to modernism's fascination with the so-called primitive. Of course it is possible to argue that it is the timeless allure of Picasso's painting that allows us to revisit the past again and again, that the painting serves as a placeholder for reflection on, and critique of, this unique historical moment. This is possibly true; but it is equally true that the painting's canonical status (not to mention financial importance to the Museum of Modern Art) ensures its existence as a fulcrum of scholarly and popular attention while resisting any real counterdiscourse about its cultural significance. Wilson's iconoclastic gesture depends upon this fact but also works to challenge this hegemony. Whether "high" or "low," Wilson reveals that "primitivism" can be understood not only as a noun but also as a transitive verb, as something that is done *to* someone or something. Wilson's installation effectively questions the role of museums in creating the status of "great" works of art and in defining the perniciously persistent notion of "primitive" culture, but the rhetorical power of *Primitivism High and Low* lies in its refusal to disassociate the ways in which institutionalized racism applies to works of art, artifacts, and living people; all are shown to suffer the consequences of the primitivism *effect*, of being primitivized both ethnographically and aesthetically.

In his efforts to bring attention to representations of race or ethnicity in museum displays, Wilson (who is himself of Carib and African American descent) generally refuses to reduce his critical analysis to a simple binary of black/white positions, but rather insists on the historical complexity through which ethnicities and cultural ideologies are formed. While many of his installations use a polemical visual rhetoric, the work never ascribes fixed roles to racial types. Instead, the artist revisits the uneven past of racial formations through the social, cultural, and even scholarly institutions that guard history's narratives.

Wilson's installation *Panta Rei: A Gallery of Ancient Classical Art* (1992) delved into one of history's most hotly debated issues at the time: the cultural and aesthetic ties between Egyptian and Greek antiquity and, by implication, the question of their African origins. The sculptural figures that populated the gallery space were an unusual yet elegant array of plaster casts of ancient and classical sculptures in black and white; but they were not simple reproductions, they were unexpected ruptures. Canonical antiquities were transformed into new hybrid creatures through apparently violent grafts that left shards of broken plaster strewn on the floor: the head of Hermes was replaced with the jackal likeness of the Egyptian god Anubis; in turn, the Greek goddess Artemis lost her head to the feline Egyptian god, Bast (figure 2.6). Walter Benjamin writes, "He who wishes to approach his own buried past must act like a man who digs.... Because facts of the matter are only deposits, layers which deliver only to the most meticulous examination what constitutes the true assets hidden within the inner earth: the images which, torn from all former contexts, stand—like ruins or torsos in the collector's gallery—as treasures in the sober chambers of our bleated insights."[38] The title *Panta Rei*—Greek for "things in flux"—aptly described the sense of active metamorphosis and disorder in the space where ruins appeared to reveal new historical truths. Wilson was attentive to historical detail in producing his hybrids: just as the Greek god Hermes was responsible for conducting the dead through Hades, so too was the Egyptian Anubis responsible for leading the dead to judgment. Wilson's anatomical reformulations, inspired in part by Martin Bernal's controversial book *Black Athena* (1987), suggest strong links between the older Egyptian gods and the more recent Greek incarnations.[39] While it is well known that both Greek and Egyptian statues were originally painted with bright colors, Wilson's choice to present them in black and white demonstrates the way Western history has framed them—Hellenistic Greek culture as the origin of an Aryan Europe, and Egyptian culture as preclassical and racially distinct. A statue of Atlas carrying on his shoulders, in place of the world, a stack of Western art history books reiterates the point. Tucked beneath his feet is one slim volume devoted to African art. The double implica-

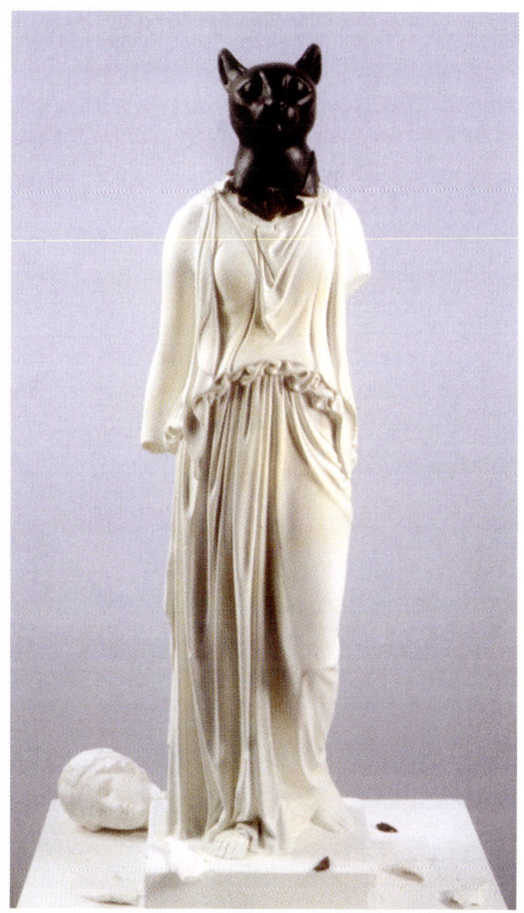

2.6 Fred Wilson, "Artemis/Bast" in *Panta Rei: A Gallery of Ancient Classical Art*, 1992. Courtesy of Pace Wildenstein.

tion is clear: European art has been built on a foundation that includes Egyptian art, yet history refuses to acknowledge these African origins. As Maurice Berger has argued, the works serve as allegories of "art history's long-standing state of denial about the sources of Western art."[40]

In his gallery installations, Wilson places artificial or hybrid artifacts in pseudomuseums to demonstrate how the display of material objects, and the subjects to which they refer, constitute a particular instance of racial formation. Both the subjects of address (the gallery visitors) and the objects on display are integrated into a network of relations designed to reveal the emergence of race discourses that define and delimit canonical museum display practices. Wilson's strategic selection and placement allows no sign to float free from its latent racial, or racially inflected, content. To be clear: it is not that Wilson finds "race" to be a concept worth supporting, he is rather engaged in the investigation of how race becomes a form of domination that operates through cultural institutions that collect, preserve, and exhibit objects or material culture. At the Whitney Museum Biennial in 1993, the artist exhibited one of his more direct and literal critiques of the "raced" object. In a small installation called *Reclaiming Egypt* that included some faux ancient artifacts and contemporary Egyptian tourist souvenirs, the artist included a large reproduction effigy of the head of Pharaoh Ankenaten. When one approached the imposing bust, painted gray and hung high on the wall, a voice triggered by a motion sensor asked, "What race am I?" After a short pause the voice replied, "Wrong," then continued, "What race are you?" After another short pause, "Hmmm." Finally, the voice asked, "What is race?" By posing these questions, the work both undermined the idea that the concept of race is self-evident and also underscored the way that works of art and historical artifacts are read through discourses of race and valued accordingly. Egyptian artifacts are from Africa obviously, but are they racially black? An Egyptologist might argue, correctly, that it is anachronistic to apply the idea of race (a relatively recent invention) to an ancient object. Wilson's work does not make such an anachronistic argument; instead it raises our awareness of the systems of representation and the logics of cultural difference that lay a veneer of race—an epidermalization—on all objects. His installations provide a stage for demonstrating how an object or artifact comes to be raced by its location, use, presentation, or affiliation with a racially defined community. When Wilson delves into the archives of public museums, this process is even more clearly articulated.

Mining Museums: Archeology of the Archive

In 1992 Fred Wilson was given his first opportunity to create an installation within the walls of a public museum resulting in *Mining the Museum,* an innovative display of archival objects from the Maryland Historical

Society. Jointly sponsored by The Contemporary, Baltimore, *Mining the Museum* was a collaborative effort that allowed the artist to have open access to the historical society's permanent collection, and gave him several months to interview its staff and plan an exhibition. Applying the display strategies developed in gallery works to the museum's archives, Wilson brought to light histories that had been buried in the museum's basement for decades, particularly those of African Americans and Native Americans in Maryland. Wilson's project was, in fact, part of a conscious effort by the historical society to make its collections more relevant to greater Baltimore's largely African American population. The exhibit was an unexpected success; serendipitously opening during the annual conference of the American Association of Museums, held that year in Baltimore, it attracted thousands of museum professionals. Running for eleven months, it was the most popular, and the most controversial, show in the thirty-year public exhibition history of the Maryland Historical Society.[41] Fred Wilson and the Maryland Historical Society gained widespread notoriety for their groundbreaking collaboration, which changed both the internal workings of the institution and the artist's own methodology.

Lisa Corrin, the curator responsible for organizing the collaboration with The Contemporary, contrasts *Mining the Museum* to Wilson's earlier works: "For it is one thing to talk about race and museums in an alternative space or hip commercial gallery," she writes, "but it is quite another to address it in an established museum by using its own collection and its own history."[42] Skillful in its rhetoric of display, *Mining the Museum* delved into the institution's archive to offer a new vision of Maryland's past that was not without its darker moments. The word *mining*, as Judith Stein observes, functioned for the artist as a three-way pun: "excavating the collections to extract the buried presence of racial minorities, planting emotionally explosive historical material to raise consciousness and effect institutional change, and finding reflections of himself within the museum."[43]

For Wilson, the work was intended to make visitors think critically and raise questions about the authority of the museum as a social institution. An introductory video reminded viewers that curators always bring their own perspective into the exhibits they construct and announced that *Mining the Museum* reflected Wilson's personal response to the Maryland Historical Society. Although legible as a form of institutional critique, the show was framed by informative disclaimers at the outset (whether this decision was originally the artist's or the museum's is unclear). Nevertheless, visitors were encouraged to raise questions rather than seek answers in the exhibit, prompted by a set of questions posted in the elevators such as: "What is it? Where is it? Who is represented? How are they represented? Who is doing the telling? What do you touch? What do you feel? What do you think?"⁴⁴ These questions allowed Wilson to raise the issues of ownership and knowledge, recognizing the lack of access for many communities to archives and cultural heritage, and to invite reflection on the limited range of behaviors traditionally allowed in institutional contexts such as museums.

Exiting the elevator on the third floor of the building, where *Mining the Museum* was installed, visitors were first greeted with an enormous golden globe emblazoned with the word *truth*. Known familiarly as the "Truth Trophy" until the 1920s, the globe was awarded to commercial organizations for truth in advertising—an innocent sense of truth that seems nearly quaint today. Inside a glass case, the trophy was surrounded by several transparent acrylic mounts, each numbered and labeled "Acrylic Mounts, Maker unknown, ca. 1960s, Plexiglas." The empty mounts signaled that neither the museum nor the artist had a monopoly on truth, that the apparatus of display was as much under scrutiny as the objects presented, and that any version of the truth would be necessarily incomplete. Displayed in the same room, three pedestals supported the carved marble and white plaster busts of Napoleon, Henry Clay, and Stonewall Jackson (each borrowed from the permanent collection, but none who were native to Maryland), while three black pedestals labeled Harriet Tubman, Benjamin Banneker, and Frederick Douglass (all famous Marylanders, but not represented in the museum's collection) remained empty.

In eight adjoining rooms the exhibition unraveled an unorthodox and unflattering narrative of Maryland's past, emphasizing the period in which Africans were enslaved but making links to more recent history. In the gallery adjacent to the Truth Trophy, a map on the wall marked the various indigenous tribes that once inhabited the Chesapeake Bay before colonization. In a nearby case filled with dozens of arrowheads, their cataloging numbers visible to the visitor, the label read "Collection of numbers, 76.1.25.3—76.1.67.11" and the medium was listed as "White drawing ink, black India ink, lacquer." In a reversal, the arrowheads, like the Plexiglas mounts, became the ground for the display of a system of cataloging that assigned them a precise location within the institution. They also served as a subtle reminder that the United States' Bureau of Indian Affairs used to keep track of Native Americans with numbering systems, such as the Dawes roll numbers in the nineteenth century. When Wilson was planning the exhibition, he inquired about the local descendents of indigenous populations in Maryland but was told that none remained. After a bit of research the artist unearthed a series of recent photographs of American Indian families from the archives at the Maryland Commission on Indian Affairs. He placed these portraits opposite a row of cigar store "Indians" from the museum's collection, thereby effecting a face-off between the wooden fantasies of the past and the contemporary subjects, who are dwarfed by comparison (figure 2.7).

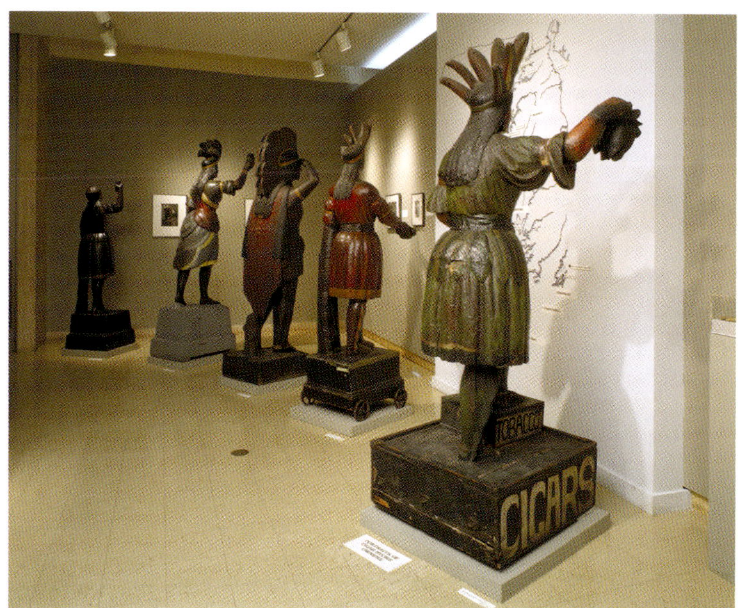

2.7 Fred Wilson, "Cigar Store Indians" in *Mining the Museum,* 1992. Maryland Historical Society, Baltimore. Courtesy of the artist.

In another room, devoted to the material culture of the land-owning classes, the artist installed one of his more powerful juxtapositions. "Metalwork 1793–1880" grouped Baltimore repoussé-style silver vessels with a single, oxidized pair of iron slave shackles (figure 2.8). Iconic of the interdependence of slave labor and a luxury economy, the visual contrast of fine silver craftsmanship and crude ironwork, as well as the position of the abject slave shackles amid the tall goblets and elegant decanters, implied the vast gulf dividing the subjects of Maryland's past. Because museum collections have typically been composed of the objects belonging to the ruling class and the wealthy elite (who have comprised the museum's audience as well), the material culture of the working class, and certainly of the slave class, would never be—indeed had never been—shown side by side with such signs of bourgeois privilege. The unlikely but felicitous category "metalwork" encompassed both silver and iron, while the nearly one-hundred-year time span from 1793 to 1880 also marked the gradual abolition of slavery in the Americas from the 1793 Anti-Slavery Act of Ontario, Canada, to the abolition of slavery in Cuba in 1880. The years 1793–1880 also correspond to the exact dates of the life of Lucretia Coffin Mott, a founder of the American Anti-Slavery Society (1833) who served as president of the Philadelphia Anti-Slavery Society before most women considered joining the movement and made her home a stop on the underground railroad in the 1850s. The dates chosen by Wilson are not arbitrary then, but significant for those who are familiar with American history.

Through the simple pairing of silver goblets and slave shackles, Wilson also calls attention to the ideological function of an institution that has

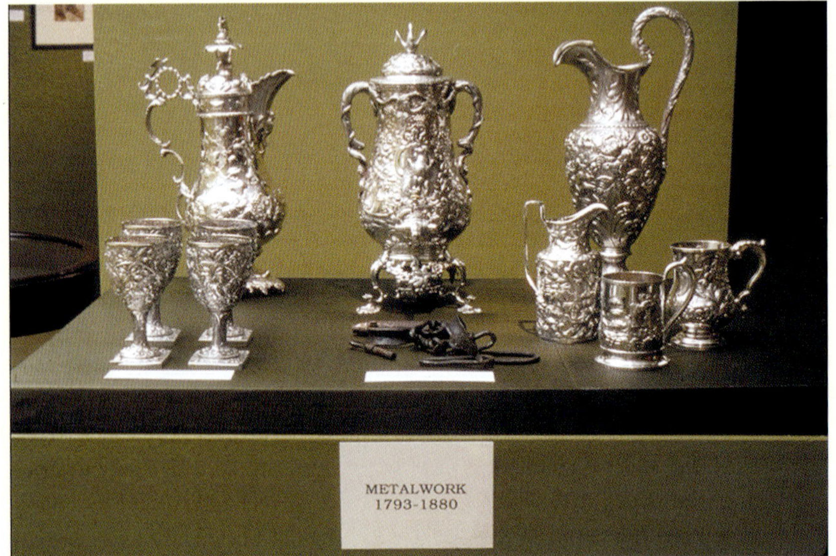

2.8 Fred Wilson, "Metalwork 1793–1880" in *Mining the Museum,* 1992. Maryland Historical Society, Baltimore. Photo by Jeff Goldman. Courtesy of the Contemporary Museum, Baltimore.

traditionally kept such objects apart. "As I see it," he comments, "juxtaposition is one way of unlocking [history] without a didactic tone—allowing the objects to speak to each other. I feel that there is a dialogue between objects—sometimes subtle dialogue, sometimes pronounced dialogue, depending on how diverse the objects are and depending on who is seeing them, too."[45] When a museum decides to display one object as decorative art and another as historical artifact, it does not merely establish a hierarchy of aesthetic values; it also limits contact between such objects and thereby restricts the stories such objects tell together. If, as Gaston Bachelard has suggested, "the hidden in men and the hidden in things belong in the same topoanalysis," then any archive also serves as a topological map of human relations, producing its own geography of concealment in the process of preservation.[46]

Fred Wilson's efforts are perhaps best understood as a rhetorical topoanalysis—every buried secret and every surface becomes part of a new logic that maps the institution's history. His attention to already visible but marginal signs even includes, for example, the margins of oil paintings. In several of the Maryland Historical Society's eighteenth-century group portraits of children, white children of the landed class are pictured with black children, probably their slaves. Often barely visible because of the dark tone of the pigments used to paint their skin, the African American children are also depicted in the margins, literally pushed to the edges of the picture frame, gazing admiringly at their masters. To focus attention on these hidden figures, Wilson used a motion sensor, triggered by passing museum visitors, to activate a spotlight and audiotape. For the young black girl who stands at the edge of *The Alexander Contee Hanson Family* portrait (Robert Edge Pine, ca. 1787), a voice asks, "Where is my mother? Who combs my hair? Who calms me when I'm afraid?" For a portrait of *Henry Darnall III* (Justus Engelhardt Kuhn, ca. 1710), pictured with his estate and a nameless slave retained by a metal collar around his neck, a voice asks, "Am I your brother? Am I your friend? Am I your pet?" (figure 2.9). Wilson's interrogative interjections address the familial, emotional, and hierarchical relations among children in a slave economy, offering his own thoughts as a contemporary viewer who identifies with the slave, not the master. The Darnall portrait was originally hung in another gallery at the historical society; when Wilson took it for his own exhibition, he left behind in its place a small leather dog collar resting against the wall, just where the metal slave collar would have been.

The rules of slave ownership that underlie the logic of these eighteenth-century portraits require that black bodies be on display as property, but the images also reveal the slave as the origin of the gaze that guarantees the status of the master—from the margins. The portraits were allegories for the museum itself, which guarantees the status of those who are made visible or invisible by it. Directly addressing museum visitors, the installations foregrounded the often-unconscious processes of identification—or disidentification—that visitors experience in front of works of art and artifacts. Instead of a narcissistic gesture, the use of "I" and "mine" in *Mining the Museum* invites identification between the viewer and those subjects whose history has been summarily ignored or institutionally erased.[47] It is a radical gesture, not trivial or quaint, to offer first-person status to the slaves in the portraits who remain nameless to this day.

For "Modes of Transport 1770–1910" the artist gathered in one room an eighteenth-century sedan chair, a wooden model of a slave ship, and several baby carriages from the early twentieth century. This incongruous collection was contextualized by a set of images: an oil painting, *Maryland in 1750* by Frank B. Mayer, ca. 1856, depicting a white woman seated in a sedan chair, her black porters waiting nearby, and an early-twentieth-century photograph of African American nannies with white children in carriages. From a distance the carriages appeared innocent enough, but many visitors were shocked to find a full-size Ku Klux Klan hood nestled in one (figure 2.10). The hood had been anonymously donated to the museum in an earlier era, and, much to the institutions' embarrassment, Wilson insisted on its display. The museum's director of education, Judy Van Dyke, recalled that the Klan hood created a wide variety of reactions:

> One black man said to me that it was almost humorous. I was blown away. Nobody in any of my other groups had thought it was humorous. And another black man said, 'Well, I don't see anything funny about it. To me it's not funny at all. I've had personal experience with the Klan in Louisiana and I can hardly look at this. I am sweating right now, just looking at it.' There was more of a general discussion and a white woman in the group moved on toward the [next room] and said, 'I think we've been here long enough. I think it's time to move on.'"[48]

A set of even more explicit juxtapositions in the adjoining gallery explored the violent relations between slaves and their masters, the disciplinary, sexual, and psychological abuse that forms a part of the legacy of human relations in much of the United States. The barrel of a large punt gun, used for hunting game birds in the Chesapeake Bay during the nineteenth century, was aimed at the entering visitor and at a cluster of antique wooden duck decoys in the midst of which stood a jointed, dark-skinned doll in a civil war Zouave uniform. The Zouave were originally a colonial French infantry unit composed of Algerian recruits, but during the civil war some Union Army units patterned themselves after these predecessors, wearing similar uniforms and identifying themselves by the same name. In the installation, a parallel is drawn between the "track-

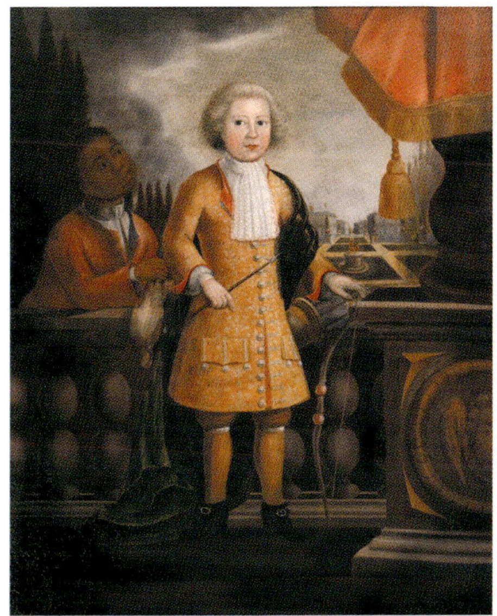

2.9 Justus Englehardt Kuhn, *Henry Darnall III*, ca. 1710. Oil on canvas. Courtesy of the Maryland Historical Society.

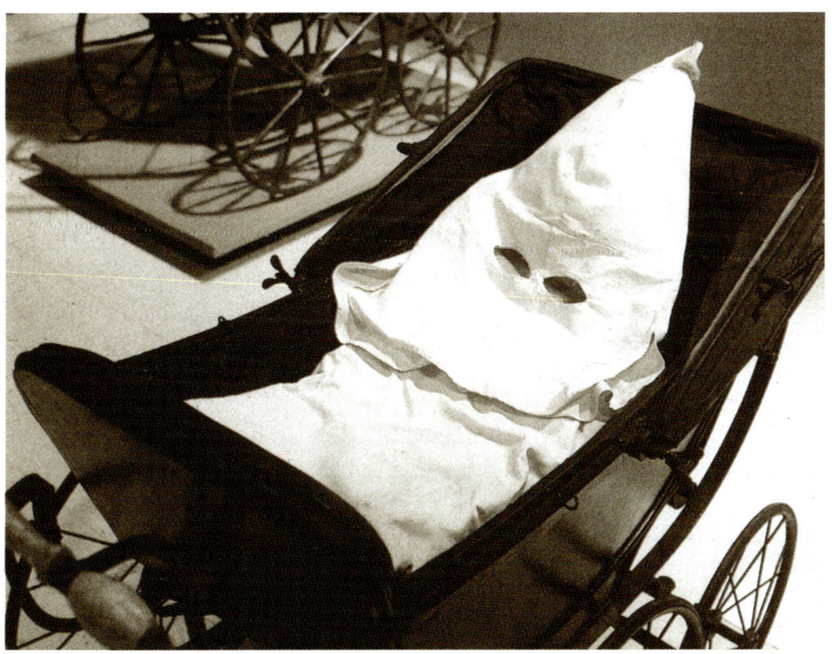

2.10 Fred Wilson, "Modes of Transport 1770–1910" in *Mining the Museum*, 1992. Detail of Ku Klux Klan hood. Maryland Historical Society, Baltimore. Courtesy of the artist.

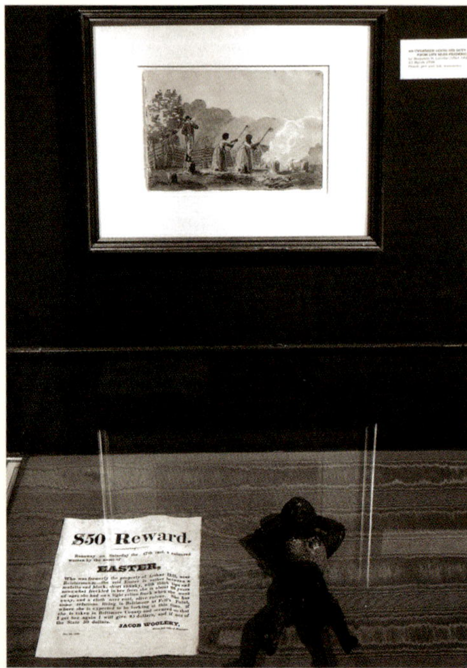

2.11 Fred Wilson, "Easter" in *Mining the Museum,* 1992. Installation view. Maryland Historical Society, Baltimore. Courtesy of the artist.

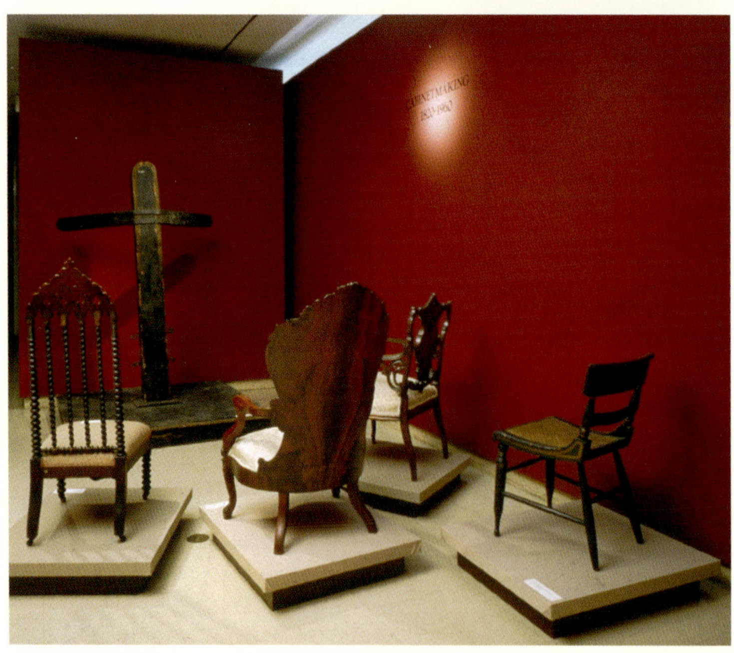

2.12 Fred Wilson, "Cabinet Making 1820–1960" in *Mining the Museum,* 1992. Installation view. Maryland Historical Society, Baltimore. Courtesy of the artist.

ing" of slaves and the "tolling" of ducks, both forms of hunting that make use of dogs to capture their prey. Copies of reward notices for runaway slaves hung on the walls with phrases in the text highlighted: "stutters a little," "leg which is a little crooked from having been once broken," "a scar on the back of his hand," "hesitates when spoken to," "ruptured and wears a truss." The bodily traumas suffered by these runaways testified to their brutal treatment and simultaneously produced those identifying marks that might lead eventually to their recapture. Another reward notice, for twenty-two-year-old "Easter," a runaway female "mulatto," was placed in a glass case beside an iron bootjack from the 1880s that took the form of a scantily clad dark-skinned woman. Called "Naughty Nelly," the bootjack woman had legs spread wide to hold the heel of the boot. To complete the display, Wilson included the watercolor *An Overseer Doing His Duty, Sketched from Life near Fredericksburg* (Benjamin H. Latrobe, 1798), depicting a white man, wearing boots, watching two barefooted slave women working in the field (figure 2.11).

What emerged from these historically researched and carefully juxtaposed displays was the overwhelming sense of the complex ideological intersection of power and violence with high culture and the fine arts that allowed for, and depended upon, a slave economy to survive. "Cabinet Making 1820–1960," installed further on, consisted of a grouping of four finely crafted nineteenth-century chairs arranged like a theater audience around a wooden whipping post (figure 2.12). Solid, tall, and cruciform, the whipping post became a sign of violent punishments, of abjection in the face of power and privilege. Maryland's legal code made numerous crimes punishable by the lash, and the whipping post was actually in use until the middle of the twentieth century.[10] 1820 was the year of the Missouri Compromise, when the U.S. Senate voted to admit Missouri as a slave state and simultaneously to admit Maine as a free state. Although human bondage would continue in the South, abolitionists succeeded in drawing a line of demarcation, north of which slavery would no longer be allowed in any future requests for statehood. Within the frame of these dates it is also possible to read the installation as a response to the legal history of the U.S. government that has used the issues of slavery and civil rights as political leverage. The Civil Rights Act of 1960 was introduced to penalize the obstruction of voting rights and to formally establish a Civil Rights Commission. The reference to "cabinet making" implicates presidential cabinets in the production and maintenance of power and law in relation to the black body, enslaved and free. Wilson's sensual and decidedly corporeal juxtaposition of chairs and whipping post provided a visual distillation of such divisions and demarcations between North and South, enslaved and free, oppression and emancipation. But the installation also implied an enforced exhibitionism and a privileged voyeurism, a kind of imagined martyrdom taking place in front of a theater of onlookers. Who occupied these fine furnishings, who left their sweat and blood in the wood grain of the whipping post? Although no black body or white body is present, the dynamics of optical domination resonate with a history of racial encounter.

The last section of the exhibition displayed a collection of journals kept by the eighteenth-century mathematician and astronomer Benjamin Banneker. A free Marylander, Banneker was respected for his *Pennsylvania, Delaware, Maryland, and Virginia Almanack* published in 1792. The almanac went through several dozen editions and earned Banneker attention from Thomas Jefferson and a place on the surveying team of a new federal district.[50] By highlighting the successes of this Marylander, Wilson showed that above and beyond the racist legacy of slavery, there was much to be discovered about African American history still hidden in the archive of the historical society.

In the year before *Mining the Museum* opened, Wilson met with museum curators, staff, and docents once a week. In discussing the process of collaboration that takes place in his museum interventions, and in particular his work at the Maryland Historical Society, the artist has commented,

> *Mining the Museum* was really about African American and Native American culture—that was the first thing that was important to me. But as I would say to all the different groups and the docents, this was about African American history specifically, but what are all the other histories that are missing? I could have done other histories in that exhibition, such as women's history, and that became clear to the curators.[51]

In the exhibition catalog, Lisa Corrin included the statements of several docents who confessed to recognizing their own prejudices concerning the museum as an institution of knowledge and authority. Others talked about the emotional responses of the visitors they guided through the exhibition. One docent recounted, "I had a woman who stood at the painting where the little girl says, 'Where is my mother?' and she broke down. She said, 'My grandmother said that she never saw her mother, that she was always with these little white girls.'"[52] Wilson's addition of voiced questions allowed both docent and visitor the opportunity to look beyond the aesthetic qualities or historical status of the oil painting to the more intimate narrative of individual lives pictured within. A selection of visitor responses appears in the back of Corrin's catalog and includes a wide variety of comments: "As an African American woman, I found my own history to be in the shadow and the backgrounds of all the pictures/paintings."[53] But the exhibit also raised the ire of some visitors, including one who wrote: "'The worst and most racist display I have ever seen in a museum!' (self-identified 62-year-old Caucasian, retired dentist),"[54] and another who remarked, "'I found *Mining the Museum* to be 'artsy' and pretentious' (self-identified 57-year-old Jewish engineer)."[55] Another commented, "'Keep exhibitions like this up. In my opinion they are much more interesting than other exhibits' (self-identified 10-year-old Polish American)."[56]

A number of museum directors and curators shared this last opinion, and in subsequent years Wilson was invited by dozens of institutions to "mine" or to reinstall their permanent collections. Each offered a new set of challenges for the artist, not only because each collection was unique, but also because the final result relied on the quality of his working relationships with museum management and staff who played a large collaborative (or occasionally obstructionist) role. *The Museum: Mixed Metaphors* (1993) at the Seattle Art Museum offered Wilson the challenge of working with an already installed museum exhibit. Unlike the Maryland Historical Society, the Seattle Art Museum had recently opened its new facilities, and its exhibits and displays were freshly mounted. Moreover, the collection reflected a wide variety of arts from around the world. There were fewer embarrassing secrets hiding in the basement and, because of the diversity of the collection, fewer intersecting narratives to construct from fragments of evidence.

As a result, Wilson focused less on the associative power of individual objects-as-signs and more on the rhetoric of display found in the institution. Dispersed across the third and fourth floors of the museum, *The Museum: Mixed Metaphors* wryly highlighted the visual tropes of display design that guide visitors' interpretation of the architectural space—drawing attention to its rhetorical effects. In the catalog to the exhibition, the artist writes, "The museum space often tells us what we should think about a work of art and the artist before we can grasp the significance of the work for ourselves. The wall text, the lighting, and the overall design of the space can tell us more about the society of the curator and the exhibition designer than any cultural information that we may be getting about the art."[57]

In the gallery of art devoted to modern European and American art from 1910 to 1950, for example, the artist returned to his earlier installation techniques, transforming the "white cube" environment by painting two adjoining walls dark green, the same color used in the museum's largest gallery of African art. A raised platform, also a copy of those found in the museum's galleries of African and Native American art, served as the base for a cluttered and crowded display of modernist works by Giacometti, de Kooning, Picabia, and others—seven sculptures and five paintings by different artists placed one in front of another (figure 2.13). At the base of the platform, an explanatory illustration carefully outlined each object and added a numerical code to match an accompanying list of names and titles. One visitor commented, "Marvelous! I was walking around very proud of myself that I got the joke and didn't have to be enlightened until I got to where all the modern European art was bunched up in the corner the way the art of other cultures always is, and I got irritated. These idiots squished the Picabia back in the corner where I can't see it! Touché."[58]

In addition to the reinstallation of existing displays, Wilson added new elements to the mix. The museum's large collection of African textiles and sculpture consisting largely of elaborately embroidered gowns, carved wooden statues, and thrones was enhanced by the addition of a mannequin in a gray flannel suit, crisp white shirt, and silk tie (figure 2.14). A caption written by the artist reads: "Certain elements of dress were used to designate one's rank in Africa's status-conscious capitals. A gray suit with conservatively patterned tie denotes a businessman or member of government. Costumes such as this are designed and tailored in Africa and worn throughout the continent."[59] Mimicking the explanatory language of the other African-textile museum labels, the artist draws attention to the familiar museum practice of ignoring the contemporary culture of Africa in order to address the cultural traditions of its past. To further disrupt this tendency, the artist included a television monitor with contemporary African music videos as well as footage of a contemporary Nigerian dance performance. The final touch was an unusual photographic survey of innovative architecture from five different African countries, compiled with the help of local and international architects. What had been an exhibit of aesthetic objects, made exotic by their display, became a glimpse into the lives of modern-day Africans.

The same operation was performed in the galleries devoted to the Native American populations in the Pacific Northwest. At the time of Wilson's installation, the Seattle Art Museum proudly exhibited elaborate traditional house posts, dance regalia, and carved masks from several indigenous communities in a hushed and darkened gallery. Signs from the contemporary life of these same communities were nowhere to be found. After conducting research in and around Seattle, Wilson invited local artists—Philip Red Eagle, Glenda J. Guilmet, Annie Hanson, Raymond Colby, and Larry Ullaaq Ahvakana—to each produce a videotape for the exhibition. From musical performance to readings of short stories, interviews with war veterans to an artist's studio tour, the videos offered a view of Native American life as it is lived today. Installed in the gallery on five different monitors, the voices of a current generation were meant to demystify and enliven the artifacts of the past. While some of the curators and visitors found the monitors intrusive in the hushed temple of the gallery, Bruce Barcot writing in the *Seattle Weekly* noted, "Wilson's installation in the Pacific Coast Native American gallery is so good the museum should consider leaving it there permanently. By introducing live Native Americans into the gallery via the video, Wilson takes the native works out of the Edward S. Curtis realm."[60] Privileging the past

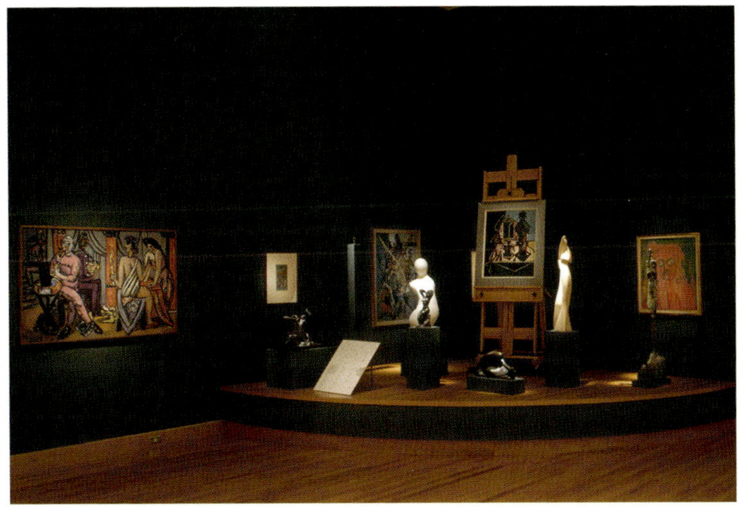

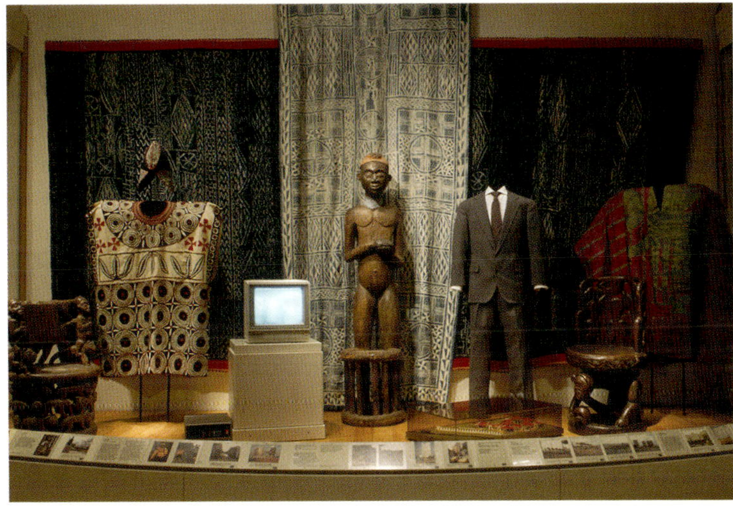

2.13 Fred Wilson, "Re-Seeing Modernism" in *The Museum: Mixed Metaphors*, 1993. Installation view. Photo by Susan Dirk. Courtesy of the Seattle Art Museum, Seattle.

2.14 Fred Wilson, *The Museum: Mixed Metaphors*, 1993. Installation view of African art and culture display. Photo by Susan Dirk. Courtesy of the Seattle Art Museum, Seattle.

over the present, this reporter recognized, reveals a largely nostalgic and perhaps unconscious investment in exploration, discovery, and domination. Wilson notes, "General art museums say they are multicultural museums. To my mind museums of this nature are about as multicultural as Great Britain in 1914. The 'empire' includes many cultures, but who decides what is important in that culture? Who speaks for that culture? Who chooses what is kept of that culture?"[61]

If the visual discourse of race relies upon the act of beholding and perceiving, then among the most telling artifacts of this activity are portraits produced cross-culturally. In the Seattle Art Museum's archives, Wilson discovered a number of porcelain figurines and small portrait drawings of Europeans, Africans, Asians, and Native Americans, as seen by the others. The striking fact of their eclecticism registered not merely the ideological valence of some (the British depicted Africans with devil's horns), but also the radical variation in the representation of human facial features (such as the culturally specific representations of eyes, nose, or mouth) as each demonstrated an effort to use traditional means of representation to depict "unfamiliar" racial subjects. The collection was displayed together as a series of photographs titled "Portrait of s.a.m." (Seattle Art Museum) (figure 2.15). The exhibition catalog claims that through this juxtaposition Wilson demonstrated the failure of each culture to accurately depict the "other," but this interpretation misses the point that each portrait reveals precisely the culturally specific modes of vision that underlie its production. As with all portraits, rather than revealing the truth of their subject, they make evident the representational techniques and social imaginary of the artists who produce them. The portraits *are* accurate, in fact, within the cultural and aesthetic paradigms of those who produced them. Although much of Fred Wilson's archeological activity retrieves the forgotten, the omitted, and the invisible, his primary object of inquiry in museum installations is the ideology of display. In a recent interview he commented, "My work is based not so much on revealing African American history—who doesn't know about slavery?—but on the notion that a point of view can be so complete that you don't even begin to think of other ways of seeing things."[62]

Later museum installations such as *Speaking in Tongues: A Look at the Language of Display* (1998), *The Greeting Gallery* (1998), and *Aftermath* (2003) continue Wilson's exploration of the logic of taxonomies, labeling, archiving, and displaying. As with the tactical reversal performed in the

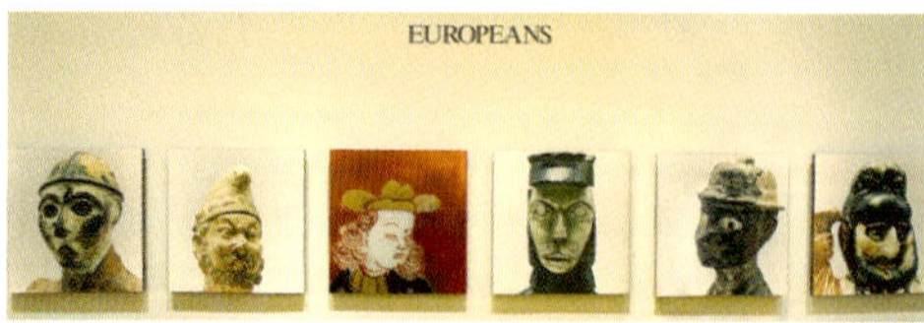

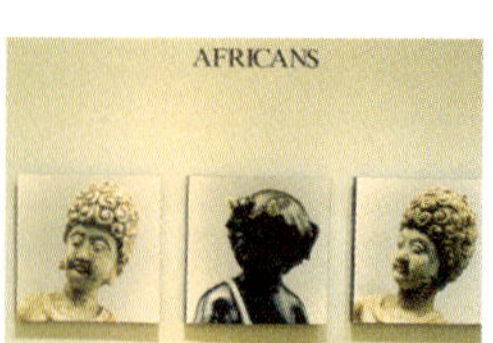

2.15 Fred Wilson, "Portrait of s.a.m." in *The Museum: Mixed Metaphors*, 1993. Installation view. Photo by Paul Macapia. Courtesy of the Seattle Art Museum, Seattle.

Seattle Art Museum, *Speaking in Tongues* applied the narrative structure of the wall text for a display of African art in San Francisco's M. H. de Young Memorial Museum to a small display of objects from the museum's European and American collection. The introductory wall text began: "Europe and the United States are characterized by tremendous diversity. The environments in which people live vary widely, ranging from tundra to desert and from mountain to plains." The text explained that "European and Euro-American sculpture is often made of wood, fiber, hair, and other organic materials that rarely survive well in extremely hot, cold, or humid climates." A marble bust of Christopher Columbus is identified as "Ancestor Figure (as a Boy): Italy, 19th Century, Marble." The descriptive text reads: "It is believed by some scholars that Christopher Columbus is among the most honored mythological figures in western culture, specifically among United States devotees.... As tradition dictates, one day of the year is set aside for the veneration of this ancestor. The mythological character of the man is captured in this sculpture, as the carver could not have seen an image of Columbus as a youth."

Generalizations about cultural diversity, attention to climate as a condition for aesthetic practice, reduction of artistic expression to a consideration of cultural myth, and the anonymous status of the "carver" all signal the manner in which art and artifacts from non-European, and particularly African cultures, have been traditionally framed by museums in the United States. Because the language used in the introductory text and the labels precisely mimics that which can be found in the adjoining gallery, where African materials are on display, it is all the more effective in demonstrating to viewers who walk through both exhibitions the different linguistic devices used to frame collections throughout the rest of the museum.

It can be argued, of course, that museums address a culturally specific audience with a relatively predictable domain of knowledge, necessitating the kinds of explanatory texts Wilson parodies. Nevertheless, Wilson demonstrates how all museums *speak in tongues* to a target audience, guaranteeing that group as the museum's privileged addressee. Classification is the way of maintaining the order of any system; anything that breaks the classification disrupts the order. This is true of the museum objects that appear "out of place," as well as of the language used by classification, which is itself "out of place" when applied to the wrong objects. Even the museum visitor who walks through Wilson's installations can feel "out of place" precisely because the installation as a *place* is not familiar, not part of an expected geography of things or ordering of discourse. Wilson's methodology is not the exposure of error but is rather the process of persistently looking into how truths are produced. Museums have specific modes of address, and Wilson reminds us that they always construct an imagined subject of that address. His work

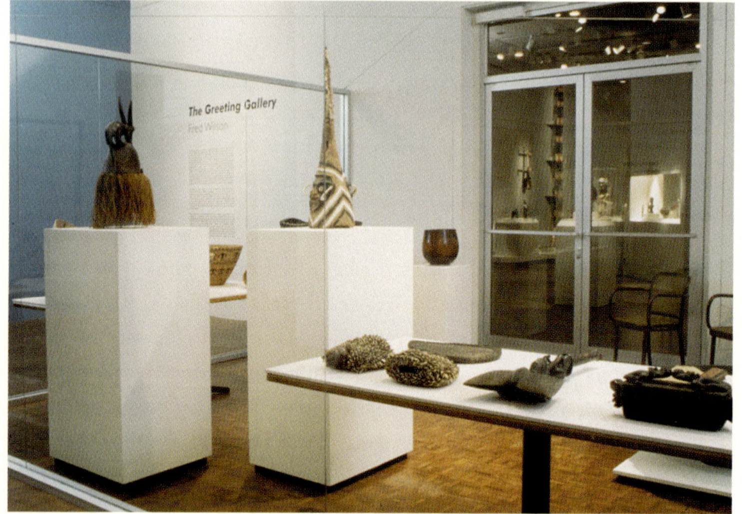

2.16 Fred Wilson,
The Greeting Gallery,
1998. Installation view.
M. H. de Young Memo-
rial Museum, San Fran-
cisco. Courtesy of the
Yerba Buena Center for
the Arts.

makes evident how a museums' power lies in its ability to interpellate its audience into this imagined subject position in order to define social membership, legitimate historical narratives, and determine access to cultural knowledge.

When visitors are alienated by museums it is not, or not only, because available educational materials are inadequate; rather, the museum as a whole, as an ideological home, does not welcome us equally. This is made painfully clear when museum archives hold ancestral cultural material to which others lay claim, either for the sake of repatriation or for use in traditional rituals.[63] In some cases such visitors are granted access to the permanent collection, but more often than not access is severely limited or simply refused. Collaborating with museum staff at both the Yerba Buena Center for the Arts and the M. H. de Young Memorial Museum, Wilson staged a sanctuary in the museum designed to facilitate access to Native American materials in a protected environment. *The Greeting Gallery,* installed simultaneously with *Speaking in Tongues,* consisted of a small, locked room with glass walls, through which the public could see tables and chairs, floor mats and art objects, and a number of other artifacts (figure 2.16). A sign on the door read "Greeting Gallery, Open Mondays, By Appointment Only." By creating a designated space in the museum where "only ethnic groups whose cultural legacies had been appropriated were permitted access for viewing, venerating, and possibly repatriating their objects,"[64] the artist provided the opportunity for a different sort of ritual domain where cultural protocols could be followed in privacy, on days when the museum was not open to the general public. By creating two display spaces, each with its own rules of access, Wilson experimented with his audience's perception of their own privileged, or disadvantaged, position in the museum.

Hal Foster has pointed out a number of real pitfalls that attend artworks, such as Wilson's, that are created in the museum or institutional context they are designed to critique. For Foster, art based on institutional critique always runs the risk of being illegible to the public, or appearing "hermetic and narcissistic."[65] And, given that most installation and site-specific work is commissioned by cultural institutions, the critical power of the work may be subsumed under the "shadow" of these institutions (museums, galleries, corporations) and be "detoured" for public relations or other ends.[66] This argument is echoed in scholar Miwon Kwon's critique of Fred Wilson when she observes that his museum commissions "can easily become extensions of the museum's own self-promotional apparatus."[67] Moreover, Kwon points out that Wilson's strategy, when enacted at numerous institutions, may fall into a repetitive pattern, "reflecting what has become a familiar museological practice—the commissioning of artists to rehang permanent collections."[68]

These are valid concerns, but they also miss the critical potential of the *détournement* provided by the artist. While it is certainly the case that Wilson's work can be, and has been, used by institutions as a "self-promotional apparatus" both to increase their audience and perhaps to assuage some historical guilt, it is not necessarily the case that Wilson's work is therefore repetitive and lacking in criticality. Even if the method and strategy are essentially the same, the institutions where Wilson has worked, and the staff he has worked with, are always different. Part of Wilson's project is not only to produce interesting exhibits for the public, but also to use his time at the museum to critically engage the curators, docents, and others who work day to day with the collection, to encourage them to approach their work with more attention and sensitivity to the underlying race politics of the institution. This leads not only to a variety of approaches and critical themes in his projects, but more important it ensures that the audience in each instance will be new. Even if the installations are similar in conceptual method or approach, they are always formally and temporally unique. In this respect I agree with scholar Frazer Ward that it is both incorrect and unproductive to argue that critical art practices engaged in institutional critique always end up serving the institution they wish to criticize. The museum, in Ward's analysis, functions as one in a complex array of institutions of publicity, as one term in an expansive set of social relations.[69] He writes, "[Hans] Haacke and [Fred] Wilson's insistence about the role of the museum is precisely about performing art's function as publicity within a prescribed and always already compromised cultural space, in order to wrest from it a partial and contingent critical publicity, in terms of which a correspondingly mobile and perhaps strategic public might form."[70] This strategic public, or what Muñoz might call a "counterpublic," does not exist prior to the exhibition, but emerges from the exhibition and is produced by it.

Wilson's archeological method has been likened by several scholars, including Hal Foster and Irene Winter, to the method of analysis defined by Michel Foucault in *The Archeology of Knowledge*.[71] This comparison is apt; Foucault's method examines the structure of systemic discourses that produce disciplinary orders on the world (the sciences and social sciences in particular).[72] An archeology of knowledge is not a geological excavation; rather, it is a scholarly attempt to outline the historical, material, and intellectual conditions that permit a particular discourse or discipline to arise—it marks the interface between systems of language and the systems of objects in the world they seek to order.[73] More significantly, Foucault is interested in not only what he calls the "enunciative" function of discourse, but what might also be called the "silencing" function of discourse. As Hayden White observes, "The aim of [Foucault's] 'archeology of ideas' is to enter into the interior of any given mode of discourse in order to determine the point at which it consigns a certain area of experience to the limbo of things about which one cannot speak."[74] Wilson's archeology reveals the museum to be a quintessentially discursive space, where disciplinary logics place some objects in carefully ordered systems while consigning other objects to the potentially permanent limbo of the archive. By reproducing this spatial logic of museum displays, he confronts archive with archive, revealing the gaps in discourse—primarily historical discourse—that have excluded both objects and subjects. The installations demonstrate how a given "order of things" reveals its bias when consciously re-ordered, when traditionally mute objects are given the opportunity to "speak."

This opportunity is of course constrained by the politics of the archive, its topology, its laws, its systems of access. Archives are social and domestic; the objects and documents stored in them are marked by cultural privilege and atemporality. Neither past nor future, an archive preserves the past *for* the future; it ensures a place in the future for the past—that is, for a very specific and circumscribed version of the past. The temporality of any archive or museum collection is the future anterior, the "will-have-been" of the present. As Jacques Derrida suggests, archives are also places of *consignation,* where objects are not only entrusted to a permanent location but also put in the company of other objects, in a collection of signs (*consigns*) that are meant to produce a coherent corpus, system, or synchrony.[75] When Wilson delves into the archives of museums, he begins the process of unraveling the corpus or system that assigns fixed places to objects-as-signs, drawing attention to the fact that *things* are *actants* in a social network. It is not only the forgotten objects in unseen or invisible storage spaces that he brings to light, but also the public space of the museum-as-living-archive. By foregrounding the spectral inventions of the past that continue to haunt the present—the friendly natives, the "primitives," the cigar store Indians—and by transforming museum displays to emphasize their inherent bias or their latent content, Wilson's installations change the *promise* these archives make with the future.

Representing Black Bodies: The Visible and Invisible
Throughout his work, Wilson attends to the site, location, and form of the black body in visual representation. Although his work is primarily about the institutional and discursive framing of cultural difference, and he has explicitly commented that his approach is not intended to foreground "race" over other cultural discourses, there is a recurring attention to the idea of skin color in his works, and its role in the framing of subjects and their subjection. From the condition of the dark-skinned museum guard, who is invisible yet always on display, to the presence of African American slave children, nearly hidden in the corners of eighteenth-century American paintings, Wilson's installations offer a spatialized study of the circulation and display of black bodies in visual and material culture. Wil-

son shares with Renée Green and James Luna an attention to the forms of visibility and invisibility that support a cultural logic of placement or location; in other words, they each attend to how black, red, and other bodies have carefully assigned sites and values, whether in popular culture or in museum culture, so that they are susceptible to being seen, or disappearing from view. For it becomes clear both in Wilson's installations and in the broader social contexts to which they refer, that the status of the black body is a monolithic, fabricated concept that extends beyond any single historical subject. It is this monolith, its maintenance, and its intersection with living subjects that Wilson's critical practice asks us to contemplate.

What does it mean to be both excessively visible and virtually invisible? Ralph Ellison's book *Invisible Man* is among the more penetrating testimonies to this condition of invisibility and institutional erasure operative as a matter of course for black men in the 1940s and 1950s. Responding in part to this classic text, Wilson's 1993 installation *An Invisible Life: A View into the World of a 120-Year Old Man* addressed the relation between biography and invisibility through a carefully crafted domestic display. Produced in conjunction with Capp Street Project in San Francisco, the installation occupied a Victorian-era home, recreating in meticulous detail the life of the previous inhabitant: Baldwin Antinous Stein. Rooms were filled with objects that mapped a history as complex and subtle as it was incredible (figure 2.17). Docents informed visitors of the extraordinary life of this unique individual, who was born in the Caribbean (slavery had been abolished in Puerto Rico in 1873, 120 years earlier) and became a world traveler, professional portrait photographer, polyglot, friend to the photographers Eadweard Muybridge and Alfred Stieglitz, and an acquaintance of Marcel Proust in Paris. Although his ethnicity is undetermined, the clues offered suggest that he could be of mixed racial heritage.

On the first floor, as docents led visitors from room to room explaining the architectural and historical details, recorded voices could occasionally be heard. From an armchair in the living room the voice of a young man whispered, "Am I alone? Is it only me? Is there no one else?" while across the dining room table two older men's voices praised the merits of Socratic dialogue. On the second floor of the house, in the library and bedrooms, hundreds of photographs—portraits of men of different ethnicities— cluttered the shelves and tabletops like so much Victorian bric-a-brac. There were turn-of-the-century photographs of sailors, athletes, gentlemen in business suits, and other men lounging outdoors (figure 2.18). The house was also filled with memorabilia, statuettes of men wrestling, and other art objects from around the world. Books sitting on tabletops, such as *Love in Ancient Greece, Of Human Bondage, Nijinsky,* and *Proust and the Art of Love,* were interleaved with yellowed bookmarks that read

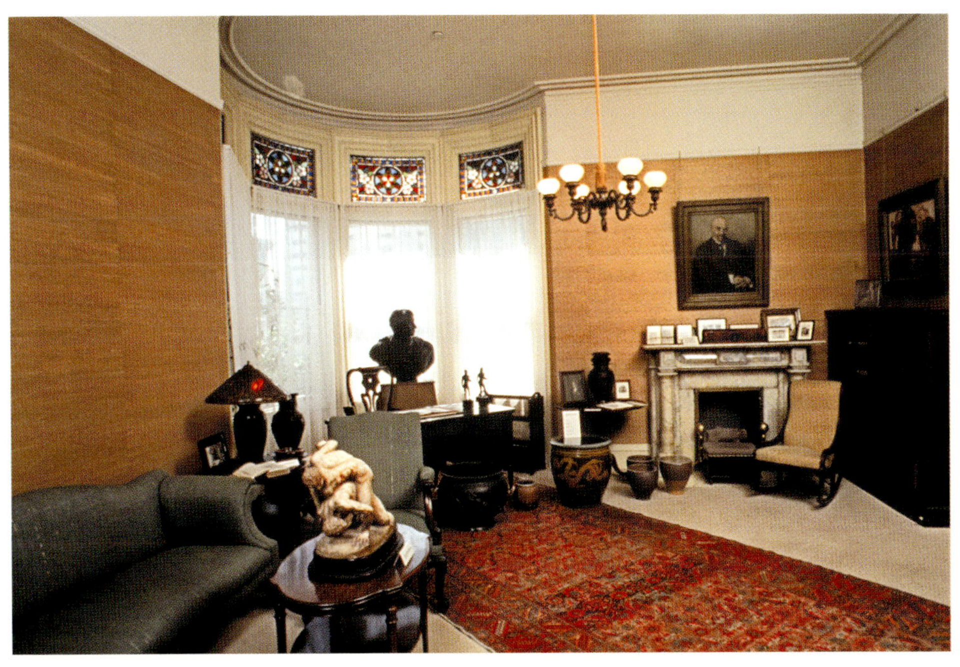

2.17 Fred Wilson,
*An Invisible Life: A
View into the World of
a 120-Year Old Man*,
1993. Installation
view. Courtesy of Pace
Wildenstein.

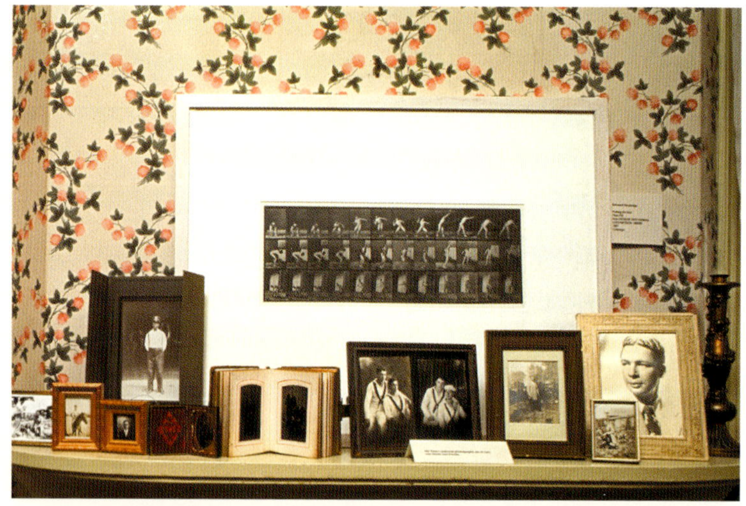

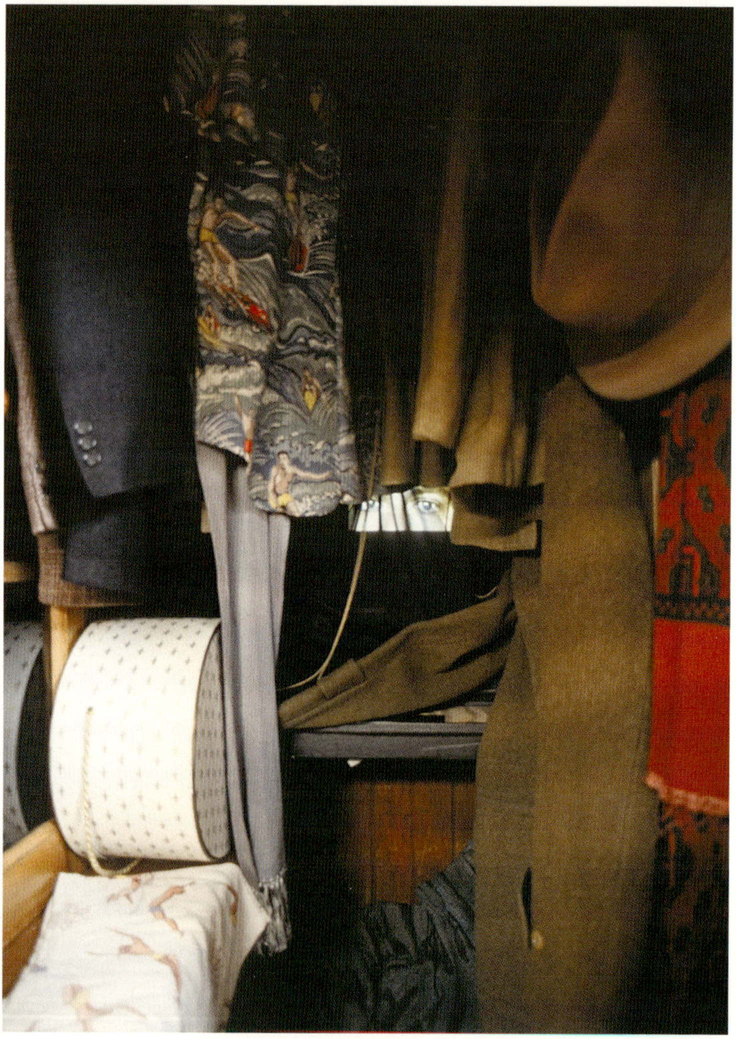

2.18, 2.19 Fred Wilson, *An Invisible Life: A View into the World of a 120-Year Old Man*, 1993. Detail of photographs and of closet. Courtesy of Pace Wildenstein.

"a mystery created, page 104" and "a history denied, page 117." Although never explicitly stated, an observant visitor could piece together the visual and textual evidence of Stein's gay desire—a desire that may have been "closeted" all of his life. Literalizing the metaphor, Wilson installed a silent video image showing only the eyes of various men (the artist and others) looking out from the back of the bedroom closet, barely visible among the clothes (figure 2.19). Looking into the closet, each visitor saw a different pair of eyes and thus formed a different image of the racial or ethnic identity of the "closeted" man.

Stein was, of course, an entirely fictional character. The artist produced a suggestive script for the docents to read that highlighted the "faux finishes" and "hidden" architectural details of the house, as well as conflicting evidence about Stein, to suggest to visitors that "all was not what it seemed."[76] Yet visitors were mostly surprised and sometimes dismayed to learn at the end of their tour that Stein was not a real person.[77]

An Invisible Life: A View into the World of a 120-Year Old Man enabled the artist to make evident both the degree to which visitors invest museums and their docents with an unquestioned authority, and the degree to which life histories of men like Stein—educated, cosmopolitan, gay men of the last century—have generally been rendered invisible. The absent body is made to appear, the invisible life is rendered visible, yet this rendering also proves to be fictional—a circular predicament that is not unlike that of the visible/invisible black body in visual culture. Stein stands in for the lives of all men across the span of 120 years whose freedom is yet uncelebrated. As in Cheryl Dunye's film *The Watermelon Woman* (1996), Wilson created a fictional character to tell the story of actual lives. The work is also autobiographical to the degree that it establishes an identification between this fictional character and Wilson, whose own life as a gay artist of Caribbean and African descent might equally be rendered invisible by history or by art criticism. The fiction of Baldwin Antinous Stein was an *autofiction* for Wilson, an alter ego, an imaginary life, an intimate mythology that procured signs of the past for the sake of the present.[78] Working from what might be called the *evidence effect* of artifacts, Wilson's display allowed for an otherwise inexpressible history to be imagined through a materialist *autotopography*.

A different evidence effect was operative in *Collectibles,* Wilson's 1995 exhibition at Metro Pictures that examined the interdependence of racial formation and the circulation of commodities in late capitalist culture. "Mammy" cookie jars, "Uncle Tom" salt and pepper shakers, "Aunt Jemima" candy dishes, porcelain and plastic figurines arrayed on white oversized tables, grouped together in clusters, echoed the sparse and rarified displays of merchandise in the nearby retail spaces of SoHo. The walls of the gallery were also hung with beautifully rendered close-up photographs of the same objects, glossy and slick. Although Wilson was reworking familiar territory—Carrie Mae Weems depicted similar racist stereotypes in her "American Icons" photographs of the late 1980s, and Betye Saar's 1972 assemblage work *The Liberation of Aunt Jemima* certainly worked to turn such objects from docility to rebellion—he was also engaging the question of the practice of collecting, and the relationship between the collector and an acquisitive, obsessive desire. Representative of popular racist stereotypes of Africans and African Americans, these "collectibles" are commonly assumed to have thoroughly devolved into the irony of kitsch, their grotesque features considered too obviously exaggerated to merit serious critique. Indeed the ubiquitous banality of these caricatures, their presumed ideological innocence, and their persistent reproduction and recirculation formed the ground of Wilson's archeology. In an interview I asked the artist about his interest in collecting:

> **WILSON:** I am always collecting things. And so I began to see more and more of these so-called black collectibles—you know these Mammy cookie jars and Uncle Tom salt shakers and other things. I became interested in how these objects have become collectibles and commodities and how expensive they've become.
>
> **GONZÁLEZ:** Very expensive?
>
> **WILSON:** Very expensive. So there is a whole host of items that white Americans and African Americans collect now.... One of the reasons that African Americans collect them is to remember the past and this horrible history. But I find it ironic (a) that they are expensive and (b) that you can buy reproductions of those things also at a high price.
>
> **GONZÁLEZ:** They are making reproductions?
>
> **WILSON:** It gets even weirder. You can also buy really cheap versions—and the cheap versions are not being sold as a remembrance of the past, but for the same reasons that the originals were sold.
>
> **GONZÁLEZ:** Where are they being sold?
>
> **WILSON:** All over the country. If you look for them, you see them. And it's global. I've found things in Spain, Italy, Japan, Taiwan—not for export but to be sold to the people there. So these images have become not only a representation of the past but also reproductions for those people who cannot afford the originals but who think they are "cute.".... What I find fascinating is the collecting of these things. Because I think a lot of African Americans collect these things because they feel by collecting them, they recuperate them and kill them. By collecting

them, they have power over them. And I don't particularly agree with that. It is interesting because I have had to collect them in order to do this piece, and you really do stop seeing them as what they are.

GONZÁLEZ: As racist.

WILSON: Yeah. Because you start getting into the thrill of the hunt.... It is all wrapped up in American capitalism, and what capitalism does to any kind of consciousness. These things really show up what that whole process does.

GONZÁLEZ: It makes that process concrete.

WILSON: And it makes it obvious what it is. Because these things are not nice things; but because you get so involved with the collecting of them you tend not to see that any more. That is the same with anything, with the commodity system here. It doesn't matter what it is, it is all wrapped up in the buying and in the collecting and the owning.

In the installation, the mock innocence of these objects is transformed into a sinister caricature of human relations; each of the many clusters of figurines is carefully arranged to perform an implied narrative. A white porcelain child towers over a miniature Mammy; a white woman in nineteenth-century dress stands on the apron of an Aunt Jemima figure who lies flat on her back, face frozen in a ludicrous smile; an Ubangi "plate-lip" candy dish offers an exaggerated open mouth, upon which is placed, as though on a pedestal, an educated white man in university cap and gown. Here is the strange but undeniable history of race and class domination in the United States, a history that is not behind us. Wilson draws our attention to the contemporary mass reproduction of these objects through his large-scale photographs. "About Face II" (figure 2.20) pairs two close-up portraits of nearly identical porcelain Mammy cooks, one with dark skin and saucerlike eyes, the other with only a residue of black paint flecks on her otherwise white cheeks and forehead; the new and the old versions side by side testify to the fact that the past is never entirely past, and the degree to which the past is revived nostalgically, excessively, signifies the degree to which it has not *passed on*. In his preface to *Invisible Man*, Ellison writes eloquently that what is commonly assumed to be past history is actually a vital part of the living present: "Furtive, implacable and tricky, it inspirits both the observer and the scene observed, artifacts, manners and atmosphere, and it speaks even when no one wills to listen."[79]

Wilson took an ambivalent revenge against the tenacity and longevity of these collectible objects in the downstairs gallery of the exhibition. Here one video monitor showed the newly reproduced red and white Mammies being smashed into tiny pieces, again and again in an endless loop. On another monitor, the artist himself silently strikes the poses of the antique artifacts he has collected. A porcelain boy servant is coyly depicted with one shoe slipping off his heel, so Wilson carefully arranges his own shoe in the same position; a cast-iron pickaninny toy bank with a row of white teeth swallows pennies and rolls its eyes, so Wilson does the same, maintaining a toothy grin; an ashtray in the form of a head holds a cigarette inside its exaggerated open mouth and releases plumes of smoke from its nostrils, so Wilson—it is difficult to watch—does the same (figure 2.21). With increasing discomfort, the viewer is forced to come to terms with the sinister implications of even the most trivial objects and the iconic violence perpetrated by their mechanistic acts. To resignify a history through the collectible artifact transforms the pseudoinnocence of the object into a testament to the pervasiveness and persistence of racism, all the more chilling precisely because it is presented as innocent: a candy dish, a child's penny bank, an ashtray.

Spike Lee's film *Bamboozled* (2000), which tells the story of a young television executive who is unwittingly forced to produce a comedy based on racist minstrel shows, demonstrates the way race discourse dangerously reproduces itself in the form of stereotyped farce. The film ends with a nightmarish scene in which the porcelain and iron caricatures collected by the protagonist come to life, haunting their owner with toothy grins and snapping teeth. Scholar Bill Brown suggests that the racist caricatures in Lee's film can best be defined as an "American uncanny" because they oscillate between animate and inanimate, human and thing, and become the subject of both repulsion and fascination.[80] In the case of such caricatures, a collector's identification with his collection is strangely perverse, as Wilson suggests. The "crushing objecthood" that Franz Fanon identifies as the fate of the black subject is here materialized in the artifact and performed on the body at the same time. A reluctance to look seriously at the history of these collectible objects, Brown argues, reveals an "apprehension that within things we will discover the human precisely because our [American] history is one in which humans were reduced to things."[81] Of course, this apprehension—which is both a fear and a recognition—will be inevitably different for different subjects. Wilson's video performance acts out in the flesh the irrational violence that is imbedded in the object: it is a violence that, as Wilson demonstrates, is deeply biographical, corporeal, and kinetic for black subjects. A different apprehension and fascination animates the onlooker, the witness, the one who does not identify, the one who laughs. Wilson's installation invites us to asks, What kind of violence is done to *both* subjects by the act of manufacturing, marketing, and collecting objects such as these?

If *Collectibles* demonstrated how the historical fantasies of the black body infiltrate mass culture as low-end kitsch, *Speak of Me As I Am,* Wilson's 2003 exhibition at the United States Pavilion of the Venice Biennale,

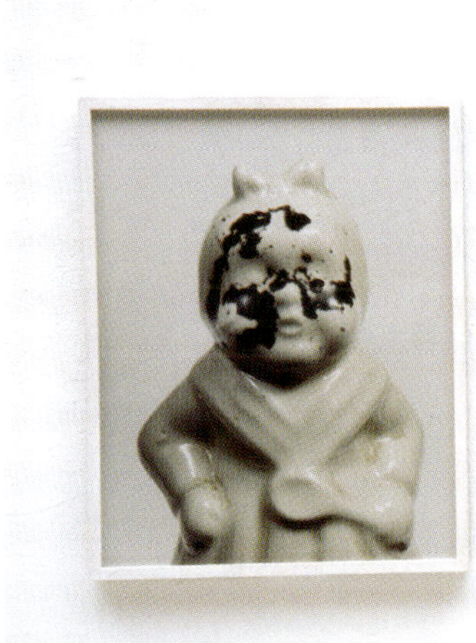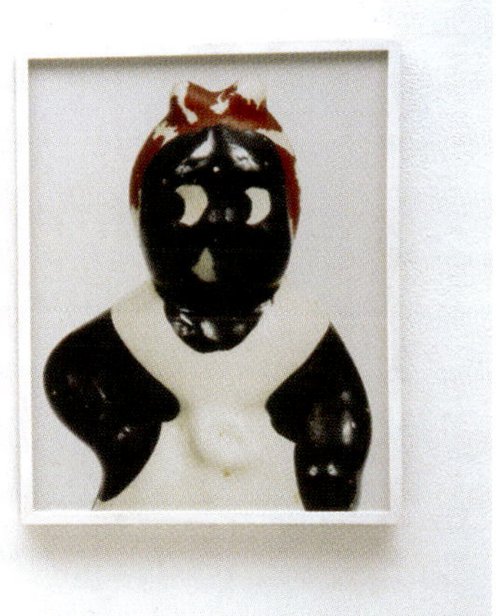

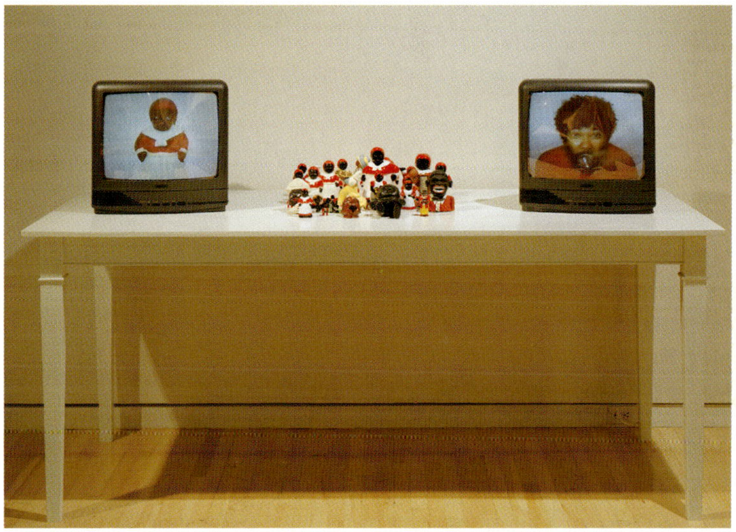

2.20 Fred Wilson, "About Face II" in *Collectibles*, 1995. Courtesy of Pace Wildenstein.

2.21 Fred Wilson, *Collectibles*, 1995. Detail of video monitor and performance. Courtesy of Pace Wildenstein.

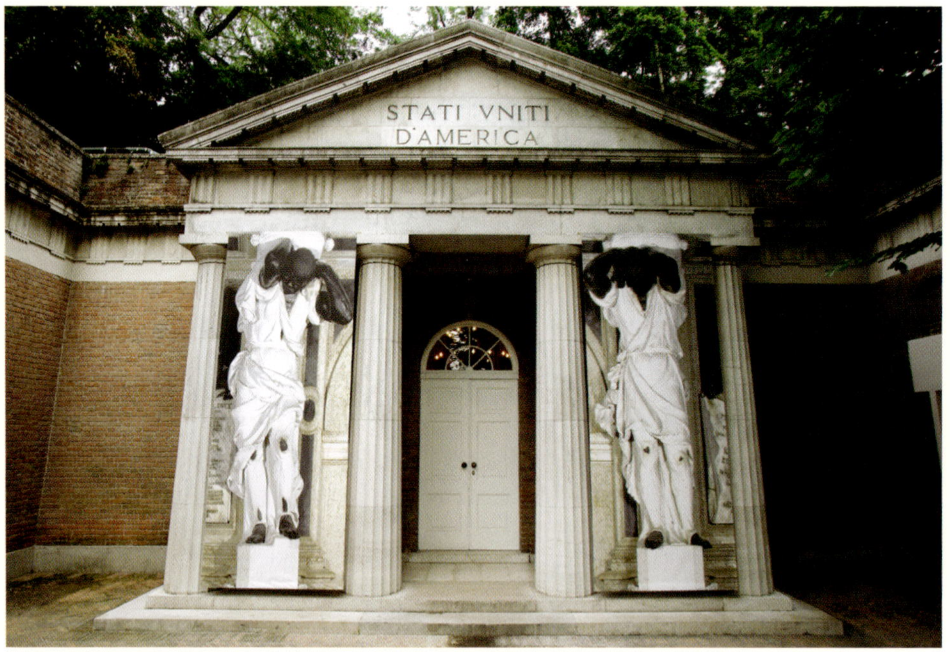

2.22 Fred Wilson,
Speak of Me As I Am,
2003. Portico. Photo
by R. Ransick and A.
Cocchi. Courtesy of
the artist.

examined a similar visual discourse that is operative in high-end kitsch and the fine arts. The title is taken from a line spoken by the tragic Moor in Shakespeare's *Othello,* whose life in Venice was anything but untroubled. Having loved "not wisely but too well," he states, "when these unlucky deeds relate / Speak of me as I am; nothing extenuate." Othello's plea for veracity from those whom he suspects may falsely represent him becomes the underlying narrative for Wilson's exploration of a centuries-long visual discourse of the black body in the Venetian imaginary. Not the first African American artist to represent the United States at the Venice Biennale, he was certainly the first to focus on the history of Venice itself. Exploring the city's museums and combing the contents of shops and marketplaces, Wilson mined the urban landscape of Venice as yet another rich and provocative archive.

Playing off the visual opportunity provided by a neoclassical portico at the entrance to the United States Pavilion, Wilson hung two full-length banners between the fluted columns on either side of the entrance. The banners depicted two black slaves dressed in rags with heads bowed who, so positioned, seem to support the weight of the structure on their shoulders (figure 2.22). The originals are two of four relatively well-known statues that adorn one of the more elaborate baroque tombs in Venice, Baldassare Longhena's tomb for Doge Giovanni Pesaro, at S. Maria Gloriosa dei Frari (1669). Atop the portico of the pavilion a stone frieze inscribed "United States of America" invited viewers to interpret the slaves as American, to see their bodies as the sign of labor upon which the wealth of the nation was constructed. This potential misinterpretation allowed Wilson to strategically exploit the found images for a double purpose, drawing parallels between the commercial, cosmopolitan Venice of the past and the wealth and power of the United States today.

Inside the pavilion rotunda, an ornate chandelier made entirely of Venetian black glass shimmered eerily, somehow both alluring and impenetrable in its dark opacity (figure 2.23). With an economy of means and an elegant deftness, Wilson compressed the long history of crystal chandeliers and their relation to class privilege, to whiteness, and to light into a single object. Its opulence is second only to its optical uncanniness. (Pepón Osorio's *El Chandelier,* makes for an interesting comparison.) At the back of the rotunda Wilson placed a black statue in fancy dress, one of many commonly found holding serving trays in numerous tourist hotels and businesses throughout the city. By replacing the statue's head with a black globe, the artist reminded his viewers that this Venetian icon was really a transnational subject and a transnational object. In adjoining galleries, one found kitsch reproductions of baroque and other period depictions of blacks in positions of servitude or submission, both docile and consumable in carved wood and plaster, painted in bright colors and gold leaf: a small boy holding a tray, a group of glass-blown candelabras (one transformed into a Molotov cocktail), and a gas lamp in the shape of a young black man encircled with rubber tubes attached to tanks of explosive gas (figures 2.24 and 2.25). The incendiary details, such as the Molotov cocktail, gestured toward the explosion or destruction of these tenacious myths. Other apparently harmless, romantic souvenirs of the Venetian Moors purchased by the artist in typical tourist shops were shown to participate in a visual discourse of popular consumption: a box of "Othello" chocolates, dark cookies called "Moor's bread," and cheap earrings with heads of Moors hanging from them. As with the objects in *Collectibles*, these decorative and popular artifacts signaled an imaginary fantasy of the black body as either docile or literally digestible, and pointed to the material history of their commercial production. Again the questions arise: Who profits from the stereotype? What role does tourism play in the maintenance of this stereotype? What fantasies of domination are maintained, "purely" for the sake of fantasy? And where does fantasy merge with real race domination in contemporary Venice?

Wilson also took up the history of the fine arts in Venice, which has a rich tradition of painting that includes historical and fanciful depictions of black Moorish subjects. Master works and reproductions borrowed from local museums, among them Andrea Mantegna's *Adoration of the Magi* (1460s), Vittore Carpaccio, *Miracle of the True Cross* (1494), Marco Marziale's *Supper at Emmaus* (1506), and Paolo Veronese's *Feast in the House of Levi* (1573). Also, a sixteenth-century portrait of a Medici prince who may have been part black, an early modern work of the goddess Diana surrounded by nymphs, one of whom is black, and an eighteenth-century depiction of King David being served by a black youth. These works are accompanied by a photographic collage of details shot from well-known early modern paintings that appear in museums throughout the city, mostly representing blacks as servants or as exotic cosmopolitans. Interspersed with these historical citations are images of blacks taken on the streets of Venice today—tourists, residents, and street vendors—whose presence has been the focus of some controversy in the recent resurgence of Italian nationalism (figure 2.26). As Blake Gopnik points out in his review of Wilson's exhibition, "Italy's African peddlers represent about the lowest stratum in its society, no longer considered people truly exotic and interesting and worth rendering in art, as they were in the Renaissance, but now only worth ignoring, unless they get so much in the way that they become a problem to be solved."[82] On the one hand, mixing the contemporary photographs with the historic images of black bodies sets up a parallel between past and present that may appear simplistic, or strangely and inappropriately anachronistic. On the other hand, Wilson's juxtaposition is jarring not only because of this temporal gap, but more so because he once again brings to our attention our own viewing apparatus, namely, the spectator's position vis-à-vis the black body as

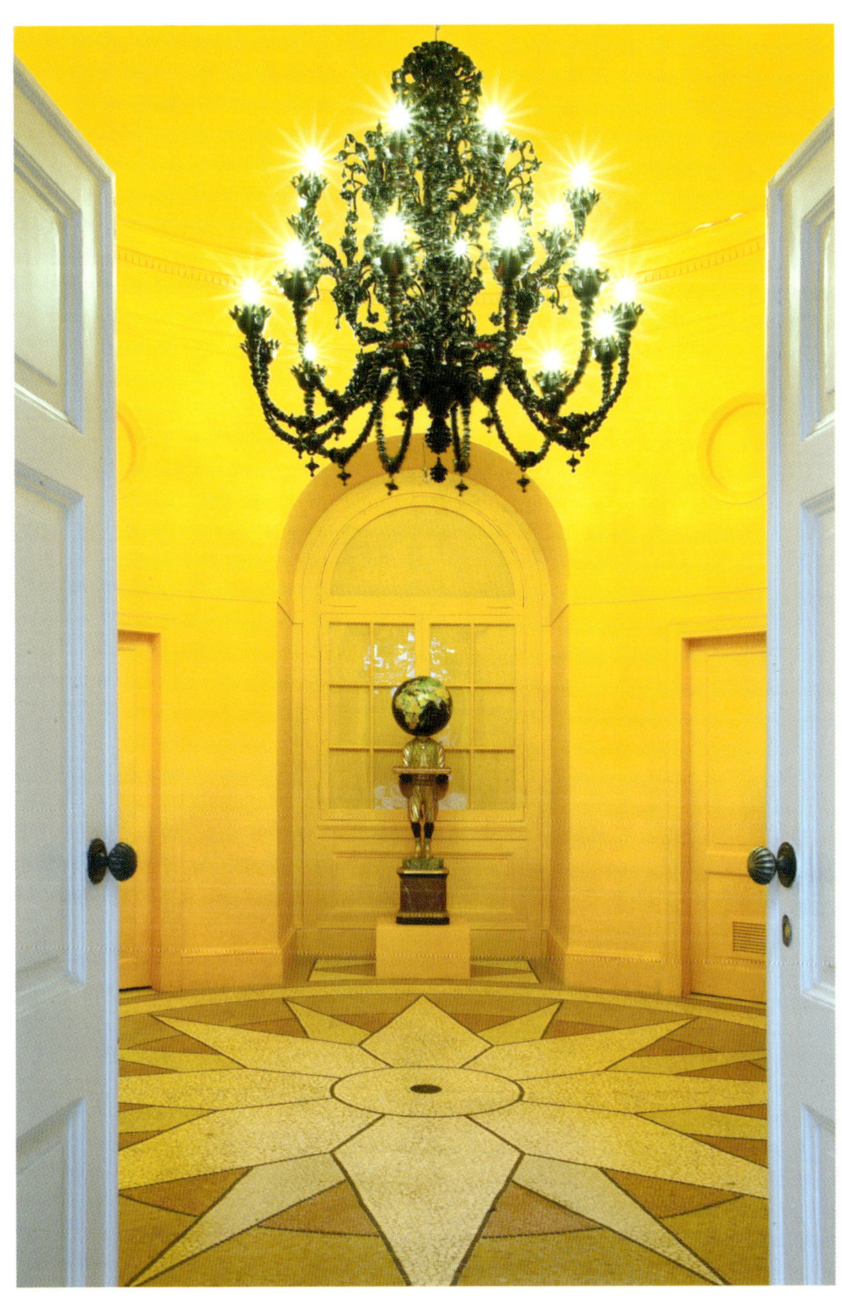

2.23 Fred Wilson, "Chandelier Mori" in *Speak of Me As I Am*, 2003. Rotunda. Photo by R. Ransick and A. Cocchi. Courtesy of the artist.

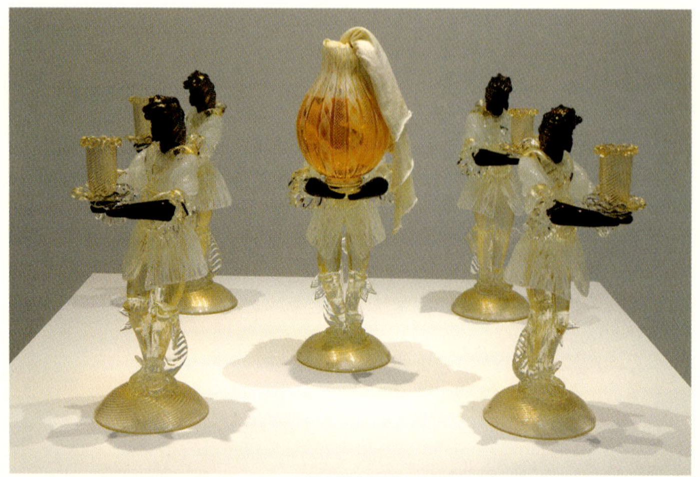

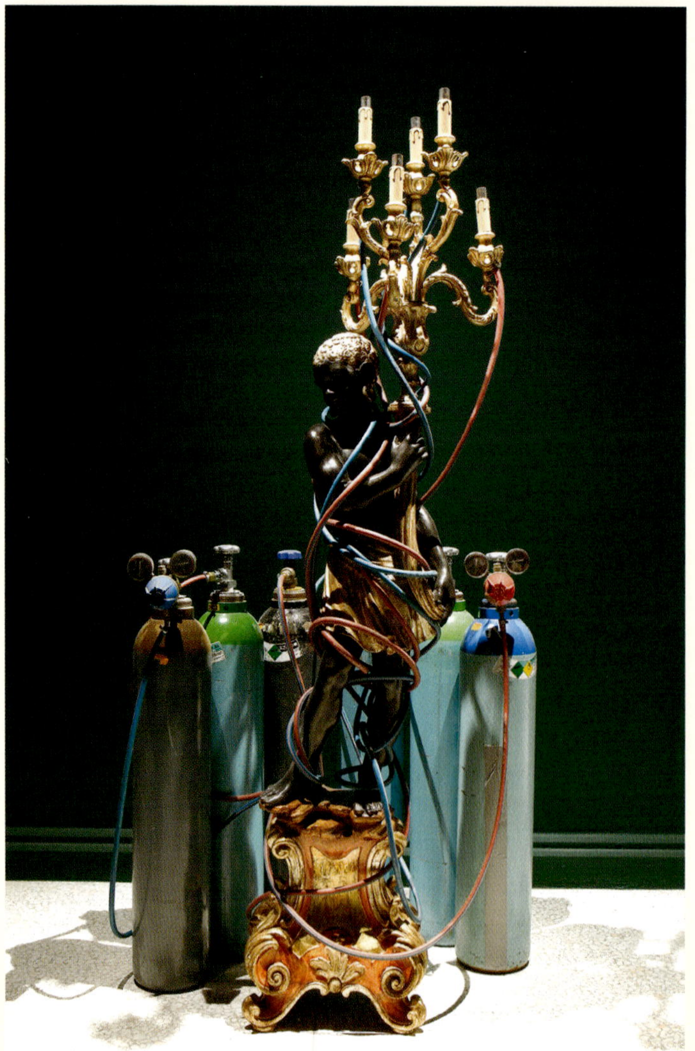

2.24 Fred Wilson, "Shatter" in *Speak of Me As I Am*, 2003. Photo by R. Ransick and A. Cocchi. Courtesy of the artist.

2.25 Fred Wilson, "Spark" in *Speak of Me As I Am*, 2003. Photo by R. Ransick and A. Cocchi. Courtesy of the artist.

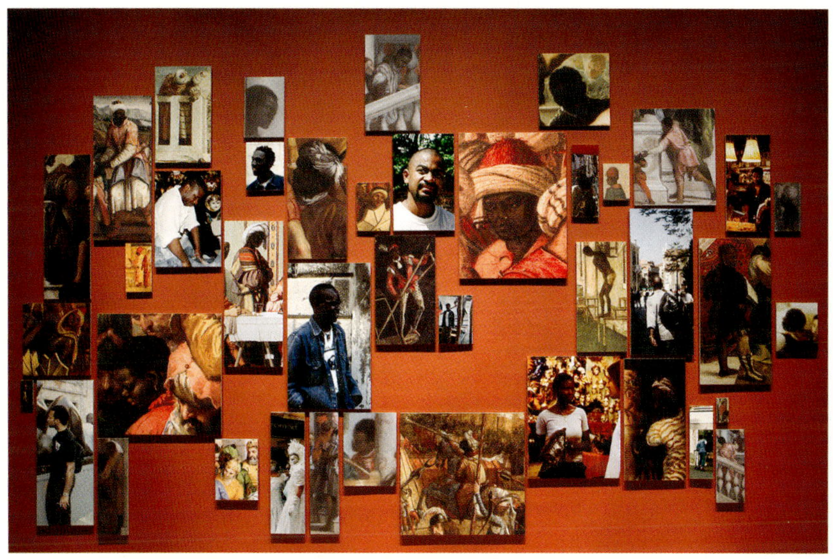

2.26 Fred Wilson, "Una Confluenza degli Africani" in *Speak of Me As I Am,* 2003. Photo by R. Ransick and A. Cocchi. Courtesy of the artist.

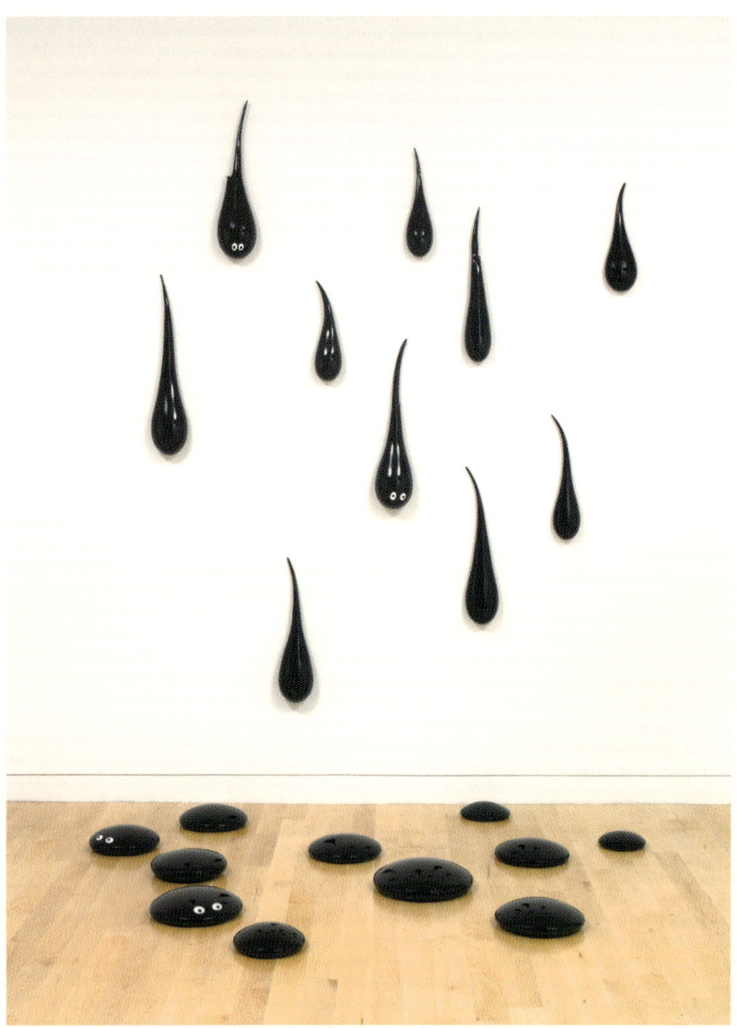

2.27 Fred Wilson,
Drip, Drop, Plop, 2001.
Photo by R. Ransick
and A. Cocchi. Cour-
tesy of the artist.

object and subject. Particularly for those who venerate the Italian masters of the pre- and early modern periods, this collage insures that the contemplative attitude of the connoisseur's gaze is disrupted by images that are effectively documentary and mundane. In short, the work is as much about activities and habits of vision as it is about black bodies per se. For many, the historic black body can be romantically incorporated into a cosmopolitan image of the city's past, whereas the contemporary black body is virtually invisible.

Wilson also included some works from previous exhibitions such as an unusual glass installation against one wall titled *Drip, Drop, Plop* (2001), which combined the simplicity of minimalist sculpture with racist caricature. Black glass tears and circular black drops arrayed on the floor and wall seemed to hang suspended in the whiteness of the gallery (figure 2.27). Small white eyes painted on several of the drops produced a cartoonish anthropomorphism, while the assemblage as a whole invited a variety of material interpretations; the molten glass could signify tears, crude oil, tar, ink, or simply blackness. It certainly seems to represent the degree to which the black body experiences degradation in mainstream Euro-American culture, devolving into little more than shapeless gobs. It is also possible, given Wilson's previous works and his points of reference, to read this piece in relation to a scene in Ralph Ellison's *Invisible Man* when the protagonist is working in a paint factory. While mixing the company's best-selling color, "Optical White" (which paradoxically entails adding ten drops of black paint to each can), the *Invisible Man* recalls, "Slowly, I measured the glistening black drops, seeing them settle upon the surface and become blacker still, spreading suddenly out to the edges."[83] The white walls of the United States Pavilion serve as the ground for Wilson's ten black teardrops against the wall—here the presence of the black body primarily signifies its own disappearance into the optically white environment. In the context of the Venice Biennale, Peter Erickson argues, *Drip, Drop, Plop* also suggests a connection to Othello's call to "speak of me as I am," which is followed with this lament: "one whose subdued eyes / Albeit unused to the melting mood / Drop tears as fast as the Arabian trees / Their medicinal gum."[84] In an email interview with Erickson the artist commented, "I wanted to heighten the fact that Shakespeare's Othello is a representation of blackness, of Africanness, and not the real thing. That Shakespeare himself was using race as a historical marker, a visual cue, a point of bias to make the story complex and exotic as well as familiar to his audience."[85]

In addition to these scattered references, one section of the exhibition was dedicated to the theatrical interpretation of Othello. A grid of four video projections showed different film and operatic versions of the play, with clips of only the most violent scenes of rape and murder running backward in slow motion, frame by frame. In Wilson's selection, which includes versions by Orson Welles and Stuart Burge, Othello's character was played as Shakespeare imagined, by white actors in blackface. It is of course the white man's violence, and fantasies of violence, that are ultimately depicted in slow motion.

Across from the silent film clips in a small room tiled in a checkerboard pattern of black and white, called "Turbulence II," a layered sound element of repeated citations from Shakespeare's play created a humming, nearly unintelligible, noise. Written on the grout *between* the tiles were notes about freedom and imprisonment. Two black mirrors reminiscent of Felix Gonzalez-Torres's paired blue mirrors suggesting the twinning of gay identity and desire hung against one wall. They were echoed in two black circular holes in the floor filled with black ink, perhaps in reference to the history of written discourse or the black tears of Othello or even to oil wells. The historical moment of the exhibition and its title implied that "Turbulence II" might have also made reference to the destruction of the Twin Towers in New York City where the artist lives. The only sanctuary in the room was a large clay vessel containing what appeared to be the remnants of a nomadic life; some clothes, a teacup, and desk lamp, some reference books, pillows, and blankets. Here the private life of the individual subject, perhaps the artist himself, might be temporarily protected from the harsh, artificially binary environment of the black/white grid in the room beyond. As with all sanctuaries, the protection of this imaginary vessel was limited and contingent, and could eventually become its own form of imprisonment. "Turbulence II" articulated not only the metaphorical but also the phenomenological dimension of spatial limits for subjects trapped between two domains of habitation and two models of racial subjectivity.

Wilson's title *Speak of Me As I Am* invites viewers to see African and Afro-European subjects in a historically and ontologically richer context, and it refers to the invented artificiality of Othello as a black man created—like so many of the other objects in the exhibition—entirely out of white fantasies. In these projects, the artist emphasizes both the complexity and diversity of blackness on the one hand, and the narrowness of its popular representation on the other. It seems to be precisely in opposition to the possibility of there being a simple representation of a black body that Wilson works. His juxtapositions demonstrate the flatness, the vacuousness of the image of blackness that appears in contemporary caricatures, while also demonstrating that their very ubiquity is the source of their insidious persistence.

Wilson's artworks stage an interpretive response to those hegemonic systems of representation that have traditionally positioned some subjects in culturally subaltern positions. In Wilson's works, the traces of history found in ethnographic museums or the canonized master works of classical antiquity are shown to take part in an institutional topography of cultural privilege and hierarchy. He illuminates legacies of cultural patrimony that haunt art museums as well as the scholarly discipline of art history. If museums of art provide the site for "civilizing rituals," as Carol Duncan suggests, Wilson reminds us that all museums, in fact, stage an account of "civilizations" by positioning viewers as either insiders or outsiders in a spatial and cultural ritual. Perhaps this is why Wilson's work resonates with, and irritates, his critics—the work is both too obvious and too accurate; too literal and too disruptive. Indeed, the antiracist arguments posed by the artworks were already familiar by the late 1980s and early 1990s, but the form of their presentation was Wilson's innovation. Neither sloganeering nor proselytizing, Wilson's approach is more demure and ultimately more devious; it depends upon the familiar, passive, and receptive viewing behaviors of museum and gallery goers that treat these architectural interiors as silent, sacred spaces where unquestioned truths and aesthetic wonders are presented. Wilson disrupts this viewing pleasure, along the lines of Bertolt Brecht or Jean-Luc Godard, by drawing the frame to the fore and then creating the conditions for a kind of theatrical farce. His critiques of race discourse are materialist engagements with the past that make use of historical objects in order to produce strategic juxtapositions. His approach is archival, research-oriented, and highly self-conscious about the spatial practices of display operative in the public sphere, especially museums. All of his works rely upon the metonymic relations between artifacts and the larger world they signify, as well as a sophisticated understanding of the rhetorical use of architectural spaces in the construction of ideologies of inclusion and exclusion. His iconoclastic approach may appear cavalier to some, but to others it is nothing less than an indispensable activist gesture. It is perhaps best to understand the installations as forms of serious play, ironic and self-conscious about every detail but deeply concerned with the real-world consequences of racial injustice.

AMALIA MESA-BAINS

DIVINE ALLEGORIES

SAINT TERESA OF AVILA was known for her corporeal passion—her heart pierced by Christ's golden arrow during an ecstatic vision, leaving her body "wholly on fire." As unconventional as she was influential, the sixteenth-century nun and patron saint of lace makers was known for miracles of healing, visionary writings, and the founding of convents. A shrine constructed in her honor by Amalia Mesa-Bains, *Altar for Santa Teresa de Avila* (1984), was among the first of the artist's works to link the tradition of home altars and *ofrendas* with a feminist recuperation of Catholic iconography (figure 3.1). Pearls, a lace fan, and a mantilla adorned the base, while flowers and framed images of the saint covered the stacked tiers that ascended to a central, arched niche emblazoned with a sacred heart. Draped in black folds reminiscent of a nun's habit, afire with symbolic flames, and crowned with a halo of silk, the altar doubled as an icon of the saint herself. For Saint Teresa, the body serves as a passionate altar. The artist's altar represents not only a holy female body hooded with a sacred garment, but also the beatification on a larger scale of its secret, enfolded organ of pleasure. The viewers' revelation comes when what initially appears as a traditional homage is recognized as a visual allegory of female desire enshrined in the frame of Catholic ritual.

Working within a culturally specific lexicon of religious traditions and Chicano critical politics, many of Mesa-Bains's early works draw upon Mexican American Catholic iconography and community-based art practices. Her later works take this formal and conceptual framework in new directions, addressing a broader history of cultural contact between Europe and the Americas during the period of colonial conquest. In parallel with these concerns is an unwavering critical attention to the place of women—particularly *mestizas* (women of mixed blood)—within the visual and material discourses of display, a political commentary in the form of symbolic and iconographic narratives that are also autobiographical. With her own interpretation of a distinctly Chicana feminist practice, the artist challenges familiar aesthetic distinctions between tradition and innovation, and temporal distinctions between cyclical and linear time.

Focusing on the domain of private spaces to explore larger historical themes, Mesa-Bains addresses the intensely social and ideological character of women's interior lives. By definition and by design, installation art is an architectural practice that operates as a prosthesis to architecture proper. Partial, fragmentary, and suggestive, Mesa-Bains's installations turn to the home altar, boudoir, curiosity cabinet, harem, library, and garden as spaces of reverence and mourning, comfort and desire, enclosure and preservation, knowledge and contemplation. Each characterized by its unique practice of collecting and display, these sites belong to a topology of primarily feminine intimacy. Mesa-Bains emphasizes spaces where individual attention is focused, daily activities are choreographed or routinized, and subject formation takes place: those mirrors, tables, and closets, those inner sanctums where relics are archived and knowledge about the body, particularly the female body, is transmitted or enforced.

Altar-Installations

The 1970s Chicano civil rights movement in California included a revival of Mexican cultural traditions as a form of critical resistance to an American imperative of assimilation. Rubén Salazar wrote that a Chicano is "a Mexican-American with a non-Anglo image of himself."[1] In addition to demands for better educational opportunities and decent labor conditions, the Chicano civil rights movement saw cultural reclamation as part of its long-term social and political mission to recuperate a lost indigenous heritage.[2] Many Chicano/a artists experimented with hybrid forms of artistic practice, working across traditions from both Mexico and the United States, producing murals, paintings, films, posters, theatrical productions, and other art forms that flourished in an atmosphere of political urgency, emphasizing public activism and public address.[3]

Having received her MFA in painting in 1966, Amalia Mesa-Bains came to the movement after the first wave of political activist art began to influence the work of more traditionally trained artists. As part of an effort to leverage aesthetics in the name of cultural politics, many artists began creating collaborative *ofrendas* (offerings) in local gallery spaces and community centers for special cultural events such as *Día de los Muertos* (Day of the Dead) in the early 1980s.[4] An indigenous memorial ritual reworked with a Catholic veneer in the sixteenth century and revived in its current popular form in the United States by Chicano/a artists in the 1970s,

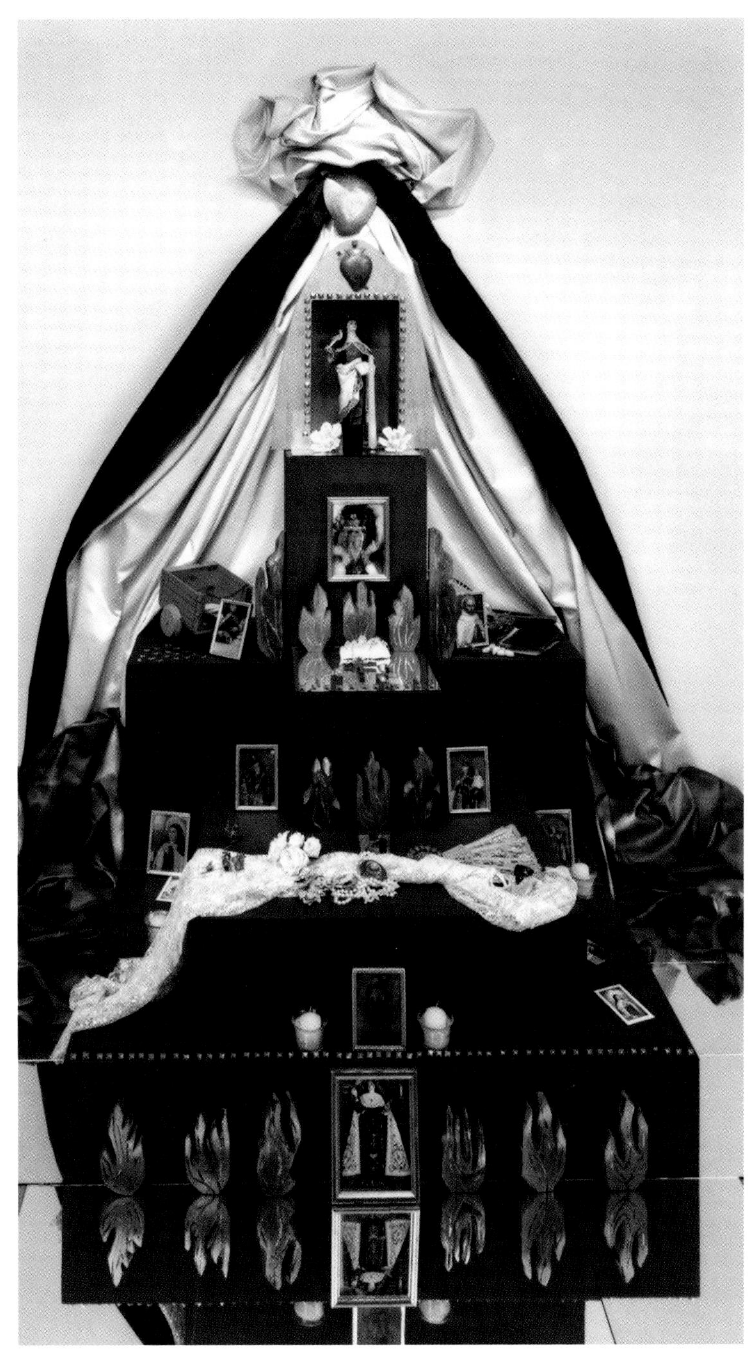

3.1 Amalia Mesa-Bains, *Altar for Santa Teresa de Avila*, 1984. Courtesy of the artist.

the traditional memorial practices of Day of the Dead include cemetery vigils, elaborate feasts, and the building of temporary altars to celebrate the memory of the deceased each year on the second day of November.[5] These temporary memorial installations celebrate the lives of ancestors with traditional multitiered structures displaying an array of objects including photographs and brightly colored flowers, candy skulls, festival foods, and decorative embellishments, such as *papel picado,* strung marigolds, and votive candles. A threshold between the living and the dead, the Day of the Dead altar was part of the cultural reclamation effort of Chicano community centers across the United States.[6]

From this early experience with community altar building, Mesa-Bains developed new methods for constructing elaborate displays of material culture, moving from the formal visual tropes of home altars in the Mexican Catholic tradition to more experimental modes of installation art. The vernacular traditions of building home altars or *ofrendas* thus became the structural and ideological ground on which the artist developed innovative alternatives for subsequent gallery exhibitions.[7] Although some scholars use the terms "altar" and "*ofrenda*" interchangeably, the artist creates a distinction by observing that traditional home altars frequently serve as the permanent, ongoing record of a family's life framed within a religious idiom of saints and other icons, while *ofrendas* are usually temporary offerings that are mounted for memorial events and festivals. Altars tend to display multigenerational memorabilia, photographs, and statues of favorite saints, whereas *ofrendas* honor a single deceased individual with objects that are associated with or dedicated to that person.[8] Familiar with the social and historical role of these vernacular practices, Mesa-Bains worked between the paradigms of altar and *ofrenda* by enlisting the archival impulse of the former, and the ephemeral or laudatory function of the latter. The idea of impermanence plays a central role in Mexican and Chicano cultural ideologies, from the recognition that death is an integral part of life to an acceptance of the transitory nature of youth and beauty.[9] It is precisely because life is fluid and cyclical that it is celebrated in elaborate rituals that engage the past; the *ofrenda* lasts only a few days before being disassembled, its objects and icons dispersed for another year. At a time when temporary and site-specific installation art had gained mainstream acceptance as a legitimate art form, Mesa-Bains worked within and across this framework by incorporating traditionally ephemeral and impermanent practices from Mexican popular culture in her gallery installations. Linking these two social and artistic practices, the artist recognized and emphasized the parallels between genres of display from two distinct cultural domains.

To emphasize their double valence, Mesa-Bains has described her early works as "altar-installations."[10] First exhibited in 1984, the *Ofrenda for Dolores Del Rio* (figure 3.2) exemplifies this mix of formal innovation and cultural tradition, while also inaugurating a transitional move to a more autobiographical and historical focus of the artist's later installations. One of her better-known works, it has appeared in a number of group and solo exhibitions, most notably the CARA/Chicano Art: Resistance and Affirmation traveling exhibition in 1991. With cascading flounces of pink satin and white lace, crushed rose petals, and bright glitter, the *Ofrenda for Dolores Del Rio* paid homage to a secular icon of cinema through an ornamental canonization in the space of the gallery. In its symmetry and abundance, the multitiered, mirrored, altar-installation elicits a certain genuflection and identification from its audience who can be seen reflected within. Mirrors are the locus of beauty rituals, where women are invited to inspect and scrutinize their bodies critically as they slowly age. Offerings of gold and silver fruit surrounded the jewel-encrusted shrine housing a film still of Del Rio who, covered in a *reboso,* resembled a sultry Madonna. Vertical rows of photographs on both sides of the altar acted as narrative images, referencing the stained-glass panels found in Gothic chapels as well as the film star's many roles. Laid at the base of the structure, a collection of silver painted film canisters also referenced a career on the silver screen. A Mexican national who found early recognition in Hollywood, Del Rio starred in silent films such as *The Loves of Carmen* (1927) and *Ramona* (1928) before making the transition to sound films such as *Flying Down to Rio* (1933) and Orson Welles's *Journey into Fear* (1942). Despite her success in the United States, Del Rio was commonly typecast as Mexican and eventually decided to return to Mexico where she continued to enjoy financial and critical success as an actress, making more than sixty films before her death in 1983.

The installation also overflowed with intimate, personal objects: discarded tissues imprinted with lipstick kisses, letters, and photographs, as well as devotional elements, candles, and religious icons. An opposition of private and public life also revealed the distance between a Mexican childhood (signified by photographs of Del Rio's parents, a doll, and a Mexican flag) and Hollywood stardom (signified by an elegant fan, cosmetics, bottles of perfume, and photographs of leading men). Placed on opposite sides of the *ofrenda,* the two groupings of artifacts suggested the conflicting conditions of an identity split between a Mexican heritage and a Hollywood career. To formulate a visual argument about the role of Del Rio as a central figure in Chicana history and in her own imaginary, Mesa-Bains developed a material rhetoric or topographical map of cultural and institutional affiliations grounded in symbolically charged artifacts. Scholar Tomás Ybarra-Frausto argues the *Ofrenda for Dolores Del Rio* allowed the artist to "focus inward, exploring her feminine psyche and generating an ancestry or lineage of women significant to her own life."[11]

The simultaneously historical and hagiographic framework of the *Ofrenda for Dolores Del Rio* suggests the duality of what Julia Kristeva has called

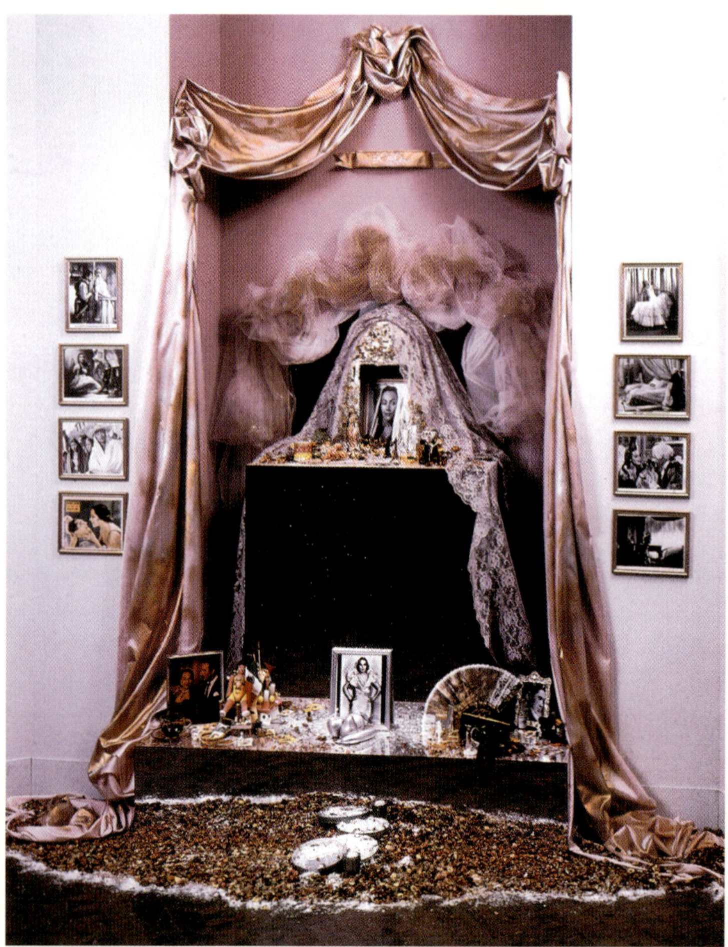

3.2 Amalia Mesa-Bains, *Ofrenda for Dolores Del Rio,* 1984. Wright Gallery, University of California, Los Angeles. Courtesy of the artist.

"woman's time," which engages both cursive time (the time of linear history) and monumental time (the time of life cycles and private rituals).[12] The figure of Dolores Del Rio is the source of both mythological identification and historical recuperation. The spatial rhetoric of the work is joined by a temporal component of remembrance and memorial, functioning as a monumental site of ritual for both Mesa-Bains and her imagined spectators. By transforming this historical figure into a canonized cultural icon, the artist adds Del Rio to a pantheon of feminine role models with which she and other Chicanas can identify. Ybarra-Frausto argues that the underlying aim of the work is "to shift perception of Dolores del Rio from being merely a fashionable commodity to her recognition as a woman of significant accomplishment—the first Mexican superstar breaking the racial taboos of mainstream Hollywood."[13] Dedicated to Mesa-Bains's mother, Marina Gonzales Mesa, who introduced the artist to Golden Age Mexican cinema, the Del Rio *ofrenda* stands as a symbol of glamour and an autobiographical meditation on beauty and aging.[14]

As systems of display, private altars and *ofrendas* have traditionally been the province of women, specifically household matriarchs. In "Mexican-American Women's Home Altars: The Art of Relationship," Kay Turner suggests that home altars provide the means of expression for an otherwise marginalized female community.[15] It is also here that gender and race discourse intersect, because it is on the home altar that the material signs of cultural affiliation are gathered. The European Catholicism exported to the Americas during the Spanish conquest had a racial bias that included its own history of violence against indigenous populations. Today, centuries later, Mexican and Mexican American Catholics have a negotiated respect for the "white" iconography of saints and virgins that constitute the dominant visual culture of the faith. The dark-skinned patron saint of Mexico, the Virgin of Guadalupe, is frequently found on home altars along with family photographs and often signs of ethnic or national affiliation such as a flag or mementos from Mexico. The home altar, in other words, is a cumulative form of expression that draws objects from different cultural, historical, racial, and religious traditions into a single, unique, and generally private display. For women, this symbolic, domestic, ritual activity provides the means to imagine a set of social relations to family, community, and even the divine, beyond the strict confines of the male-dominated church. Mesa-Bains's decision to choose the altar as the format for her early installations suggests an awareness of these gender-specific connotations that might have successfully worked against the more heroic, masculine bias inherent in Chicano art of the time.

While the *Ofrenda for Dolores Del Rio* might appear to some as a glorification of a hyperfeminine woman, Mesa-Bains's feminist gesture is to honor Del Rio—a secular, professional woman—with the woman-centered, culturally specific practice of home altar building. In the same way that earlier feminist artists validated women's creative work by eschewing the traditional art media of the academy and favoring sewn fabric, soft felt, or quilting, Mesa-Bains's installation brought creative work from the domestic sphere, defiant of patriarchy and white Catholicism, into the public space of the art gallery.

Other Chicana artists, notably Carmen Lomas Garza, Yolanda López, and Ester Hernandez, took part in this broader feminist project, visually transforming female cultural icons such as Frida Kahlo and the Virgin of Guadalupe into powerful figures of resistance and strength. Mesa-Bains's art practice emerged out of contact and conversation with these and other artists who saw that a new vision of female emancipation might be built on already cherished and familiar icons. Lomas Garza was one of the first Chicanas to eulogize the independent-minded artist and political figure Frida Kahlo, using the form of an altar dedicated in 1978 for a Day of the Dead celebration. Chicana artists looking to the past and to Mexico for inspiration and role models of independent and politically engaged female artists revered Kahlo long before she became an icon in mainstream popular culture. Similarly, the indigenous Virgin of Guadalupe became a central figure in numerous works by Chicana feminist artists. Scholar Yvonne Yarbro-Bejarano observes that as a "syncretic fusion of the Catholic Virgin Mother and the preconquest fertility deity Tonantzin, Guadalupe signifies the racial construction of Mexican national identity as the *mestizo* or hybrid product of the sexual union of Indian woman and male Spaniard."[16] For her *Guadalupe Series* (1978), López produced a triptych of oil pastel portraits of herself, her mother, and her grandmother as incarnations of the Virgin of Guadalupe. Posed as family matriarch, working seamstress, and young marathon runner, the grandmother, mother, and artist transform the Virgin from a passive and submissive figure into an active, mobile, and self-sufficient woman who has power and mastery within her own life.[17] In a similar gesture, Hernandez pictured the Virgin of Guadalupe as a powerful kickboxer in *La Virgen de Guadalupe Defendiendo los Derechos de los Xicanos* (The Virgin of Guadalupe Defending Chicano Rights) (1975), which appeared on the cover of a student magazine. Of course, women artists were not the only members of the Chicano movement to recuperate such iconic figures as symbols of cultural identity and religious affiliation. César Chávez and the United Farm Workers Association also made use of the traditional image of the Virgin of Guadalupe as a symbol of piety, protection, and a *mestizo Mexicanidad*. Nevertheless, Chicana artists redefined, and continue to redefine, these female icons as signs of liberation rather than obedience, freedom rather than conformity.[18] The early work of Amalia Mesa-Bains can be understood as engaging with this larger Chicana feminist project.

Mesa-Bains's altar-installations are neither a simple enactment of religious tradition nor a purely secular art installation, but rather a hybrid genre intended for a new Chicano/a-identified audience able to decipher the multiple iconographic references in both a Mexican and U.S. historical context. This audience is able to appreciate the way in which the work is simultaneously traditional and irreverent, paying respect to cultural heroes and heroines while criticizing more rigid social mores. By purposefully crossing the categorical boundaries between site-specific conceptual art and folk tradition, the artist also sought to develop a new practice of reception and engagement. Like many other Chicano/a artists trained in mainstream art schools, Mesa-Bains worked within two paradigms and two visual idioms: the postconceptual framework of the art establishment of the late twentieth century, and the politically focused, culturally specific idiom of Chicanos under a U.S. cultural hegemony. In this way, the works participated in a redefinition of aesthetic frameworks prevalent at the time.

Paradigms of innovation that shape both art history and art criticism usually ignore the possibility that works of art, particularly those produced during the second half of the twentieth century, might be designed to preserve or maintain cultural traditions from earlier eras. Under these conditions, it becomes difficult to address models of art practice that cannot be defined in terms of originality only but must be understood in terms of ritual, repetition, tradition (not only fine art traditions), and cultural reclamation that is part of a larger anticolonialist endeavor. Nestór García Canclini writes that many Latin American art works that

> practice the ephemeral but refuse to insert themselves in the ahistorical metaphysics of a present without substance, remain occasions to re-encounter something that folklore represented: not the melancholic nostalgia for what can no longer exist, nor the fundamentalist dogmatization of vanished images or knowledges, but the experience of social relations as the product of a continuity, and the conviction that that continuity can point the way toward living the conflicts between traditions and modernities more intensely—toward being at one and the same time, responsible for and critical of memory.[19]

This slippage between "folk" art and "fine" art, between tradition and innovation, between memory and revision of memory, is also characteristic of Mesa-Bains's altar-installations, which operate within and across these conceptual categories.

In *Grotto of the Virgins* (1987), for example, memorial *ofrendas* dedicated to Frida Kahlo, Dolores Del Rio, and the artist's grandmother Mariana Escobedo Mesa were brought together in a single display space, inviting the audience to draw parallels among the three women who served as female archetypes for the artist. Typically a small cave or cavern found in nature, the grotto has been identified, at least since the sixteenth century, as a site where one might commune with the "muses." Artificial grottoes were frequently constructed in aristocratic gardens of early modern Italy, France, and England to provide a proper site for social or intellectual meditations on nature.[20] Referencing this tradition in the gallery space, Mesa-Bains surrounded the entrance with stone tiles and shards of broken mirrors and covered the floor with rocks, tree branches, and flower petals.[21] *Grotto of the Virgins* was the first of Mesa-Bains's works to extend the traditional altar form into an environmental artwork using earthy materials scattered across the floor and piled in corners to convey a sense of a rocky cave, but also a tomb or a burial site.[22] The arched doorway with its mosaic surface of mirrors reproduced the decorative style of outdoor *capillas* (little chapels) that serve as enclosed yard shrines of many Mexican American households. A spatial ambiguity created by the layered materials on the gallery floor meant that visitors were unsure about where they were allowed to step, about whether they were "inside" or "outside" the artwork. To some degree, Mesa-Bains was working within a well-established tradition. Walter de Maria, Robert Morris, Robert Smithson, and others had long since blurred the boundaries between artwork and exhibition space in the 1960s by scattering rocks, earth, and other nontraditional materials on the floors and in the corners of gallery exhibition spaces.[23] When *Grotto of the Virgins* was installed two decades later, this use of materials was already familiar, or at least not surprising, to an artgoing public, but its semiotic function had shifted. No longer exploring the phenomenological, perceptual questions raised by this earlier generation of conceptual and minimalist artists, Mesa-Bains turned to rocks and earth for their symbolic, allegorical valence, linking the lives of her muses to the earthly substance to which they returned at death.

Each individual altar-installation played off the tradition of *ofrendas* in a different way. The altar dedicated to Kahlo focused on her struggles with illness and injury and her confinement to the home and to bed, where she produced many of her best-known paintings. On the altar stood a miniature bedroom with tiny reproductions of Kahlo's works surrounded by candied skulls, dried leaves, one of Kahlo's self- portraits, and twisting branches and vines, serving as an ode to creativity, decay, and the passing of time. Perched on a shelf was a pair of antlers very much like those in Kahlo's self-portrait *The Little Deer* (1946), which depicts the painter as a wounded animal pierced with arrows, lying on the floor of the forest. Mesa-Bains's altar recalls this scene for those familiar with Kahlo's work, and thus works as an intertextual reference to the history of Mexican painting, but it also reminds viewers of Kahlo's vulnerability, her suffering, and her remarkable resilience to both racism and patriarchy in her own time.[24] Del Rio's altar replicated the shimmering, baroque quality of its earlier incarnation, framing femininity in the context of glamour and desire. Finally, the grandmother's altar took the form of a simple church confessional placed against one wall; spectators were required to kneel in order to peer through a wooden lattice to see a traditional home altar with images and artifacts that made reference to Mariana's life: black-and-white family photographs, personal letters, roses in a vase, the Mexican national flag, a votive candle, and an image of Christ.

Viewed together the three altar-installations invited comparison, creating parallels among the lives of these very different women. All are shown to have lived complex and difficult lives, negotiating their way through sexuality, marriage, and the ambivalent process of forming national or cultural identities. By presenting Frida Kahlo, Dolores Del Rio, and her grandmother Mariana as virgins, Mesa-Bains suggests that these extraordinary women deserve the reverence normally accorded to the most holy of Catholic icons, despite their decidedly worldly existence. By referencing the tradition of the grotto, the work implies that the women serve as the artist's muses, each reflecting characteristics, desires, or ways of life that have been influential in shaping the artist's own feminine and feminist consciousness. The decorative quality of the display and the mix of sacred and secular icons, in both the *Ofrenda for Dolores Del Rio* and *Grotto of the Virgins,* are elements borrowed from vernacular Chicano/a traditions. With their playful irreverence and eclecticism, they display an aesthetic sensibility that can be best described as *rasquache.*

Domesticana, a Chicana Rasquachismo

What does it mean to be *rasquache*? In his essay "Chicano Movement/ Chicano Art," Ybarra-Frausto argues:

> In the realm of taste, to be *rasquache* is to be unfettered and unrestrained, to favor the elaborate over the simple, the flamboyant over the severe. Bright colors (*chillantes*) are preferred to somber, high intensity to low, the shimmering and sparkling over the muted and subdued. The *rasquache* inclination piles pattern on pattern, filling all available space with bold display. Ornamentation and elaboration prevail and are joined with a delight in texture and sensuous surfaces.[25]

Flamboyant, glittering, full to the margins with an abundance of heterogeneous objects, Mesa-Bains's early altar-installations are most certainly informed by a *rasquache* aesthetic. Ybarra-Frausto clarifies that *rasquachismo* is an underdog perspective: "Resilience and resourcefulness spring from making do with what is at hand. This utilization of available resources makes for syncretism, juxtaposition, and integration."[26] Linked to a working-class position of marginality or lack, *rasquachismo* suggests clever resourcefulness, flexibility, attentive intuition, and a creative mix and juxtaposition of aesthetic forms.

Feminist scholars have also developed a language for the critical analysis of traditional and vernacular aesthetic practices by women, emphasizing their inventive or recuperative modes of production. Turner writes, "At the home altar women remake and reinvent the usefulness of cultural symbols, both sacred and secular, according to their own histories, purposes, needs, desires, and beliefs."[27] Although the formal organization of a home altar is not rule bound, Turner suggests that there is a certain aesthetic of "femmage" that characterizes its composition. A term coined by feminist artist Miriam Schapiro to suggest a feminine form of collage or montage, femmage is a name given to "the process of collecting and creatively assembling odd or seemingly disparate elements into a functional, integrated whole"[28]—a process that Turner claims is evident in many forms of women's traditional domestic art making. Schapiro's term validates practices and methods derived from home craft traditions across generations. In the context of a male-dominated art world, the concept of femmage offered a legitimizing frame for experimentation with decorative materials, fabric, and other nontraditional media in the production of new works.

In her essay "*Domesticana*: The Sensibility of a Chicana Rasquache," Mesa-Bains offers a theoretical analysis of a specifically Chicana form of "making do." Although it is unusual in the discipline of art history to use an essay authored by the artist as an interpretive framework, Mesa-Bains's theory of *domesticana* is an important conceptual innovation that is central to comprehending not only her work but also that of other Chicanas. Combining the word *Mexicana* (used to describe cheap tourist art from Mexico) with the *domestic* (the culture of everyday home life), Mesa-Bains follows in an activist tradition of deconstructing stereotypes by redefining them. Mesa-Bains sees *Domesticana* as the feminist affirmation of cultural domestic *values* in combination with emancipation from traditional feminine *roles*. She writes, "A defiance of an imposed Anglo-American cultural identity, and the defiance of restrictive gender identity within Chicano culture, has inspired a female *rasquachismo*."[29] Using "techniques of subversion through play with traditional imagery and cultural material," *domesticana* transforms "feminine" space from its traditional isolation under patriarchy into a public representation of the lived experience of Mexican American women.

Mesa-Bains's act of naming this critical aesthetic practice parallels other forms of enunciation that lay claim to conceptual and linguistic territory. Neologisms in the arts tend to appear when the conceptual vocabulary used by art critics and theorists fails to adequately address the important conceptual or culturally specific elements of contemporary art practice. While their unchecked proliferation is something to be avoided, neologisms signal a politics of language that parallels a politics of representation in a broader social sphere. By introducing the notion of *domesticana*,

Mesa-Bains participates in a necessary form of self-naming that can also provide a new analytic framework for future critics, scholars, and artists. For example, her essay includes an analysis of Celeste Olalquiaga's *Megalopolis: Contemporary Cultural Sensibilities* and Gerardo Mosquera's essay "Bad Taste in Good Form" in an effort to correct what she sees as the oversimplified use of the concept "kitsch" to describe her own version of Chicana art practice. Olalquiaga's work provocatively delineates first-degree, second- degree, and third-degree kitsch in order to argue for the collapse of Clement Greenberg's historical distinction between kitsch and the avant-garde. Olalquiaga suggests, for example, that a plastic virgin statuette performs on the level of first-degree kitsch when "the relationship between object and user is immediate, one of genuine belief."[30] Second-degree kitsch is explained as "a popularization of the camp sensibility, a perspective wherein appreciation of the "ugly" conveys to the spectator an aura of refined decadence, an ironic enjoyment from a position of enlightened superiority."[31] Last, in third-degree kitsch, "iconography is invested with either a new or foreign set of meanings, generating a hybrid product."[32] Olalquiaga's argument is insightful and compelling, but she unintentionally misreads the work of Mesa-Bains as an example of this third-degree kitsch, arguing that the artist's ironic use of religious iconography replaces "the transcendental with the political."[33] While Mesa-Bains is willing to concede that any number of artists described by Mosquera and Olalquiaga may have a purely ironic, calculated relation to their use of kitsch, Mesa-Bains distinguishes this notion from the *rasquachismo* or *domesticana* of her own work and of other Chicana artists. For Mesa-Bains, the use of religious figures and motifs is not purely ironic, not entirely a question of opportunistic *détournement*. Rather, the work connotes the sacred *and* the secular, the political *and* the transcendental, the feminist *and* the pious—what Olalquiga might call both first- *and* third-degree kitsch.

For Mesa-Bains, kitsch is itself a problematic concept because it is used to designate "poor taste" that is always first defined by, and then ironically appropriated by, an elite, privileged class. This cultured sense of taste that evolves through years of formal education within a rarified social milieu is rejected by a *rasquachismo* aesthetic precisely because the underdog or outsider, aware of the multiple social domains through which aesthetic signs circulate, also recognizes that "good taste" is a culturally relative term. The very idea of taste is inseparable from the process of education and breeding, discrimination and sensibility inherited within a context of cultural homogeneity and class hierarchy. Mesa-Bains's essay makes a helpful, indeed crucial, distinction between the ironic insider use of kitsch as an opposition to "good taste" and the critical outsider position of *rasquachismo* that produces its own invented forms. Mesa-Bains's altar-installations are just this kind of invented form, using a familiar visual idiom that borrows from working-class memories and domestic culture to revise the narrow range of possible role models for women.[34] As a form of Chicana *rasquache,* *domesticana* becomes the method by which the complex material iconography of a gender-specific domesticity is brought into the public space of exhibition to actively construct a new ideology and iconology of display.

Matter and Metaphor of History

Following her experiments with the format of the altar-installation, Mesa-Bains turned to new forms of installation practice and to the idea of history as itself a field of scattered artifacts whose story is unfinished. Addressing European colonial expansion and its relation to the construction of New World epistemologies and typologies, Mesa-Bains draws on the practices of collecting and display found in cabinets of curiosity and still-life painting, borrowing also from the literary tropes of the baroque emblemists of the sixteenth and seventeenth centuries, whose allegorical juxtapositions of image and text served in the instruction of moral and religious doctrine. These installations articulate how secular sites of collecting and display have always served to confer value on objects and to elicit veneration and awe in their audiences. Indeed, many similarities exist between the home altar and the cabinet of curiosity, not only formally but also historically and ideologically. In this series of works, Mesa-Bains explores the intersection of colonialism, collecting, and the politics of display with the history of the conquest of indigenous populations of the Americas.

Curiositas: The Cabinet (1990), first installed at the M.A.R.S. art space in Phoenix, Arizona and again in The Decade Show in New York (1990) referenced the interdependence of colonialism in the Americas and the development of European cabinets of curiosity—the precursor to modern museums (figure 3.3). Like her altar-installations, the work staged a kind of still-life tableau against one wall of the exhibition space. A mock domestic interior with a wooden and glass cabinet, an armchair, and a Persian carpet were surrounded by mounds of fresh earth and dried flower petals, sprinkled with shimmering gold. Floating on this artificial terrain a few inches off the ground were two toy Spanish galleons, a plastic horse, and two strategically placed indigenous dwellings, all painted in glistening gold. Part miniature diorama, part iconic map of historical relations, the tongue-in-cheek use of the toys referenced contemporary mass production while gesturing to the lust for gold that brought ships and soldiers to the new world. Inside the glass cabinet, indigenous and pre-Columbian artifacts were placed beside small piles of domesticated grain and pottery shards, along with sinister instruments of torture and bondage.

There can be no doubt that a fascination with the flora and fauna of the New World fueled the aristocratic collection and display of specimens (human and nonhuman) from the Americas in Italian *studiolos* and German *Wunderkammers*. Giganti's *studio* of Bologna in 1563 contained

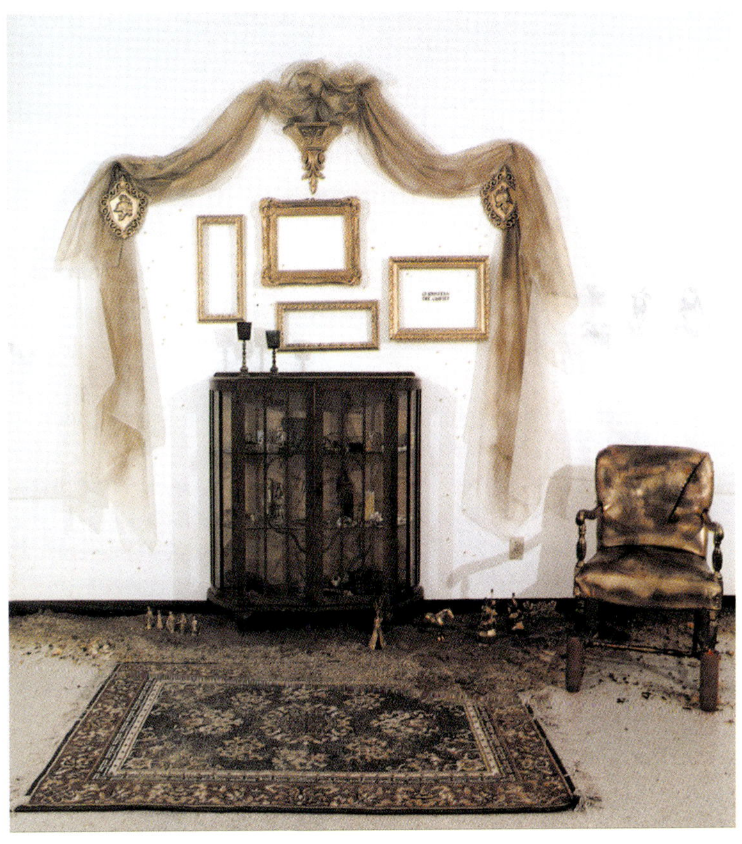

3.3 Amalia Mesa-Bains, *Curiositas: The Cabinet*, 1990. Photo by Robert C. Buitrón. Courtesy of the photographer.

many pre-Columbian objects such as maps and codices, feather head-dresses, and stone idols.[35] In the collection of Archduke Ferdinand II, Elisabeth Scheicher speculates that the most famous objects were the pre-Columbian feather works that the Archduke dismantled to adorn his own wedding garments.[36] And in describing the Munich *kunstkammer* assembled in the 1560s, Lorenz Seelig writes, "In terms of quantity, the cultures of Latin America and especially Mexico were strongly repre-sented."[37] Such fascination was not only driven by delight in the rare and beautiful; as Gerard Turner points out, these symbols of far-flung empire came to represent "the means of development, the raw material of trade and prosperity."[38] For Amalia Mesa-Bains, such cabinets of curiosity are a record of New World domination powered by two driving principles of colonialism: the desire to see (*speculari*) and the desire to know (*curiosi-tas*), both appearing in her work as a material rhetoric of display.

In "Shrines, Curiosities, and the Rhetoric of Display," Stephen Bann links the conventions of display in medieval churches to those in cabinets of curiosity of the sixteenth century. By drawing parallels between forms of symmetry, devotion, and performative narration, Bann suggests that cabinets of curiosity were concerned with a drive to recuperate the strat-egies of display that had been dropped from religious practices during an iconoclastic era. The very mode of "curiosity," Bann suggests, was that of mourning: the mourning accompanying the loss of sacred relics as well as the mourning evident in a general shift to a new, scientific paradigm.[39] As epistemological categories of the sixteenth century, the notions of curi-osity or wonder also enjoyed "a temporary spell in power, an interim rule between those of theology and science."[40] This interim period roughly coincided with what is euphemistically called the 'age of discovery' in Europe. It is hardly surprising that strange and new forms of cultural life across the Atlantic would elicit curiosity and wonder. They also, however, threatened not only theological but also scientific and cosmological para-digms, and this threat ultimately led to their destruction or domination.

Curiositas: The Cabinet presents artifacts in a synechdochic reliquary. As an act of critique and mourning for the lost treasures and cultures of the indigenous populations killed and enslaved by the Spanish conquerors, the artist's reconstruction also signals the hidden history for which the original cabinets of curiosity acted as a fetishistic screen. The objects in Mesa-Bains's cabinet are not merely objects of wonder, rare and mag-nificent—such as those adorning European collections—but are also the mundane traces of commerce and domination. Similar to Fred Wilson's juxtaposition of slave manacles with silver goblets that reveal the rela-tions of race and class under slavery, Mesa-Bains's installation stages an intersection of objects that tell the sad history of conquest in the Ameri-cas. The violence that underlies the very existence of such collections also haunts the installation, hovering in ghostly, nearly transparent portraits of slain indigenous figures on the walls, and in the anthropomorphized armchair with its brown leather upholstery slashed through in several places suggesting both a wounded and absent body.

The artist observes that in the original cabinets of curiosity indigenous cultures were "being classified and represented in relationship to one another in a fragmentary and disordered way by European subjects who put artifacts together in absurd ways, which in the end become the ways we are forced to relate to each other."[41] Many cultural expressions of the non-European world "were reordered and misapprehended."[42] Her comments are confirmed by scholar Anthony Alan Shelton, who writes that in many Renaissance collections "the civilizations of the New World—Aztec, Toltec, Mixtec, Maya—were conflated, and the inhabitants of distant city states and regions were subsumed under general rubrics," such as the pagan and the marvelous.[43] Mesa-Bains's installation implies not only that cabinets of curiosity—and by association, the history of early museums—are inseparable from the history of conquest, but also that their inherited categories and Eurocentric world view play a role in determining the ways in which even contemporary subjects are defined, interpellated, and eventually "forced to relate to each other." Barbara Kirshenblatt-Gimblett echoes this observation when she writes, "Not only do ordinary things become special when placed in museum settings, but also the museum experience itself becomes a model for experiencing life outside its walls."[44]

Exploring the colonial logic of the baroque period appears to have inspired other works such as the two-part installation *Emblems of the Decade: Borders* (1990) and *Emblems of the Decade: Numbers* (1990). Part of The Decade Show at the Studio Museum in Harlem, the work took its inspiration from baroque emblems of sixteenth- and seventeenth-century Europe. Victor Zamudio-Taylor writes that in both Spain and the Americas baroque emblems taught religious doctrine through a dynamic relationship linking an *inscriptio* or motto, a *pictura* or visual depiction of the concept, and a *subscriptio* or epigram that served as commentary on both.[45] While emblem books were occasionally directed at children to teach proper moral behavior, they were also forms of ideological persuasion for adults, treating issues such as love, death, knowledge, ignorance, and friendship with pithy poems and visual allegory. Employing this literary and pictorial tradition as metaphor in three dimensions, the artist combined material objects to produce a *pictura* with both accompanying *inscriptio* and *subscriptio*. Emblazoned on the gallery walls, the words "Borders" and "Numbers" clearly demarcated two parts of the installation: a domestic interior and a scientific laboratory, respectively. Like emblems of old, the work was presented as unambiguously didactic, though the lessons to be learned are ones that are generally repressed in mainstream culture. Structured as a dialogue between a quantitative and qualitative mapping of migra-

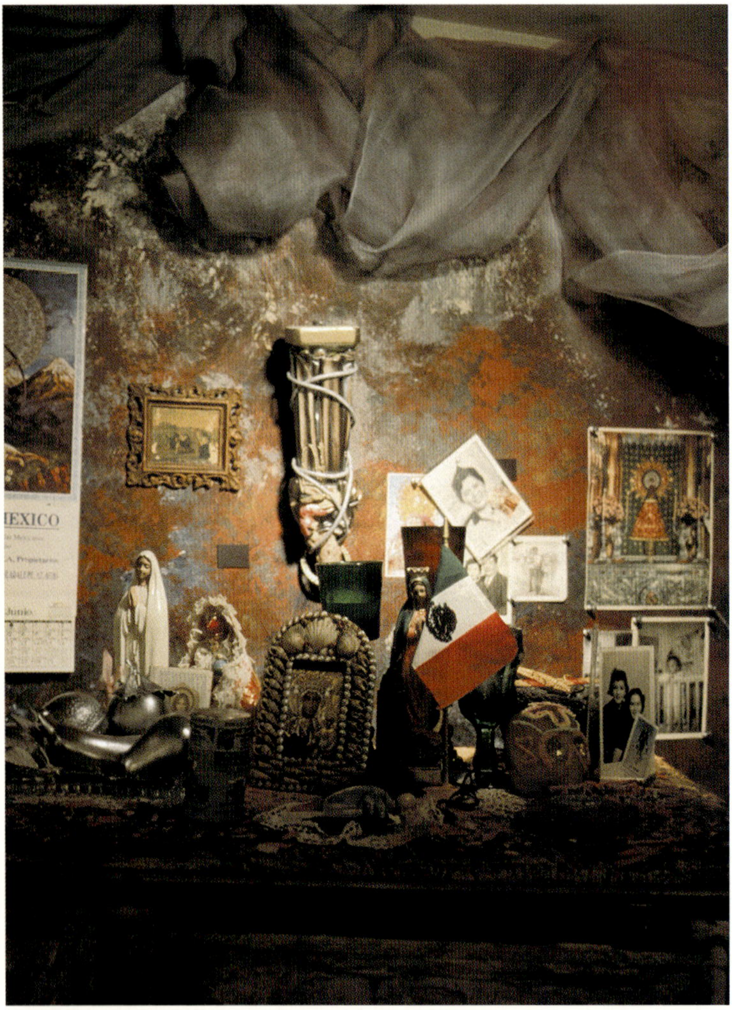

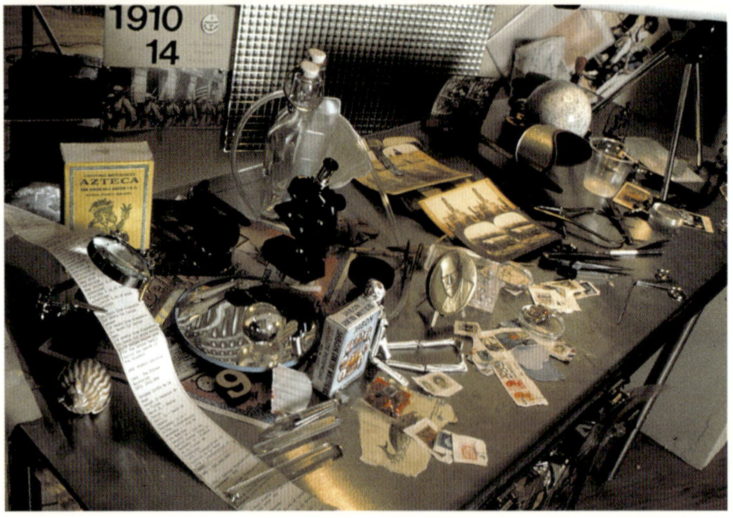

3.4 Amalia Mesa-Bains, *Emblems of the Decade: Borders,* 1990. Detail. The Studio Museum in Harlem, New York. Courtesy of the artist.

3.5 Amalia Mesa-Bains, *Emblems of the Decade: Numbers,* 1990. Detail. The Studio Museum in Harlem, New York. Courtesy of the artist.

tion experiences, the work focused on immigrant communities and the struggles these communities face in the process of moving from one cultural context (Mexico) to another (the United States).

Emblems of the Decade: Borders was primarily composed of a large chest of drawers surrounded and overflowing with black earth. Narratives of migration were written on letters that spilled from a suitcase on the ground, telling stories of hardship, loss, and longing that are part of cross-border experience.[46] Wall text offered a second-order *subscriptio* as a first-person tale of a young boy who is smuggled across the border: "The *coyote* put me in a sack in the back of a truck with potatoes and told me to be totally quiet until he came. I was so hot I couldn't breathe. I cried with no sounds. After hours he came to get me. We had gotten across but, where was my mother? She had given me an address but I didn't know how to get there and was afraid to ask for help." *Coyote* is the colloquial Spanish term for the person who smuggles immigrants across the U.S.-Mexico border. A child's individual memory of transition is a poignant reminder of familial ties broken by economic hardship. "The globe shrinks for those who own it," Homi Bhabha writes, but "for the displaced or the dispossessed, the migrant or refugee, no distance is more awesome than the few feet across borders or frontiers."[47] As a metaphor for memory, the bureau drawers filled with earth appeared to reference a buried past as well as miles of ground covered in the process of transition from one place to another. On the top, a makeshift home altar mixed sacred with secular souvenirs: the Virgin of Guadalupe, the Empire State Building, a candy skull souvenir from Day of the Dead celebrations, the Mexican national flag, and family photographs that seemed to maintain a sense of continuity with the past (figure 3.4).[48] St. Anthony, the patron saint of lost things, was also displayed above the altar, bound and hung upside down—a common vernacular punishment of the saint who would be "freed" when the lost object, or lost person, was found.

In contrast to the domestic and intimate quality of the *Emblems of the Decade: Borders* installation, *Emblems of the Decade: Numbers* offered a scientific and empirical laboratory site. A television monitor silently ran a video loop, a visual narrative linking the photographic portraits in the former to the statistical information provided in the latter. Here the *subscriptio* consisted in the multitude of numbers large and small, posted on the wall and written in books, that included statistics on a contemporary Chicano/a experience such as median income, numbers of AIDS cases, teen pregnancies, as well as dates of major historical events such as land annexations, acts of genocide against indigenous populations, revolutions, political independence, and finally numbers with religious, spiritual, and symbolic significance.[49] Also included were historical lists and inventories copied from original ledgers of centuries past and placed in hanging folders or pasted to the wall. These lists and inventories were linked by association to the activity of scientific analysis and exploration. A long, highly polished chrome table, evocative of a cluttered laboratory, displayed a variety of viewing instruments and scientific apparatuses such as telescopes, magnifying glasses, and microscopes (figure 3.5). There were also instruments of measurement (calipers and compass) and dissection (surgical scissors and knives). Smaller artifacts were "preserved" in transparent boxes while others were jumbled together: seashells, centuries-old drawings of sea creatures, stamps from letters sent and received across the Atlantic, a global star chart, a miniature skeleton, iron spikes from railroad ties, a wooden rosary, coins, even a box depicting an American Indian in feathered headdress bearing the word "Azteca" across the front. All of these found objects became a kind of working vocabulary for the artist, recurring later in works exploring the same themes, each time from a slightly different perspective.

In this apparent clutter, so stylistically different from the minimalist aesthetics of other installation artists working with historical artifacts and collections, Mesa-Bains makes reference to the activity of European sea passage, the written correspondence of migrant populations, the untimely death of the indigenous populations of Mexico, the influence of Catholicism, and the role of the railroad, capitalism, and economic domination in the commodification of the native population. Zamudio-Taylor writes of Mesa-Bains's work, "History is rendered in the works as a piling up of fragments, an accumulation of the debris and ruins from the first encounter onwards where a layering of the diverse cultures make up the Latino identity."[50] History takes the form of objects placed next to one another in a critical, dialectical, and sometimes unpredictable relation. Mesa-Bains reminds her audience of the variegated terrain across which cultural formations are forged and, simultaneously, through which antagonistic and hegemonic systems are maintained.

In an interview Mesa-Bains has commented, "As I went to graduate school, and was studying Adorno, Lacan, Benjamin, and Fanon, all of these critical thinkers started to become part of my vocabulary."[51] When investigating Walter Benjamin's theories of allegory and the writings of other members of the Frankfurt School, Mesa-Bains was particularly drawn to the kinds of dialectical materialist history that Benjamin himself sought to explore in his *Passagenwerk* with pictorial representations of ideas that seemed to be modeled on the baroque emblemists.[52] Just as Benjamin saw decorative mirrors and bourgeois interiors as emblematic of bourgeois subjectivism, or mechanical dolls as emblematic of workers' daily existence under industrialism, Mesa-Bains's curiosity cabinet is emblematic of a European expansionist logic, while *Emblems of the Decade: Borders* and *Emblems of the Decade: Numbers* are emblematic of contemporary hardships and oppressive conditions faced by Chicano/as that have their roots in the colonialist past.

Rather than a future-oriented, progressivist understanding of history that can only be sustained by an active process of forgetting, Mesa-Bains, like Benjamin, looks backward in order to bring the past forward. A tiny detail in the *Emblems of the Decade: Borders* installation references Walter Benjamin's angels of history, delicately hung in front of mirrors, looking back over the ruins of history. It is not only the form of Mesa-Bains's work, as I have suggested in the discussion of her revival of the home altar tradition, but also the allegorical content in the work that produces a social critique. For Craig Owens (and Walter Benjamin), allegory demonstrates a capacity to rescue from historical oblivion that which threatens to disappear. It is characterized by a conviction of the remoteness of the past and a desire to redeem it for the present, and is therefore a key ingredient for all forms of historical revivalism. Allegorical imagery is always appropriated imagery; the allegorist does not invent images but *confiscates* them. Antithetical to a desire for pure innovation, the allegorical mode was seen by many early-twentieth-century modernists as "contaminated" by the past. Owens argues that allegorical art of the 1980s and 1990s self-consciously explores the social and historical conditions of its own systems of representation.[53] Mesa-Bains's installations, with their attention not only to the politics of display and its rhetorical structures but also to the historical traces of the past, clearly fall within this kind of allegorical framework. "With all that talk about allegory," the artist once joked, "I was sure that Craig Owens must secretly have been a Chicano."[54] By staging material culture in the context of familiar spatial registers of the home, the laboratory, or the museum, the artist asks her viewer to consider how each architectural domain provides a logic of legibility and a set of connotations for the objects presented there.

These concerns return in the artist's 1993 installation *Vanitas: Evidence, Ruin, Regeneration,* which might be read as a companion piece to *Emblems of the Decade.* As a participant of the Revelaciones/Revelations: Hispanic Art of Evanescence group exhibition hosted by the Johnson Art Museum at Cornell University, Mesa-Bains returned to her ongoing investigation of the historical and spatial connotations of colonialism and material culture, this time through the *vanitas* tradition in painting wherein the transitory nature of life—its false knowledge, mortality, and conceit—is depicted by images of worldly goods and signs of luxury imbedded with signs of death and decay (figure 3.6).

Entering the installation, visitors passed beneath one of two decorative archways of strung marigolds (commonly found on Day of the Dead altars). The fresh flowers first wilted, then dropped their petals slowly over the course of the exhibition, enacting in real time the ephemeral condition of life. Several separate areas of the installation represented different historical moments marked by death: a display case with Teotihuacán pottery, a *vanitas* painting from the seventeenth century, an altar dedicated to the recently deceased César Chávez, and in the center a table that served as a *vanitas* assemblage displaying scientific instruments, notebooks of cranial studies, and a replica of a human skull. Also arrayed on the table (a surgical autopsy table borrowed from Cornell's School of Veterinary Medicine) were feathers, animal skins, glass vials filled with grain, dried citrus fruit (to prevent scurvy on sea voyages), and old maps. From a distance the table looks like a jumble, but on closer examination it is possible to see that objects have been carefully juxtaposed to invite associative readings: the African diaspora and indigenous populations (represented by tiny figurines and historical images) were subject to devices of observation, speculation, measurement, and investigation (represented by the magnifying glasses, telescopes, and microscopes seen in *Emblems of the Decade: Numbers*). Staged as a kind of sacrificial altar, the surgical table implied that the history of scientific practice, despite its secular pretensions, was also a profoundly moralistic and ritualistic endeavor.

A life-size reproduction of the painting *Vanitas with Negro Boy* by David Bailly (1584–1657) hung on the wall behind. Nearly invisible in the shadow of the worldly possessions of his master, the "negro boy" depicted in the seventeenth-century painting recalled a history of slavery that was materialist in all its forms. As an object to be put on display, the dark-skinned body of the young boy became a sign of wealth and power for the absent master. Like the portraits of slave children that Fred Wilson reinstalled in *Mining the Museum,* this image had no pretense of presenting its human subject as anything other than property. Framed in green satin, the replica, the original of which belongs to the Johnson Art Museum, became a site of eulogy for this anonymous slave but also a site of contested institutional control. After being told that she would be able to use the original *Vanitas with Negro Boy* painting as part of her installation, Mesa-Bains was disappointed to discover she would be given a replica instead. She has commented, "I ended up with an amusing simulacrum. I wasn't allowed to decontextualize [the painting], but I could do whatever I wanted with the image of it."[55] To draw attention to this subtle institutional censorship, the artist wrote the director's comments (that he was "afraid the artist would undermine the integrity of the object") on the wall of the installation itself. Apparently also concerned that the painting's original title might cause offense, the director simply dropped the phrase "with Negro boy" from the official museum label. These two gestures, while apparently minor and innocuous, speak volumes about the museum's attitude toward working artists and to the racially complex history of its own collection.

Outside the museum, Cornell University had its own racial tensions during the time of the installation and exhibition of Revelaciones/Revelations: Hispanic Art of Evanescence. Anonymous students had spray-painted swastikas and white supremacist epithets on an outdoor work by Daniel Martinez titled *The Castle Is Burning*. The incident incited the

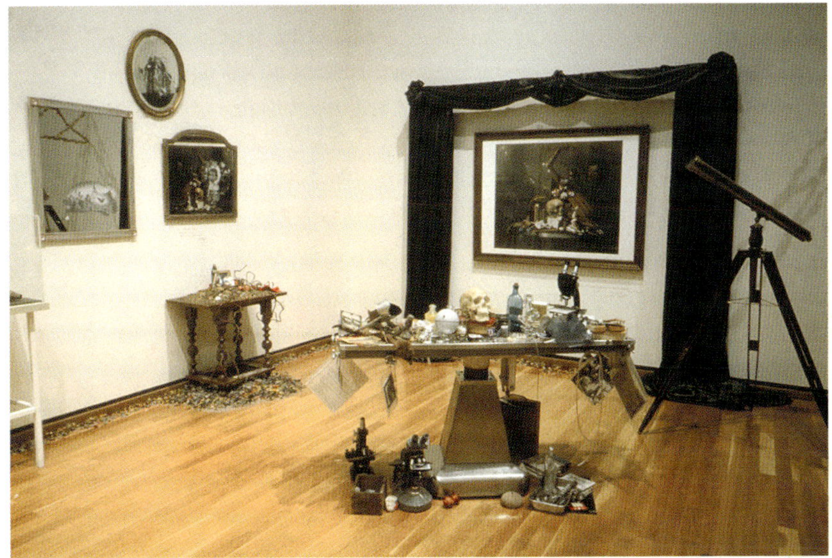

3.6 Amalia Mesa-Bains, *Vanitas: Evidence, Ruin, Regeneration*, 1993. Installation view. Herbert F. Johnson Museum, Cornell University, New York. Courtesy of the artist.

Chicano and Latino students, who were already demanding greater curricular and institutional support, to stage a sit-in at the administration building that lasted for several days. After the incident, students who were assisting the artist with her installation researched newspaper articles reporting on the 1969 armed black student demonstrations at Cornell. Mesa-Bains decided to add these articles to a reading area in her installation, positioned near the *Vanitas with Negro Boy* painting.

Ironically, the display case containing pre-Columbian figurines from Teotihuacán demonstrated the hierarchy of value placed on museum objects. These were not replicas, but originals also borrowed from the university's permanent collection. A double standard applied: the artist was given carte blanche to work with these indigenous artifacts but was not allowed to touch or reinstall the European fine art.[56] By foregrounding the overlap of these categorical domains—art and artifact—Mesa-Bains joined Fred Wilson and James Luna in revealing the power of museum taxonomies to organize, collect, and display objects in a racially inflected way.

In Mesa-Bains's installation, a critique of the power/knowledge dyad that displaces the history of the oppressed through a calculated rhetoric of display is shown to enact this displacement precisely in its selection of metonymic signs. In other words, unlike still-life painting of the early modern period that eagerly demonstrated the rare beauty and abundant resources of the New World by capturing it in a meticulous painted image, Mesa-Bains's installations uses a slightly different selection of objects to memorialize the fatal effects of global trade that turns subjects into objects, in both the past and the present.[57] In this work, material culture functions as a *sign* of historical evidence, not as historical evidence per se. The play between the factual and fictional function of the artifact is an explicit part of the work. Visual tropes borrowed from ethnographic, archeological, or fine art museum displays are thus a formal device, used as a tactical critique of the unquestioned legitimacy of these disciplinary domains.

Envy, Intimacy, Interiority

In the mid-1990s, Mesa-Bains began a continuing study of contradictions that women face within a network of social institutions, both religious and secular. Encouraged to emulate a range of possible female ideals, women are shown to be constantly negotiating a complex path through a web of expectations and demands that shape and constrain relations of power, sexuality, and knowledge. In her *Venus Envy* series, the artist examines idealized feminine roles and their sites of enforcement through the spatial metaphors of intimacy and interiority. The installations stage typically private spaces that double as psychological interiors. Souvenirs and mementos, clothing and photographs, heirlooms and sentimental possessions are often arranged in a spatial representation of autobiography—what I have earlier called an autotopography. Its own form of prosthetic territory, this private-yet-material memory landscape is made up of the more intimate expressions of values and beliefs, emotions and desires that are found in the private collection and arrangement of objects, used to anchor a life narrative. As an artistic method, this autotopographical approach shares qualities with a Chicana feminist literary tradition of producing "creative nonfiction" or "testimonial autobiographical fiction" that uses life events as the basis for a compelling fabulation.[58]

When *Venus Envy I: First Holy Communion Before the End* (1993) opened at the Philip Morris branch of the Whitney Museum of American Art, it signaled a return to the conceptual concerns that had occupied Mesa-Bains in a number of her earlier works, such as the *Ofrenda for Dolores Del Rio*. Revealing the process through which the artist and the women of her community negotiate the terrain of a Catholic and Mexican subjectivity in the United States of the late twentieth century, the installation examined the subtle conflicts between sexual desire and religious devotion that are materially counterpoised with the political battles that face an economically disadvantaged community trying to maintain the rituals of its ethnic heritage. Ritual spaces and everyday spaces—the church and the home—often intersect in their ideological control of the action and freedom of those who inhabit them. Sexuality is one such domain of organization and coercion that is frequently tied to architectural context. In his discussion of gender and architecture, scholar Mark Wigley points out, "Place is not simply a mechanism for controlling sexuality. Rather, it is the control of sexuality by systems of representation that produces place."[59] Rituals, which are repetitive by definition, produce a locus of enforcement by their very enactment. In the Catholic Church, First Holy Communion, as the artist perceives it, "occupies in the feminine landscape a fork in the road where the soul and the body are forced to separate."[60] This momentary ceremony, where confession is used to crystallize the consciousness of sin, marks a young girl's first loss of innocence.

Venus Envy I: First Holy Communion Before the End occupied a gallery lined on three walls with rows of framed mirrors reflecting not only the faces of gallery visitors but also ghosts from the past—photographs of the artist as a young girl, of her ancestors, and of admired female icons that haunt the interior of the glass where the reflective silver coating had been rubbed away. The audience was invited to consider the process by which they see, reflected in themselves, the faces of others (parents, grandparents, ego ideals) from their own past—a past mediated or framed in large part by photography. In the center of the room, five display cases were covered with glass. Large and low to the ground, each case contained a different kind of memorabilia suggesting an autobiographical collection of artifacts that represented ceremonial rites of passage. One was layered with dresses from a First Holy Communion, a confirmation, and a wedding—all pure white (figure 3.7); another case contained the somber

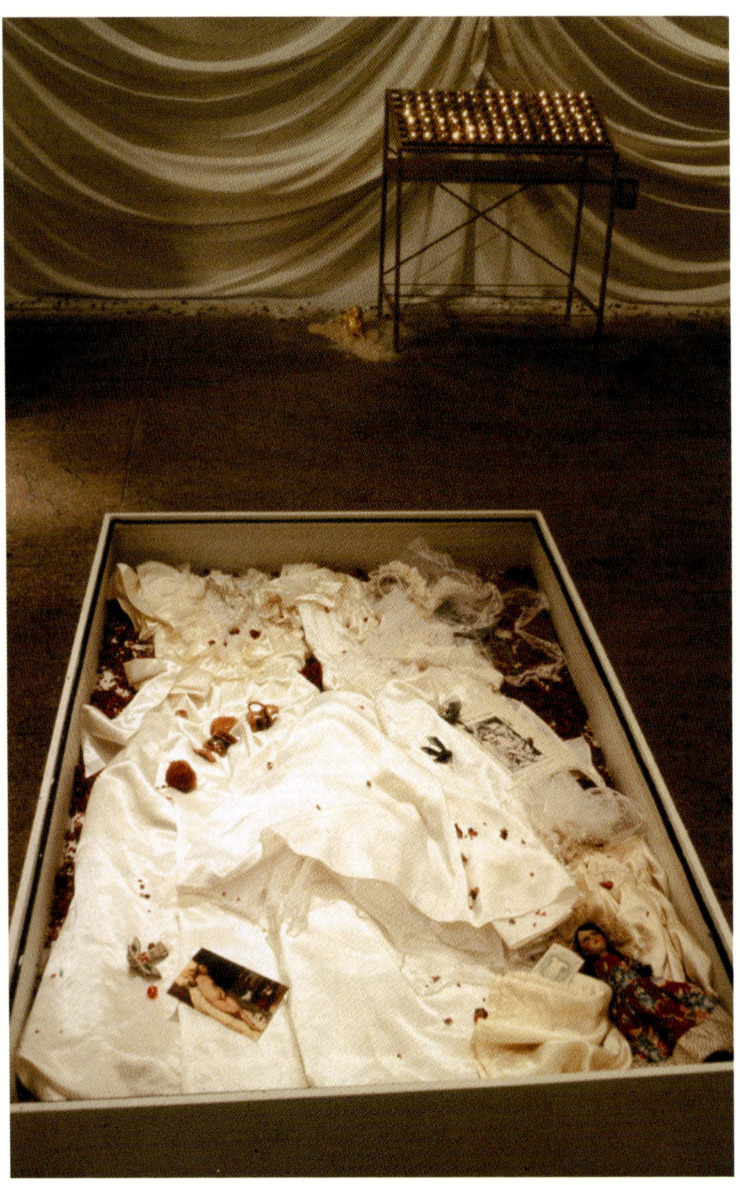

3.7 Amalia Mesa-Bains, *Venus Envy I: First Holy Communion Before the End*, 1993. Detail of display case. Photo by George Hirose. Courtesy of Whitney Museum of American Art, New York.

3.8, 3.9 Amalia Mesa-Bains, *Venus Envy I: First Holy Communion Before the End,* 1993. Detail of display case with photographs and of installation view of boudoir chapel. Photos by George Hirose. Courtesy of Whitney Museum of American Art, New York.

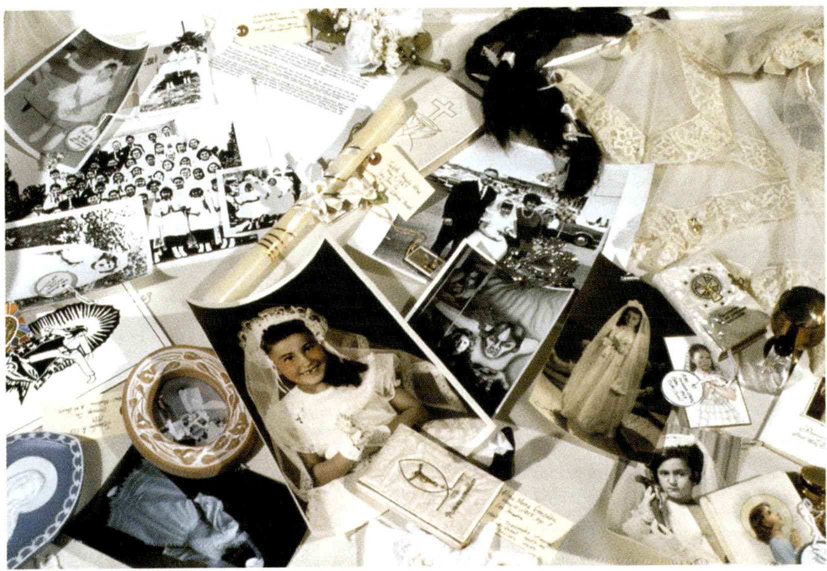

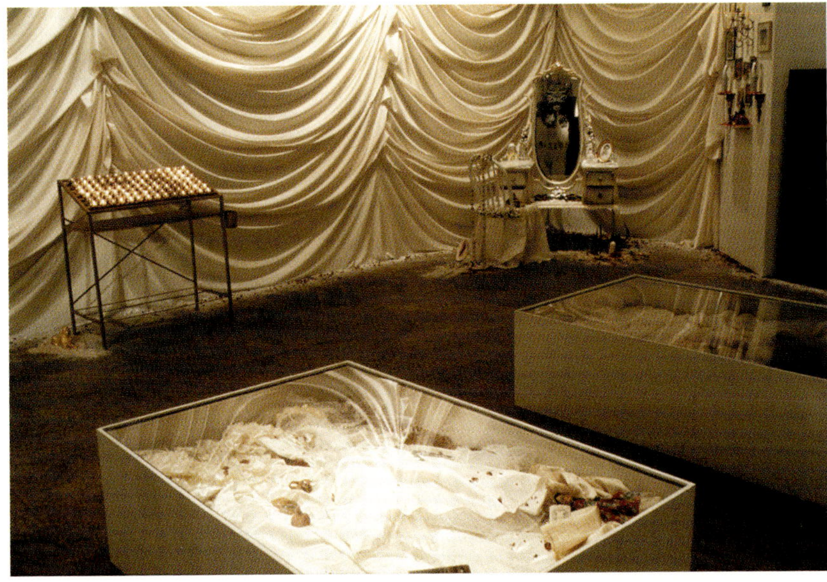

habits of Catholic nuns, displayed with the flowered crowns worn at ordination and at burial. Reminiscent of French artist Annette Messager's *Histoire des Robes* (1990–1991) or the dresses and other framed garments in Betye Sarr's more recent *Colored: Consider the Rainbow* (2002), Mesa-Bains's dresses suggest their own unique biographical narratives. Fragile artifacts and images strewn on the surface and tucked into the folds of creamy satin and delicate lace include antique dolls, a postcard image of Titian's *Venus of Urbino,* crushed red rose petals (looking like drops of blood), dried fruit, and tiny Mexican ceramic jars. These items function not only as evidence of major life events but also as metaphors for the *psychic effects* of these events on the female subject (i.e., identification, desire, repression). The white dresses and habits become costumes for the rituals of obedience and for the three possible life paths assigned to the good Catholic woman: the virgin, the bride, or the nun.

In another display case, photographs of young Mexican American girls, again in the full regalia of Catholic ritual, were interspersed with images of powerful adult females who project an entirely different sense of femininity (figure 3.8). Next to a snapshot of a young girl (the artist) dressed in gloves and veil, hands demurely posed in prayer, lay a reproduction of Hernandez's *La Virgen de Guadalupe Defendiendo los Derechos de los Xicanos,* mentioned earlier, that depicts the virgin as an energetic kickboxer. While creating a rhetoric of antithesis, such juxtapositions also serve as a developmental narrative for contemporary Chicanas. The cultural institutions (economic, religious, familial) that shape the identity of the female subject are filled with inherent contradictions: to be delicate and to be strong, to be pious and to be filled with desires. The virgin, the nun, and the bride are the ground upon which, and against which, new images of womanhood are projected. But elsewhere in the installation, the artist offers a series of alternatives to these iconic roles and a rearticulation of their social function.

Along one wall of the gallery, yards of white silk were draped behind a stand of votive candles and a vanity table—what the artist called a "boudoir chapel"[61] (figure 3.9). In front of the table a diminutive decorated chair with satin skirting, a bridal bouquet, and other baubles suggested the seat of dainty femininity. Hung from the back of the chair was a heavy burden—giant rosary beads draping three feet to the ground, encumbered with the weight of Catholicism. At the end of the rosary was not a cross, however, but a large iridescent seashell; other large conch and abalone shells, as well as animal horns were placed strategically in the installation to suggest influences from an indigenous or syncretic system of belief (figure 3.10). The somber gaze of Coatlicue, the Aztec deity whose double-serpent head is believed to symbolize moments of death and rebirth, emanated from the oval mirror (figure 3.11).

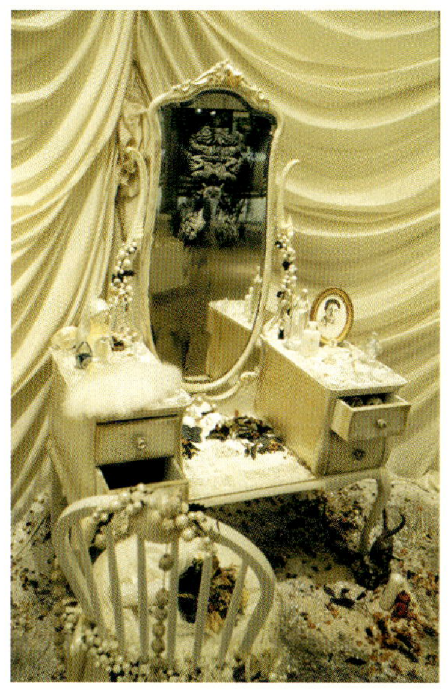

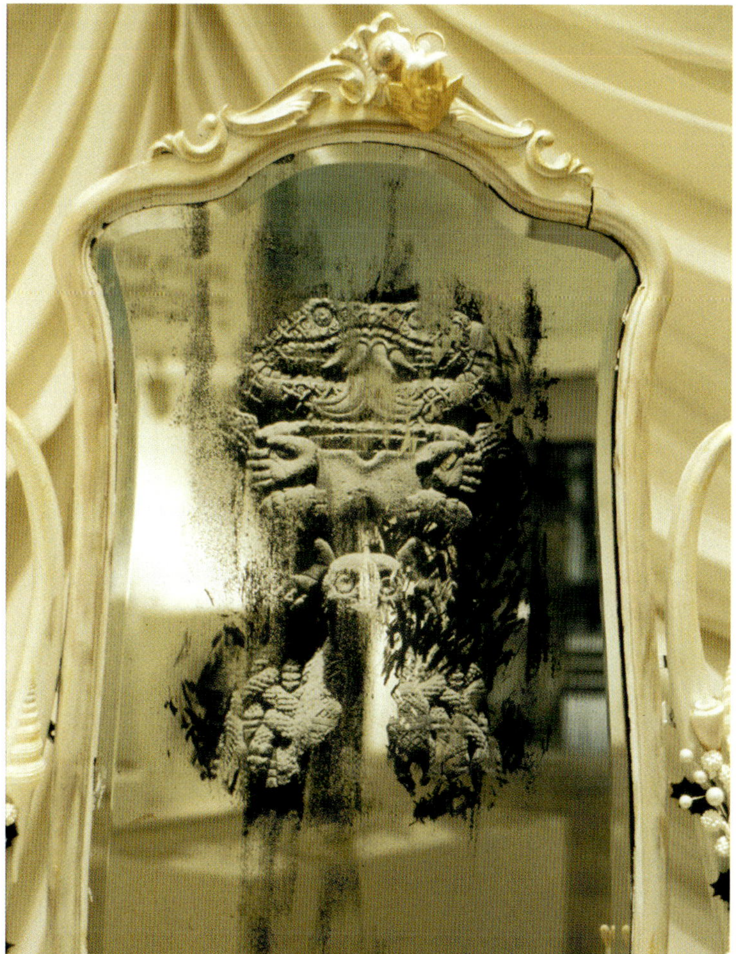

3.10, 3.11 Amalia Mesa-Bains, *Venus Envy I: First Holy Communion Before the End,* 1993. Detail of boudoir chapel and of boudoir mirror. Photo by George Hirose. Courtesy of Whitney Museum of American Art, New York.

Borrowed from the ancient Aztec culture around which the Chicano political movement established a myth of origins in Aztlán, the figure represents those indigenous traditions that were lost with the imposition of Catholicism as well as the racial difference of that indigeneity. The image of Coatlicue has been used by numerous Chicana artists to signify a strong and powerful female presence.[62] Writer and scholar Gloria Anzaldúa seems to echo the intent of Mesa-Bains's installation when she writes:

> There is another quality to the mirror that is the act of seeing. Of seeing and being seen. Subject and object, I and she. The eye pins down the object of its gaze, scrutinizes it, judges it. A glance can freeze us in place; it can "possess" us. It can erect a barrier against the world. But in a glance also lies awareness, knowledge. These seemingly contradictory aspects—the act of being seen, held immobilized by a glance, and "seeing through" an experience—are symbolized by the underground aspect of *Coatlicue, Cihuacoatl,* and *Tlazolteotl,* which cluster in what I call the *Coatlicue* state.[63]

For Anzaldúa, the Coatlicue state is one way to articulate the confluence of contradictory positions—both internal and external—that cross-cultural, and in some cases cross-gendered, subjects are able (and obliged) to occupy. In Mesa-Bains's installation, the mirror frames the imaginary transparency between the subject and that sign, or set of signs, which interrupt its simple reflection. If *Venus Envy I: First Holy Communion Before the End* is about the teleology of beauty, love, and marriage that are imposed upon young girls in a patriarchal, Catholic tradition, the image of Coatlicue appears as an internal, indigenous resistance.

Taking Coatlicue as an idealized symbol, Anzaldúa and Mesa-Bains participate in a larger Chicano recuperation or appropriation of Aztec images that has its own complex racial politics meant to valorize the non-European elements of Mexican heritage, and to offer an alternative iconography and cosmology for Chicanos living in the U.S. Southwest. Art historians and archeologists have been ambivalent concerning the use, misuse, or reinterpretation of borrowed images from Aztec history in works by contemporary artists. They tend to worry that the popular reproduction or reinterpretation of important archeological finds, such as the imposing stone sculptures of Coatlicue, will obscure or exaggerate their historical relevance. Scholars Davíd Carrasco and Eduardo Moctezuma have argued that Mesa-Bains's claims about the central importance of Aztec cosmology in the construction of a Chicano communal sensibility are somewhat exaggerated, and have suggested that Chicano artists in general have tended to idealize Toltec, Aztec, and Mayan cultures to serve strategic and political needs.[64] Creative writers and visual artists are generally less concerned with historical precision, and more interested in the iconic valence of such images and their potential for critical or political expression.[65] Valorizing an indigenous past, Mesa-Bains strategically borrows from a racially inflected domain of visual culture in order to expand the narrow repertoire of subject positions allowed her under a white hegemony. Whether Mesa-Bains is descended from Aztecs is not the issue in question. Her political gesture is to imagine a space of interior subjectivity inhabitable by both the ancient earth deity Coatlicue and Titian's 1538 *Venus of Urbino* painted during the period of conquest, by both the "good" Catholic girl and the rebellious, sexually mature woman.[66]

Handwritten script on the gallery walls, for example, included quotations from the female religious order of the Beguines of the fourteenth century, along with texts by other religious women of the period, demonstrating that women have long resisted the confining traditions of the church. The Beguines sought a religious life outside the walls of the convent, and were consequently considered heretical by many. Refusing to separate the pleasures of the body from those of the spirit, they wrote poetry about the physical quality of spiritual pleasures. Mesa-Bains copied out lines such as "The holy bread strengthened her heart; the holy wine inebriated her, rejoicing her mind; the holy body fattened her; the vitalizing blood purified her by washing.... Sometimes she happily accepted her Lord under the appearance of a child, sometimes as a taste of honey, sometimes as a sweet smell, and sometimes in the pure and gorgeously embellished marriage bed of the heart."[67] Far from maintaining a celibate life, the Beguines were free to marry, although many chose not to, preferring the homosocial world of women. In short, the artist layers the internal contradictions of the social institutions of religion onto the subject's identi fication with them. Not only might a woman be impelled to disidentify with roles dictated by institutional paradigms, those very paradigms can demonstrate internal contradictions and serve as sites of resistance.

Of course, *Venus Envy I: First Holy Communion Before the End* can also be read as a pun on the Freudian concept of penis envy in girls (a desire to have access to the power and privilege accorded to males and to masculinity under patriarchy) and, simultaneously, an acknowledgment of a feminine sexual desire linked to fantasies of love and beauty. On the wall next to the vanity table an altarlike arrangement of candles and miniature reproductions of Chicano and Chicana art—the *Virgen de Guadalupe* by Yolanda López, *Black Virgin* by Patssi Valdez, and *La Butterfly* by John Valadez, among others—had as its central focal point a memorial homage to Eva "Venus" Garcia who had worked at San Francisco's Galleria de la Raza and had died a year or two before. Multiple references to Venus in the piece allowed viewers to speculate about the intersecting discourses of contemporary Chicana life and the history of art, the history of colonialism, and the history of Catholicism. Gender is represented as a complex set of behaviors that are produced through an ambivalent relation to cultural hierarchies and imposed feminine roles that are also read through a specific race discourse of the mestiza.

Venus Envy I: First Holy Communion Before the End additionally created a new discursive formation for the interpretation of material culture. It organized the context and legibility of everyday relics and icons so they might be read as part of a system of acculturation. Each sign referred to the interior of the self, and to the female body as part of an extended sign system of objects.[68] Shifting the connotations of familiar signs by removing them from an isolated discourse and placing them in the context of other visual discourses—discourses of sexual desire or activism—Mesa-Bains reveals the interior lives of Chicanas through the spatial and architectural tropes of archive and museum display, shrine and sanctuary. In this work, it becomes clear that the female subject is *subject to* the play of visual and material signs, of ritual costumes, of family photographs, of collected souvenirs that come to define or demarcate the limits of her experience.

The second phase of the *Venus Envy* series, entitled *Venus Envy II: The Harem and Other Enclosures,* opened at Williams College in Massachusetts in 1994. Divided into three separate enclosures—the garden, the harem, and the library—the installation explored how women over the centuries have been protected and empowered, as well as confined, by private spaces dedicated to the spirit, the body, and the mind. Each pseudo architectural recreation of these private "interior" spaces evinced traces of a missing inhabitant.

"The Garden," bounded on one side by a low lattice fence covered with living green vines and on the other side by an ornamental painted dado or

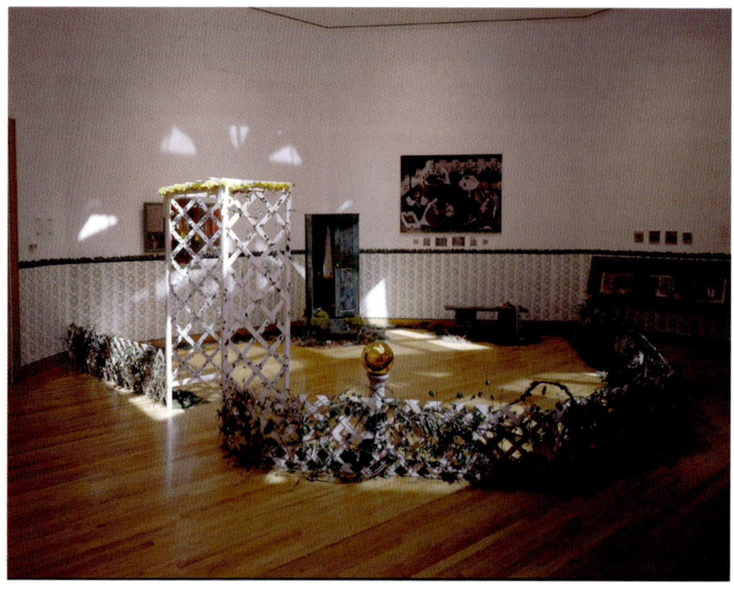

3.12 Amalia Mesa-Bains, "The Garden" in *Venus Envy II: The Harem and Other Enclosures,* 1994. Installation view. Courtesy of Williams College Museum of Art, Williamstown, MA.

wainscoting topped with artificial leaves, suggested a hybrid mix of domestic interior and verdant oasis. On one wall an enlarged reproduction of a small, lyrical painting—the *Little Garden of Paradise* by the Master Of Frankfurt (ca. 1410)—depicts the Virgin and Child with angels and attendants quietly playing and reading in a walled garden filled with flowers and abundant fruit trees (figure 3.12). In Mesa-Bains's garden, a statue of the Virgin shared the space with a stone bench, vanity mirror, and elaborate wardrobe that served as the installation's centerpiece (figure 3.13). Its wide doors opened to magically reveal an interior world. Holy garments made of blue and pink satin embellished with golden fringe and pearls, directly copied from paintings of the vestments of the Virgin, shared space with miniature trees, dried gardenias, leaves, and grass. It gave the impression of an inhabited world with a landscape of earth and dried vines spilling forth from the darkened interior, silver cherubs floating among sacred garments high above moss-covered virgins and tiny wanderers. Pearl necklaces and other jewels, images of saints, and photographs crowded the peat-filled drawers, suggesting that even the Virgin would have private mementos in her possession.[69] For many women, the wardrobe houses garments delimiting a range of possible selves. Here the Virgin is shown to have her own choice of dress, referencing the long tradition in Catholicism of icon adornment. By providing the viewer with an opportunity to imagine wearing the garments themselves, trying on the role as well as the raiment, the transcendental, transhistorical subject of the Virgin is effectively brought down to earth.

Installed opposite "The Garden," "The Harem" offered a romanticized abstraction of a Moorish arcade that formed a hexagonal interior glowing with light filtered through brightly colored gels covering the gallery's windowpanes (figure 3.14). A row of transparent curtains created a diaphanous, billowing veil through which the audience might pass. The floor of "The Harem" was set with white tiles softened around the edges by a border of white sand. In the center of the harem a blackened pyre of love letters, books, photographs, and souvenirs was tinged with ashes. Dried pomegranates scattered on the floor signified the reconciliation of diverse elements within an apparent unity, their many-seeded compartments a sign of fecundity.[70] In the context of "The Harem," pomegranates may stand for the diverse women who inhabited such sites as well as the sexual services that some of the women provided. Historically, a harem was not only the lodging for wives and concubines, but also the homosocial environment for other women of the court (musicians, dancers, servants), and often created a strong network of female support.[71] Written on the wall, below the solitary portrait of a young woman, were the words "desire, longing, possession, separation, death." A row of mirrors offered a glimpse into the Orientalist fantasies produced in European representations of the harem, primarily reproductions of nineteenth-

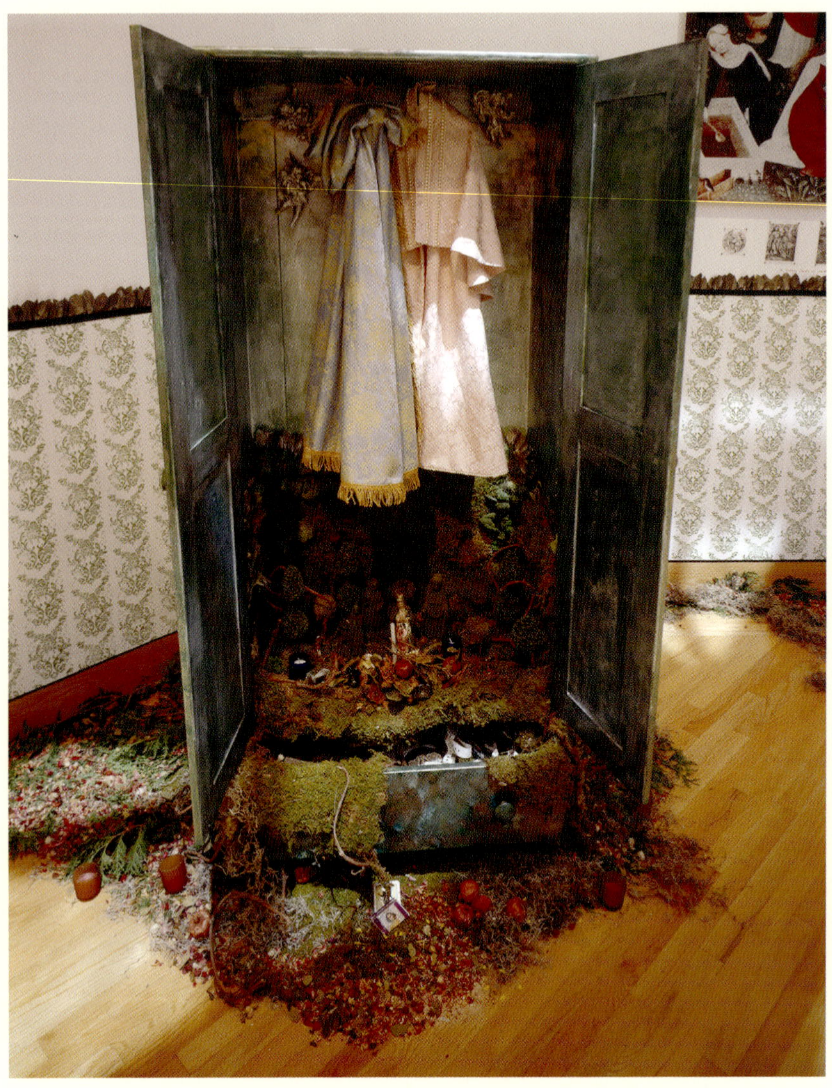

3.13 Amalia Mesa-Bains. "The Garden" in *Venus Envy II: The Harem and Other Enclosures,* 1994. Detail. Courtesy of Williams College Museum of Art, Williamstown, MA.

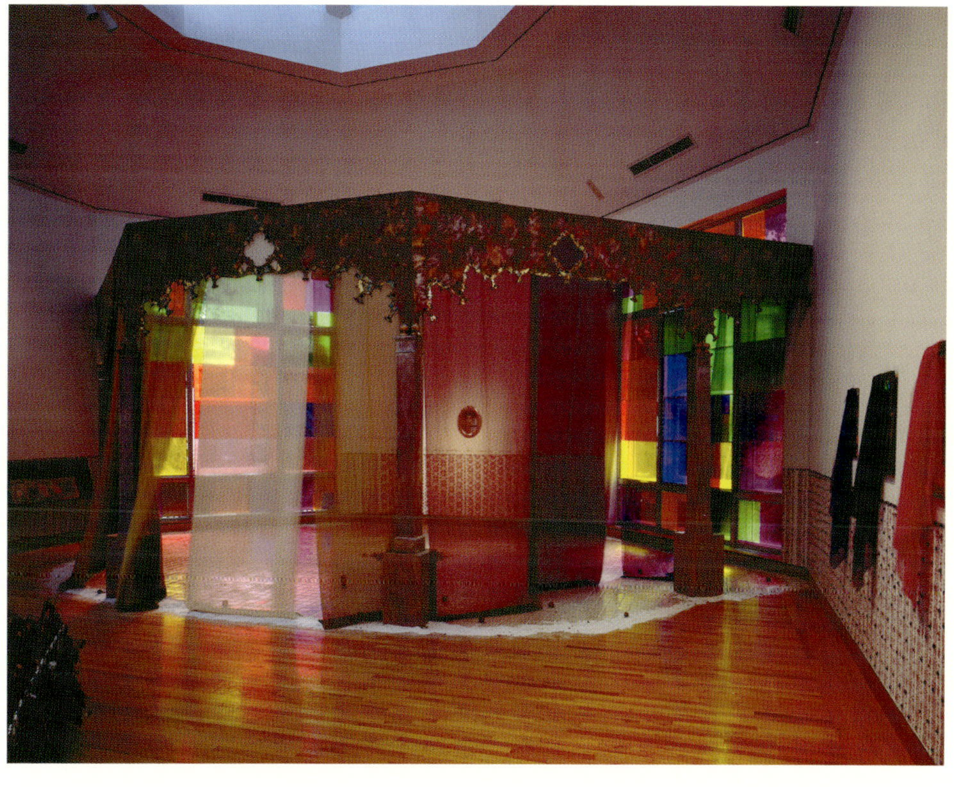

3.14 Amalia Mesa-Bains, "The Harem" in *Venus Envy II: The Harem and Other Enclosures,* 1994. Installation view. Courtesy of Williams College Museum of Art, Williamstown, MA.

century paintings, some in the permanent collection of the Williams College Museum of Art. By placing the images behind the mirror's surface, Mesa-Bains implicated the viewer's identification with these Orientalist fantasies, both their production and reproduction. Delicate veils of different colors were draped over one corner of each image. Historically, according to the artist, they were "part of an elaborate color code; each color means something different. Pink is tenderness, purple is longing, one is for passion, another for separation. When members of the harem went out, they wore these veils as signs to their lovers on the outside."[72] Yet, of the three spaces, this seems the most forlorn and empty, and only narrowly escapes an Orientalism of its own. For all its references to the sensual aspects of life, "The Harem" is also an abandoned enclosure, filled with ashes from love letters burned and forgotten.

The third space of the exhibition, "Sor Juana's Library," formed a mythical reconstruction of the study once inhabited by the seventeenth-century Mexican scholar, poet, and ecclesiastic Sor Juana Inés de la Cruz (1648–1695). Originally a member of the court of New Spain, Sor Juana eventually lived as a nun, engaging in intellectual activity generally forbidden to laywomen of the time. A prolific writer as well as an investigator of the natural sciences, she was probably the first woman in the Americas to argue for the intellectual rights of women within the hostile institution of the Catholic Church. Of aristocratic but illegitimate birth, Sor Juana found sanctuary in learning, in the library, and in the convent. In his biography, Octavio Paz writes that the library was, for Sor Juana, "a treasure consisting of books made by men, collected by men, and distributed among men. To possess that collected learning, she must do what all thieves do, not excluding the heroes of myth: disguise herself. Masculinity is a disguise imposed on Juana Inés by society, as is her profession as a nun. Her bastard origins and her father's absence lead her to the library, and the library, to the convent."[73] Sor Juana's library in the convent functioned as a room-sized cabinet or study. As Orest Ranum observes of early modern architecture, "Studies and cabinets increasingly became the expression of the individual as creator and intellectual, yet they continued to bear traces of their origins as a place for study, prayer, and seduction."[74] At the same time, such sanctuaries could be seen as an escape from narrowly defined ecclesiastical traditions: "It was only during the development of secular architecture in the Renaissance that the modern studio emerged to express a new individualism and a freedom of scholarly inquiry apart from the authority of the Church. The *estudiolo* became a place filled with private artifacts of knowledge (books, painting, globes, and scientific instruments)."[75]

"Sor Juana's Library" mimics just this kind of semisecular *estudiolo* housed within the walls of a religious order. It features a desktop littered with papers and books, rocks and gems, inkwell and quills, test tubes and beakers, maps and musical instruments (figure 3.15). Sor Juana believed that scientific research into natural phenomena would inspire spiritual devotion rather than challenge religion. Both intellectual and nun, Sor Juana was frequently at odds with the power of the Catholic Church, with which she maintained an ambivalent but devoted relationship. From 1672–1690 she was favored by the Viceroy of New Spain, and her convent cell served frequently as a salon for intellectuals and literati. In 1690 she became embroiled in an ecclesiastical debate about the education of women and wrote her famous *Reply to Sor Philothea* where she argues: "Many fathers prefer leaving their daughters in a barbaric, uncivilized state to exposing them to an evident danger such as familiarity with men breeds. All of which would be eliminated if there were older women of learning, as Saint Paul desires, and instruction were passed down from one group to another, as in the case with needlework and other traditional activities."[76] The archbishop did not agree. He confiscated her books, musical instruments, and scientific equipment, along

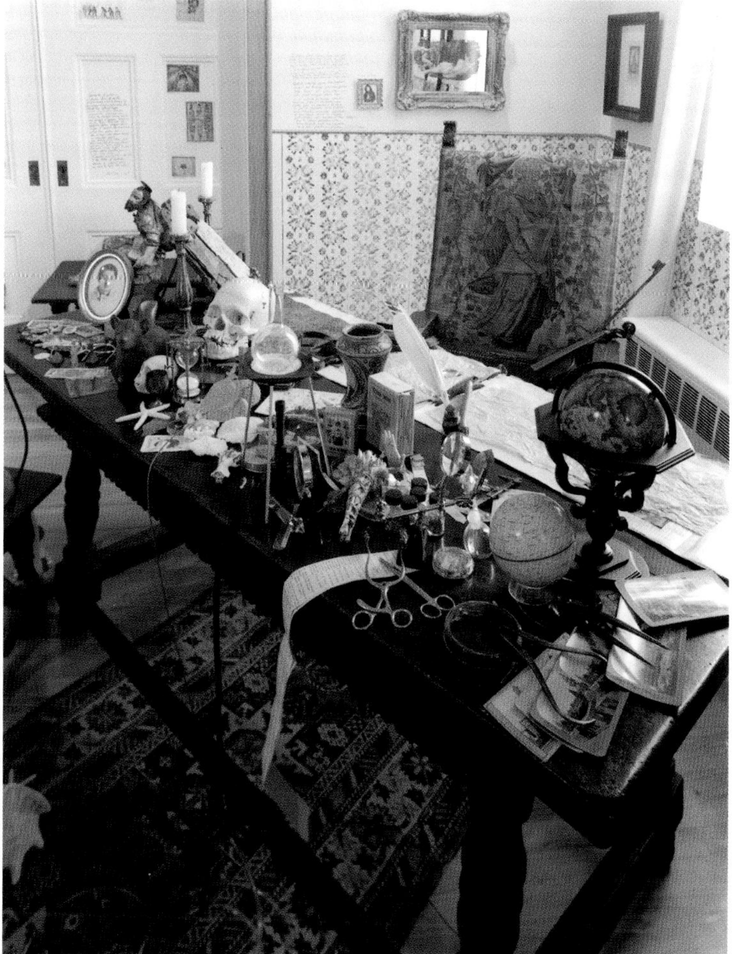

3.15 Amalia Mesa-Bains, "Sor Juana's Library" in *Venus Envy II: The Harem and Other Enclosures,* 1994. Detail of desk. Courtesy of Williams College Museum of Art, Williamstown, MA.

with many of her other possessions. Near the end of her life, Sor Juana was thus effectively ordered into silence.

The exhibition of "Sor Juana's Library" was a strategic choice for Mesa-Bains. Quite by chance, a number of female students at Williams College had staged a protest to demand the hiring of a Latina professor just prior to the artist's visit. Mesa-Bains gathered informational articles about the protests and added them to the installation. Videotapes were also made of the protests and sent to the artist. Mesa-Bains chose several stills and included them on the wall of the library, next to a portrait of Sor Juana herself. The message was clear: the struggle for institutional support of the intellectual endeavor of women, particularly those from disenfranchised communities, continues.

"Sor Juana's Library" also served as a metaphorical archive representing traces of the clash of Spanish and indigenous cultures of Mexico. The imposing portrait *A Knight of Santiago* (1626), painted by the infamous Spanish inquisitor Francisco Pacheco, was hung above a translated text by an indigenous poet that appeared in *Historia de Tiatelolco*: "All these misfortunes befell us. We saw them and wondered at them; we suffered this unhappy fate. Broken spears lie in the roads; we have torn our hair in grief. The houses are roofless now and their walls are red with blood.... We have pounded our hands in despair against the adobe walls, for our inheritance, our city, is lost and dead. The shields of our warriors were its defense, but they could not save it." As with her installation at Cornell University, the artist provided reading material on a wooden lectern including notebooks of colonial and contemporary drawings, etchings, and articles for the viewer to peruse (figure 3.16). Small tables displayed statuettes from the Spanish baroque and the pre-conquest Americas suggesting the cultural transformations and intersections of material culture in a colonialist era.

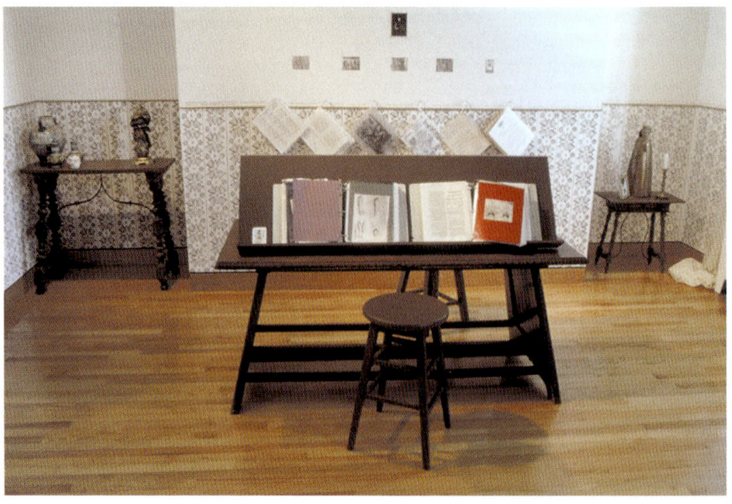

3.16 Amalia Mesa-Bains, "Sor Juana's Library" in *Venus Envy II: The Harem and Other Enclosures*, 1994. Detail of bookstand. Courtesy of Williams College Museum of Art, Williamstown, MA.

In contrast to a history that reads the *estudiolo,* laboratory, or archive as, by definition, a scientific or spatial discourse gendered masculine, Mesa-Bains offers "Sor Juana's Library" as a simultaneously imaginary and historical view of a female and feminist intellectual domain. If Sor Juana stands as a figure who called for the equal education of women, her library-within-a-convent represents those important and generally invisible architectural sites where women's intellectual endeavor took place in parallel with, or outside of, a patriarchal logic of knowledge production and acquisition. "Sor Juana's Library" is an allegorical staging for the "intellect" in balance with the "body" ("The Harem") and the "spirit" ("The Garden"), each conceived as a protective enclosure where women are educated, seduced, or sanctified. Yet the protective immurement of women in these cloisters concurrently stages a form of bodily and ideological imprisonment, revealing how the history of sexuality and power is also a history of social confinement that women have negotiated for centuries. By staging the spaces as environment or installation, the artist invites the viewers to temporarily inhabit these sites of enclosure and to recognize them as interior states of consciousness as well.

In the third chapter of her series, *Venus Envy III: Cihuatlampa, the Place of the Giant Women* (1997), Mesa-Bains turned from the domestic and historical sites of the previous works to the imaginary space of myth and legend. In Aztec cosmology, Cihuatlampa is the place where women's spirits linger in the afterlife if they succumb to death during childbirth, their honorable sacrifice considered comparable to that of a male warrior. Acknowledging and revising this concept to celebrate the lives of heroic women generally, the artist produced an imaginary set of garments and props for a woman of great, untamed spirit: a giant woman, a transgressive woman, a powerful woman. Natural elements such as earth, air, and water served as the organizing rubric. At the entrance to the installation a vanity mirror nearly five feet high, embellished with glittering seashells, announced the shift in scale viewers could expect inside. Reclining like a verdant island on the gallery floor was an oversized anthropomorphic *Cihuateotl (Woman of Cihuatlampa),* her broad sculpted hips and large breasts generously proportioned and covered with a fine moss, like rounded hills in a lush landscape. "Vestiture…da Ramas" (Vestiture…of Branches), an elaborate copper mesh gown with long metallic tubes and tendrils of wire reaching out from within, suggested a rhizome or arboreal strength, a tree with deep roots. Towering ominously in the center of the room, its delicate armor with a single breastplate also referenced the legend of the single-breasted Amazon warriors who appear in the writings of Herodotus. At the far end of the gallery, cascading like a waterfall, a great plumed cloak more than nine feet high presented a fantastical version of the spectacular feathered capes of Aztec and Inca royalty (figure 3.17). With thousands of carefully sewn feathers in blues, greens, and gold,

"Vestiture…Emplumada" (Vestiture…of Feathers) signified the majesty of the sky. With an emphasis on sculptural innovations and painstaking manual construction, the installation was engaging on a formal level, but it was not as conceptually or as historically complex as the previous works in the series.

More interesting was the fact that the artist had included a supplementary exhibition in a separate space of the gallery behind a dividing wall. There, a table covered with dirt and sand, bones, and magnifying glasses treated the subject of the artist's own life as an archeological dig. Personal souvenirs or mementos were interspersed with objects saved and collected from previous installations. An orderly display of these trinkets and artifacts, along with books and other research materials, were stored against the wall on the bare white shelves of a makeshift "Der Wunderkammer" (figure 3.18). Rather than including miniature versions of her own works of art, as in Marcel Duchamp's *Boîte-en-Valise* (1935–1941), Mesa-Bains offered a temporary, transitory museum for her ongoing materialist practice. Her metadiscursive recuperation of fragments also revealed the recursive interdependence that exists among her works of art, the framing discourses of a Chicana identity, and the archival apparatus of collecting and display itself.

Decolonial Vision

The *Venus Envy* series and other works by Mesa-Bains demonstrate the artist's investigation of historical, social, and political concerns through the guise of the memorial or monument. By reviving *and* revising traditional aesthetic practices and their methods of display, the artist interrogates the process of subject formation through the material conditions of its replication. The work draws parallels between forms of oppression and regimes of vision, as well as between life cycles of the past and the present. For Mesa-Bains, material culture signifies as the sentimental evidence of psychological states. Objects serve as metaphors to memorialize the meeting of internal desires and external forces.

The lives of Chicanas are the artist's starting point for exploring race discourse as a process of ongoing cultural colonialism. Her works suggest the continuities between present-day racisms that fuel, for example, anti-immigration sentiment along the U.S.-Mexico border or the cultural hierarchies of university education, and the long history of conquest, domination, and exploitation that characterized European nation building in the Americas. A parallel concern includes the continuities between the patriarchal power structures of the past and the ongoing struggle by women to negotiate sexual desire, intellectual freedom, and independence. The work reveals how these continuities shape not only a politics of the public sphere but also the private, interior domains of the subject where they are felt as wounds to the psyche or enclosures for the body.

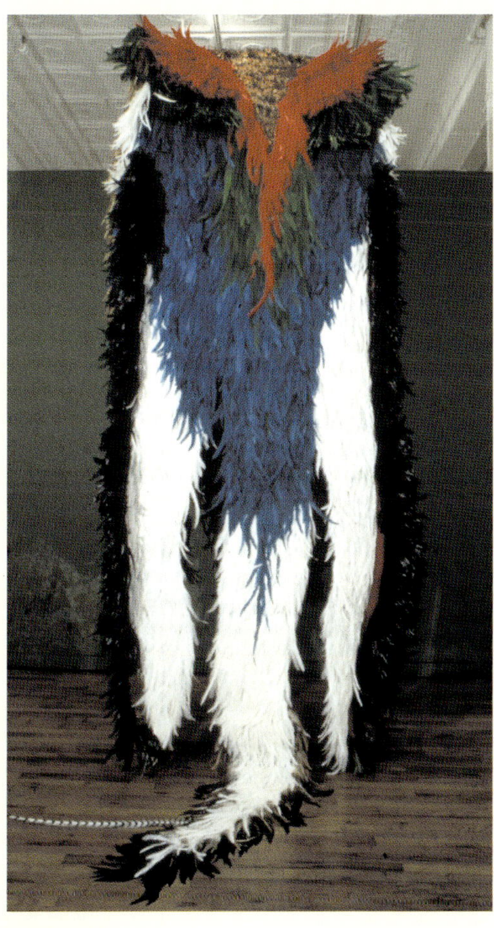

3.17 Amalia Mesa-Bains, "Vestiture . . . Emplumada" in *Venus Envy III: Cihuatlampa, the Place of the Giant Women,* 1997. Bernice Steinbaum Gallery, New York. Courtesy of the artist.

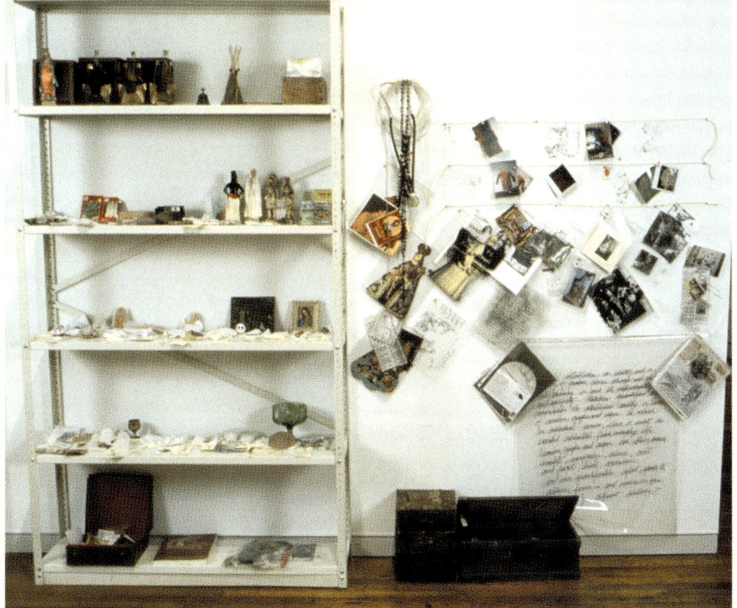

3.18 Amalia Mesa-Bains, "Der Wunderkammer" in *Venus Envy III: Cihuatlampa, the Place of the Giant Women,* 1997. Bernice Steinbaum Gallery, New York. Courtesy of the artist.

It is also possible to conceive of the installations as a series of carefully articulated portraits, each providing more than a mere mimetic representation of significant female icons recuperated from historical erasure. The indexical lipstick traces, perfume bottles, artifacts, and photographs that comprise the details of Mesa-Bains's installations offer a reality effect in tension with their metaphorical enterprise. It might be more accurate to identify Mesa-Bains's formal choices as a kind of "progressive realism." Ella Shohat and Robert Stam write, "Many oppressed groups have used 'progressive realism' to unmask and combat hegemonic representations, countering the objectifying discourses of patriarchy and colonialism with a vision of themselves and their reality 'from within.'"[77] At the same time, Mesa-Bains's critical and deconstructive approach resists realism in a naïve or mimetic sense. A mestiza identity is shown to be both more real and less substantial than the "reality effect" of its historical construction. Taken as portraits, the installations suggest the confluence of myth and history that support any form of cultural identity or life narrative.

Mesa-Bains recalls the past not with a sense of nostalgia but rather with a sense of urgency, with a desire to unravel the way that past is understood in order to produce a different future. In this way the work may also contribute to a *decolonial imaginary,* defined by Emma Pérez as a rupturing space or alternative to that which is written in history, as "that time lag between the colonial and the postcolonial, that interstitial space where differential politics and social dilemmas are negotiated."[78] The work of Mesa-Bains can thus be read as a decolonizing gesture that repositions the gendered body of the mestiza through a critical transformation of the politics of display, contributing to a much longer semiotic struggle over conditions of representation that began with the conquest of the Americas and continues to this day.

CHAPTER FOUR

PEPÓN OSORIO

NO LIMITS

Urban geographies are typically characterized
by strictly bounded neighborhoods connected by liminal zones of contact. A single avenue can mark the edge of poverty or wealth, alienation or belonging. Communities are separated physically, ideologically, and historically from each other by conditions of power that perpetuate inequality, while the environment of city streets requires a complex literacy to be properly deciphered. To be "at home" in the city is to be literate in the *space* of the city, to articulate a language of daily practice that is based on rhythms and regularities that form a routine. Most urban dwellers live within their own *limit politics,* in a network of circumscribed spaces linked together by the transit population that inhabits buses, trains, subways, and cars. Only rarely do people breach familiar limits, only rarely do they cross into unknown territory—whether that territory is a street, a neighborhood, or an art museum.[1]

Pepón Osorio works within and through this limit politics to draw our attention to the boundaries that define and circumscribe the everyday movement of men and women in urban communities, as well as the commodity culture that entices and envelops them. Many of Osorio's works can be read as a response to the effects of cultural displacement on Puerto Ricans living in and around New York City—a displacement felt by the artist himself who arrived in 1975 at the age of twenty from Santurce, Puerto Rico. Mixing culturally specific aesthetic traditions with a critical look at U.S. commodity culture, his early works trace the common effort on the part of immigrants to make a home away from home while negotiating the seduction of consumption as a method of assimilation. After a decade in the South Bronx,

Osorio turned to the politics of violence as the basis for another series of works about the material conditions, cultural traditions, and gender politics of masculinity. In the process of producing these installations, Osorio's working method became one of interaction and participation, conversation and collaboration. Many of his later installations are conceived, developed, and constructed with members of youth groups, neighborhood associations, schools, and social service offices. By involving communities outside the art world in the process of production, and by installing the works in neighborhood storefronts, Osorio extends the reach of his work beyond museum and gallery exhibitions. The artist's most recent works emphasize the uneven social relations that produce hierarchies of class and race, revealing the necessity of bringing people face-to-face with their own limit politics.

Drama and Domesticity

Osorio's early collaborative performances with dancer and choreographer Merián Soto involved the production of set designs that eventually formed the basis of his sculptural and installation work that followed. In 1985 the artist produced the set for *Cocinado* (Cooking), a multimedia performance choreographed by Soto that used the narrative of a land rescue effort as a metaphor for the recuperation of Puerto Rican cultural traditions more generally.[2] Osorio modeled his set design on the resourceful spontaneity of the *rescatadores* (rescuers), echoing a period of Puerto Rican history when grassroots social movements of the 1960s claimed land rights for the rural dispossessed. *Los rescatadores de terrenos* (rescuers of the land) built small dwellings or *casitas* on unoccupied territory, eventually gaining ownership through squatters' rights.[3] Understood at the time as a reclamation of land that would otherwise be lost to the elite of a neo-colonialist government, the activity also privileged the rights of individual families and neighborhoods over those of larger economic and political systems.

The legacy of *rescatadores* is visible today in the vacant lots of Manhattan's Lower East Side. Osorio and I took a walk through this neighborhood in 1995 to view different styles of *casita*; each "little house" with its own verdant garden, modest furnishings, and neighborhood membership seemed an oasis tucked between the grim, low-income apartment buildings. In his study of Puerto Rican barrios, Luis Aponte-Parés observes, "*Casitas* . . . are generally located in neighborhoods that witnessed massive population displacement in the past three decades and now suffer from extreme poverty."[4] Borrowing construction techniques of rural workers' housing, the *casitas* in Manhattan serve as a community space for neighborhood meetings and social events. Aponte-Parés argues that the *casita* is a source of Puerto Rican pride in the otherwise anonymous space of the city: "The decline and loss of institutions, bodegas, churches, social centers, schools, friends, and neighbors has led to a collective need for people to play an active role in rearranging the environment, and thereby restoring the community's sense of well being."[5]

For each performance of *Cocinado,* actors built a *casita* from scratch in front of the audience. As the story unfolded, the domestic scene came to life, complete with hanging laundry, live chickens, dancers, and musicians.[6] For his innovative set design referencing this vernacular architectural tradition, Osorio won the New York Dance and Performance (BESSIE) award. Many of the critical concerns the artist has subsequently pursued were condensed in this work: a recuperation of vernacular traditions, an attention to the spatial politics of neighborhoods and urban communities, a sympathy for the experience of displacement, and a squatter's penchant for temporary, site-specific architectures.

As part of the design for *Cocinado,* Osorio included elaborately decorated props, such as *La Bicicleta* (The Bicycle) (1985), inspired by the bicycles ridden by local street vendors in his hometown of Santurce (figure 4.1). With reflective papers tied to the spokes, strings of plastic beads and streamers hung from the handlebars, and white plastic roses, golden leaves, and faux pearls glued on every surface, the bicycle shimmered with color and light as it moved across the stage. Closely viewed, *La Bicicleta* also revealed miniature palm trees, colorful fish, toy action heroes, and gilt crucifixes. In addition to serving as a lively prop, *La Bicicleta* presented a microcosm of the island experience, boyhood fantasies, and religious upbringing of the artist's past. "At the very beginning," Osorio has commented, "I was using artifacts as a way of dealing with my memory, dealing with my childhood, dealing with images of being a child."[7] Speaking as a self-proclaimed *embelequero* (embellisher), Osorio has explained his impulse to customize commercial objects such as the bicycle: "Having been denied a national identity, Puerto Ricans never accept things as they are given to them. . . . They forge a self-identity by giving things a personal touch."[8] This decorative imperative is more than an aesthetic gesture on Osorio's part; it mimetically reproduces a common critical response of many minority communities to the condition of living in a material world driven by an economy of mass production and cultural uniformity. *La Bicicleta* further signifies a life wheeled from place to place: a life of transition, of immigration, of cultural diaspora.

Another work to originate as a theatrical prop, and the first to be staged as part of a room-sized installation, *La Cama* (The Bed) (1987) was designed for an interpretive performance by Soto at the Longwood Gallery in the Bronx (figure 4.2). The performance commemorated rites of passage from birth to death, from childhood to adulthood, and from innocence to knowledge. According to Osorio, the prop was inspired by a personal dream in which, fearfully hiding behind a tomb or deathbed, the artist waits to introduce Soto (his light-skinned future wife) to Juana (the

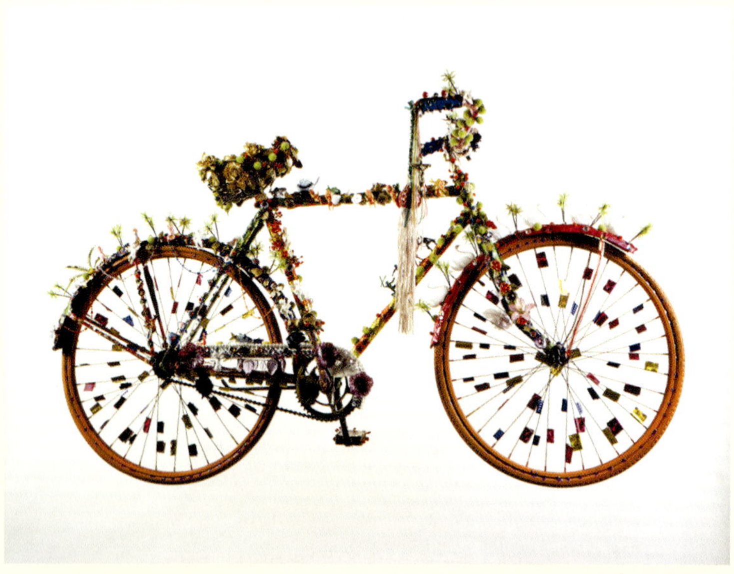

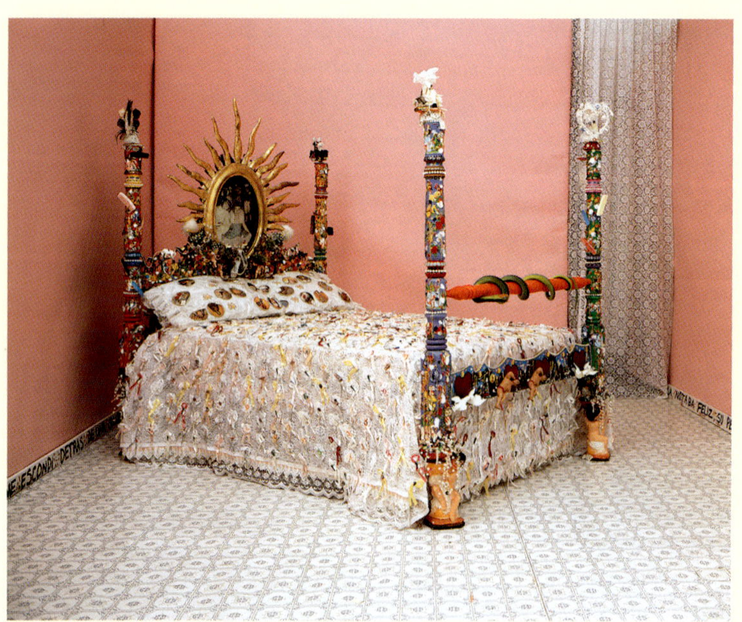

4.1 Pepón Osorio, *La Bicicleta*, 1985. Photo by Tony Velez. Courtesy of El Museo del Barrio, New York.

4.2 Pepón Osorio, *La Cama,* 1987. Installation view. Collection of El Museo del Barrio. Photo by Tony Velez. Courtesy of El Museo del Barrio, New York.

dark-skinned maid who raised him as a child). In the dream, Juana lifts herself from the bed and gently whispers a few words in Spanish and in an African language to tell him she approves.[9] *La Cama* was thus a memorial to Juana—an offering of material opulence for the dead—as well as a celebration of Osorio's future marriage. Painted hearts, lovebirds, and cherubs adorned the base and frame of *La Cama,* while Catholic saints and virgins in frames of gold appeared as offerings on the pillows. The white lace coverlet was studded with a layer of *capias* or *recuerdos*—popular tokens of affection exchanged at baptisms and anniversaries—each carefully attached to the bed by a ribbon. Of course, a bed is a highly overdetermined object in a household: the site of intimacy, of the primal scene, of birth and of death. It is not by accident that Osorio reads his relationships to the women in his life through this material trope. Nevertheless, *La Cama* was more than a repository for personal fears and desires; it worked metaphorically to illuminate the artist's interrogation into the binary logics of racial identity and familial bonds. Atop the bedposts, paired figures posed in tiny emblematic scenes of life's stages: a black baby and a white baby, a black groom and a white bride, a skeleton dressed in black and one in white. The black/white binary was repeated in the placement of two portraits back-to-back on the headboard. On the front, a golden halo encircled the large oval photograph of a young girl (Soto) dressed in a ballet tutu of blue satin. On the back, a portrait of Osorio as a child was surrounded by leopard-spotted rays, an alternating pattern of plastic cigars, cloves of garlic, miniature shoes, and tiny men in tuxedos, each with a different skin tone, the majority dark

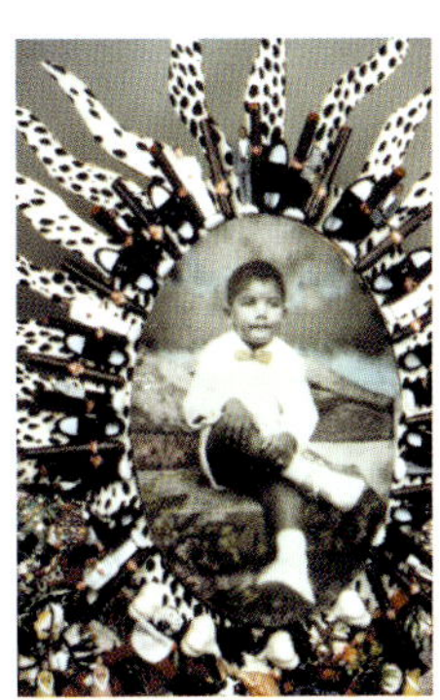

4.3 Pepón Osorio, *La Cama,* 1987. Detail of back of headboard. Collection of El Museo del Barrio. Photo by Tony Velez. Courtesy of El Museo del Barrio, New York.

(figure 4.3). In our interview the artist remarked, "I realized the toys, the figures, that I was using in my work were not reflecting my skin tones. And that was when I began painting, out of anger, all of the different toys. You will see in a lot of the work that the toys have very dark painted skin—that I did myself."[10] Osorio is dark-skinned, Merián light-skinned. *La Cama* also maps an allegory of racial difference that historically would have prohibited their union. Taken as a whole, the sculpture produces a portrait of two people and the broader story of their cultural heritage, economic class, religious faith, and social networks.

Consciously working in layers of intelligibility, Osorio understands his audience to be a culturally eclectic population of artists, critics, neighbors, and community members. Sensitive attention to the distinct visual literacy of these groups motivates the artist to speak in multiple visual discourses simultaneously. Describing the objects that adorn *La Cama*, for example, the artist has noted that the plastic cigars (and their imaginary smoke) represent transcendence, the shoes represent a social network of men, the garlic decorations are a form of protection, and so on.[11] "So these things from the very beginning you might say are very kitschy, or funny, but they have meaning behind them that, if you did not have that cultural pre-contact, you would not understand."[12] Osorio's reference to "cultural pre-contact" implies that specialized knowledge will unlock the full symbolic significance of the piece, to which interpretive access is not universally available. Although his works are not intentionally hermetic, they tend to participate in several iconographic paradigms at once, effectively redistributing the power that attends interpretative knowledge. In this respect, they resemble the works of the other artists discussed in this book. Each addresses a local or insider audience while also attending to a history of artistic precedents. *La Cama*, for example, clearly responds to the installation genre innovations of Robert Rauschenberg's *Bed* (1955), Claes Oldenberg's *Bedroom Ensemble* (1964), and Edward Keinholz's darker and more ominous *While Visions of Sugarplums Dance in Their Heads* (1964), each of which involved the interrogation of desire, mass culture, domesticity, or nightmares. The iconography of *La Cama* was also inspired by the invocation of loss in the song "La Cama Vacia" (The Empty Bed) by Filipe Rodríguez, whose "La Protesta de los Reyes" in 1974 struck a chord in the hearts of Puerto Ricans for its affirmation of cultural pride.

A mix of vernacular religious symbolism, art-historical allusions, and popular culture references may be transparent or opaque to Osorio's diverse audiences. This is a risk the artist has taken self-consciously, but that has occasionally resulted in critical misinterpretations. For example, one of Osorio's better-known works, *El Chandelier* (The Chandelier) (1988), was generally misread by mainstream critics who described the colorful work as either a postmodern revival of kitsch or a baroque pastiche of humorous junk (figure 4.4). Critic Joan Ross Acocella's reading, while otherwise sympathetic to the artist's work, is symptomatic in its characterization of *El Chandelier* as a "knickknack heaven" and an example of Puerto Rican "pop richness." A miniature reproduction of Saint Lazarus—a symbol of suffering and healing in the Puerto Rican *Santería* tradition—is listed simply as a "plastic leper" by Acocella, who mentions it along with the "plastic rhinos and giraffes and monkeys" that also decorate the piece.[13] She does not follow through with a metaphorical or metonymic reading of the objects chosen, or their placement within a complex hierarchical structure. The New York-based artist and writer Coco Fusco has rightly remarked that "appreciation of Osorio's oeuvre usually stops at the surface; viewers revel in or rail against its sumptuousness and presume a nonreflexive recapitulation of a 'naïve' vernacular cultural practice. Within a

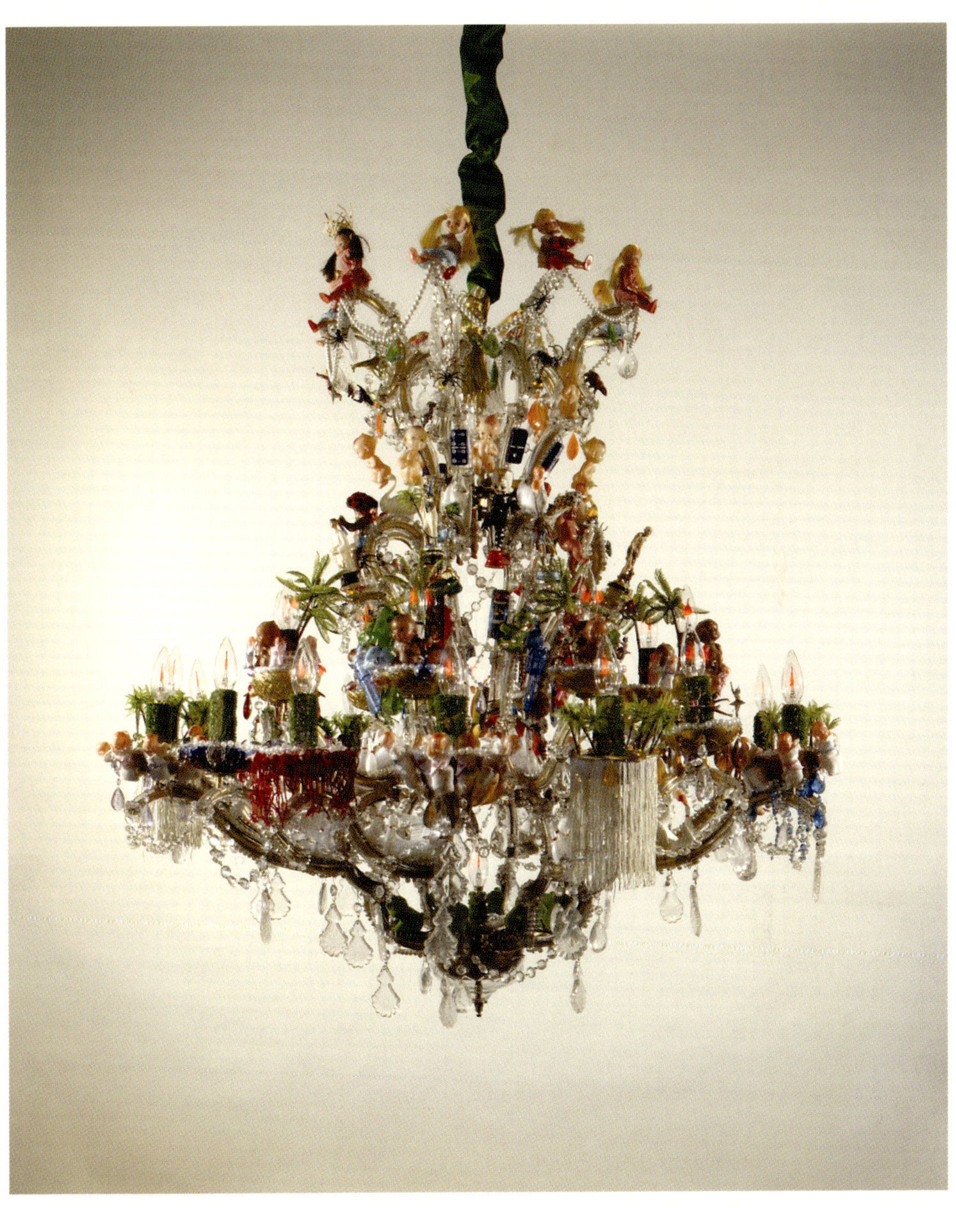

4.4 Pepón Osorio, *El Chandelier*, 1988. Photo by Beatriz Schiller. Courtesy of El Museo del Barrio, New York.

culture like that of the United States, informed by minimalist notions of elegance and a Puritan disdain for decoration, it is all too easy for even a highly calculated use of kitsch to be perceived as unselfconscious."[14] Osorio himself has commented, "Perhaps *El Chandelier* is among the least understood, although it depends upon who you ask. If you ask the people in the Bronx, they understand it perfectly well."[15]

El Chandelier was inspired by Osorio's observation that, even in the poorest homes of New York's Lower East Side, it was possible to glimpse shimmering glass chandeliers through the windows of otherwise drab interiors.[16] Scholar Kellie Jones observes, "In *El Chandelier,* for instance, the majestic European-identified lighting fixture is weighed down with signs of these missing elements from the cultural story. Dominoes, black babies, and palm trees are attached to a lamp already oversaturated with mass-produced jewels."[17] As a microcosm of the social relations that produce hierarchies of economic status, *El Chandelier* presents an ascending order of race and class strata. Nested in the base of the lamp, green frogs signal the tropical and fertile life of the island, while farther up a row of lights encircles plastic palm trees. The next tier is inhabited by a variety of dark-skinned and light-skinned dolls, plastic guns, and toy police cars, creating a visual transition between the rural and urban context, between the lush vegetation of the island and the threats of city life. Encircling this domain are miniature religious figures including Saint George and Saint Lazarus. And finally, at the top, are eight dolls seated on the outermost tips of the chandelier's crown. Seven of the dolls have light skin and blond hair, but the eighth, with dark brown hair and a miniature *pava* (a loosely woven straw hat worn by farmers and laborers of Puerto Rico), serves as a token representative of the Latino population in the upper classes. Osorio has commented, "I understand that there is a level of misunderstanding between classes in the Latino community—and that is something that I am interested in bringing into the work."[18] By using trivial or toy objects in the construction of *El Chandelier,* Osorio appears to make light of a serious situation. But it is this combination of levity and critique, of literalness and exaggeration that materializes in Osorio's politics of display. Paralleling characteristics of a Chicano *rasquachismo,* Osorio's philosophy that "more is better" is here used ironically to address conditions of privation.[19] For immigrant communities, the space of the home can be a haven, a momentary escape, from that which is strange, new, hostile, or foreign. At once a site for the affirmation of cultural traditions and private memories, this intimate domain can also facilitate forms of cultural assimilation as new consumption practices slowly change the accumulated shell of material objects that fill the domestic sphere.[20]

Whether changing the skin color of a plastic doll, or infecting the logic of the tourist souvenir, Osorio's material transformation of commodity objects is an inherently political act in a market economy where individual consumers are defined by objects they own and produce. Osorio has commented:

> A lot of stores are selling things marketed at a specific ethnicity. T-shirts of Malcom X are mass-produced.... So what you find around are people who will wear the "x" and who will sell the "x" on things because they know people who have some kind of identity with their culture or their race will buy it. Hair extensions are sold everywhere and they are manufactured by people who are outside of your culture. And yet they can become the identifying fact of your culture. What does this manufactured object that deals with my identity have to say to me? And what does it mean to me when I bring it home? Because I may be associating with it as an African American or as a Puerto Rican or Latino. So I have to then turn it around so that it can *really* fit my home, my position, my environment, and so on.[21]

Détournement or "turning around," from its Duchampian and surrealist to its situationist elaboration, has been understood as a critical appropriation and reuse of both artistic and consumer culture. Osorio articulates the politics of critical *détournement* operative not only in his own work, but also in the everyday lives of subaltern populations of the United States. As with the skilled artisans of low-rider car culture, *customizing* becomes a form of *tactical critique.*[22] In Osorio's work, this transformation is part of an effort to remap the terrain within which mass-produced objects are legible, to make the conditions of their circulation visible as a politics of social organization and manipulation. At the same time, Osorio's transformations of found objects serve a narrative purpose, producing newly fashioned artifacts that tell the story of an elided population. This critical methodology, linked to a spatial politics of display, recurs in his room-sized installation works.

In *Scene of the Crime (Whose Crime?),* produced for the 1993 Whitney Museum Biennial, Osorio continued his focus on the home by staging a life-sized living and dining room interior in the space of the museum gallery.[23] Produced as a diorama into which viewers gazed from a missing fourth wall, the installation recreated the tragic aftermath of domestic violence in a small Nuyorican apartment (figure 4.5). In the center of the living room space, richly decorated with lush red and white satin curtains, a gold vinyl semicircular divan and armchairs upholstered with the flag of Puerto Rico, lay an artificial corpse, the body of a woman, covered with a white and bloodied sheet. One of the chairs had been overturned, a woman's high-heeled shoe lay on the floor, glass and china figurines were smashed and scattered, and other items had fallen from the shelves. Security tape (not unlike a museum guard rope) cautioned us not to cross into the space. Carefully labeled plastic bags of incriminating "evidence" were also placed within view. These last details were the result of an invitation Osorio had extended to a detective from the New York Police Department's crime unit to "investigate" the scene of his art installation before the opening. (Osorio had come to know the detective during his time as a social worker.) It was the detective who bagged the evidence and hung the security tape in the presence of the artist and slightly disconcerted curators. While this touch of realism was probably lost on most viewers, it constituted a unique breach of museum etiquette and served as a device for transforming the display space of the gallery into a public investigation site.

The realism of the interior was, at the same time, eclipsed by its artificial theatricality and excessive iconicity. Hundreds of photographic portraits were placed on the coffee table, framed in wall niches, tucked into the edges of mirrors, or in folding lockets decorating the blue vinyl bar dividing the living room space from the dining room. Myriad faces, young and old, male and female, black and white gazed back at the viewers amid an abundance of decorative elements, porcelain figurines, and *chucherias* that covered every ledge. The sheer abundance of elements made the room feel densely populated. Viewers were invited to draw a metonymic link between image and object, between individual portrait and fragile figurine. Against the back wall, the artist installed a large decorative mirror, through which a video screen was visible. On the screen an urn, apparently filled with blood, falls in slow motion to the floor and shatters. The urn is then reconstituted in reverse, only to fall again. Strategically placed around the room, amid the debris, are seven large plaster reproductions of Catholic saints, doubles for *Santería orishas*, gazing on the body of the deceased. Osorio has commented, "There are seven saints in the work—they are all placed there as the witnesses to a crime."[24]

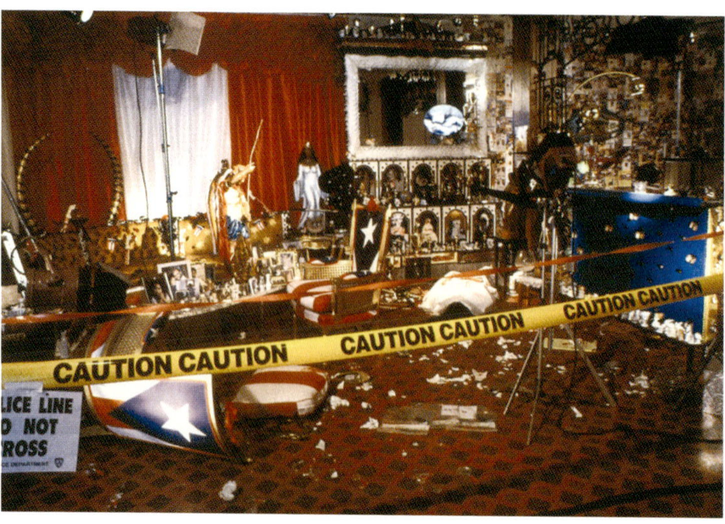

4.5 Pepón Osorio, *Scene of the Crime (Whose Crime?)*, 1993. Installation view. The Whitney Museum of American Art, New York. Courtesy of the artist.

References to Santería, a syncretic religion of African (Yoruba) and European (Catholic) traditions practiced throughout the Americas and the Caribbean, operate as a parallel visual discourse within the staged "realism" of Osorio's installation format, but are generally ignored by scholars and critics. Both Robert Farris Thompson and Arturo Lindsay have offered important studies of the role of Santería in other contemporary art practice.[25]

For those unfamiliar with Santería, it is worth expanding slightly on its iconographic logic.[26] As with Christian saints, Santería potentates are associated with specific objects, powers, personalities, and even colors. In some cases, an equivalence is created between a particular Christian saint and a Yoruba deity. Seven primary gods or *orishas* form the core of Santería religious practice.[27] Babalú-Ayé, the African god of smallpox and epidemic, represented by the color purple, is often associated with Saint Lazarus, because of the sores of leprosy covering his body. Ogún, male god of war, iron, and weapons, is equated with Saint George the dragon slayer and is often represented with metal objects, swords, and guns. Oshún, goddess of love and "sweet water," is represented with golden-colored things: brass, liquid honey, yellow flowers, ochre earth.[28] Shangó (Changó in Afro-Caribbean Creole), the god of thunder and lightning, is linked with Santa Barbara and the colors red and white together, either as a single red stripe on a white ground or as an alternating pattern.[29] Yemayá, a Creole version of the African river god Yemoja, is the goddess of the Atlantic Ocean, of living bodies of water, and of the sea. She is represented by the color blue, seashells, and porcelain vessels with an opalescent shine. Sometimes Yemayá is associated with the Catholic Virgin Mary, who is frequently depicted in blue robes. Oya is the goddess of night, wind, cyclones, and sudden destruction. She is often represented as a pair of horns (which are sometimes struck together to call her forth) or a mound of earth.[30] The last, Obatalá, is the "saint among saints," the honest judge with a pure heart, represented by silver and white objects, birds with white feathers, or transparent white cloth such as lace or gauze. Also deriving from a Yoruba and Santería tradition is the symbolic use of leopard spots. These painted spots, usually white on a dark ground, appear from time to time on African and Afro-Caribbean altars dedicated to the *orishas*. They function as a symbol of strength, power, initiation, and leaps of faith. Leopard spots therefore indicate an ability to make an existential jump and are sometimes used in an intricate pattern—almost hieroglyphic—to represent communal relations between people.[31]

Within a Santería framework, the leopard spots on the back of *La Cama* surrounding the image of Osorio, who is about to be married, clearly signify a leap of faith. The circle of saints that surround *El Chandelier* can also be read as Santería equivalents, and the artist's choice of color in each work takes on a new semiotic valence. Indeed, the most accurate way to

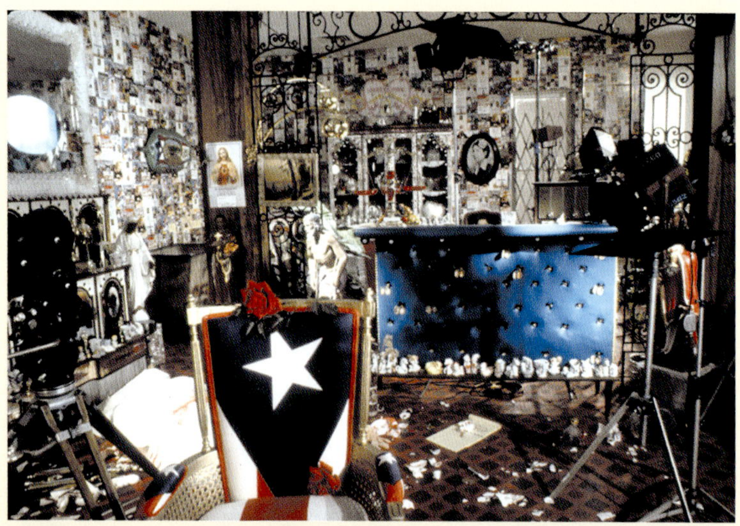

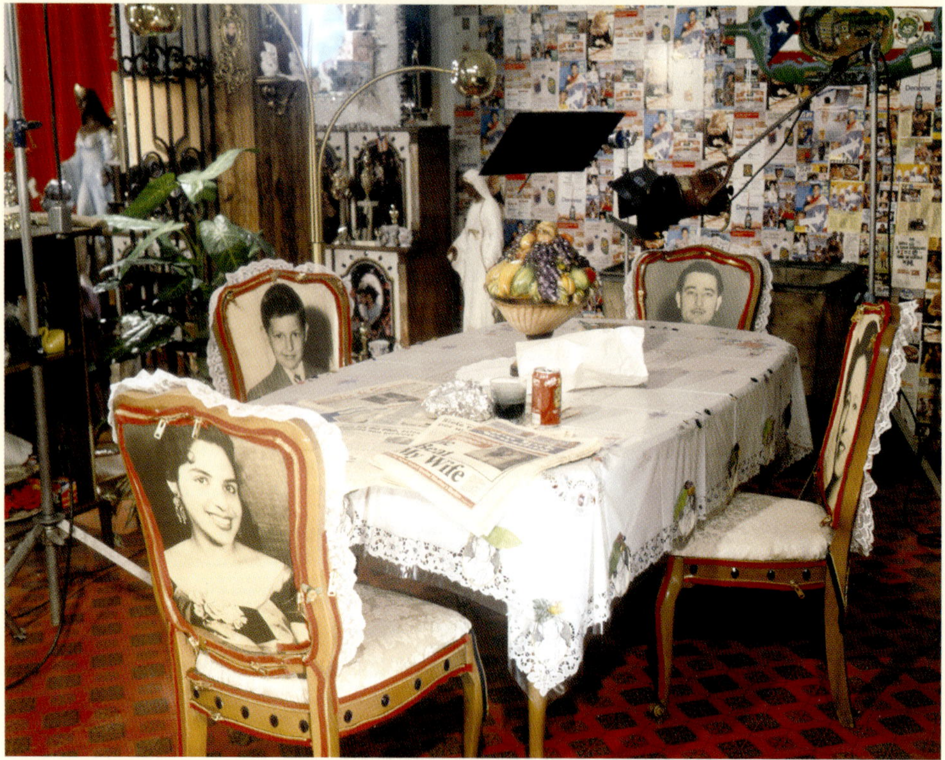

4.6, 4.7 Pepón Osorio, *Scene of the Crime (Whose Crime?)*, 1993. Detail of living room and of dining room. The Whitney Museum of American Art, New York. Courtesy of the artist.

understand the role of Santería in Osorio's work is as a conceptual, chromatic palette with culturally specific associations. These associations are to be read not literally, but as a subtext within a larger visual argument. In *Scene of the Crime (Whose Crime?)*, the red and white curtains, the golden divan, the blue vinyl bar, and the pristine white lace that adorns the china cabinet can all be read as part of this palette through which Osorio invokes the presence of the *orishas*. This invocation speaks to an audience of initiates while also introducing a use of form and color rooted in a Caribbean cultural tradition, rather than an academic or European tradition.

In addition to staging the aftermath of domestic violence, *Scene of the Crime (Whose Crime?)* also represented the "scene" of a larger social crime. The bright glare of spotlights flooded the installation while a film camera focused on the prostrate body, transforming the scene of a crime into another scene—a movie set, a fictional drama (figure 4.6). Osorio's installation implies this is the scene of a crime in which the *crime itself is the staging of such scenes*. With his title *Scene of the Crime (Whose Crime?)*, Osorio asks who is responsible, ultimately, for the production of such scenes. Is it the people living in Latino communities, or is it the mass media, the film industry, and the newspapers that perpetuate images of violence? Shelves of videotapes that lined the outside walls of the installation made these questions explicit. All of the listed titles were films perpetuating Latino stereotypes—particularly those of a violent nature. Each tape was labeled with a statement taken from interviews Osorio conducted with Latino men. When asked how they have been affected by representations of Latinos in Hollywood film, some responded: "We are either seen as violent, horny, or on welfare. They never show our humanity or our struggles and empowerment," and "You see the negative stereotypes portrayed in the movies so many times that at some point you start believing them yourself."[32] In the dining room portion of the installation (figure 4.7), tabloids are strewn across the table with headlines in Spanish and English reporting the latest rape or murder while the chairs, upholstered with oversized black-and-white photographs of a nuclear family, personify a happy and innocent ideal. Again using domestic furnishings to condense the traditions of the portrait and still life, Osorio treats the image as an object, and the object as image, in order to animate the space with otherwise absent subjects. The effect is a dreamlike displacement or condensation of people and things. Found images, both on the furniture and in the tabloids, perform as personifications of systemic problems. The clash of photographic genres and their domestic intersection is materialized through this condensation; family portraits depicting warmth and conviviality are invaded by depressing images of death and destruction in the popular press.

Scene of the Crime (Whose Crime?) is a domestic melodrama, in which every element is intentionally exaggerated and overplayed: the colors, the profusion of photographs and knickknacks, the film apparatus, the various religious persona and silent "characters," the police presence, and the female victim's draped body. In our historical moment in the United States, violence is normalized by film and television, newspapers and magazines. Racially inflected violence becomes a familiar narrative, with familiar protagonists, told again and again. Artist Adrian Piper has shown in drawings and photomontages such as *Vanilla Nightmares* or *Ur-Mutter #5* how newspapers and advertising images perpetuate visual stereotypes of Africans, African Americans, and other blacks as violent, poor, or starving while simultaneously presenting images of white Americans as happy and prosperous.[33] In a similar way, Osorio targets the film, television, and newspaper industries by showing how a story of violence in Latino communities is presented as a relentless, predictable narrative. As Victor Burgin observes, "We can no longer unproblematically assume that 'Art' is somehow 'outside' of the complex of other representational practices and institutions with which it is contemporary—particularly today those which constitute what we so problematically call the 'mass media.'"[34] Taking a theatrical approach, Osorio installed a staged encounter between an idealized Puerto Rican domestic sphere and the race discourse of the dominant media environment in which Latinos find themselves both the subject and the object of an artificial racial melodrama.

Scene of the Crime (Whose Crime?) was the first of Osorio's works to be exhibited in a large mainstream museum, rather than Latino-oriented exhibition venues, such as El Museo del Barrio. Unfortunately, the literal-mindedness of interpretive responses, along with stubborn racial stereotypes held by the museum-going public and critics, surprised the artist—who overheard visitors discussing *Scene of the Crime (Whose Crime?),* for example, as if it were an ethnographic portrayal of a real Puerto Rican household.[35] Recognizing that "the experience implicit in museum and gallery exhibition has not been one to which the Puerto Rican people have been historically welcomed, especially for the contextualization of their culture,"[36] Osorio resolved to locate his subsequent installations in sites that would attract a more diverse audience. In order to address more directly this de facto excluded audience, Osorio began to apply his skills of collaborative art practice to innovative public art projects, attempting to bridge the cultural and economic divide between museum spaces and city neighborhoods.

Remaking Latino Masculinity

The first of these projects, *En la Barbería No Se Llora* (No Crying Allowed in the Barbershop), opened in the summer of 1994 on Park Street in Frog Hollow—the heart of Hartford, Connecticut's Puerto Rican community. According to the executive director of Real Art Ways (the organization that invited Osorio to create the project), Frog Hollow had been the site

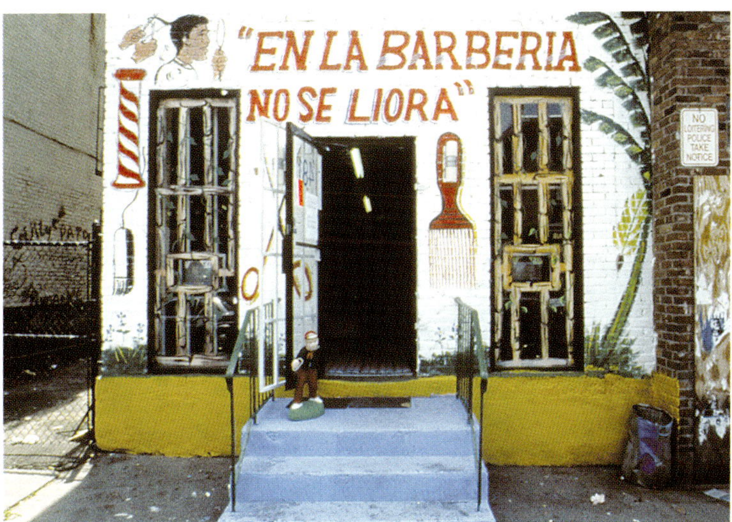

4.8 Pepón Osorio, *En la Barbería No Se Llora,* 1994. Façade. Park Street, Hartford, CT. Commissioned by Real Art Ways. Collection of Museo de Arte de Puerto Rico, gift of Diana and Manolo Berezdivin. Courtesy of the artist.

of many violent confrontations and prolonged gang fighting.[37] In the previous year alone, sixteen youths had been killed as a result of street warfare.[38] At the same time, Park Street remained a vibrant central artery for the community that had grown tremendously and whose members comprise almost a third of Hartford's population.[39] Osorio began his project by visiting the neighborhood and talking with residents, local social organizations, and merchants. Through these casual conversations, the artist began to trace connections among gang activity, domestic violence, and even the spread of AIDS, and the patriarchal hegemony that grows out of a narrow yet persistent articulation of masculinity. In considering where and how masculinity develops, Osorio thought about the social spaces that produce, define, and regulate masculine behavior, about the environments designed to encourage conformity in boys and men, and about his own days as a child spent listening to gossip and fearfully awaiting his haircuts at the local barbershop.[40]

For *En la Barbería No Se Llora,* the artist transformed an abandoned building, easily accessible to pedestrian traffic, into a recognizable social institution—a barbershop (figure 4.8). The welcoming façade of Osorio's *barbería,* brightly painted with vines, banana trees, and flowers, was easily distinguishable from the surrounding urban landscape. On the outside walls, a candy-striped column and giant scissors were painted next to an image of a young man gazing into a mirror, shedding a single tear, as a pair of hands prepared to cut a lock of his hair. Inside, a reception desk, waiting area, and five reclining chairs furnished the space; the floor was simple linoleum and the lighting, a commercial, florescent glow. When the show opened, free haircuts were offered outside, and in the following weeks several people walked in thinking it was an operating barbershop. This ambiguity was important to Osorio, who saw the installation as part of an ongoing conversation that begins with a few individuals and eventually spreads, perhaps like a rumor, through a neighborhood. In an interview with Hans-Ulrich Obrist, he comments:

> That kind of back-and-forth conversation is important to me. For example when the work is in the storefront, people look at it and, little by little, go inside the exhibition space in their neighborhood. What happens to them is that they are not prepared to see a work of art. When you go into the specific space or structure our society has devised for exhibiting art, that space preconditions and limits the experience of the viewer. But when you look at art unexpectedly…you look at it with a more visceral reaction.[41]

At the entrance to the space, a small waiting area displayed scores of framed photographic portraits—of men only—from floor to ceiling (figure 4.9). Most of those depicted were recognizable Latin American and Caribbean athletes, politicians, and entertainers: Che Guavara, Fidel Castro, Roberto Clemente, Ruben Blades, José Serrano. The largest portrait was that of Osorio's father, Benjamin Osorio. Their collective male gaze invited (or perhaps intimidated) male viewers into an identification with a masculine lineage. A woman entering the installation would at least be made immediately aware of its masculine aura. Yet the collective *machismo* achieved by this pantheon of heroes clashed with the overtly feminine wallpaper—a pink and yellow floral print—that covered the walls. The artist has commented, "Placing all these different pictures of men in the waiting room is a way of really imposing the color pink—which has been associated with women—into the man's world."[42] This chromatic imposition is not so much a threat to the masculine space of the barbershop as it is a feminine "opposite" against which, or in relation to which, the space is defined (figure 4.10). It is as if the artist wished to use discrete feminine signs to infiltrate, or mitigate against, the masculinity of the space, to soften its rough edges, to balance its gender bias. By exaggerating gender stereotypes, Osorio reveals their artificiality, contingency, and tenacity. In a traditional, heterosexual context, women are allowed to cry, men are not; women are supposed to attend to beauty and preen in front of mirrors, men are not. Fusco observes, "Osorio quite openly asks his viewers to acknowledge the very spectacular and narcissistic aspects of male identity, underscoring an internal contradiction of Latin machismo that to look macho one must make oneself up, not unlike a woman."[43]

At each of the barber stations, this contradiction played out as a face-to-face video encounter between the "clients," represented by the barber chairs, and images reflected opposite in the wall of mirrors.[44] In the partially transparent mirrors, men enacted their machismo in a variety of

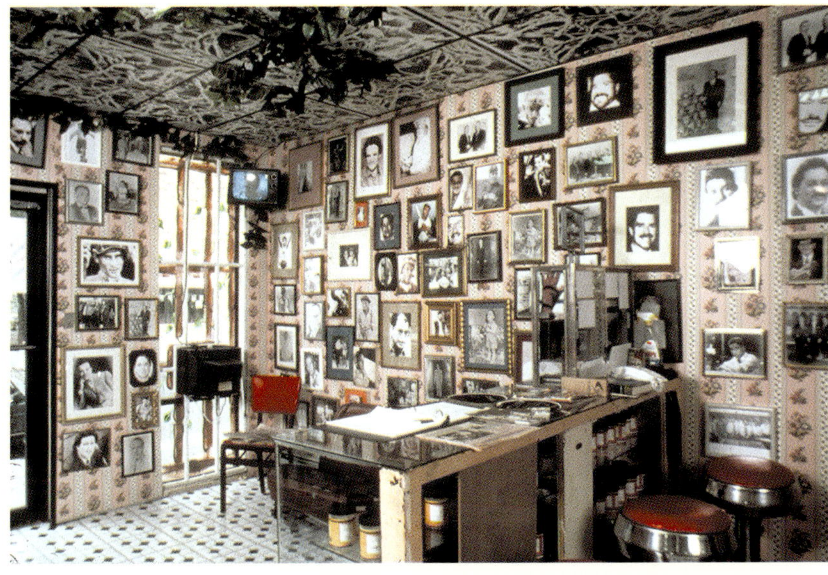

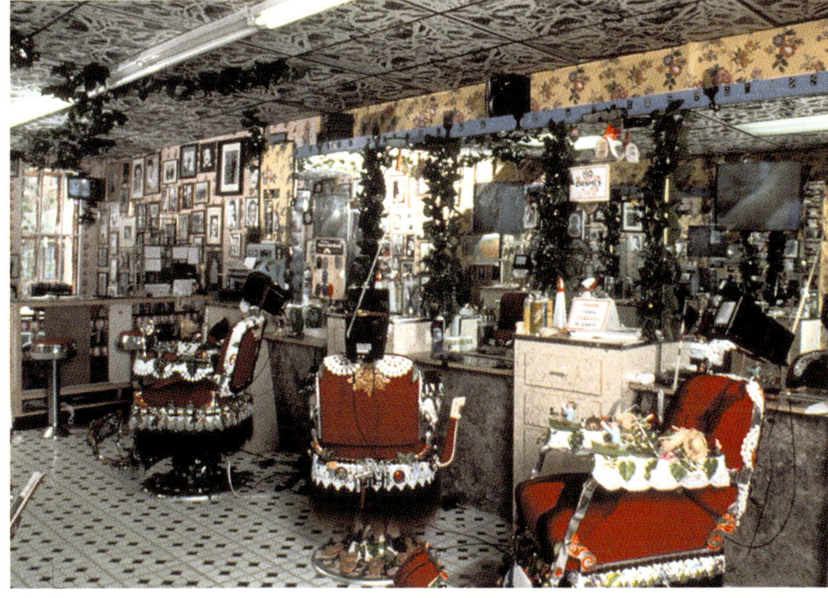

4.9, 4.10 Pepón Osorio, *En la Barbería No Se Llora*, 1994. Installation views. Park Street, Hartford, CT. Commissioned by Real Art Ways. Collection of Museo de Arte de Puerto Rico, gift of Diana and Manolo Berezdivin. Courtesy of the artist.

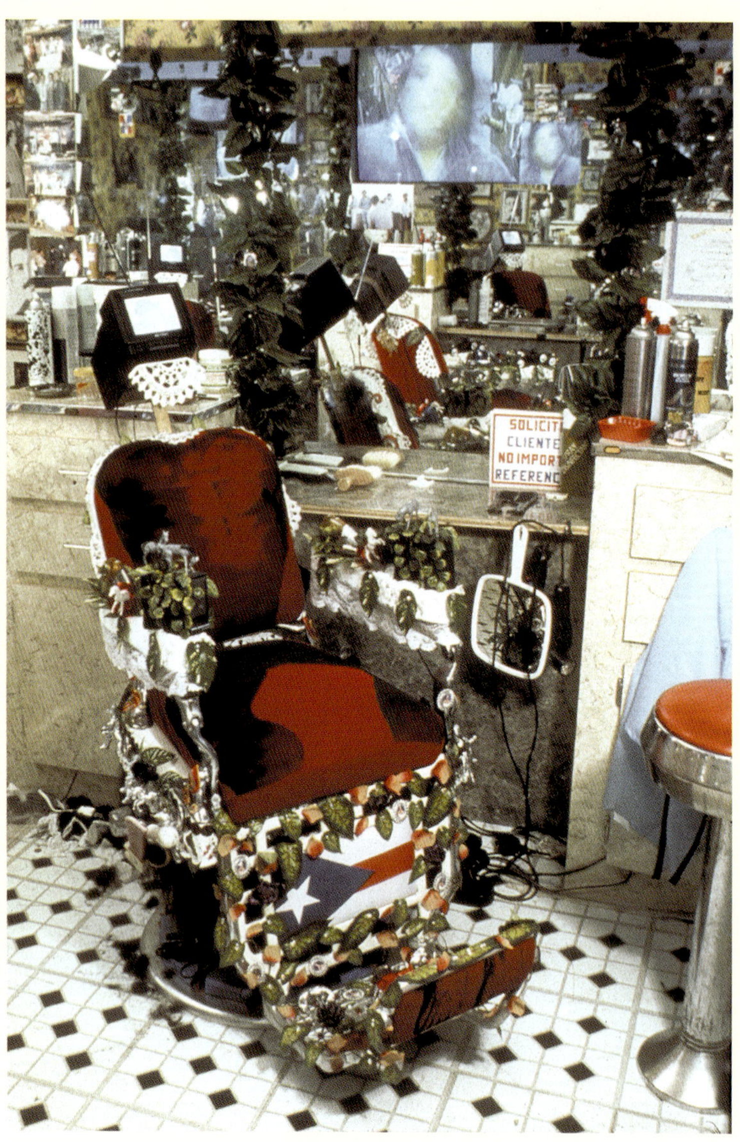

4.11 Pepón Osorio, *En la Barbería No Se Llora,* 1994. Detail of chair. Park Street, Hartford, CT. Commissioned by Real Art Ways. Collection of Museo de Arte de Puerto Rico, gift of Diana and Manolo Berezdivin. Courtesy of the artist.

ways: they lifted weights; they displayed their tattoos; they strutted with other men in parades; they dressed themselves in formal attire; and they engaged in everyday forms of gender normativity. Without presuming a Lacanian intent on the part of Osorio, one finds it obvious that these men inhabiting the mirror served as ego ideals and a source of identification for the barbershop patrons (figure 4.11). By contrast small monitors, welded to the chairs in place of a headrest, showed men silently weeping. Almost animate, each chair had its own "face" (displayed on the monitor), and its own "body"—the nude torso, legs, and feet of an adult male lightly silk-screened on the plush red upholstery. Sexually suggestive, the silk-screened bodies also made visible the kind of exposure and vulnerability that grown men may experience when in tears. Unique collections of artifacts also added character: one chair was decorated with old baseballs and miniature baseball caps, another covered with toy horses and receipts from offtrack betting, and another with plastic fishermen and a multitude of plastic fish. Each thematic embellishment implied not only the recreational preferences of a single person but a homosocial world of male bonding. One chair that stood out from the others embodied Osorio's childhood fears: it was covered with scissors and razors, and around its base an uncanny pile of artificial ears added a strangely macabre and humorous touch. The back wall of the barbershop was also covered with these ears, interspersed with framed photographs of mouths wide open. *En la Barbería No Se Llora* is that space where one hears the local gossip— a posted sign reading *"no chismes"* (no gossip) suggests as much—as well as where one learns how to be or *become* a "man," how to listen selectively, or perhaps how to not listen at all. All the ears on the floor and walls, all the silent, open mouths, imply a cacophony of male-to-male communication and all of its possible failures.

En la Barbería No Se Llora topographically recreated a kind of surreal social space in order to demonstrate how a human subject is produced as a *male* subject, one who must engage in a series of promises and repressions in order to negotiate his own relation not only to masculinity but to Latino machismo. The term *macho* has both negative and positive connotations within and outside of Latino culture. For those outside Latino culture the word macho can bring to mind an overbearing, aggressive male, while within the Latino community it might also represent a responsible, fatherly male, or a heroic, tough male. Osorio's work does not reproduce these stereotypes; instead, it frames the conditions of their emergence. Just as there are varieties of racial formations, there are many varieties of masculinity. Terms like machismo and masculinity are abstractions used to define behavior but also to subsume, and perhaps even repress, otherwise boundless gender permutations. In other words, machismo as a term might well work to create a conceptual limit on the many forms of masculinities operative at any given time, in any given community.

Indeed, this may be its primary function. By exposing the working logic of the barbershop as a social institution through spatial and iconographic metaphors, Osorio's installation provided viewers the opportunity to see the degree to which traditional concepts of masculinity are a limiting frame, open and susceptible to change. Henri Lefebvre writes, "The spatial practice of a society secretes that society's space; it propounds and presupposes it, in a dialectical interaction; it produces it slowly and surely as it masters and appropriates it. From the analytic standpoint, the spatial practice of a society is revealed through the deciphering of its space."[45] It is possible to see how Osorio's installation offers a critical interpretation or deciphering of spatial practices in their structural and ideological forms by being situated in a dialectical relation with parallel sites (i.e., real barbershops). Lefebvre's circular claim that the spatial practices of a society *produce* that society's social spaces, reveals the iterative process of living in a complex socioarchitectural environment. Osorio's public installations are inserted into the otherwise seamless flow of spatial practices to draw our attention precisely to this iterative process; more than a representation, imitation, or copy of "real" social spaces, the installation works as an analytic study. With a mix of humor and serious intent, *En la Barbería No Se Llora* presents machismo as both a social fact and an abstract concept that can be interrogated through spatial means.

Osorio's exploration of masculinity continued to be one of the primary subjects of his next project, *Badge of Honor* (1995), an installation that first appeared at 33 Broadway, in Newark, New Jersey, again in the heart of a working-class, Puerto Rican neighborhood. After its street-level exhibition, the installation then traveled to the Newark Museum (the institution that commissioned the work) and was exhibited from September 1995 to February 1996. As with previous works, *Badge of Honor* developed out of discussions with people living and working in the surrounding area of Newark. According to Joseph Jacobs, curator of painting and sculpture at the Newark Museum, the title of the work derives from Osorio's discovery "that for some adolescents, an imprisoned father is often literally considered a 'badge of honor' that invests the youths with a special status among their peers."[46] At a time when economic survival is difficult, and racism remains a powerful force against which such youth must struggle daily, this unlikely appellation is perhaps the only way to transform an otherwise bleak situation into a source of pride. But to wear such a badge of honor is also to carry a heavy burden. Osorio decided to tackle the topic by focusing on the complex relations between a real father (Nelson "Senior" who was incarcerated in New Jersey's Northern State Prison) and son (Nelson "Junior," age 15). Their private story became the basis for a publicly staged yet intimate tableau.

Situated on a busy commercial street between two discount furniture stores, *Badge of Honor* could have been taken for another retail shop, but for the large-scale portraits of father and son (made by Newark artist Manuel Acevedo) that filled the storefront windows (figure 4.12). The enigmatic exterior worked to Osorio's advantage, because he was able to entice into the space an audience that would not normally have attended either art galleries or museums. Inside, two fully furnished rooms, divided by a thick wall and situated side by side were in stark contrast: one a prison cell and the other an adolescent boy's bedroom. As with *Scene of the Crime (Whose Crime?),* visitors were required to remain spectators, standing outside the installation space to observe both rooms from a missing fourth wall or through the bars of a prison cell.

The prison cell was bleak, empty, almost devoid of objects or color (figure 4.13). Its walls were painted a faint yellow, smudged and dirty, the floor was black linoleum, a simple mattress jutted out from the back wall, and a stainless-steel toilet and sink were in a corner near the floor-to-ceiling bars of the cell doors through which the audience looked. The only material signs of an inhabitant were neatly folded clothes lying on the bed, several boxes of cigarettes, and several color photographs taped to the wall. The cell clearly mapped the barren living conditions of Nelson Senior, against which was contrasted the material plenitude and tenuous adolescent fantasies that filled the bedroom of Nelson Junior. Papered with baseball cards and posters of sports heroes that covered every inch of the walls, a television and massive sound system, sports shoes and a mountain bike, trophies, and a personal computer, the teenage boy's bedroom was clearly the recreated phantasm of projected consumer desires and masculine ideals (figure 4.14).

But the resemblance to a normal boy's bedroom ended there, as dark-skinned hands protruded from the walls, wearing expensive watches and rings and holding out the promise of economic success in the form of

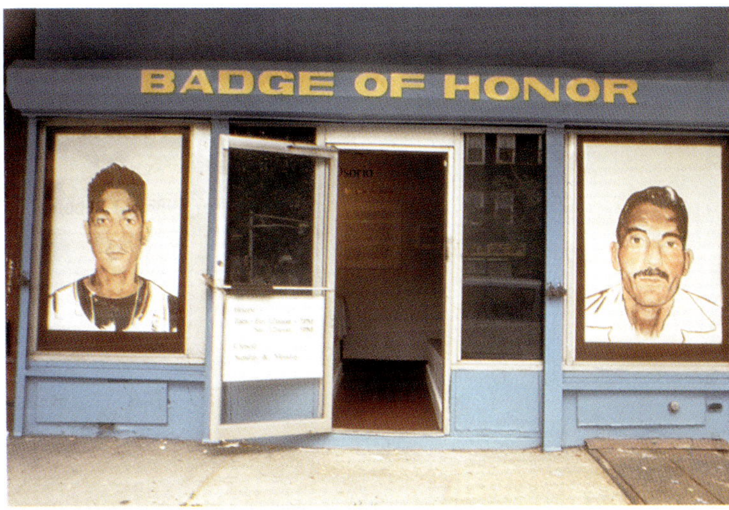

4.12 Pepón Osorio, *Badge of Honor,* 1995. Storefront view. 33 Broadway, Newark, NJ. Commissioned by the Newark Museum. Courtesy of the artist.

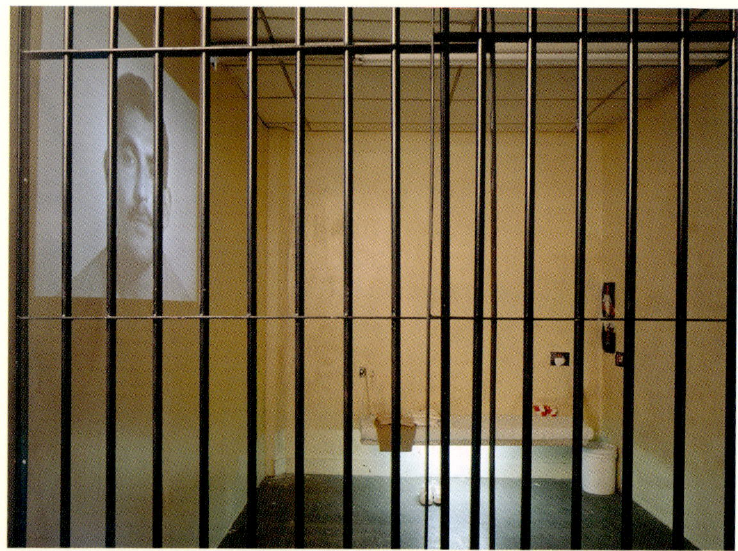

4.13 Pepón Osorio, *Badge of Honor*, 1995. Father's prison cell. 33 Broadway, Newark, NJ. Commissioned by the Newark Museum. Photo by Sarah Wells. Courtesy of the artist.

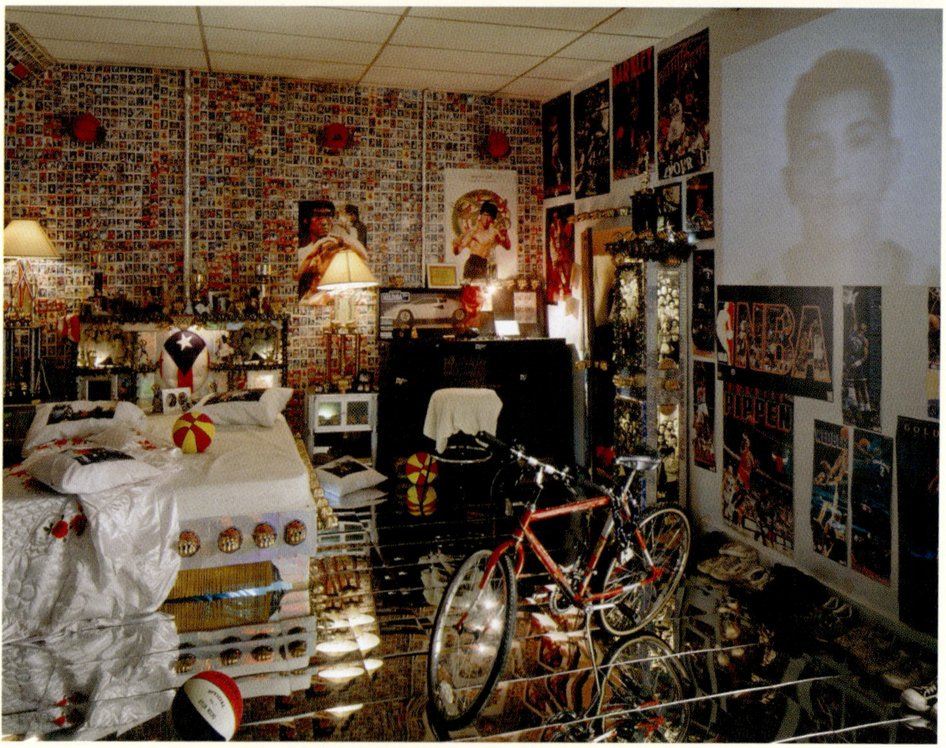

4.14 Pepón Osorio, *Badge of Honor*, 1995. Detail of son's bedroom. 33 Broadway, Newark, NJ. Commissioned by the Newark Museum. Photo by Sarah Wells. Courtesy of the artist.

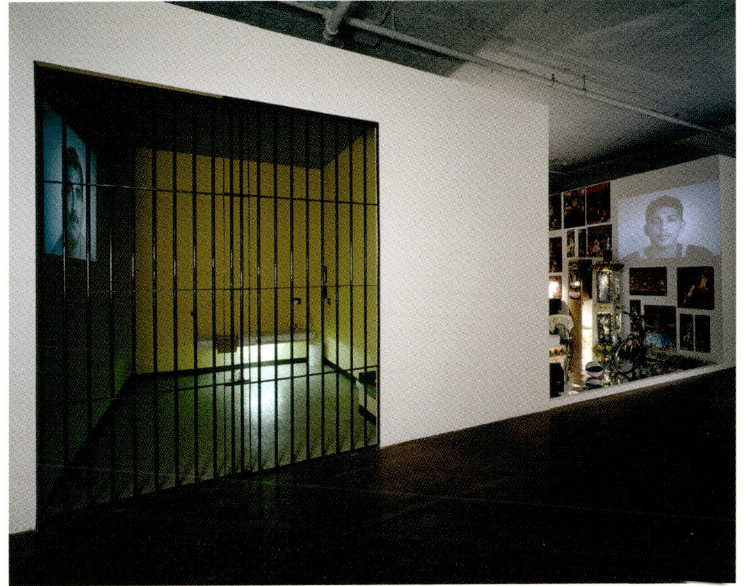

4.15 Pepón Osorio, *Badge of Honor*, 1995. Installation view. Courtesy of the Ronald Feldman Gallery.

bright orange basketballs. Archival photographs representing Latino boys and young men in the neighborhood during the 1950s were also placed on the doors of the closet and around the room, tying this boy's life to local ethnic history and the economic circumstances of those who came before him. In contrast to the brightly colored images of sports heroes, these archival black-and-white images were somber reminders of the gap between a popular culture system of ego ideals and the real circumstances of life for many Puerto Rican youth in Newark. The floor was a pool of silver light, tiled with square mirrors that reflected and redoubled the objects in the room and also suggested the lack of a stable foundation. Rows of golden fists on the bed, cabinets, closets, walls, and even doors added a surreal hint of aggression or strength. Simultaneously protective and threatening, their abundance made reference to the boxers and other athletes (such as Bruce Lee) pictured around the room. In our interview, Osorio has offered further insight into this particular element of display:

> On the cabinet [pointing to a photograph of the installation] do you see the hand fists? Those are car air fresheners. One of the biggest patrons of the arts (his daughter is a curator) [has] a corporation; you know those car air fresheners that look like crowns? They became very popular. Well, what he does is, uses the Black Panther fist and makes that into an air freshener. So what happens? All the African Americans are going to buy it right away—they are going to take that and bring it into their cars. They are going to use it as a way of thinking that they will be empowered by it. So…I decided I wanted to buy a whole bunch of them because I wanted to recontextualize that and change them and give them a different meaning—dealing with the issue of anger, dealing with the issue of masculinity and mass empowerment."[47]

Impressive in their iconographic difference, the two rooms set the stage for a remarkable dialogue. Projected as four-foot-high talking heads on the walls of their respective rooms, the father and son speak to each another, each facing the barrier of the thick wall that separates them (figure 4.15). Osorio and his assistant Irene Sosa videotaped the son and then the father in an alternating sequence for several weeks so that the two could ask each other questions. Each would receive a reply, delivered by Osorio or Sosa one or two days later, on videotape. For the installation, the tapes were edited so that the father and son appear to be having a dialogue. They challenge each other with questions about responsibility and family obligation. They discuss their relationship, especially the impact of the father's absence on the son. The son announces, "I am willing to give up anything for you to be home with us. Anything." Although the video projections revealed the private desires and fears of Nelson Senior and Nelson Junior, the roles the father and son play in the work are primarily iconographic. If the installation were comprised of nothing but the two videotapes, the audience might have felt like eavesdroppers on a private, if compelling, family conference. Instead the work depends on the semiotic potential of mass culture objects to plot the links between this intimate story and the broader population to which it alludes: the disproportionate numbers of Latinos and African Americans that inhabit the prison industrial complex of the United States.

Osorio's installation reveals that this tragedy is not merely a question of racial hegemony played out on the bodies of disenfranchised men, but that the consequences of an economic reality that leads to crime and recidivism also create a configuration of social space such that prison cell and domestic life appear to exist in tandem. The wall that separates the prison cell from the bedroom is impenetrable; in this way, *Badge of Honor* demonstrates the profound emotional impact of spatial separation on relationships between fathers and sons. Yet by placing the two spaces next to one another, the artist implies that there is only a thin line between the boyhood fantasies of Nelson Junior and the harsh realities faced by his father.

In order to entice a local audience into the space at 33 Broadway, Osorio requested a Spanish-speaking guard be hired to encourage passersby to stop in for a look. In fact, many of those who were most moved by the work were the most hesitant to enter. At the opening of the exhibit, two such visitors, middle-aged men, had a powerful reaction: "Standing on the sidewalk in front of the store, right hand resting against his heart, one man told the other how *Badge of Honor* reminded him of his own childhood, when he was separated from his father who was in prison. His friend, slowly shaking his head in amazement, kept saying over and over, 'This is powerful. This is how it is.'"[48]

As a redefinition of limit politics, *Badge of Honor* cut across a number of social and cultural domains. Not only did the artist work to negotiate his way past prison walls to bring the story of life on the 'inside' out to the public, he encouraged an unsuspecting audience from the streets to encounter this story via contemporary installation art. Osorio also used *Badge of Honor* to rethink the function of the New York gallery system. After traveling to the Newark Museum from 33 Broadway, the show was installed at the Ronald Feldman Gallery in Manhattan's SoHo district. The gallery owner allowed the artist to invite a variety of curators, critics, and scholars, myself included, to attend an informal discussion with the family whose lives were depicted in the work. Present to answer questions for one hour were father, son, mother, and the artist. (The father was given special permission to come to the event by New Jersey's Northern State Prison, to which he returned thereafter.) While some audience members asked questions about the production process, most seemed curious to know about the impact of the installation on the lives of the family members. Some were concerned about a possible invasion of privacy. The family members responded with candor: the father claimed that the process had inspired him to "change his life around" and gave him an "opportunity to accomplish something"; the son was primarily surprised that the exhibition had such widespread impact; the mother commented that "the family was brought closer by the videotapes" and that her son and husband communicated through this medium in a way they never would have in person.[49] In this way *Badge of Honor* provided the opportunity for not only a discussion of art's redefinition as social praxis but an important family exchange as well. It is precisely this kind of conversation—unpredictable, unscripted, and often uncomfortable— that Osorio's work tends to elicit.

Questions of paternity and masculinity that arose in the making of *En la Barbería No Se Llora* and *Badge of Honor* were further explored in a 1998 installation called *Las Twines* (mixing Spanish and English to render a Spanglish version of "The Twins"). Based in the South Bronx, *Las Twines* was inspired by conversations between the artist and the youth group UNITAS whose purpose is to pair local teenagers with younger children in a system of surrogate parenting. In his conversations with members of the group, Osorio encountered a series of recurring themes: the loss of parents and/or parental guidance, a general lack of knowledge about family history or heritage, and the perceived need for systems of formal and informal adoption of young children who would otherwise be without proper support and protection. In addition to their pragmatic concerns, the group also raised the social and emotional issue of racial difference within and beyond their local community. Skin color surfaced as the site of identity and the origin of conflict for many in the group. Finally, underlying all of their concerns, the artist observed, was a desire for material wealth.

In *Las Twines,* Osorio addressed these conceptual concerns (paternity, identity, and consumption) in the form of a fictional landscape. Wall text at the entrance to the installation told the fable of twin girls born alike in every respect except for their hair and skin color. One was light-skinned with blond hair; the other was dark-skinned with black hair. Their mother had died when they were still young, so they set out into the world in search of their unknown father. Crossing the seven seas and scouring the continents, their quest for patrimony brought them fame and fortune but was finally in vain, for no man would step forward to claim them.

With this narrative introduction in mind, viewers entered a dark installation space filled with floor-to-ceiling mirrors, video projections, and life-like mannequins that formed a strangely haunting scene. "Papa…Papa …Papa…!" The voice of a young girl echoed through the interior of *Las Twines,* its rhythmic refrain starting quietly and slowly, increasing in vol-

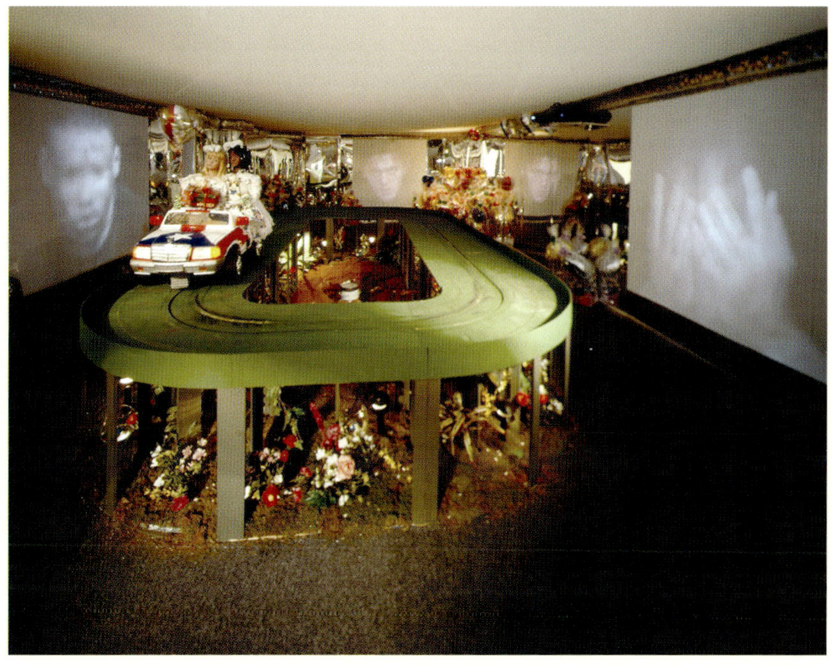

4.16 Pepón Osorio, *Las Twines,* 1998. Installation view. Courtesy of the Ronald Feldman Gallery.

ume and urgency, and then ceasing abruptly. Taking center stage were the twins, two mannequins whose realistic faces were cast from a young girl who lived in the neighborhood. Wearing white dresses, they rode in a toy car embellished with the Puerto Rican flag, circulating on a miniature elevated highway structure, never stopping and never arriving at "home" (figure 4.16). Around the walls were large video projections of young men washing their faces to the quiet murmuring sound of splashing water. Projected in slow motion, the close-up images of their faces were at once beautiful and unsettling. As their wet hands slid across forehead, nose, and chin, streaks of color were removed, transforming white skin to brown, brown skin to white, revealing new tones underneath. Washing away a layer of color, each boy shook his head as if in disbelief or denial, exposing the simultaneous transparency and opacity of identities, the permanence and impermanence of race as a marker between generations in a family. The young men appearing in the video images were in fact members of UNITAS and may have been surrogate parents themselves.[50] Unraveling the fixity of race categories, *Las Twines* demonstrated the necessary disjunction of identity from race, and race from color. It also countered the naturalized categories that fix complex subjects into the simple black/white binary.

Exploring race discourse in *Las Twines* is also part of the artist's larger project of drawing attention to the history of race relations between dark-skinned and light-skinned Puerto Ricans, both on and off the island, a preoccupation that first appeared in his installation *La Cama*. The postcontact demographics of the island included a significant majority of African slaves and a minority of European colonists (and very few indigenous inhabitants) by the seventeenth century, while antimiscegenation laws were in place by the late eighteenth century.[51] Nevertheless, racial mixing was more the rule than the exception, and like other Caribbean islands, Puerto Rico developed a diverse spectrum of terms for racial difference that was markedly different from the tendency toward the black/white binary operative in the United States. Sociologists have commented on the situation of Puerto Ricans in the United States as existing somewhere between black and white. Scholar Clara E. Rodriguez suggests that Puerto Ricans, racially speaking, belong to both categories, yet ethnically and culturally belong to neither. "It is not just a matter of black and white families within a community," she notes. "It is more often a matter of a Negro-appearing brother and his Anglo-appearing sister attending the same school."[52] In the United States, Puerto Ricans are not always accepted as a culturally distinct, racially integrated group, but are rather perceived and consequently treated as either black or white. Skin color becomes a powerful mode of racial interpellation in the United States in ways that are different from racial interpellation in Puerto Rico.[53] Osorio's critical insight is to link cross-cultural *skin interpellation* to mass production, consumption, and the formation of subjectivity, particularly masculine subjectivity. In these installations, the artist resurfaces and repurposes everyday objects, kitsch, and commodities, to either demonstrate or deflate their ideological valence. Not only artifacts but also people are given a new skin. In a distinctly materialist analysis of the inherent race discourse of contemporary capitalism, Osorio's work invites his audience to consider the deep ties among bodies, objects, and inhabited spaces.

Institutional Displacement

In 1999 Osorio received the MacArthur Foundation "genius" award, and in 2000 the Museo de San Juan, the Museo de Arte Contemporáno de Puerto Rico, and the Museo de Arte de Puerto Rico joined forces to hold a major retrospective of his works. Titled *De Puerta en Puerta/Door to Door,* the exhibition provided a thorough overview of the artist's work to date, including a reinstallation of several large works including *Badge of Honor* and *Scene of the Crime (Whose Crime?).* With the retrospective behind him and the MacArthur in hand, Osorio began a new phase of work that entailed an extended period of research with the Department of Human Services (DHS) in the city of Philadelphia, where he had recently moved with his family. The MacArthur grant facilitated the artist's volunteer status as the first ever artist-in-residence at the DHS. The new director, Alba Martinez, enthusiastically supported Osorio's proposal to explore the relationship between caseworkers and their clients as they navigated a maze of government bureaucracy. To some degree, Osorio was return- ing to a set of concerns from his youth when, before becoming a full-time artist, he worked for the Child Abuse and Abuse Victims Unit for the City of New York. The harsh realities Osorio witnessed during his years serv- ing as a social worker rendered him skeptical of the way human lives are flattened into little more than paperwork in public agencies.

For about one year the artist interviewed and observed a group of DHS caseworkers, as well as higher-level managers and other employees, including security guards. He visited the office on weekends and did everything he could to learn about the culture, the people, and the day- to-day working environment.[54] *Face to Face* (2002) was the end result: a full-scale, meticulously recreated office interior with computers, file cabinets, cubicles, and copy machines installed at the Ronald Feldman Gallery. Amplified details such as family photographs and tourist souve- nirs were piled on the desks, while discarded soda cans and hand-written notes revealed the human side to an otherwise dehumanizing govern- ment agency (figure 4.17).

While many of the artist's previous installations focused on masculinity and masculine spaces, one striking feature of the DHS installation was its clear focus on women (particularly African Americans and Latinas), both

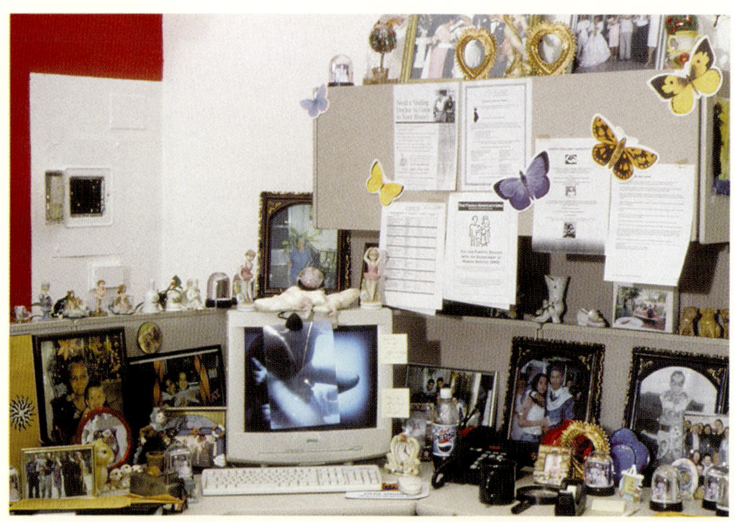

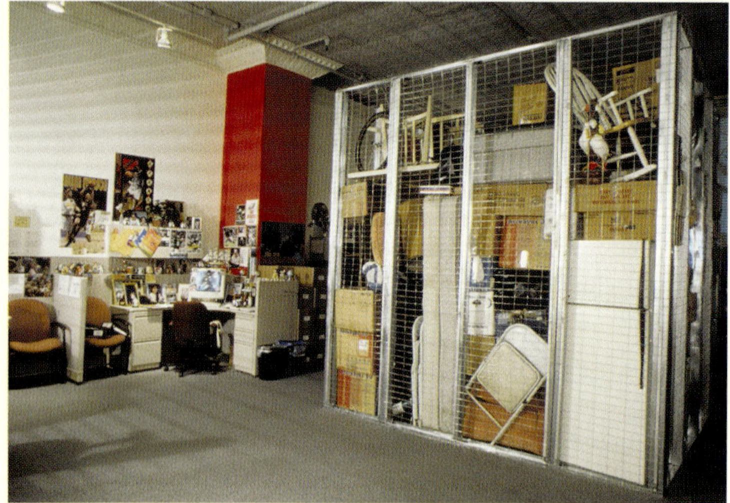

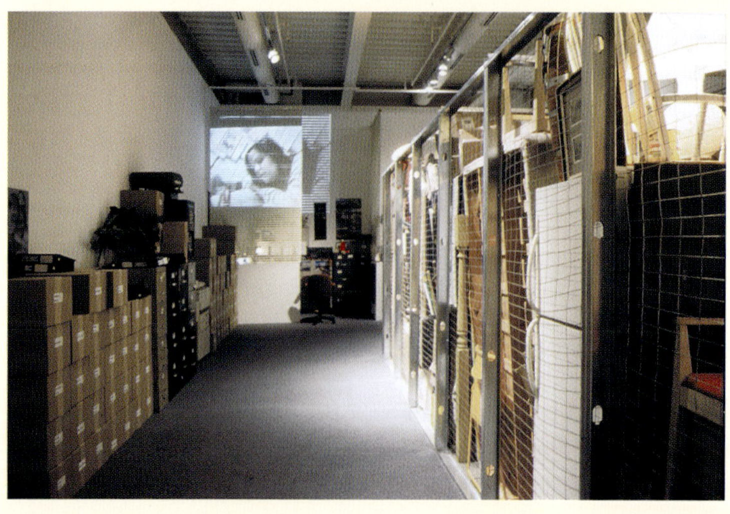

4.17 Pepón Osorio, *Face to Face*, 2002. Detail of desk. Courtesy of the Ronald Feldman Gallery.

4.18, 4.19 Pepón Osorio, *Face to Face*, 2002. Installation views. Courtesy of the Ronald Feldman Gallery.

as caseworkers and as managers—reminding viewers that "social" and "service" work in our contemporary moment is still largely performed by women. Each cubicle was unique, each with its own character, its own memorabilia, its own topography of subjectivity functioning as a bulwark against the anonymity and uniformity of a bleak institutional work life. Committed to creating the least possible disturbance during his residency, Osorio had the photographs and papers he found on the caseworkers' desks carefully copied during their lunch hour, making certain all their possessions were where they left them on their return.[55] In the exhibition, viewers could satisfy a voyeuristic urge by examining every element of these "private" spaces up close. Despite the realism of the installation, it became clear that the artist had embellished even this space by multiplying and exaggerating the details slightly: an overabundance of plastic toys, photographs, calendars, family souvenirs made the cubicles appear somewhat overstuffed. Still, the workers whose desks he had replicated commented on the meticulousness and believability of the recreation as a whole, and the artist claims many of the original cubicles were so filled with decorative items and papers that it was literally difficult to turn around.[56]

In the center of the gallery space, the artist included a large wire-mesh cage, stacked with furniture, boxes, and other household items (figure 4.18). Similar to the caged storage spaces used by the welfare office to store the belongings of families "in transition," the artist's recreation was, in fact, a real collection of property belonging to a homeless family who could not afford to store their belongings anywhere else. Tucked between the many cardboard boxes and well-worn pieces of furniture, a small monitor showed home video clips from the life of a sixteen-year-old boy, personalizing an otherwise anonymous collection of private property. The artist thus transformed the Ronald Feldman Gallery into a temporary site for the support of the larger mission of the DHS office, while devising an innovative function for installation art.

Video projections in corners of the room showed social workers writing intake reports, a glass-enclosed room recreated the soundproof chamber used by the office to interview new clients, and a recorded voice near the storage space recounted the narrative of one person who was facing difficulties trying to find a new place to live (Osorio received permission to tape actual exchanges). Each of these elements allowed the verbal discourse of caseworkers and clients to emerge as the crucial moment of encounter when the system decides how to "place" its subjects. The computer monitors on the desks also displayed an image of a young woman; a large magnifying glass placed over the screen invited close scrutiny, but appeared to distort as much as reveal her character. A large projection on the louvered mini-blinds separating several of the cubicles showed a caseworker laying down her head in exhaustion, over and over again (figure 4.19). The installation suggested that in most social services offices, clients are little more than a file in a stack of folders, while caseworkers are little more than cogs in a machine. Yet it also brought the workers to life, with their personal stories, tragedies, possessions, and family relations, turning a two-dimensional bureaucracy into a three-dimensional landscape of human labor and affect.

The title signifies the kind of face-to-face encounter that is at the heart of many social services activities, from counseling to direct assistance. As it happens, the Ronald Feldman Gallery is situated directly across the street from a Social Security Administration office. Although they are "face-to-face," the buildings are separated by a social chasm that guarantees the population circulating in one space will not cross over to the other; this separation plays itself out not only in economic but in racial terms as well. Osorio's project offers a concrete echo of the concerns of philosopher Emmanuel Levinas in its emphasis on the ethics of encounter and the situation of the subject who is face-to-face with an Other in a material and historical situation of both personal and, in this case, bureaucratic responsibility. Through Osorio's installation, a largely affluent and predominantly white gallery audience is also brought face-to-face with the dilapidated yet lovingly encrusted everyday working environment of social service departments, face-to-face with the tragic consequences of poverty, and perhaps face-to-face with their own privilege.

In 2004 Osorio reinstalled *Face to Face* at the Philadelphia Institute of Contemporary Art as part of a larger exhibition called *Trials and Turbulence: Pepón Osorio, An Artist in Residence at DHS*. In addition to the original installation, two new works were displayed: a simple yet haunting video installation titled *Run, Mikey, Run* (2004), showing a young boy silently running—whether in flight or for fear is unclear—visible behind a wall of industrial-looking wooden pallets, and *Trials and Turbulence* (2004), based on a recreation of the interior of the Philadelphia district Family Court. During his stay at the DHS, Osorio became familiar with several young people who had been in and out of the foster care system, some who had benefited, and others who had suffered through constant transitions and feelings of displacement.

One young African American women, Adrienne Stinson, who goes by the name "Angel," recounted her feelings of loneliness and the loss of privacy that was inevitable when moving from foster home to foster home. Frequently, her only refuge in the house was the bathroom, where she could close the door and sit quietly apart from the rest of her foster family. Osorio asked Adrienne's permission to use her story as the basis for an artwork about the relation between the lives of foster children and the legal system that determines their futures. Leveraging his position as artist-in-residence with a government agency, Osorio also managed to convince a sympathetic judge to loan him used courtroom furniture for the project, including a full bench with witness stand, clerk's desk, wall clock, and seating for the public.[57] Anyone who has been in a courtroom might recognize the determined drabness and stale uniformity of the surroundings, recreated by the artist with striking realism (figure 4.20).

Yet this, like all courtrooms, was only the backdrop for a confrontation of public laws with private life. Adrienne's story inspired the sculptural centerpiece of *Trials and Turbulence*: an elegant, enclosed room made from wood and glass salvaged from a large revolving door. The enclosed oblong structure perched in the middle of the courtroom on large rolling casters was furnished with a full-sized bathtub, sink, and commode, lace curtains, a clothes rack, flowering plants, and other sundry objects that might be found in the bathroom of a teenage girl (figure 4.21). Projected on the undulating shower curtain was a film loop of Adrienne, recounting the story of her own young life: the courtroom where her case was heard, the experience of being shuttled from household to household, her fear of being disciplined, and her regrets about the court's decision to place her in foster care (figure 4.22). Visitors needed to be relatively close to the glass walls of the bathroom to hear her voice if there were other ambient noises in the gallery space. If the space was quiet, however, it was possible to hear Adrienne's story from the height of the judge's bench. Those who ventured up to the judge's seat discovered another video image, this one imbedded in the surface of the desktop, showing a white hand in black robes flipping through a dictionary and resting a finger on certain words as if they were a mystery that needed clarification—words like "home," "care," "safety," "freedom," and "anger." The attentive listener would eventually notice that the video images were perfectly synchronized such that each of the words the judge sought out in the dictionary appeared just at the moment they were spoken in Adrienne's narrative.

The installation was also a memorial to a lost childhood. Adrienne speaks of the past, not the present; her life in foster care had already ended. The courtroom became a projection of her memory, and the dictionary became an allegorical device signifying attempted but missed communication across a social, and perhaps racial, divide. *Trials and Turbulence* made evident the vulnerability of children in a court system and their repeated (revolving door) exposure to the public as if on display. Without heroes or villains, *Trials and Turbulence* demonstrated the well-intentioned efforts of the DHS to end human suffering, and the often misguided or unsuccessful attempts by large government bureaucracies to achieve this goal.

Less explicit, but nevertheless present, were the race politics underlying this endeavor. The courtroom staged legal power in the body of the judge as white and anonymous. Turning the pages of an English-language dictionary, the judge sought clarification in a regulatory text that both

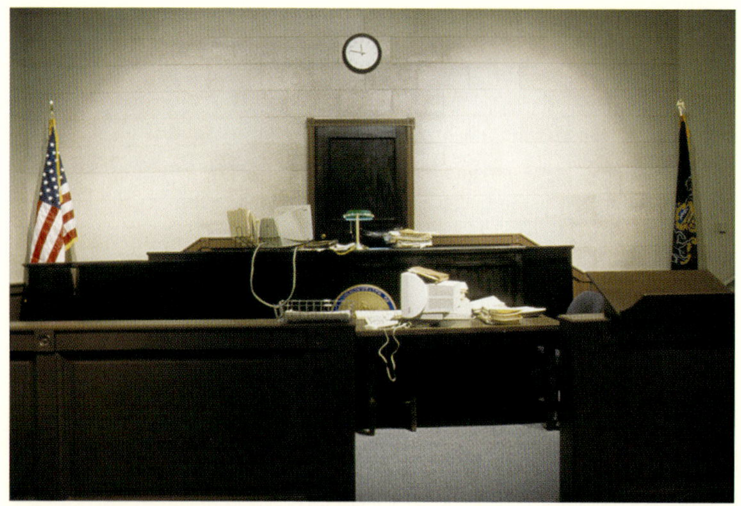

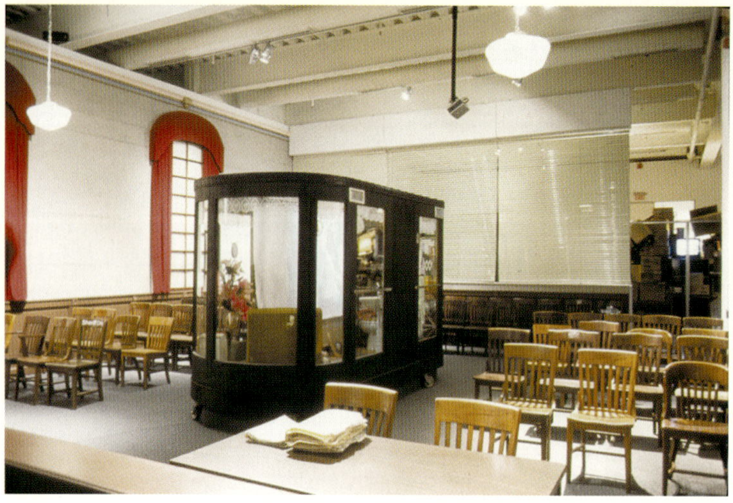

4.20, 4.21 Pepón Osorio, *Trials and Turbulence*, 2004. Installation views. Courtesy of ICA, University of Pennsylvania.

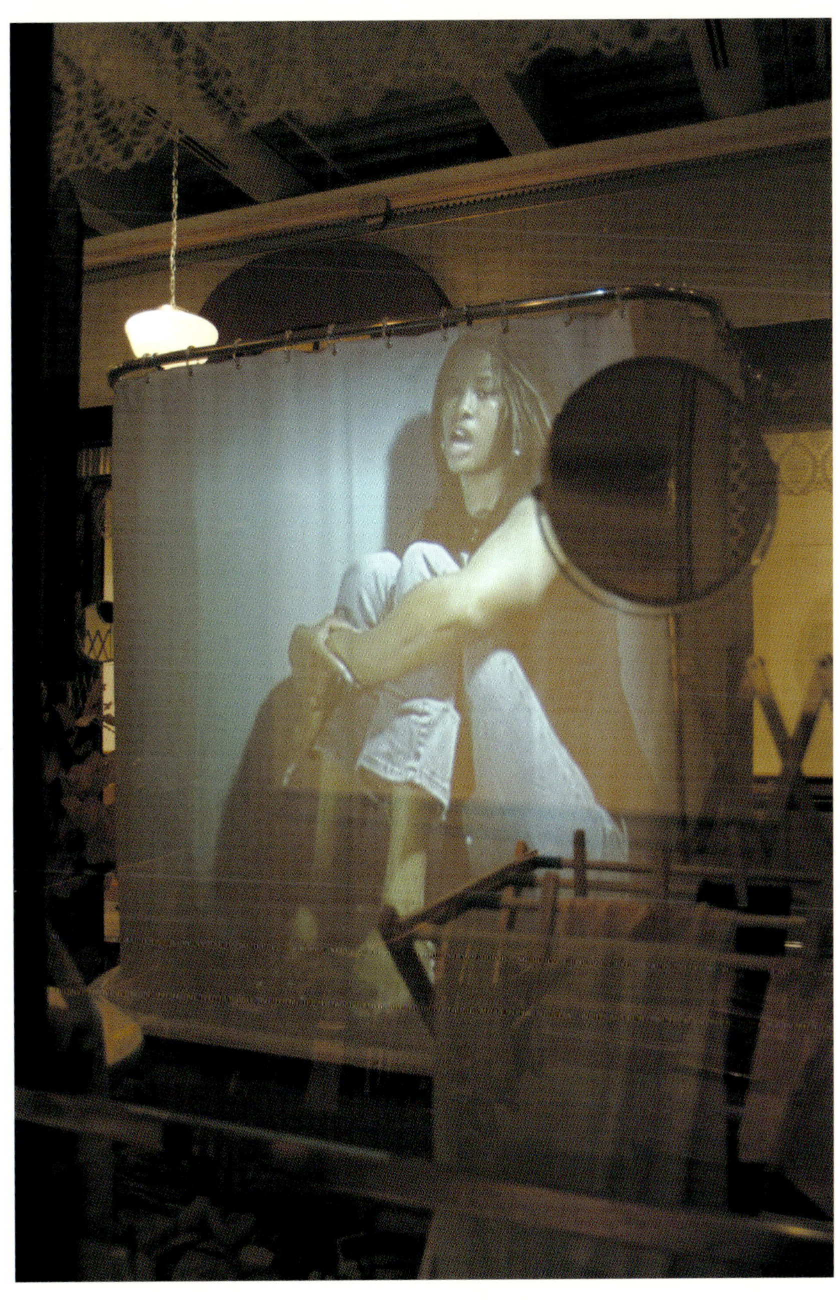

4.22 Pepón Osorio, *Trials and Turbulence*, 2004. Detail of girl's bathroom. Courtesy of ICA, University of Pennsylvania.

explained and ignored the emotional and historical resonance in the words as uttered by Adrienne. What part of "home," "safety," or "freedom" did the judge not understand? For the last two decades, critical race theory scholars have thoughtfully argued that the procedures and the substance of American law are structured to maintain white privilege, and that the legal concept of color "blindness" does not eliminate racism in the law.[58] They also challenge the notion that racism is a matter of individuals confronting individuals and argue instead that racism is best understood as a *systemic* problem of intersecting social webs of domination and subordination.[59] Osorio's installation encapsulates this condition of uneven contact between the relative unilateralism of the law and those who are unwillingly or unwittingly placed within its control.

In all his works, Osorio articulates race as an unstable and unpredictable yet aggressive force that transforms and defines social relations between subjects in their everyday lives. His work is not particularly concerned with historical analyses of race, although occasional historical references do appear in his work; instead, Osorio shows how race discourse and racialized bodies produce (and are produced by) contemporary social systems. All of his works combine the representational registers of portrait and habitat, fusing their spatial tactics in order to suggest the process of subjection that operates through a material politics: a chair becomes a body, a face becomes a threshold. Moving beyond traditional forms of institutional critique, Osorio's most recent art practice might be characterized as *institutional displacement*. Rather than producing a critical response inside an institution, such as a museum, the work recreates institutional spaces elsewhere for a different public to encounter. The installations serve as a kind of portal, as if two distant points were made to intersect or collapse by the folding of space. With this shift in exhibition tactics, Osorio clearly extends the familiar *limit politics* of neighborhoods and art institutions, and redefines the practice of "public art."

As scholar Rosalind Deutsche observes,

> The ideas that art cannot assume the pre-existence of a public but must help produce one and that the public sphere is more a social form than a physical space nullify, to a considerable extent, accepted divisions between public and non-public art. Potentially, any exhibition venue is a public sphere, and conversely, the location of artworks outside privately owned galleries, in parks and plazas, or simply outdoors, hardy guarantees that they will address a public.[60]

Deutsche's comments signal the degree to which the term *public* has widely varied definitions in different disciplines, from the culturally narrow Habermasian concept of the "public sphere" to an urban studies concept of "public agency."[61] In this framework, it is not possible to define "the public" according to general characteristics, but only possible to delineate multiple and plural *publics* that develop and change over time, and that may or may not intersect, spatially or ideologically. This definition allows a distinction to be made between a "museum" public and a "neighborhood" public while recognizing that these are not mutually exclusive categories. It can be useful to retain the geographical inflection of the term, however, because it is also necessary to recognize the spatial, material, and architectural politics that give shape to a given set of social relations. Just as individual subjects have unique spatial imaginaries and limit politics, so do the many publics that inhabit a given spectrum of social spaces.

Osorio's work, both in its production and exhibition, invites an expansion of the limits produced and maintained by these geographically and ideologically defined communities. Part of his method involves a collaborative series of conversations orchestrated with members of a given "public." In some cases, these conversations serve as an inspiration for the work; in other cases, they lead to the hands-on participation of interlocutors in the design and implementation of the final installation.[62] Unlike other community-based art practices that have been productively criticized for their unsuccessful attempts at "community representation," Osorio attempts to produce the condition for the possibility of social contact where previously little existed. A large portion of the artistic *work* is conversational and interactive, taking on a life of its own beyond the exhibition.

Although many of Osorio's projects might be, and in some cases have been, read within the rubric of site-specific art practice—given their attention to both social discourse and strategically located exhibition venues—the notion of "site specificity" has itself become so broadly defined that, as an identifying label, it does little descriptive or conceptual work. His work is closer to what scholar Miwon Kwon might call "collective artistic praxis," as opposed to "community-based art."[63] Osorio's work neither represents nor defines a "community." Conceptually his work is concerned with specific, if abstract, social practices and discourses such as violence, masculinity, racism, and poverty, and their articulation, repetition, and critique. Methodologically his work is materialist, dialogic, and collaborative on the level of conception and production. In this respect, the work is *performative* to the degree that the artist acts as a mediator between different members of a neighborhood, a bureaucratic organization, or even members of a family. Grant Kester's useful theorization of "dialogical aesthetics" might apply well to the work Osorio performs in preparation for an installation. For Kester, a "dialogical aesthetics" relies on local consensual knowledge that is only provisionally binding, grounded at the level of collective interaction, and based on a "reciprocal" rather than "sacrificial" view of social encounter.[64] Listening is as important as speaking for Kester, and for Osorio; both recognize that subjectivities are formed through discourse and mutual exchange rather than existing abstractly a priori.[65] As a result of her work with *Trials and Turbulence,* for example, Adrienne helped draft and lobby for a foster children's bill of rights in the state of Pennsylvania.

Osorio's installations serve as the material evidence, the final result, of a laborious process of social, activist work. At the same time, they are conceived as a meeting place or a site of intersection, as well as a kind of temporary habitation. The artist has commented, "I feel like a squatter, because I'm really interested in the negotiation involved with my presence there, whereas an infiltrator is really quiet, and often no one really discerns his role until he is revealed. But from the very beginning, everybody knows that I am squatting."[66] Osorio's work highlights cultural barriers that limit communication and the circulation of people, wealth, and knowledge. Of course, the kind of meeting that can take place in the context of the exhibition does not necessarily lead to communication, understanding, or mutual respect—even if these are the goals of the artist or funding institution. The outcome of this kind of dialogic work is always unpredictable. Nevertheless, it is undeniable that members of diverse publics (museum curators, neighborhood development officers, shop owners, youth organizers, public librarians, university students, gallery directors, barbers, prison inmates, art collectors, social service workers) cross paths in the production and viewing of the work. Rather than representing a community, Osorio's installations offer an opportunity for unplanned discourse and reciprocity *across* communities.

RENÉE GREEN

GENEALOGIES OF CONTACT

WE ARE BORN INTO a world full of histories that precede us; we are bequeathed its interwoven network of truths and fictions. Deep in the archive, the archivist frequently discovers that the imposed and implied coherence of its order is little more than a temporary fantasy. Artist Renée Green takes up the past as her subject; but unlike the historian who works to impose order on chaos, she works to unwind an ever-expanding network of associations that emerges out of the close examination of what seem to be already finished or forgotten stories. Methodologically, Green is a polymath. Most of her works are installations, but she also publishes books, produces videos, and records sound. Formally spare but semiotically layered, her installations tend to include as much text as image, following a post-conceptual model of linguistic analysis. Nevertheless, techniques and technologies of vision and opticality are a central thematic concern for the artist, who works genealogically to investigate the activity and the history of seeing as it intersects with the politics of colonialism and race discourse, with history and memory.

The term *genealogy* typically signifies a map that charts the descent of ancestry over time. Contemporary use of the term by artists and critical historians largely derives from the distinction Michel Foucault makes between a genealogical approach to the past—which develops a provisional account from fragments of always partial evidence—and a more traditional historical approach to the past that produces overarching explanatory narratives or general characterizations of a historical epoch. Foucault writes that a genealogical model of critical analysis is "no longer to be practiced in the search for formal structures with universal value, but rather as a historical investigation into the events that have led us to constitute ourselves and to recognize ourselves as subjects of what we are doing, thinking, saying. In that sense, this criticism is not transcendental…it is genealogical in its design and archeological in its method."[1] A genealogical approach to the past might be said to follow an interlocking, capillary spread of facts without imposing a necessarily or absolute order on things. For, despite the great efforts of traditional historians, the past is not something that can be kept in order—or kept in place. Green's genealogical method reveals an effort to chart the relations of bodies to systems of power through which they have been marked and dominated. In this respect, she follows Foucault's assertion that "the body is the inscribed surface of events…. Genealogy as an analysis of descent, is thus situated within the articulation of the body and history. Its task is to expose a body totally imprinted by history and the process of history's destruction of the body."[2]

Green offers a vision of the material effects and semiotic residues of race discourse genealogically. Each of her works compiles texts, sounds, or images from different historical periods to provide viewers the opportunity to examine the idea of not only racial difference but also cross-cultural encounter as a set of broad social conditions that are produced, and reproduced, over time. Her work invites us to consider the concrete, sensual materiality of historical subjects (slaves, aristocrats, entrepreneurs, explorers, artists, performers) at the contested sites of their mutual encounter. These subjects are never imagined simply or purely as "individuals" in the humanist tradition, but are shown to be framed, defined, marked, and measured by archives, taxonomies, literatures, and visual images. At the same time, Green pushes against the authoritative order and social power of such archives and taxonomies. Her installations reveal the result of purposeful, careful research, while also introducing an element of the unexpected, whether in chance encounters or unlikely juxtapositions. I agree with scholar Alex Alberro who argues that Green's use of found materials and recycling of images is not inspired by a postmodern turn to appropriation, but is rather a practice of citation where "the quotation marks remain in place, the originary source is self-consciously and respectfully acknowledged and indexed."[3] Of course, Green's choreography of loosely linked citations also runs the risk of appearing overly academic, on the one hand, or undertheorized, on the other. Despite this risk, her experimental works manage to gather disparate signs into new geographical and temporal models, extending or reconfiguring familiar maps of the past.[4]

Seeing Color, Reading Race

The history of U.S. race relations is a history of shifting definitions of the color line tied to the concept of biological inheritance. The one-drop rule,

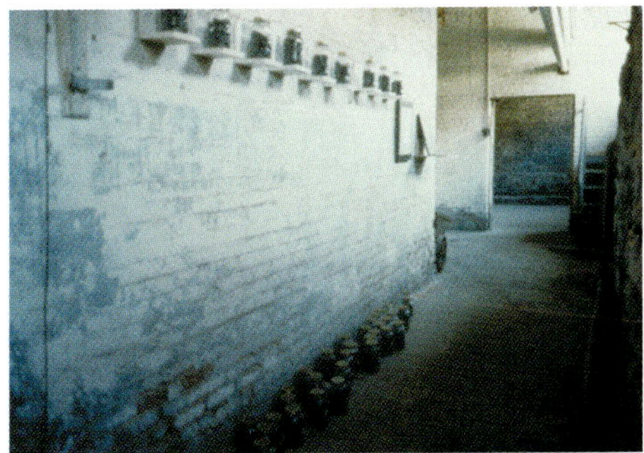

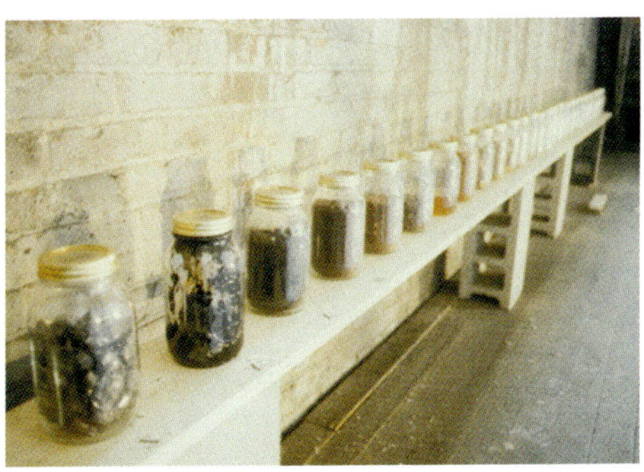

5.1 Renée Green, *Sites of Genealogy*, 1991. Detail of jars with coal. Courtesy of the artist and Free Agent Media.

5.2 Renée Green, *Sites of Genealogy*, 1991. Detail of jars. Courtesy of the artist and Free Agent Media.

adopted into U.S. law for the first time in 1910, decreed that a person with any ancestors or genetic traits outside those of the white or Northern European genetic pool (with as little as "one drop" of nonwhite blood) should be classified as colored.[5] Since that time, despite the intervening years and radical transformations of civil rights law, a direct relation remains between skin color and economic inequality in the United States. How does the optical quality of color, its visual logic, become a kind of absurdly oppressive phenomenon when tied to the power of inheritance? When applied to human bodies, what *work* does the category of color continue to perform, conceptually and pragmatically?

In an early installation at P.S. 1 Museum in Queens, New York, Green employed the architectural features of the site to metaphorically reference the relations of lightness and darkness ascribed to both interior spaces and skin color. The basement and attic were used to stage the absence and presence of luminosity. On the walls of the basement, the words "dusky," "sooty," "dingy," "inky," and "charred" were stamped beneath a row of nine numbered glass jars filled with coal (figure 5.1). On the opposite wall, lines from Richard Wright's 1940 novel, *Native Son*, were printed on plaques. In the attic, thin wooden slats were nailed to the floor and hung like window blinds from the ceiling. Printed on each slat were lines from Harriet Jacobs's *Incidents in the Life of a Slave Girl*, recounting the author's own self-imposed exile in an attic to escape the sexual advances of her master. Glass jars were present here as well, but rather than being ordered by number, they were labeled with the letters of the alphabet. The twenty-six jars contained everyday substances such as soap, marshmallows, or coffee and were arranged by color, from the lightest white to the darkest black (figure 5.2).

Titled *Sites of Genealogy* (1991), the installation created an intersecting narrative, linking the materiality of color imbedded in everyday objects and the logic of racial typologies. In the center of the attic, bounded by a horizontal lattice of white string (which created a boundary for the audience to negotiate, not unlike an orderly version of Marcel Duchamp's *16 Miles of String*), were a desk, chair, typewriter, and monumental stack

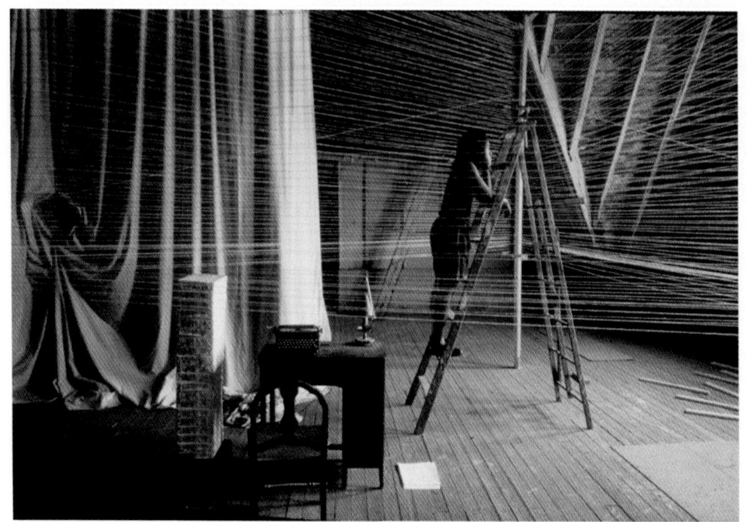

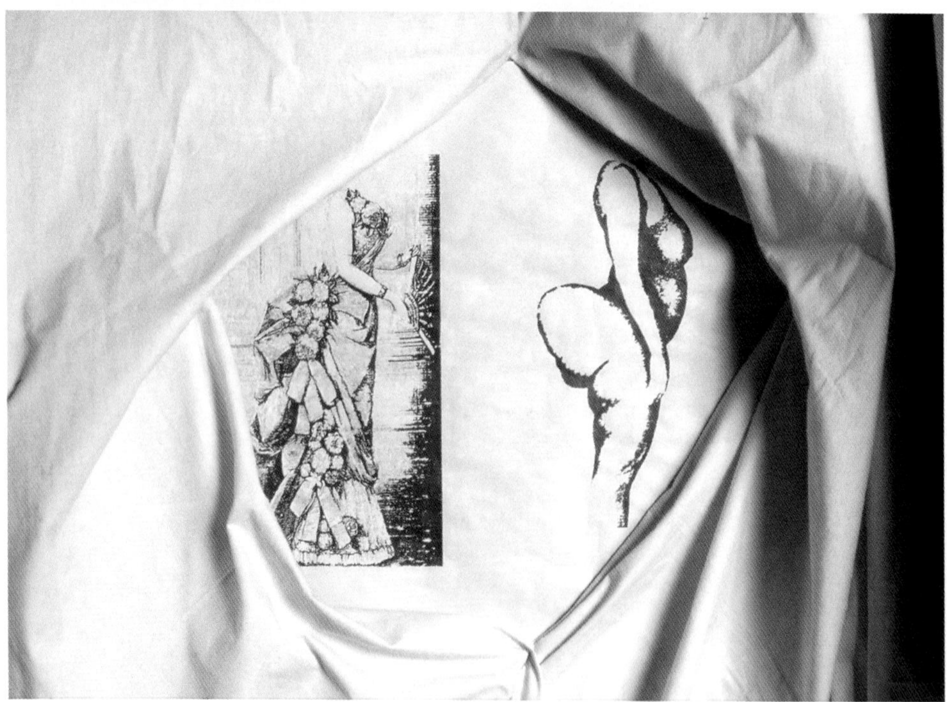

5.3 Renée Green,
Sites of Genealogy,
1991. Installation view
with artist on ladder.
Courtesy of the artist
and Free Agent Media.

5.4 Renée Green,
Sites of Genealogy,
1991. Detail. Courtesy
of the artist and Free
Agent Media.

of typing paper, as well as a tall ladder atop which a telescope perched, offering a view out of the attic window to the horizon beyond (figure 5.3). Whether the bounded space signified intellectual confinement or the possibility of escape was not immediately evident, and it is possible that it suggested both. The objects implied the tools of an explorer or writer, trapped in a confined space, but with a view to a wider world— referencing Wright and Jacobs, perhaps, bounded by a world of narrow racial schemas, rescued metaphorically by the typewriter and telescope. The text on the typewriter recounted daily life in New York, perhaps that of the artist. Hidden behind a curtain in another corner of the attic was a small engraving of Saartje Baartman, a nineteeth-century South African Griqua woman from Cape Town who was called the Hottentot Venus. Considered a curiosity by Europeans because of her large buttocks, she was brought to France by an enterprising doctor who displayed her nude as a public attraction between 1810 and 1816. Fifty years later, European women could be seen wearing elaborate bustles that mimicked (even if they were meant to disguise) exactly the same features that had once been a source of ridicule and fascination—an irony not lost on Green, who paired a Victorian etching depicting this feminine costume next to the image of Baartman (figure 5.4). Even more disturbing than this public ridicule is the fact that Baartman's genitalia, surgically removed from her body at death, were on display in a glass jar in the Musée de l'Homme in Paris until quite recently—for nearly 160 years.[6] If one is aware of this history, it becomes clear that the glass jars both upstairs and downstairs in *Sites of Genealogy* made reference to this kind of display and to those museums that have consistently disguised an ideology of cultural superiority, or even a simple prurient sensationalism, under a cloak of historical preservation and scientific analysis. The arbitrary nature of Green's numbering and alphabetizing taxonomies in relation to the different substances in each jar succinctly articulated the equal absurdity of racial categories based on skin color. The subtle gradations between white and black, and the material references used to make the distinction (i.e., coffee-colored, coal black, etc.) take her engagement with color beyond skin to the implied social and cultural connotations attached to material substances. One can draw clear conceptual parallels to works by artists Lorna Simpson and Carrie Mae Weems produced several years earlier. For example, Simpson's *Twenty Questions (A Sampler)* (1986) reveals the constructed parallels between qualities of objects and qualities of subjects when it depicts a row of identical images of an African American woman and asks, "Is she as pretty as a picture…or clear as crystal…or pure as a lily…or black as coal…or sharp as a razor?" Weems's *Blue Black Boy* from her *Colored People* series (1987) similarly pairs three identical blue-tinted portraits of an African American boy with each word in the title. The image—and by extension the child—might thus be read as blue, as black, or as a boy. The words also suggest that "blue" might refer to the emotional state of the boy or to a kind of blackness. Or, taken as a whole, the title might obliquely reference a "black" version of Thomas Gainsboroughs's famous painting *Blue Boy*. These artists, like Green, invite reflection on the connotations of race imbedded in commonplace objects, linguistic tropes, and artistic traditions.

Green's focus on color as a social discourse comprised of an intricate interdependence of visual and linguistic signs also appeared in *Color I–Color IV* (1990), a series of small-scale wall installations. *Color I*, for example, drew our attention to the names of commercial paints and their imbedded cultural references: Siamese Green, Orient Blush, Painted Lady, Empire Yellow, Indian Ivory, Brazil Brown, Deep Jungle, Mexican Orange, etc. Labeled and mounted as rectangular paint chip samples on a large gray board, the grid of colors looked like a minimalist painting from a previous era (figure 5.5). The installation also included two textual citations on printed sheets of paper that addressed the question of race and color. One was drawn from *The Great Gatsby* by F. Scott Fizgerald in which the character Tom praises a book entitled *The Rise of the Colored Empires* that warns against the contamination of the white race by immigrants: "The idea is if we don't look out the white race will be—will be utterly submerged. It's all scientific stuff; it's been proved."[7] The other text is drawn from Frances Ellen Watkins Harper's book *Lola Leroy: Or Shadows Uplifted* (1892), which narrates the encounter of two doctors who are enjoying each other's company until one reveals to the other that he is "negro": "'The blood of that race is coursing through my veins. I am one of them,' replied Dr. Latimer, proudly raising his head. 'You!' exclaimed Dr. Latrobe, with an air of profound astonishment and crimsoning face." These citations allow for a visual intersection between the literary past and present-day taxonomies of color that continue to pervade the American imaginary.

For *Color II* (1990), the artist arranged seven small glass bottles filled with powdered pigment on individual shelves—each labeled with the day of the week and the color of pigment, for example, Sunday: Red, Monday: Pea-green, Saturday: White, and, in the center, Wednesday: Black (figure 5.6). Using an aesthetic of scientific display, Green again references conceptual art from the 1960s and 1970s such as Robert Morris's glass bottles of fresh air, and the maps and charts produced by Adrian Piper or Douglas Huebler.

On one side of the bottles a text recounted a synesthetic experience of color: "When I think at all definitely about the month of January, the name or word appears to me reddish, whereas April is white, May yellow, the vowel 'i' is always black the letter 'o' white." On the other side, Harper is cited again: "Dr. Latrobe thought he was clear-sighted enough to detect

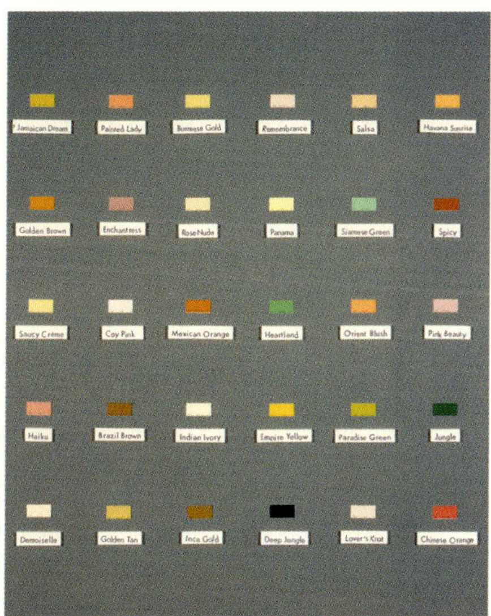

5.5 Renée Green, *Color I,* 1990. Courtesy of the artist and Free Agent Media.

5.6 Renée Green, *Color II,* 1990. Collection of Eileen Harris-Norton and Peter Norton, Santa Monica, CA. Courtesy of the artist and Free Agent Media.

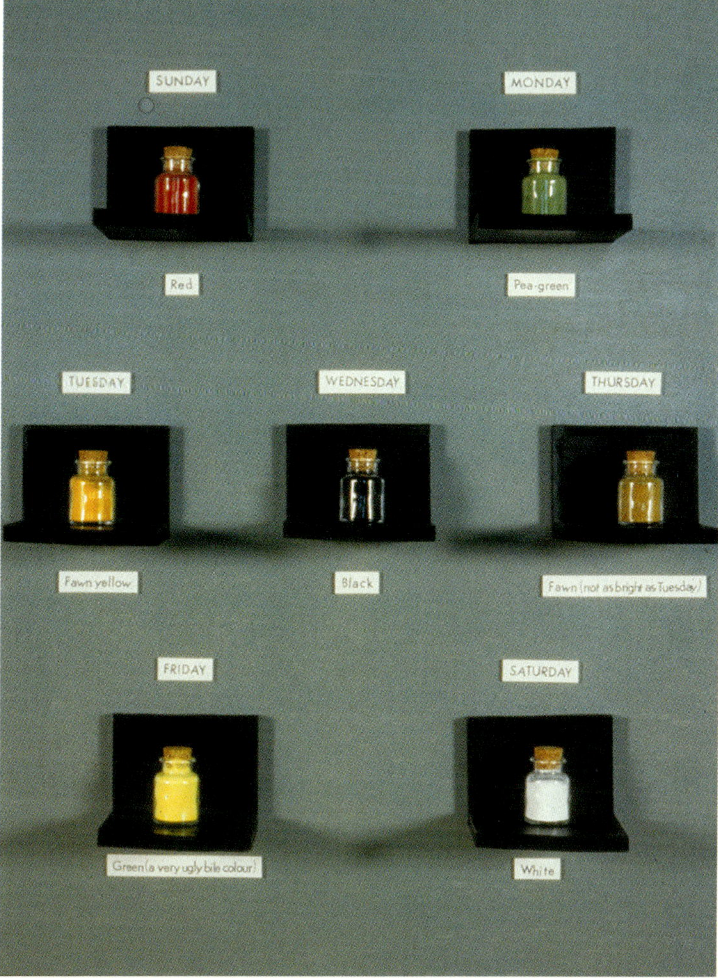

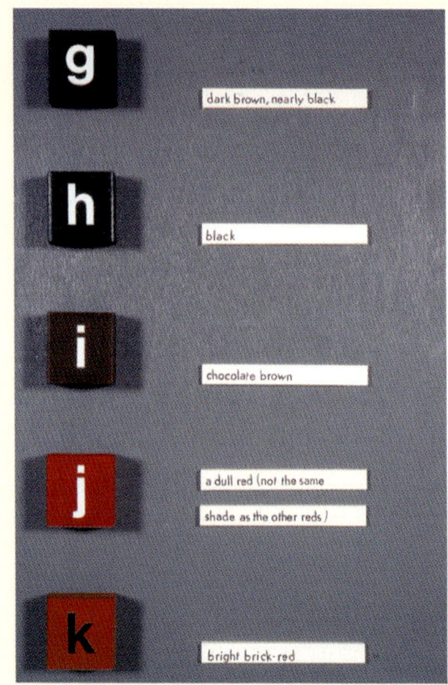

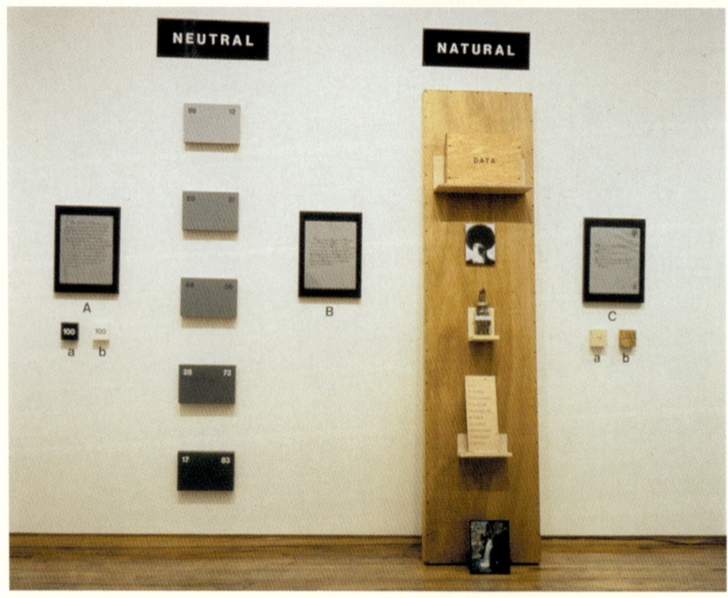

5.7 Renée Green, *Color IV*, 1990. Detail. Collection of Südwestbank LB, Stuttgart. Courtesy of the artist and Free Agent Media.

5.8 Renée Green, *Neutral, Natural*, 1990. Courtesy of the artist and Free Agent Media.

the presence of negro blood when all physical traces had disappeared. But he had associated with Dr. Latimer for several days, and admired his talent, without suspecting for one moment his racial connection. He could not help feeling a sense of vexation at the signal mistake he had made."[8] As framing devices, these texts offer two very different accounts of the strange collision of color and race at the level of everyday perception. Many people have color associations with numbers or letters—the vowel "i" as black, for example—but there seems to be no systematic logic to these psychologically unique associations. For Dr. Latrobe to announce a "clear-sighted" (i.e., visual) perception of race when "all physical traces" of race have disappeared is equally paradoxical or absurd. Yet it clearly reveals the doctor's own unconscious fantasy of seeing even the invisible traces of race.

The same strategy of taxonomy paired with text is at play in *Color IV* (1990), which included two panels with vertical rows of blocks, each painted with a letter of the alphabet and a different color (figure 5.7). Three citations, presented as "cases," were drawn respectively from an ancient text describing the four humors (pure blood, yellow bile, black bile, pale phlegm) and the colored bodies they produce, a medical case (reported in the *Journal of Abnormal Psychology* in the early twentieth century) of a person who divides all words into "dark" and "light" classes, and the nonfiction book *Black Like Me* (1961) in which journalist John Howard Griffin recounts the process of changing his skin color from white to black in order to experience living as a black man in the South. All of Green's taxonomies allow viewers to consider how color and race are mutually dependent on equally inexact categories of vision that nevertheless lead people to make uncompromising value judgments and ultimately construct categories of racial difference. Such chromatic schemas might be of particular interest to an artist whose name is "Green" but who is socially positioned in the United States as black.

In the same vein, Green's installation *Neutral, Natural* (1990) focuses on two terms that are supposed to operate in a safe (neutral) or untainted (natural) zone of color (figure 5.8). Placed against one wall under a large label reading "Neutral" were five panels of gray paint—the "neutral" mix of black and white—hung in a vertical spectrum from lightest to darkest with what appeared to be percentages of each color neatly painted in the corners. Beside these panels, under the heading "Natural," a tall wooden plank displayed a photograph of Angela Davis in her "natural" Afro hairstyle, a glass jar containing leafy plants, a photograph of a mountain landscape with a waterfall, and a list of words that are frequently prefaced by the term *natural* including "law, philosophy, science, resources, selection." Many other natural categories might have been chosen, but this particular list links concepts that have long been tied to race discourse, from evolution (natural selection), to biological determinism (natural law), to economic and political concerns (natural resources). When taken together the list summarizes a history of human thought that has relied on the fact that the term *natural* largely remains an unquestioned concept—itself made to seem natural—despite its varied applications.

Both *Neutral, Natural* and *Color I–IV* are artworks whose primary subjects are words and whose secondary subjects are the objects, concepts, and characteristics to which the words refer. Green's linguistic approach echoes Joseph Kosuth's early conceptual play in *One and Three Chairs* (1965), pointing to the intersection of language, object, and image as systems of representation that approximate an abstract idea.[9] Green's work extends Kosuth's early epistemological experiments (which were largely designed as antiformalist gestures using language as a propositional system) by making explicit reference to the long cultural history of power and privilege that always underlies systems of representation, a cultural history of language that is anything but neutral or natural. In 1978, Roland Barthes gave a series of lectures on the idea of the neutral that begins with the category "color" and proceeds with an analysis of the idea of the "colorless," turning eventually to the idea of the relation of descriptive adjectives to the social position of the subject as "Neutral." The lecture (recently translated by Rosalind Krauss) is prefaced by a personal rumination on his experience buying paint:

> I go out to buy some paints, bottles of pigment; following my taste for the names (golden yellow, sky blue, brilliant green, purple, sun yellow, cartham pink—a rather intense pink), I buy sixteen bottles. In putting them away, I knock one over . . . it was the color called Neutral. . . . Well, I was both punished and disappointed: punished because Neutral splatters and stains (it's a type of dull gray-black); disappointed because Neutral is a color like the others, and for sale (therefore, Neutral is not unmarketable): the unclassifiable is classified. All the more reason for us to go back to discourse which, at least, cannot say what the Neutral is.[10]

Barthes's confessed "taste" for the names of colors echoes Green's *Color I*, but his insights are parallel to Green's insofar as he wants to point to the impossibility of determining the substance or quality of the neutral while also recognizing its persistent, paradoxical identity as nonidentity.

Both Barthes and Green play off the relation of the concept neutral to its material forms of grayness in order precisely to draw out its larger social implications. Barthes writes, "The thought of the Neutral is in fact a borderline thought, on the edge of language, on the edge of color, since it's about thinking the non-language, the non-color (but not the absence of color, transparency); language and the coded practices that flow from it always reframe the Neutral as a color."[11] For Barthes the neutral is not really the color gray so much as it is neither black nor white. At the same time the conceptual "safety" of this position that refuses to be marked is belied by the fact of its dependence on the opposing terms (black/white) that define it. Color becomes its own social *adjective* that is imposed from the outside, disrupting the neutrality of the subject.

Green's combined materialist/linguistic strategy alludes to conceptual art in ways that are familiar to an art-world audience, while bringing an unspoken genealogy of color (and noncolor) into view. Additionally, an absent but implied body appears in each of these works. Whether and how one is socially positioned *in relation to* color is made evident in the hegemony of words and the taxonomy—or taxidermy—of colors that target the skin of the racialized body as "black" or "white" or "red" or "yellow" but not "neutral."[12] In Green's works, Fanon's concept of "epidermalization" can apply to the fetishization of the body as spectacle, even when the body or its image is absent from the work; the pigments and artifacts stand in for this body and are, in some sense, a distillation of this body-as-fetish reduced to a set of nearly abstract signifiers that allow for the emergence of a "raced" body as a visual spectacle. In addition to interrogating the image-concept of the "colored" body, Green recreates the scenes of its appearance.

This is the case with Green's installation *Seen* (1990), which was designed to place the viewer in the position of being both the subject and the object of a voyeuristic gaze (figure 5.9). On the bare surface of a raised wooden platform with steps on two sides and a wooden railing all around, Green printed historical accounts of the staged appearances of Baartman (mentioned earlier) and the popular African American performer Josephine Baker who was a nightclub sensation in Europe in the 1920s and 1930s. The texts emphasized the racial and sexual features of the two women's bodies, revealing a lasciviousness in the minds of the writers. Small images of both women could be found partially concealed behind a curtain, but in order to see them, viewers of Green's installation were required to climb the platform where they, too, would be on display. To read the historical accounts written on the floor, viewers were required to pace back and forth in the light of a bright spotlight. Placed on this temporary stage—built with the crude construction reminiscent of a platform for the sale of slaves—viewers saw their own silhouettes projected clearly on a white screen behind. In the persistent glare of the light, it was difficult not to be aware of having one's body on display while extracting information from the writing on the ground. This experience was magnified by the fact that a hole cut in the floor revealed two blue eyes—joke spectacles—peering up from below (figure 5.10). A sound recording of Baker repeatedly singing *"Voulez-vous de la canne?"* (Would you like some sugar cane?) implied the sexual delectation of women's bodies, black women's bodies in particular, who appeared on the stage. As the title implied, the work was about vision; spectacle and spectator were implicated in a nonmutual relation of the gaze.

Seen can certainly be read as a critical feminist response to the history of the black female body on display, subject to a white—especially white male—gaze; but it is also about the visual technology of race discourse. The wooden platform was crude and rough, the white screen smooth and cinematic, the projected silhouettes black and gray. While the experience of racial objectification could never be replicated by the installation, the artist provided the phenomenological conditions for the *mechanism* of this objectification. Compressed into a single installation, what appear to be diverse references to the auction block, the peep show, the movie screen, and the bright lights of the theater suggested a historical span of display technologies and their intersecting practices of viewing that have worked in concert, especially in Europe and the United States, to define the raced female body as a body that *must be seen.*

In parallel with, but in contrast to, other artworks of the late 1980s and early 1990s, such as James Luna's *The Artifact Piece* or Coco Fusco and Guillermo Gomez-Peña's *Two Undiscovered Amerindians...*, that recreated the historical conditions of viewing racial difference in museums and sideshows, Green did not use her own body as an object of display; even the images of Baartman and Baker were presented in a modest, partially covered state that required unveiling to view. Moreover, the minimal nature of the work, its bare, almost colorless construction in the blank space of the gallery was decidedly stark and visually frugal. Compared to the sensational and seductive quality of both *The Artifact Piece* and *Two Undiscovered Amerindians...*, Green's minimalism might be read as a kind of failure—a failure of aesthetic or entertainment value—but may also signal a perverse success. In *Seen,* visual pleasure is denied rather than reproduced at the "scene" where it has been historically sought out. Green offers very little to see, in fact, except a transient shadow play that provides a potentially self-reflective exercise for visitors who, in the extended space of the art gallery, become implicated in a longer history of seeing and visual pleasure.

If architectural spaces can be conceived as materialized ideological forms, then they are also subject to practices of inheritance. Green linked these two concerns—architecture and inheritance—in *Bequest* (1991), installed at the Worcester Museum of Art. Reflecting on the museum's past, the artist decided to present two histories: a family genealogy of the museum's founder, Stephen Salisbury III, and a genealogy of New England through the literary texts of Nathaniel Hawthorne, Herman Melville, Edgar Allen Poe, and W. E. B. DuBois. In an interview, Green commented, "The idea of a family genealogy can be expanded to include that of a nation, the United States, with a particular focus on New England. What

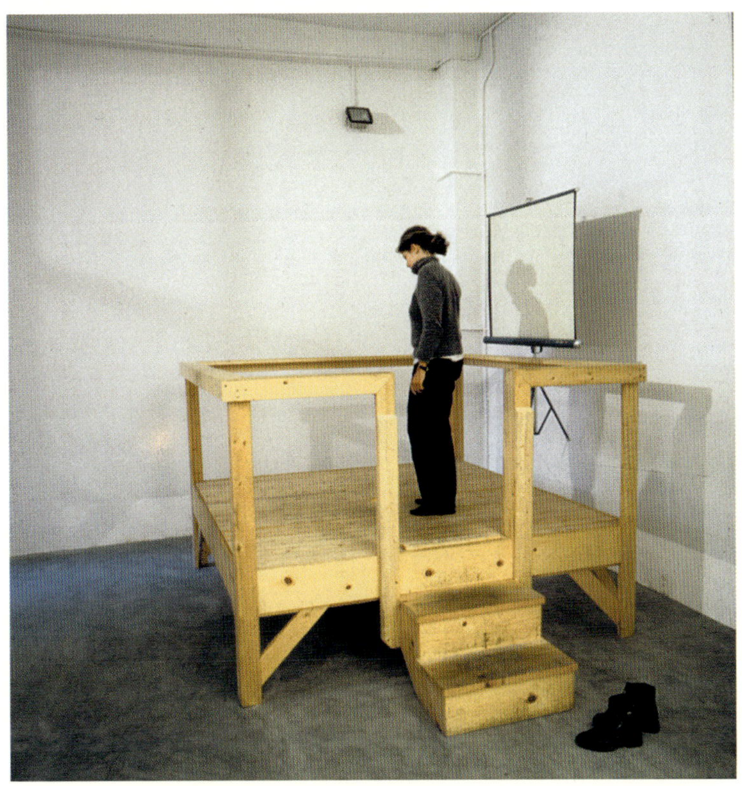

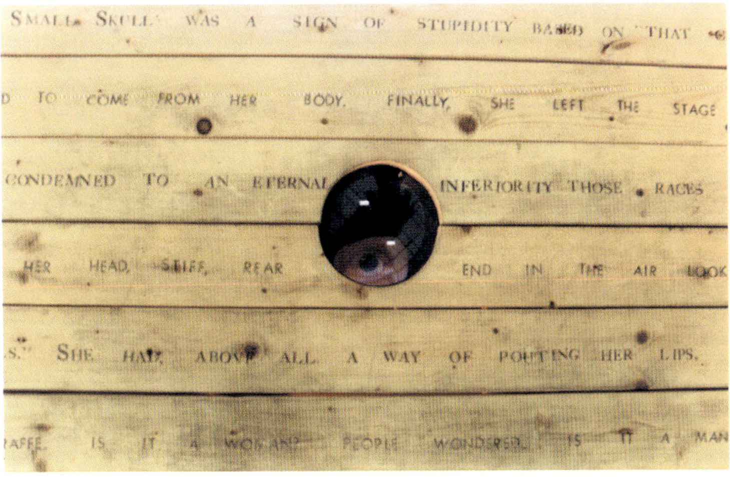

5.9 Renée Green, *Seen,* 1990. Installation view with platform. Courtesy of the artist and Free Agent Media.

5.10 Renée Green, *Seen,* 1990. Detail of spectacles. Courtesy of the artist, Free Agent Media, and Galleria Emi Fontana, Milan.

5.11 Renée Green, *Bequest*, 1991. Entrance. Courtesy of the artist and Free Agent Media.

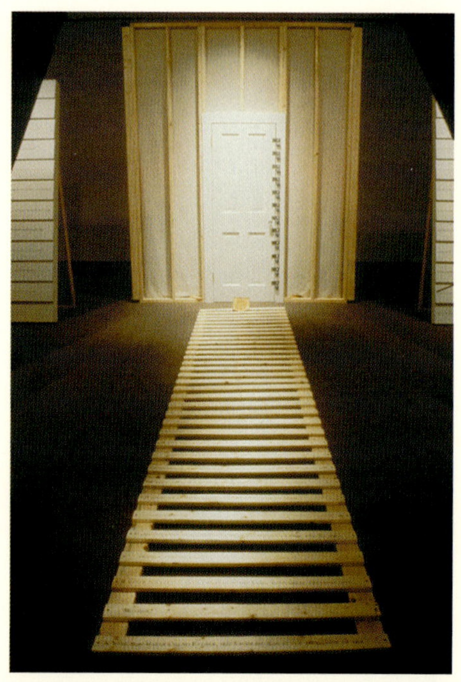

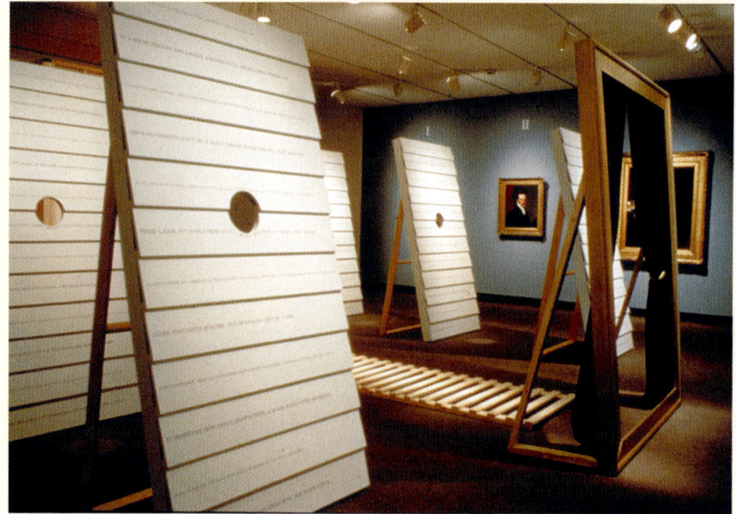

5.12 Renée Green, *Bequest*, 1991. Detail of clapboard panels. Courtesy of the artist and Free Agent Media.

5.13 Renée Green, *Bequest*, 1991. Detail of display case with heirlooms. Courtesy of the artist and Free Agent Media.

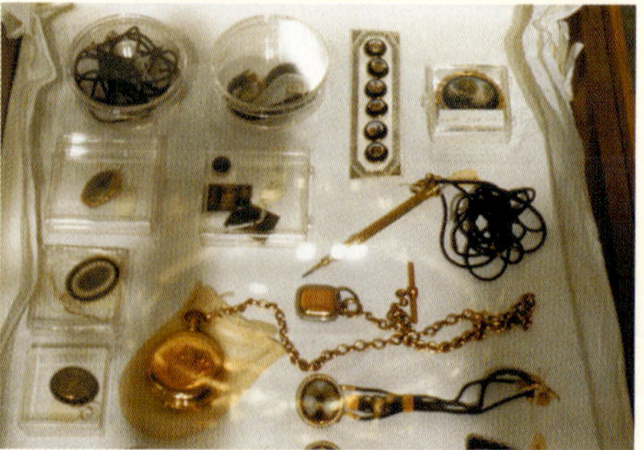

characteristics form a nation and culture? What sorts of stories are told about a nation, and which stories are left out?"[13] To enter the space of the installation, visitors walked through a golden frame hung with black velvet curtains. Wooden slats, like train tracks or a boardwalk, led from this main entrance to a white door at the far end, fastened with a vertical row of twelve padlocks, each bearing the brand name "Master" (figure 5.11). Flanking the center pathway were two rows of artificial clapboard walls, painted white, each about eight feet high and four feet wide. In the center of each wall a circular hole had been cut out, making it possible to see from one to the next, giving the strange impression of a Puritan stockade. Each clapboard panel was carefully stamped with a fragment of text by one of the New England authors (figure 5.12). The quoted passages continued on every other line so that an intertextual reading was invited. Each selection drew from passages that mention both blackness and whiteness ("The raven by its blackness represents the prince of darkness," "It was the whiteness of the whale that above all things appalled me") or citations that revealed moments of coming to consciousness about racial difference ("Then it dawned upon me with a certain suddenness that I was different").[14] By selecting citations that emphasized colors, the artist also drew attention to the colors in the room: white clapboard, gold frame, black curtains, and colonial blue walls.

The installation also emphasized the historical intersection of cultural institutions, such as museums, with the wealthy elite of the United States. Portraits of Salisbury's male ancestors were hung on the walls surrounding the installation, like a group of witnesses, and a small glass case containing family heirlooms such as gold watches and miniature portraits stood in one corner (figure 5.13). Stephen Salisbury III was the son of a very wealthy businessman; he was educated at Harvard, bought his way out of military service in the civil war, became enamored with archeology after a trip to the Yucatán Peninsula in 1862, served one term in the Massachusetts Senate, was president of the Worcester National Bank, and directed the Worcester & Nashua Railroad. He was a trustee of the Worcester City Hospital and Worcester Polytechnic Institute. As a philanthropist, he considered the establishment of the Worcester Art Museum in 1896 to be one of his greatest achievements.[15] Green did not include these biographical details in the installation, but it was made clear to visitors that Salisbury was the museum's founder and that his generous bequest supplied its collections. The installation was not intended as a critique of Salisbury, the man; rather, it pointed to the relations of economic power in one New England community that made it possible for a person of wealth to wield significant influence.

Green's early installations engage the space of the subject and the space of *subjection* within the framework of U.S. and European history. The legacy of African Americans—who worked in the boiler room, stood on the auction block, or performed on stage; who were prevented from bequeathing the vast wealth produced by their labor to their own children; who were locked out of the "master's houses" of literature or national identity—is a corporeal legacy that Green articulates through spatial metaphors.[16] Like the other artists discussed in this book, Green produces a pseudomimetic installation that positions the body of the viewer in an imaginary space that is both voluntarily and involuntarily participatory. Examining genealogies of inheritance, the artist examines the historical conditions and logic of racist practices, while also suggesting the ways these practices continue to encroach on the present.

Genealogical Tours

The professor said, "Such a tight little fence around us: caste and class, race and place, a whole list. And some of it associated with old, deep things—so familiar and so secure around us—but we, we of the mind, we can do without; we don't always want to, but we can go stand in the cold and the wind and see for ourselves."

—Maria Dermoût, cited in Renée Green,
After the Ten Thousand Things

While Foucault's notion of genealogy is important for its critique of an unequivocal "will to truth," it can lose sight of the *agency* of the individual. While recognizing, with Foucault, that history has participated in the destruction of the body, Green nevertheless seems to retain the notion that individual subjects have the power or agency to respond to the circumstances of this "imprinting." For this reason, Cornel West's theory of a "genealogical materialist analysis" offers an apt description not only of Green's practice but also that of the other artists discussed in this book. For West, a genealogical materialist analysis relies upon a Marxist materialist specificity, but replaces Marx's teleological and rationalist historical model with a Nietzschean concept of genealogy. He writes, "I hold that many social practices, such as racism, are best understood and explained not only or primarily by locating them within modes of production, but also by situating them within the cultural traditions of civilizations."[17] For West, a genealogical materialist analysis consists of three parts: a genealogical inquiry into the discursive conditions for the possibility and logic of racist practices; a microinstitutional (or localized) analysis of the mechanisms that promote and contest these practices and logics in everyday life, including the ways in which self-images and self-identities are shaped; and a macrostructural approach that addresses modes of overdetermined class exploitation, state repression, and bureaucratic domination.[18] Green's practice can be seen as a genealogical materialist practice on both macro- and microinstitutional levels. She works to demystify what might be considered familiar mythologies of race and their perpetuation through cultural institutions and taxonomies.

Standing on the deck of a ship bound for Ceuta, a port town on the northwest coast of Morocco, Green pursued the opacity of the past across the deep water and cold wind of the present. Part of the multiphase art project *Tracing Lusitania,* Green's voyage was an etymological and philosophical journey. Green began *Tracing Lusitania* by examining maps, decorative objects, botanical gardens, museums, architecture, and literary and classificatory texts that she found in Lisbon. By charting the emergence of cultural contact between Europeans and Africans, the artist hoped to "detect the intricate workings of those ideologies" which had been born in the colonial period and were still, to some degree, in effect.[19] Instead of working to examine the confines of inherited or fixed concepts of race and their naturalization in the rituals of performance or museum display, Green began to examine the translocation of people, language, and things. She embarked at Lisbon for the short trip to the first African site of conquest by the Portuguese, a busy contemporary port, as well as a nearly forgotten site in the European imaginary. Like any location of origin, Ceuta anchors a more expansive narrative of colonial imperialism and maritime power in a legacy of sea trade and human bondage that began for the Portuguese in 1415. Lusitani was the name given by the Celts to the region of the Iberian Peninsula that is now part of Portugal. The Romans conquered the area, giving it the name Lusitania, but eventually lost the territory to the Moors from North Africa in the fifth century. Eight centuries later, the Spanish pushed the Moors out of the region and a Portuguese monarchy and dynastic political system were established. Becoming one of the more powerful seafaring nations, the Portuguese charted a sea route to India, colonized Brazilian territories in the Americas and fought with the Dutch for control of the spice trade as far away as the Molucca Islands in Indonesia, where they gained control in 1511. *Tracing Lusitania* is a fragmentary account of this history, and of the Portuguese colonial period that lasted until 1974 when it ceded control of its African and Indonesian territories, embattled East Timor among them. The name Lusitania, better known to some as that of the ill-fated British passenger ship sunk by German U-boats during World War I, reappeared in 1992 as the *Lusitania Express,* a Portuguese ship sailing on a peace mission to protest the Indonesian government's military efforts to gain control of East Timor. Both the name Lusitania and the region it designates became evidentiary artifacts in a video project in which the artist traced the legacy of colonial encounter, international commerce, and uneven relations of power that continue to this day. In a self-referential way, *Tracing Lusitania* revealed how the artist's own desire for travel and exploration mirrored colonial desires.

Similarly, in *Idyll Pursuits* (1991), an installation exhibited in Caracas, Venezuela, Green examined fantasies about land and landscape central to a nineteenth-century colonization of the Americas and to the visual culture of heroic landscape painting that perpetuated the myth of undiscovered, unspoiled, and uncivilized nature. Taking American *plein air* painters as her subject, the artist constructed an installation with a freestanding easel as a centerpiece, evoking, in a stylized way, the scene of the explorer artist. Above the easel a small reproduction of snow-capped mountains was flagged with the words "El Dorado." The canvas on the easel depicted not a majestic scene of breathtaking beauty, but instead the travel itinerary of George Catlin, a nineteenth-century lawyer turned painter, who followed the trail of the Lewis and Clark expedition to record the "manners and customs" of Native Americans. His first South American expedition from 1852–1855 took him through Caracas, down the Amazon River, and eventually back through the Yucatán. Written in large letters on a blank canvas, the narrative serves as a substitute for the images he might have painted. Catlin's written itinerary extended onto the painter's palette where another travel itinerary, for the Hudson River School painter Frederic Edwin Church, begins. Church, whose travels in South America included sailing to Columbia and taking a river steamer up the Rio Magdalena, was renowned for his majestic and idyllic depictions of the natural landscape. In writing about the Hudson River School, Arthur C. Danto remarks of the paintings, "They constitute the American wing of the Protestant ethic given cultural expression. They radiate self-congratulation and an almost cosmic complacency."[20] In addition to providing a vision of unconquered possibility for a U.S. manifest destiny, Church was also carrying out a common, masculine fantasy of the time—the foreign expedition. The impact of this legacy was suggested by Green's inclusion of references to nineteenth-century literature that glorified the life of explorers, such as *Frank Redcliffe: A Story of Travel and Adventure in the Forests of Venezuela—A Book for Boys* (1883) by Achilles Daunt that offered illustrated stories of intrepid explorers who faced "untamed wilderness" and its people. Green reproduced the engraved illustrations from Daunt's book and placed them on the ground in a semicircle surrounding the easel (figure 5.14).

While clearly critical of the colonial history whose ideology of acquisition and penetration was supported, if sometimes bemoaned, by painters like Catlin and Church, *Idyll Pursuits* also points to the condition of contemporary artists who travel. Green included in the installation a small photograph of herself in Venezuela. Viewers were left to wonder what the artist's relationship was to pleasure and discovery abroad. As a contemporary version of the artist-traveler, was Green any less complicit in the production of imaginary, idyllic myths about Venezuela than were Catlin and Church?

As a genealogical materialist, Green tends to follow up on what appear to be random clues or curiosities with a process of diligent research that then becomes elaborated into a more focused study. This is the case with

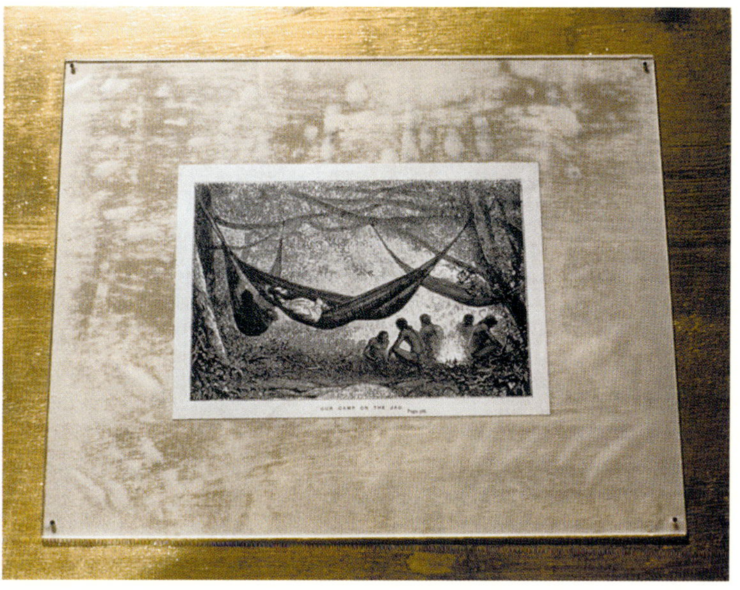

5.14 Renée Green, *Idyll Pursuits*, 1991. Detail of book page. Courtesy of the artist, Free Agent Media, and Galleria Emi Fontana, Milan.

her exploration of the history of the village of Clisson, France. Perched on the edge of the Loire River in an agricultural valley not far from the city of Nantes, Clisson boasts a long history. Its promotional materials read: "Two different époques meet at Clisson, the dark and violent Middle Ages, and the romantic 19th century Italian architecture. A very agreeable town, surprising, and inspiring. It makes you dreamy."[21] Commissioned to produce a contemporary art project for the site by F.R.A.C. Huitièmes Ateliers Internationaux des Pays de la Loire, Green began to look beyond the dream to the historical period *between* the Middle Ages and the nineteenth century to see what she might find. She brought with her, as a kind of talisman, a scrap of toile fabric found in New York depicting pastoral scenes of Europe. In the city of Nantes, she writes,

> I walked around the Jardin des Plantes where plant species from around the world were gathered, and along the port to the Jules Verne Museum. I began to notice details here and there, an African head over a doorway, a restaurant called L'Esclave, an Afro-Antilles hairdresser. I began asking local people to tell me what they knew of the city's history. I also mentioned the fabric, which was referred to as *indienne,* and which was produced during the eighteenth century in that region.[22]

Intrigued by the transatlantic slave trade that passed through Nantes, the artist explored further, discovering that the two economies of textile manufacture and slave trade were tightly linked. The wild popularity of the *toiles indiennes*—so-called because of their origin in Patnas, Madras, and other Indian cities—motivated French merchants to copy them and eventually to place a legal ban on their import from other countries. The aristocratic classes who, in a frenzy over their bright colors and tropical scenes, used the fabrics for elaborate dresses, upholstery, and curtains, eventually demanded that the ban be lifted. Nevertheless, significant profit from the sale of the locally produced fabric was used to support the purchase of slaves who were shipped to the American colonies, where they were sold, in turn, for chocolate, rum, sugar, or the raw cotton that eventually would be woven anew into *toile indienne.*

This web of historical economic transactions is charted in Green's installation *Mise-en-scène* (1992) in which the artist implicates the history of French textile production in the history of the African slave trade. In a room furnished with eighteenth-century armchairs upholstered in *toile indienne,* the artist arranged an equilateral triangle of three open file boxes filled with cards, each printed with either the names of slave ships, or African languages, or dates of slave trade in France (figure 5.15). A black box in the center labeled "Trésor Caché" (hidden treasure) was filled with photographs of the fleur-de-lis stamped on bare skin (figure 5.16). (The fleur-de-lis was used to brand the flesh of newly arrived Africans to iden-

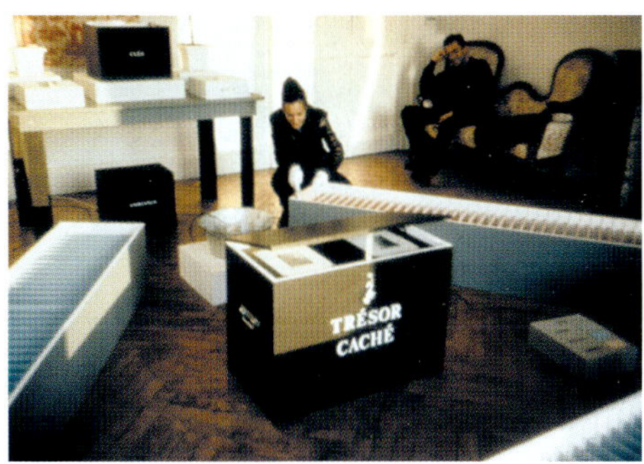 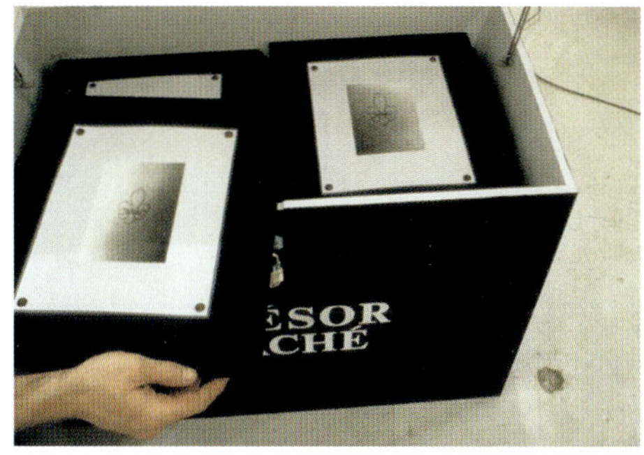

5.15 Renée Green, *Mise-en-scène*, 1992. Installation view. Courtesy of the artist and Free Agent Media.

5.16 Renée Green, *Mise-en-scène*, 1992. Detail of treasure chest. Courtesy of the artist and Free Agent Media.

tify them as property in the West Indies—the primary site of trade with the city of Nantes.) Treating the installation as itself a map, the artist provided two keys: a color-coded key and a photographic key, the latter consisting of contemporary images of Nantes and Clisson in a box labeled "Clés" (keys). Some of the photographs pictured the "clues" the artist had found during her walks in the city that precipitated her desire to unravel the complex local history of international trade. On a table framed by a hanging *toile indienne* were magnifying glasses and white gloves labeled "Outils" (tools). Utensils of observation and archival analysis, the magnifying glasses seemed to refer to the gaze of both the genealogist (i.e., Green) and the slave trader. In an interview the artist stated, "One of the things I'm interested in is how explorers, conquistadors, first arrived at a territory, saw it—and how they connected seeing the land with owning it."[23] Literally translated, the title *Mise-en-scène* means "placed in the scene," implying a set of practices that form a logic of vision and display, as well as referring to the more conventional translation of the term: a theatrical production. In Green's piece, the title appears to have several references, from the capitalist production that underlies the history of the port town, to the pretty floral scenes depicted on the textiles, to the historical incorporation of the black body, to the artist's staged "scene" where these histories intersect. Green's vision of Clisson's past was not a chamber-of-commerce dream but a haunted *mise-en-scène* of those interdependencies of wealth and violence that operated on a grand scale until well into the nineteenth century.[24]

After installing *Mise-en-scène,* Green decided to continue her work with the *toile indienne* at the Fabric Workshop in Philadelphia, designing her own commemorative pattern that included pastoral scenes of French aristocracy along with eighteenth-century found images depicting a slave in chains, a Frenchman hanged during the Haitian Revolution, and a Senegalese nun (figure 5.17).[25] More accurately depicting the historical context framing the production of *toile indienne,* in marked contrast to the pastoral visions of tropical paradise that graced the original fabric, these stark images were camouflaged as sumptuous décor in *Taste Venue* (1994), an environment of curtains, pillow covers, upholstered furni-

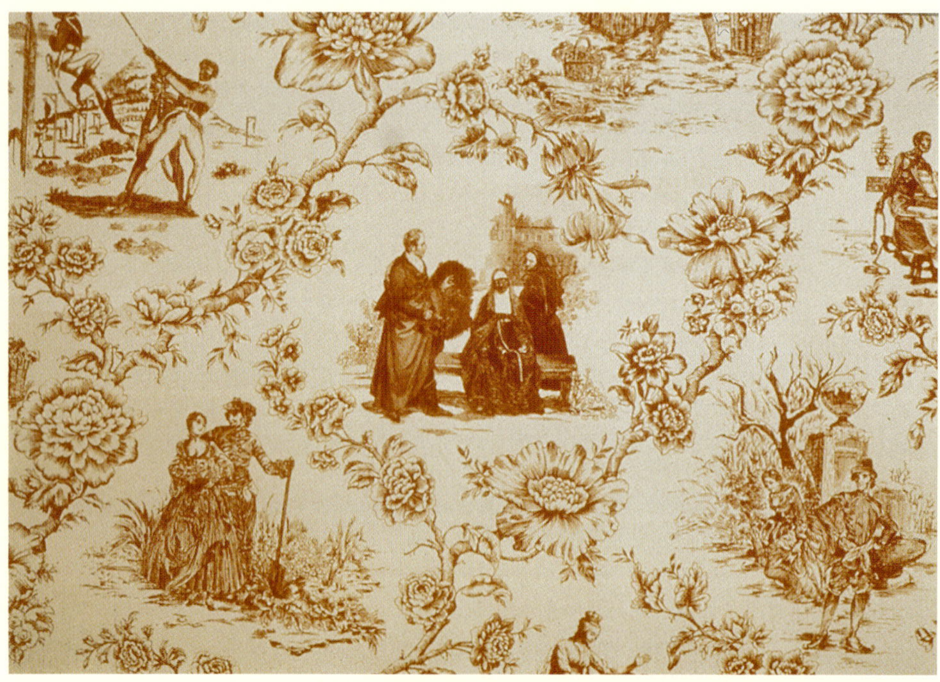

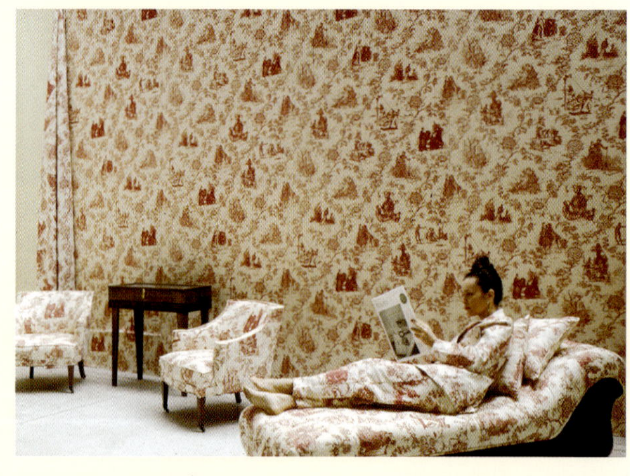

5.17 Renée Green,
Taste Venue, 1994.
Detail of toile. Cour-
tesy of the artist and
Free Agent Media.

5.18 Renée Green,
Taste Venue, 1994.
Installation view with
Pat Hearn on chaise.
Courtesy of the artist
and Free Agent Media.

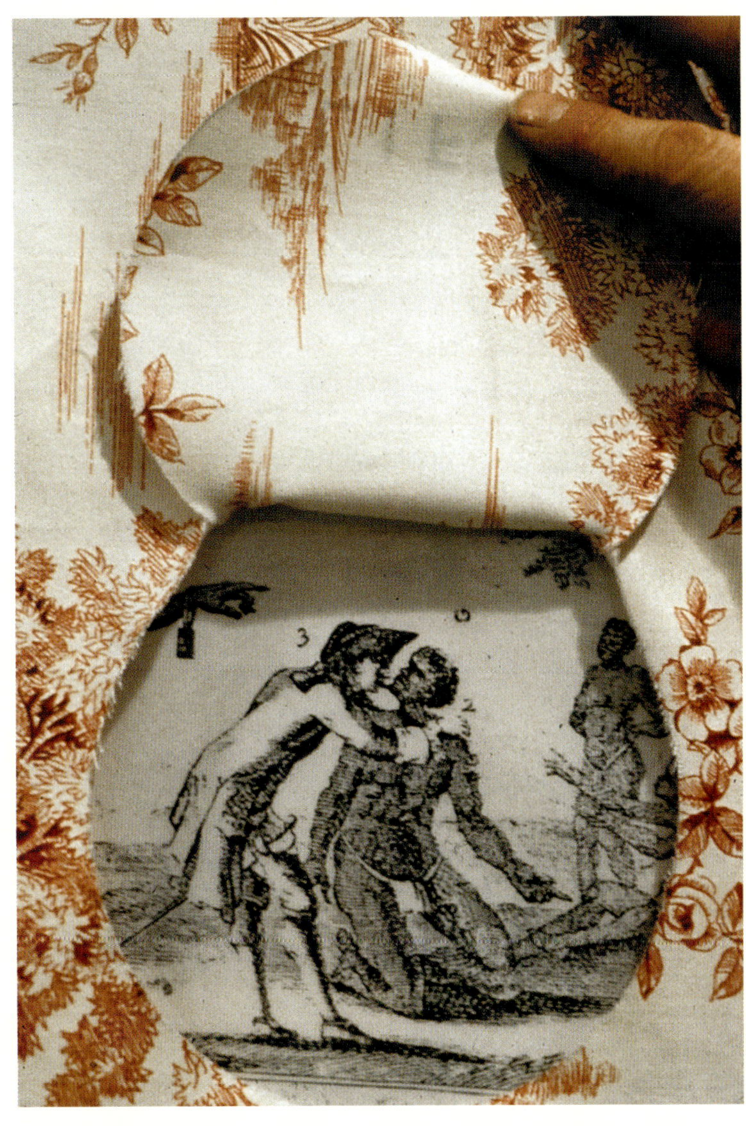

5.19 Renée Green, *Taste Venue*, 1994. Detail of man licking slave. Courtesy of the artist and Free Agent Media.

ture, and clothing staged at the Pat Hearn Gallery in New York (figure 5.18). Against one wall of the installation, under a cutaway flap of fabric, Green placed an engraved image of a slave owner licking the face of a slave, tasting his sweat in order to determine his health and therefore his monetary value (figure 5.19). Collapsing two notions of taste—the aesthetics of aristocratic décor and the nearly cannibalistic gesture of the slave trader—Green's installation also brought to mind the origin and etymology of the notion of taste as the primary eighteenth-century discourse on beauty in the arts.

As an investigator of history, unconstrained by the narrative or geographical imperatives of the academician, Green, like Wilson, uses unlikely juxtapositions to bring out parallels between forms of cultural subjection. Her work asks us to consider how testimony might take the form of objects and images, in addition to the words of the eyewitness, or the memories of the survivor. At the same time, Green seems to be clearly aware of the purely representational status of historical evidence, recognizing that it has no more legitimate claims to "truth" than any other social discourse. In reference to her own methodological practice, Green cites Giorgio Agamben's analysis of the testimony given by survivors of the Auschwitz concentration camps:

> Testimony thus guarantees not the factual truth of the statement safeguarded in the archive but rather its unarchivability, its exteriority with respect to the archive—that is, the necessity by which, as the existence of language, it escapes both memory and forgetting. It is because there is testimony only where there is an impossibility of speaking, because there is a witness only where there has been desubjectification.[26]

Agamben recognizes that testimony on behalf of another—another who has *not* survived—is always testimony to the impossibility of testimony itself. The *unarchivability* of the process or state of *desubjectification,* of rendering a subject no longer a subject, resonates with Green's reassessment of archival signs. Green compares Agamben's observations with those made in Olaudah Equiano's slave narrative, drawing the links between Agamben's example and Equiano's witnessing and survival of desubjectification under the genocidal conditions of slavery. Green's attention to the politics of archives becomes an interrogation into what can and cannot be archived, and what form archives might take if they were to be reconceived genealogically.

The archival impulse is clearly present in Green's *Import/Export Funk Office* (1992), an installation mapping international flows of music, literature, capital, and politics. A close reading of the culture industry that grew up around hip-hop music and its dissemination in the United States and abroad, *Import/Export Funk Office* took the physical form of an archive or bureaucratic space filled with unadorned, institutional metal shelves stacked with books, video monitors, audio recordings, and various texts and posters, many belonging to the German music critic Diederich Diederichsen. A contributing writer for the magazine *Spex,* Diederichsen was an avid collector of American hip-hop music, as well as books on the subject and on the history of black music in the United States. Reminiscent of spare governmental customs offices that hold international contraband and/or museum storage rooms, the work traces the intergenerational and international exchange of hip-hop music, African American political resistance, and German Marxism. The writings of U.S. scholar and activist Angela Davis and German philosopher Theodor Adorno—who was her teacher—are presented together, suggesting the links between German intellectual culture and U.S. progressive politics.

The title of the work also makes reference—if obliquely—to artist Adrian Piper's *Funk Lessons* (1982–1984) and to the German word *funk,* which means radio. One goal of Piper's performance piece involved teaching audience members how to dance to black funk music. The didactic foil of the lessons was intended to provide a context for collaboration and an opportunity for her generally white, middle-class audiences to "understand this art-form of black, working-class culture without fear or shame, and so to gain a deeper understanding of the cultural and political dimensions of one's social identity."[27] Green's project was not so utopian, but it did share an interest in exploring the question of cross-cultural translation and exchange. The installation drew attention to the materials of cultural exchange, the transference of language, fashion, and musical forms, and to their political impact and necessary transformation through translation.

In a series of humorous wall texts, the artist offered a list of slang in English and German, with corresponding notation indicating the dates when the slang was used, when its use changed, and how it was used differently in each cultural context. Under the rubric "Lexicon," terms like "buggin' out" and "fly" were posted with an accompanying definition and explanation of their historical use. The installation provided multiple points of access: books to read, video interviews to watch, audio tapes that one could listen to with headphones, and documents to peruse at the "funk stations" that were filled with files of historical ephemera (figure 5.20).

Import/Export Funk Office was a demanding work of art, like many of Green's later installations, because it required a significant investment of time on the part of the viewer to be fully appreciated. The artist included more than twenty-six hours of video interviews conducted by the artist or Diederich Diederichsen with artists, musicians, producers, and writers knowledgeable about hip-hop music or culture. Despite the abundant visual material, the installation downplayed optical pleasure in favor of

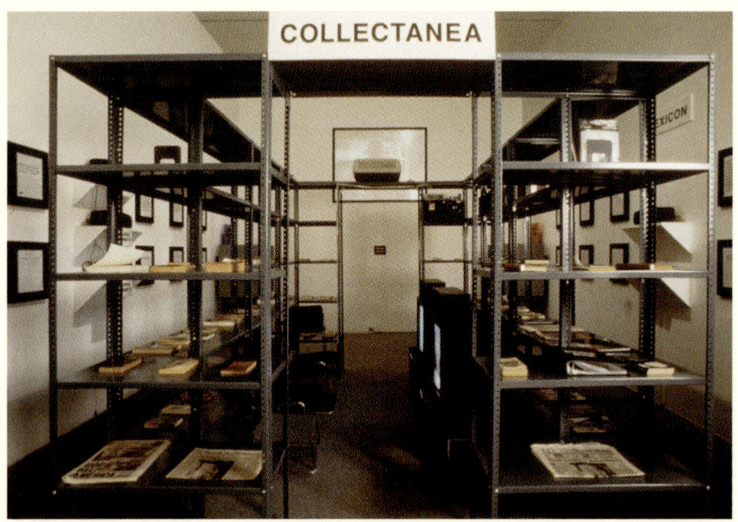

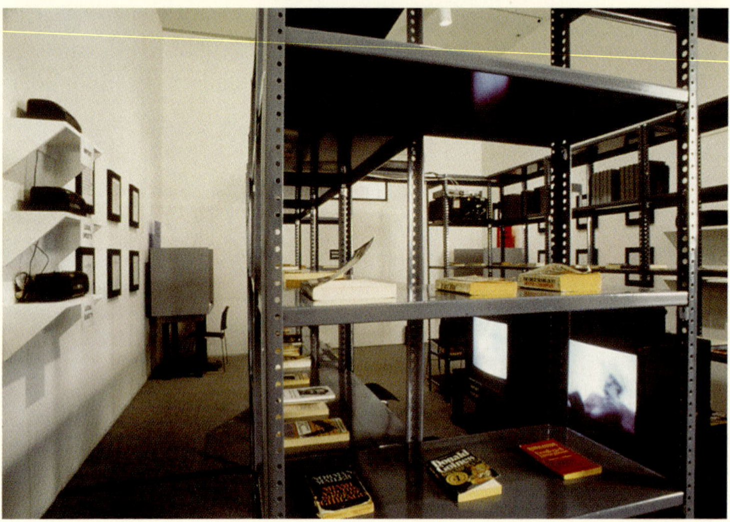

5.20 Renée Green, *Import/Export Funk Office*, 1992. Installation view. Courtesy of The Museum of Contemporary Art, Los Angeles, gift of Gaby and Wilhelm Schürmann.

5.21 Renée Green, *Import/Export Funk Office*, 1992. Detail of books. Courtesy of The Museum of Contemporary Art, Los Angeles, gift of Gaby and Wilhelm Schürmann.

a documentary approach (figure 5.21). The typical museum or gallery visitor only glimpsed a small portion of the video footage, and no doubt spent only a few minutes flipping through the available materials. With a greater investment of time, the viewer might have begun to grasp the complex web of social, political, and aesthetic exchanges that made up this nexus of cultural production. Apparently, the audience in Cologne where Diederichsen was well known spent hours listening to tapes, watching videos, and reading books.[28] After opening in Germany, *Import/Export Funk Office* was exhibited in numerous venues including New York and Los Angeles. In order to make the work more relevant to its U.S. audience, the artist included voices and images of local hip-hop culture. Unfortunately, the cult status of Diederichsen did not translate to the United States, and many of the German-language references remained opaque. The work appeared more scholarly than investigatory, despite Green's stated rejection of didacticism.[29] Nevertheless, the work certainly succeeded insofar as it emphasized that something is always lost in translation when importing and exporting music, ideas, commerce, or people. As an artificial trap or waystation for a diverse array of recording devices, *Import/Export Funk Office* operated as an archive of an otherwise ephemeral, transnational form of cultural production while also referencing the history of archives and archival practices, their essentially arbitrary order and necessary incompleteness.[30]

In Green's installations, travel appears as more than intrepid exploration and heroic return; instead, its logic is one of concentric circles, false starts, lost origins, and unexpected encounters. This may have something to do with the fact that since the early 1990s the artist has been nomadic to the degree that she, like many of her contemporaries, is requested or invited to relocate physically to implement new art projects and to survive the economic imperatives of the freelance artist. Neither naïve nor utopian about her peripatetic condition, the artist explores the inherent contradictions and impasses it poses, taking a critical look at her presence in a specific locale, whether new or familiar, and the histories that made it possible. To journey, to travel, and to transport goods (or people) became the explicit thematic concerns of these early installations.

In 1993, at the Los Angeles Museum of Contemporary Art, Green exhibited a selection of her installations entitled World Tour, bringing together *Bequest, Idyll Pursuits, Mise-en-scène,* and *Import/Export Funk Office*. Responding to the exhibition, scholar Miwon Kwon wrote, "The effort to resituate the individual site-oriented projects as a conceptually coherent ensemble eclipsed the specificity of each and forced a relational dynamic between discrete projects. Consequently, especially for an audience unfamiliar with Green's practice, the overriding narrative of World Tour became Green's creative process as an artist in and through the four installations."[31] Kwon concludes that World Tour was staged as a fairly conventional retrospective. While this may be true, by bringing these different works together—out of their original sites and under the rubric of a world tour—the artist is able to conceptually link the cultural "world tours" of aspiring middle-class artists and aristocrats and the touring itineraries of contemporary musicians to the historical "world tours" of European colonialists and the involuntary global "tour" of enslaved Africans. If the artist appears to implicate herself autobiographically in this history of wandering and touring, she also reveals how such concepts work euphemistically in a genealogy of exploration and domination.

Contact Zones

In 1994, Green organized a symposium in New York called "Negotiations in the Contact Zone" that brought together artists, cultural theorists, and academics to address the idea of cross-cultural moments of encounter. Green's use of "contact zone" was borrowed from the book *Imperial Eyes: Travel Writing and Transculturation,* in which author Mary Louise Pratt—whose use of autoethnography has already been discussed in chapter 1—coins the term to refer to "the space of colonial encounters, the space in which peoples geographically and historically separated come into contact with each other and establish ongoing relations, usually involving conditions of coercion, radical inequality, and intractable conflict."[32] For Green, the notion of the contact zone seems to imply a necessary set of ongoing semiotic negotiations across asymmetrical power relations. What is the role of the artist in contact zones? How often are artists requested to act as intermediaries between communities? Like many of her contemporaries, Green is self-conscious about the degree to which she is invited to perform service roles for arts institutions.[33] She, like Fred Wilson and Pepón Osorio, is aware of the pitfalls that attend artists who are invited to add a bit of "color" to the "scene," whether it is the scene of urban redevelopment or the art scene.[34] Green's response to these working conditions is self-recursive or self-reflective. She maps the historical and institutional *context* of her production into the production itself. The thematic focus on voyage, travel, and translation that characterized her earlier works became secondary to an emphasis on moments of engagement, face-to-face contact, and personal exchange.

One of the clearest and more controversial examples of this process appeared in her contribution to Project Unité. In the summer of 1993, a group of artists were invited to install works in one of Le Corbusier's Unité d'Habitations, a vast modular apartment complex in Firminy, France (not unlike the suburban low-income housing projects where protest riots took place in 2005). Each artist was assigned to an abandoned living space in the once classic (but now crumbling) symbol of modern architecture. The remaining apartments were still occupied by residents, mostly immigrants, living on low wages. Green's written account of the

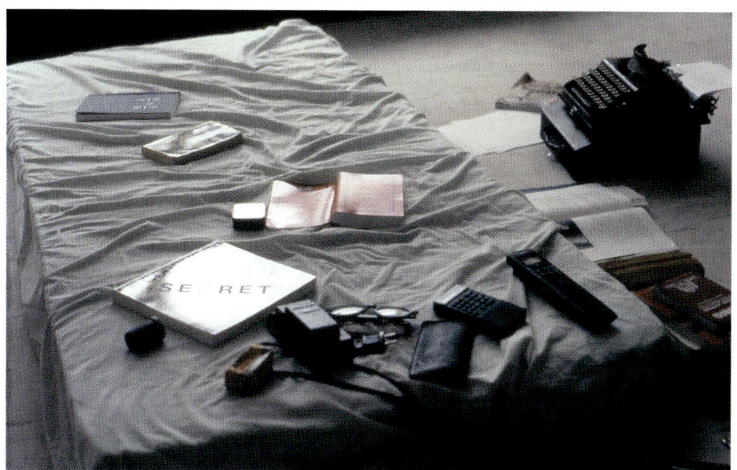

5.22 Renée Green, *Secret,* Projet Unité, Firminy, 1993. Courtesy of the artist and Free Agent Media.

event, "Scenes from a Group Show: Project Unité," offers a day-by-day diary of the week the artist spent camping or squatting in her vacated apartment while those around it were being transformed into an art exhibition space (figure 5.22). During her stay she writes, "For me it seemed important to actually use the apartment as an apartment, to the extent which that is possible. Unfortunately, the toilets and water do not function, which reflects a kind of camping or squatter situation."[35]

Charting seven days of habitation, Green vividly recounts the wind blowing in the night, the moments of boredom and calm, the occasional encounters with residents in the elevators, the 1960s decor, the search for fresh bread, the sounds of construction and construction workers, the arrival of other artists, the traumatic loss of the keys to her room, and the final art opening. Within the vast modern buildings perched in a barren suburb, the artist felt alone yet strangely surveyed. She wore a jacket with the word "immigrant" written in large letters on the back, confessing to her own status as a recent arrival and a foreigner. Mostly, residents and construction workers ignored her, but one woman of African descent pointed at her jacket and laughed knowingly. Both black women were "immigrants" in the white French imaginary, and thus shared an insider/outsider status that was precarious.

Methodologically, Green's self-reflective project was partially inspired by Michel Leiris, whose *L'Afrique Fantôme* raised the question of why the ethnographer's own reactions, dreams, and responses should not become important parts of fieldwork. Green's interest lay less in fieldwork, however, than in producing an analysis and record of her own, rather awkward, relation to the site and the goals of the art exhibition. Green's project articulates the *fact of encounter,* without pretending to comprehensively understand or accurately reveal the place or the people in it. Her diarist treatment emulates neither the strict documentary function of fieldwork nor the sweeping claims of sociology, but has more in common with the conceptual practice of "meta-art" outlined by Adrian Piper. Piper writes,

> By "meta-art" I mean the activity of making explicit the thought processes, procedures and presuppositions of making whatever kind of art we make. Thought processes might include how we hypothesize a work into existence: whether we reason from problems encountered in the last work to possible solutions in the next, or get "inspired" by seeing someone else's work, or a previously unnoticed aspect of our own; or read something.... Procedures might include how we come by the materials we use; what we do in order to get them; whom we must deal with, and in what capacity; what kinds of decisions we make concerning them (aesthetic, pecuniary, environmental, etc.); to what extent the work demands interactions (social, political, collaborative) with other people, etc.... In elucidating the process of making art on a personal level, meta-art criticizes and indicts the machinations necessary to maintain this society as it is. It holds up for scrutiny how capitalism works on us and through us; how we therefore live, think, what we do as artists; what kinds of social interactions we have (personal, political, financial); what injustices we are the victim of, and which ones we must inflict on others in order to validate our work or our roles as artist.[36]

Evidently self-conscious, Green is also self-critical, pointing to moments of conflict or failure in her own art practice. For example, the last words of her account of Project Unité in France reveal the underlying social tensions produced by the international encounter. "At the opening," Green writes,

> the inhabitants of the Unité and the artists exhibiting in the former habitations were all invited to a party in the social space on the top floor of the building.... There was a palpable tension in the air. The artists stayed in groups with other artists and art world infra-structural personnel, the tenants stayed in groups with their friends and neighbors.... A fight began. An inebriated male tenant began throwing punches in all directions. All were forbidden to leave the floor until the man could be stilled. Eventually, bruised and bloody, he left. Everyone else was also free to leave.[37]

Green's personal narrative reveals how Unité inhabitants were perhaps hostile to the presence of the artists, and unsympathetic to the cultural institution's effort to inhabit or rehabilitate their living environment. Metaphorically if not literally bruised by the process, they appear to have suffered a psychological injustice at the hands of the artists, including

Green. What we see in Green's text is an effort to assess her own complex position of racial and economic difference in relation to the Unité inhabitants. If Project Unité was an experiment in artificially constructed contact zones between the visiting artists and the inhabitants of the building, facilitated by a city bureaucracy looking for a form of social rehabilitation, then Green's response was to examine that encounter as such, producing a form of meta-art that reflected this underlying social contract and its economic imperatives.

The year following her sojourn in Firminy, Green was invited to participate as a visiting artist for a Dutch contemporary art project called the Seventh Museum, initiated by the Stroom Center for the Visual Arts at the request of the six cultural institutions comprising the Hofvijvermusea Foundation in The Hague. As an imaginary, temporary museum, without a building or collection, the Seventh Museum presented works of contemporary art in diverse sites in the Hofvijvermuseums and the area around the Hofvijver. The project guidelines reminded the participating artists of the following: "A site-specific artwork needs to consider the (art) historical, aesthetic, and political models of presentation that already exist in this area. In this list also belong the historical and architectural aspects of the Hofvijver itself, a striking stretch of water, surrounded by magnificent buildings and architectural objects reminiscent of a scattered décor."[38] In preparation for the Seventh Museum project, Renée Green visited The Hague several times, exploring the Hofvijver area on foot, looking in shop windows and exploring the government buildings and the museums. Over time, she began to notice that despite the numerous museum and tourist bookstores filled with beautiful art catalogs and travel literature in the area, there was almost no visual or literary reference to the local site itself or the ethnically diverse population who lived there.[39] Green proposed to do a book project based on the urban landscape of the city and to include the missing stories that seemed to haunt its public imaginary.

Two chance encounters provided the underlying structure of the book. The first was with Magdalena, an opera singer who briefly shared the artist's living space during her initial visit to the city. Green's first conversation with her revealed several unexpected connections: "As we were breakfasting she mentioned that she was Moluccan, part Dutch and part Moluccan. I mentioned that my mother was a classical vocalist. She told me that she directed the choir that sang Moluccan songs. I told her that my mother used to direct the church choir. Somehow I mentioned the title of a book that had been on my mind called *The Ten Thousand Things*. She said that it was her favorite book. Her uncle had been taught by the author, Maria Dermoût, who used to live on one of the 'Spice Islands,' Ambon, in the Moluccas."[40] The second encounter, during the artist's next visit to The Hague, was with a tour guide at the First Chamber of

Parliament. She writes, "His manner was relaxed and pleasant. When he asked what exactly it was I did as an artist I told him that sometimes I made video interviews with people, and that in one of these I'd focused on someone's collection habits. He then told me that he was a collector. I asked what he collected and he said that he lived over the rooms of the Parliament and he would give us a quick tour."[41] The tour revealed that the collector owned Roman and Spanish antiquities, African masks, Indonesian statuettes, contemporary Dutch art, and hundreds of other artifacts packed tightly into a small urban residence.

Maria Dermoût's novel *The Ten Thousand Things,* loosely based on an intergenerational narrative of Dutch colonial presence on the Molucca Islands, suggests the complexity of material exchange that structures local economies of wealth, cross-cultural desire, and death. Rare shells kept in special cabinets, magical talismans traded as medicine balls, deadly knives and coveted pearls pull the quietly episodic tale forward through an unstoppable flow of time. It was a local custom in the Moluccas to speak a list of the "hundred things" from a person's life at the moment of death (the names of loved ones, cherished memories, precious belongings). Dermoût closes her novel with the protagonist observing quietly in her chair that "they weren't a hundred things but much more than a hundred, and not only hers; a hundred times "a hundred things," next to each other, separate from each other, touching, here and there flowing into each other, without any link anywhere, and at the same time linked forever."[42] In the long tradition of copyists in the visual arts, Green titled her book *After the Ten Thousand Things* (1994) in honor of Dermoût's original narrative, but the title also suggests Green's interest in the urban space of The Hague, the collecting practices of its private citizens and institutions, and the parallel history of the Dutch presence in the original Spice Islands (figure 5.23). For the artist,

> The title *After the Ten Thousand Things* suggests that we are always at the beginning, no matter how many things (events, objects, people) have passed through our lives. There's no way of getting away from a beginning, a perpetual renewal: after the time in which the book itself was published, after the listing of things at the end of one's life and at the end of the book, after the accumulation of life, after the accumulation of things.[43]

On the opening and closing pages of Green's book, scores of small photographs without text or captions evoke Andre Malraux's *Museum without Walls,* but unlike his eulogistic rendering of classic works of art, these images are fragments, details, snapshots recording the path of the artist's wandering eye. The pages comprise a visual catalog of material "things" encountered in wandering through The Hague, its neighborhoods, its cultural institutions, and various private collections of objects found in

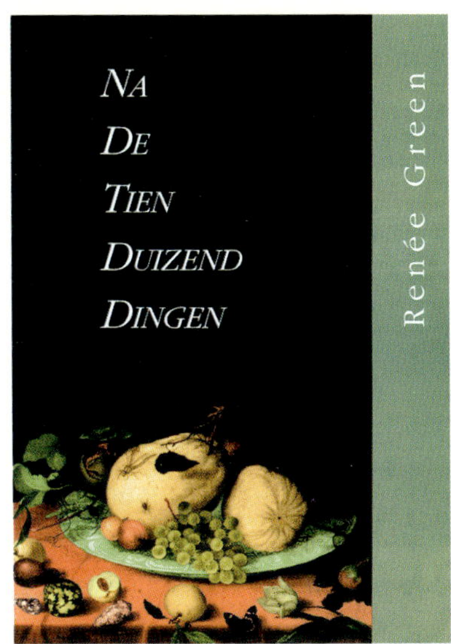

5.23 Renée Green, *After the Ten Thousand Things*, 1994. Book cover. Courtesy of the artist and Free Agent Media.

5.24 Renée Green, *After the Ten Thousand Things*, 1994. Details from interior pages. Courtesy of the artist and Free Agent Media.

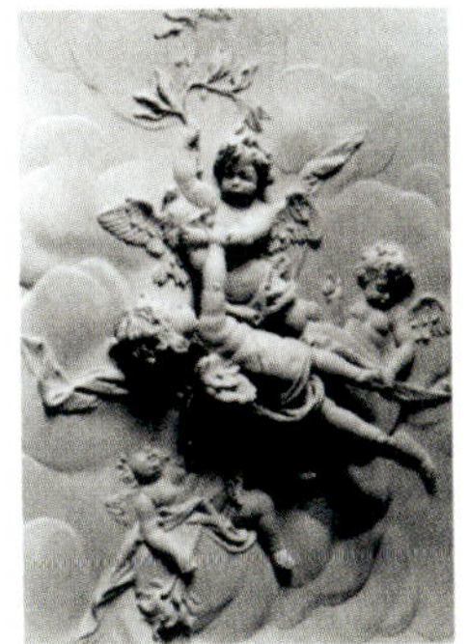
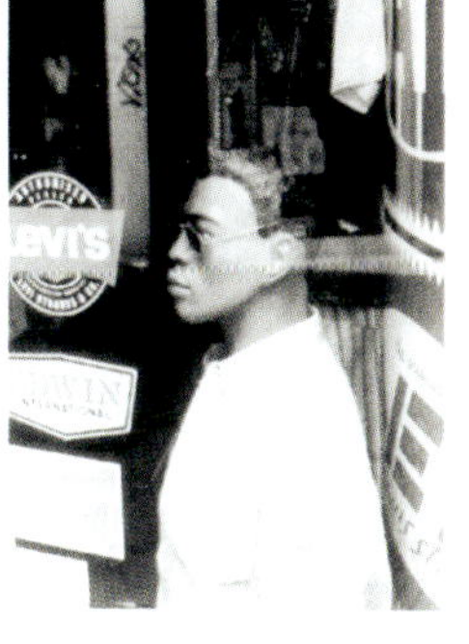
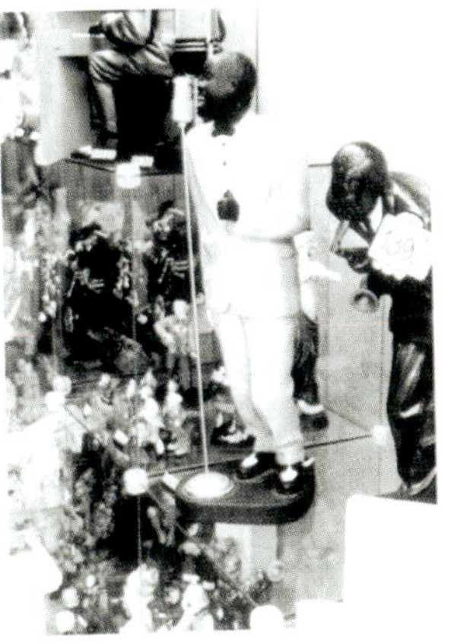
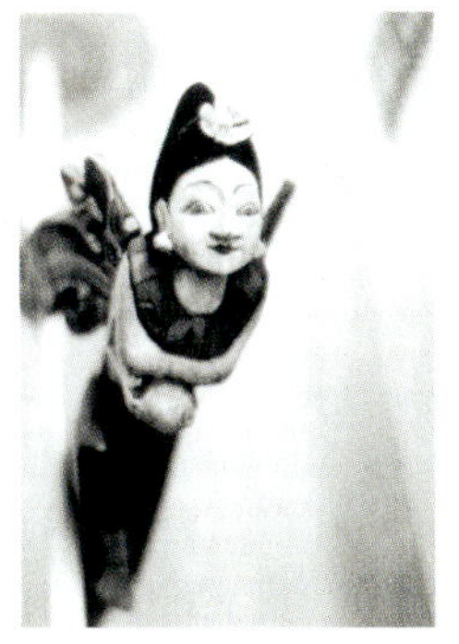

hotel lobbies and stairways, domestic interiors, museums, shop windows, and the street. The collection at first appears to be a random selection of the artist's trajectory of vision, as if the photographer-flâneur sought to record every object, every detail in the field of her gaze; but ultimately the images work together to reveal a visual, material history of cross-cultural contact (figure 5.24).

The eclectic compendium includes seventeenth-century portraits of aristocrats with their African slaves, masks and carvings from Indonesia, window displays with satirical statuettes of black Africans or black American jazz musicians (not unlike those Fred Wilson showed in *Collectibles*), street lamps adorned with Christian motifs, a colonial nostalgia shop called "Decorum" with antique world globes and nineteenth-century travel accessories, advertisements for local political groups representing ethnic minorities, the interior of the parliamentary buildings, Orientalist paintings of Arabs, eighteenth-century chairs upholstered with scenes of tropical flora and fauna, architectural decoration consisting of military coats of arms, contemporary street markets operated by dark-skinned immigrants, and so on, more than ten thousand things. By consciously directing her lens on the visual details of the city that attest to its military, colonial past and its globally inflected, racially diverse present, she produced a new portrait that moved beyond the limited scope of urban architecture as "scattered décor" implied by the curators' statement.

The South Moluccas (Maluku Selatan) existed as a separate colony of the Netherlands until 1949, when they were ceded to the newly independent Republic of Indonesia. There has been intermittent ethnic and nationalist violence on the islands ever since. At the time Green produced her text, serious unrest still existed. *After the Ten Thousand Things* brings us back to *Tracing Lusitania*. Like a musical refrain or coda, the many histories that seem so disparate and unconnected are played in Green's work as compositional notes in a larger series of movements. *After the Ten Thousand Things* reminds us that humans always enter the world in medias res, after the long history that precedes them. We are born into a language that shapes our consciousness, we are born into racial and economic hierarchies, we are born as one more *thing* in a world of things—hundreds and thousands of things. Green's associative working process presents a tangled weave of national identity, cultural memory, and the desire to collect as interdependent activities that work collaboratively to construct the conditions for and enunciations of race discourse and discord.

After the Ten Thousand Things was the third book project for the artist who has published several books to date, including *Camino/Road* (1994), *Certain Miscellanies: Some Documents* (1996), *Between and Including* (2001), and the anthology *Negotiations in the Contact Zone* (2003). Some books are experimental conceptual projects, while others primarily compile the artist's writings, interviews, and documents of exhibitions. All are published in English and a second language (German, Spanish, Dutch, or Portuguese). Green's books do not function as comprehensive exhibition catalogs; instead, like her installations, they are filled with fragments, clues, and sketches of ongoing projects.[44]

With the shift to conceptual art practice in the 1960s and 1970s and other subsequent experimental modes of temporary installation art in the present, where a final, saleable object is not the primary goal of the work, it has become more and more common for artists to produce different and multiple versions of the same work. This is certainly the case with the reinstallations in galleries and museums undertaken by all of the artists considered in this book, but it is particularly the case with Green's work, in which the unfinished nature of both form and content are foregrounded. There seem to be two primary conceptual reasons for this: the first is an attention to the fact that both memory and history (the subject of the artist's inquiry) are also always unfinished, accretive, and in the process of transformation; and the second is an interest in the technological means of preservation and archiving that follows the logic of multiple versions and revisions. This is particularly visible in a series of works that Green developed to explore the slipperiness of memory, the process of forgetting, and the necessity of renarrating the past. The first version, *Partially Buried* (1996), took the form of both an installation and a video project that mapped the intersection of a series of contemporaneous events in 1970: Robert Smithson's ideas about site-specific earth art and their manifestation in his *Partially Buried Woodshed* at Kent State University; the Kent State student protests against the Vietnam War; Green's mother's attendance at Kent State University as a student of music at the time; and Green's own memories of Cleveland, Ohio, the site of her birth and childhood.

Smithson, known for his large-scale earthworks such as *Spiral Jetty*, had been invited to do a project on the Kent State University campus in January 1970. Among his primary interests was the entropic process by which things naturally fall apart, decay, or dissipate over time. For *Partially Buried Woodshed* Smithson covered one half of an old wooden storage space with twenty truckloads of earth until the central roof beam cracked. The structure was then left to slowly transform according to the conditions of the environment; grass and trees were planted and eventually grew up as the building slowly sagged lower year after year. When the roof finally collapsed in 1985, the artwork was cheerfully bulldozed by a university administration that had long considered it an eyesore and political embarrassment. For, in addition to its identity as an innovative earthwork, Smithson's woodshed came to stand metaphorically for the antiwar protests of May 1970, when four students were shot and killed on campus by the National Guard. Six months after *Partially Buried Wood-

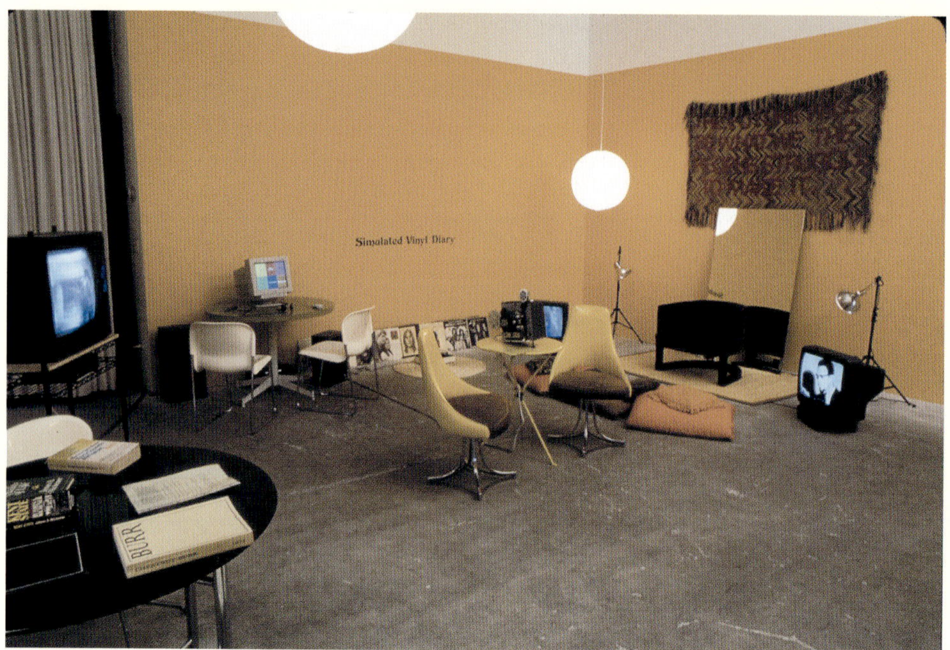

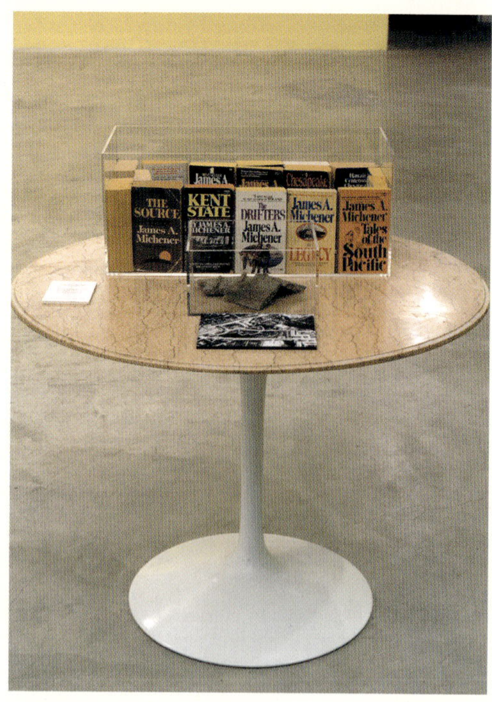

5.25 Renée Green, *Partially Buried*, 1996. Installation view. Courtesy of the artist and Free Agent Media.

5.26 Renée Green, *Partially Buried*, 1996. Detail of books on table. Courtesy of the artist and Free Agent Media.

shed was installed, the date of the massacre was anonymously painted on one of its walls, thereby turning a conceptual project about decay into a symbolic memorial for the dead.

Green's *Partially Buried* can be seen as a pseudodocumentary return to the past that consists in her own effort to unearth a history, both of art and of her own life, that has been partially buried by time and shadowed by fiction and that, alarmingly, seems to be returning as commodified style. "The seventies are in vogue now," the artist observed in her video; but what does it mean for a historical moment to be in vogue? What could be a more effective means of ideological erasure than to transform a historical period of extreme social upheaval and progressive politics into fashion? Against this erasure, Green offered her own revised mapping of the past. For the installation, the artist furnished the Pat Hearn Gallery with period furniture from the 1960s and 1970s, popular literature such as James A. Michener's *Kent State,* black-and-white photographs of the Kent State campus at the time of the protests, and concrete fragments from Robert Smithson's earthwork—all items that had been "partially buried" by history (figures 5.25 and 5.26). Leaning against one wall were rows of LP albums presented as a "Simulated Vinyl Diary," their technology out of date but their historical resonance still intact. Several areas or stations for viewing video and super-8 film, listening to music, or reading books gave the room a domestic feel, enhanced by soft cushions on the floor, tangerine orange walls, a rice paper hanging lamp, and brightly upholstered chairs. A fringe-covered banner pronounced, "The future will be what we the people struggle to make it." These words were taken from a 1976 film about the 1960s radical student activist group the Weathermen titled *Underground,* which formed the topological basis of Green's recursive project, since the installation was directly modeled on a set from the film.

Partially Buried was not a simple recuperation of, or nostalgia for, a bygone era; it was a questioning of precisely the function of the past, its ideological power, and its repressive relation to the present. Smithson's entropic earthwork served as a convenient nodal point in a larger nexus of associations and intersecting narratives. For example, when the artist interviewed her mother about that fateful day of student protest in May 1970, she found that her mother did not remember any details about the event; in contrast, the artist remembers waiting anxiously for her at home. This interview and other interviews conducted by the artist with her Ohio relatives and with professors at Kent State played on the video monitors along with clips from *Underground* and films of Green's childhood. Although the interviews gave the appearance of documentary "reality," their credibility was undermined by the multiple versions of the past that appeared in each narrative. Conflicting memories and histories of Kent State, of the student protests, and of Smithson's art project produced an overflow of meaning. "The notion of surplus in the locations of assumed absence is a current that runs through the different parts of this work," Green writes.[45] She defines this surplus as related to that which *survives,* whether in the material form of an architectural ruin, or as perceptual traces in memory. Accumulated versions of past events might also be said to follow the disordered logic of entropy and dissipation. The artist asks, "What other possibilities for reflection emerge where what appears to be decay can be viewed as transmuting traces, shifting remains?"[46]

Partially Buried creates an intersection for art history, private history, and political history by drawing these accumulated versions of the past together so that their various narratives collide. More than twenty color photographs of the Kent State campus at the present moment were hung on one wall of the installation, mixed with images of local industry, restaurants, and the remains of Smithson's *Partially Buried Woodshed* reduced to a cement foundation hidden in an overgrowth of weeds. On another wall were hung a series of photographs of the student demonstrations and the military response by the National Guard, some drawn from Michener's book that depicted primarily the white college students and some found by Green of the Black Student Union participation in the protests. Like Amalia Mesa-Bains's references to black student protests at Cornell University and Chicana protests at Williams College, Green's decision to broaden the archive of visual associations represents the history of the educational institution from an uncommon perspective. Green's installation leverages Smithson's *Partially Buried Woodshed* and the Weathermen's *Underground* to reveal the intersecting histories that cross a racial divide, but that are rarely acknowledged or recorded. I agree with James Meyer who writes that Green's project posits "a sixties that holds within itself the idea of future transformations," particularly because it presents the past as an archive that is always unfinished, unfolding.[47]

In order to account for the ways that private memories intersect with public histories, Green began the second stage of the *Partially Buried* project with a work called *Übertragen/Transfer* (1996), exploring the idea of the cosmopolitan patriot who circulates among different localities through tourism, migration, nomadism, and diaspora, while remaining attached to the particularities of a cultural home.[48] In *Übertragen/ Transfer,* Green decided to examine how the history of the United States circa 1970 was conceptualized across this kind of cosmopolitan cultural divide by conducting interviews with Germans or former German citizens who currently live in the United States. Their process of cultural *transfer* reveals early fantasies of the country they eventually came to inhabit. One of the interviewees remarked that in 1970 when she was six or seven years old and still living in Teheran before moving to Germany, her primary memory of the United States was the television broadcast of the Vietnam War along with network programming that she couldn't understand. Another remarked that he enjoys living in the United States, but that he is shocked by the political apathy: "Those people who really tried to change something in the nineteen-seventies, they grew up and somehow they…weren't able to educate the following generation in a way that they would continue a political fight."[49] The interviewees also discuss the cultural transitions they have had to make, their reasons for leaving Germany, and, in some cases, their desire to return.

Übertragen/Transfer and *Partially Buried* were installed with a final segment of the project at the Kwangju Biennial in Korea for an exhibition titled *Partially Buried in Three Parts* (1996–1999). The first segment of the exhibition touched on the life of the artist's mother, while the final segment, consisting of the video *Partially Buried Continued*, traces the father's participation in the Korean War and the artist's own voyage to Korea during the process of preparing for the biennial (figure 5.27). A series of intertitles lead the viewer through Super-8 footage, slides taken by the artist's father around Seoul, interviews conducted by the artist, contemporary shots of the city, pages of Theresa Hak Kyung Cha's *Dictée,* and video transfers from the more recent Kwangju Uprising of May 18, 1980 (during which many students were shot and killed). A local photographer, Hae Sun Kim recounts the event and shows Green historical materials from the event (figure 5.28). Comments from the father's interview reveal an encounter with race politics during the war, from the desegregation of blacks in the U.S. Army in 1951, to the comment that "my lieutenant was Chinese from California."[50] Green's video also poses its own rhetorical questions at the end: "Who owns history? Who can represent its complexity?"[51]

In these video installations, Green appears to reference Smithson's construction of "non-sites," which he defined as a 3-D logical picture that is *abstract* yet *represents* an actual site. Smithson brought mounds of rocks and earth into the gallery space as a way of referencing, abstractly but also metonymically, the "other" sites, the deserts and mountains, from which they had been gathered. Smithson writes,

> It is by this three-dimensional metaphor that one site can represent another site which does not resemble it—thus the *Non-Site.* … Let us say that one goes on a fictitious trip if one decides to go to the site of the Non-Site. The "trip" becomes invented, devised, artificial; therefore one might call it a non-trip to a site from a Non-site. … This little theory is tentative and could be abandoned at any time. Theories like things are also abandoned. That theories are eternal is doubtful. Vanished theories compose the strata of many forgotten books.[52]

Partially Buried in Three Parts uses the past as a "site" from which systems of representation (artifacts, interviews, photographs) that produce "the past" as a functioning social discourse are recuperated or transposed into the abstracted "non-site" of the video and the installation. In this respect, the artist invites her viewers to draw the obvious and sometimes not-so-obvious connections across historical time among the U.S. military presence overseas, student protests, and death; between international politics and race politics; between private lives and public spaces.

Attending to the nature of the apparatus of representational technologies, Green shoots segments of *Partially Buried Continued* on a Super-8 camera, a 35mm camera, and a digital camera—each referencing a different historical moment and the material conditions of its visualization. Green also exposes the potential fluidity of her own subject position, caught up as it is in the life narratives of her parents, of the Korean activists she encounters, of the artists and art historians who frame the parameters of her own art practice. As Foucault points out, "If genealogy in its own right gives rise to questions concerning our native land, native language, or the laws that govern us, its intention is to reveal the heterogeneous systems which, masked by the self, inhibit the formation of any form of identity."[53] Instead of simplifying one's identity, Green's work implies, genealogical analysis always complicates the picture.

Green's installations demonstrate that our relationship to the past is always a negotiation between voluntary and involuntary memory. Philosopher Henri Bergson writes, "Whenever we are trying to recover a recollection, to call up some period of our history, we become conscious of an act *sui generis* by which we detach ourselves from the present in order to replace ourselves, first in the past in general, then in a certain region of the past—a work of adjustment, something like the focusing of a camera."[54] Like a photographic snapshot, memory as the desired memory-image is brought into focus by an act of will: "Little by little it comes into view like a condensing cloud; from the virtual state it passes into the actual; and as its outlines become more distinct and its surface takes on color, it tends to imitate perception."[55] By contrast, Sigmund Freud asserts the necessarily *involuntary* nature of memory, most clearly outlined in his discussion of *screen memories*.[56] Unlike the transparency of Bergson's camera metaphor, this notion immediately implies the crucial blockage of information that takes place in the act of remembering. The idea of a screen memory, tied to a notion of visual perception and its resistance, comes from Freud's attempt to understand how it is that certain very vivid memories, especially of childhood, do not seem to have any particular purpose or reason, while other more traumatic events are not remembered in the least. He hopes to explain this phenomenon by suggesting that the vivid memories are in fact a substitute for and a guard against other, unconscious, remembrances. The concept of screen memory thus "owes its value as a memory not to its own content but to the relation existing between that content and some other, that has been suppressed."[57] This relation is usually one of association: "It is a case of

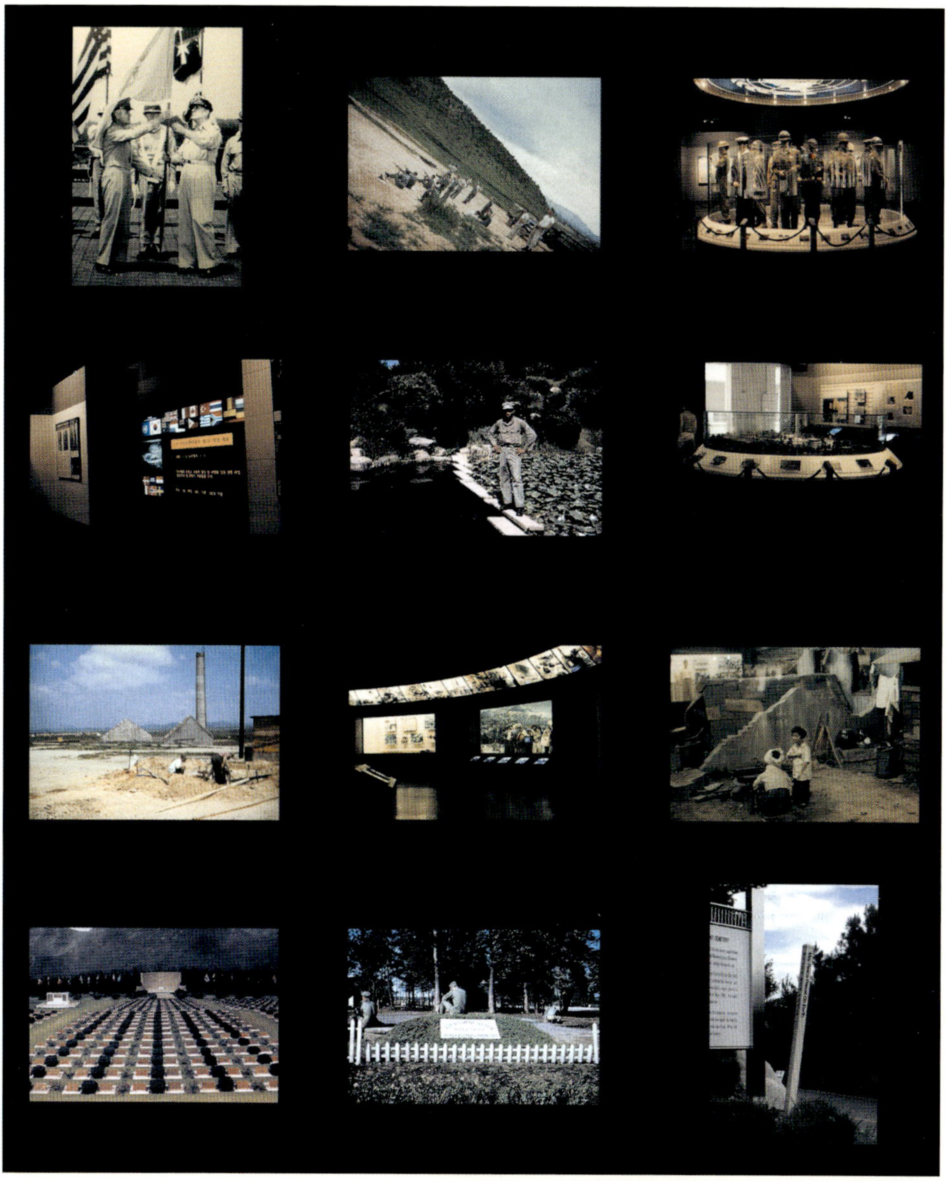

5.27 Renée Green,
*Partially Buried Con-
tinued,* 1996. Stills.
Courtesy of the artist
and Free Agent Media.

5.28 Renée Green,
*Partially Buried Con-
tinued,* 1997. Still of
Hae Sun Kim. Courtesy
of the artist and Free
Agent Media.

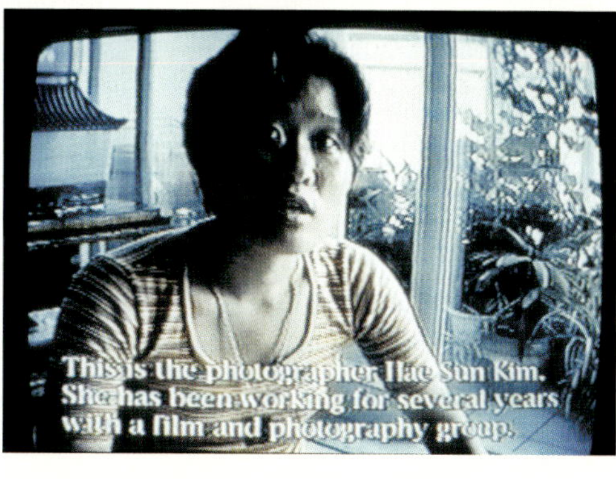

displacement on to something associated by continuity; or, looking at the process as a whole, a case of repression accompanied by the substitution of something in the neighborhood (whether in space or time)."[58]

Green's *Partially Buried in Three Parts* investigates both models of memory. Charting an investigatory path to a historical moment of the 1970s, the artist trains her lens on particular scenes and moments. At the same time, the work emphasizes the essentially irretrievable quality, the opacity of that past—from screen memories that might be at work in her mother's inability to remember traumatic events, to her father's snapshot memory of Korea, to the way the Kent State University campus participates in the erasure of Smithson's work. Green also examines the intersection of private memories with collectively received representations of the past such as cinema, television, music, or literature by including images from public archives or clips from live broadcasts in order to reveal the extent to which public histories of the past contribute both to its revival and its erasure. Just like the private workings of the unconscious, public memory also demonstrates the desire to screen out historical trauma. In Green's work, memory and history are shown to be forms of human *labor* characterized by both voluntary and involuntary actions that work inextricably in concert.

Sedimented Evidence

For Green, race discourse is imbedded in transnational transactions, as one element in a genealogy of historical relations. The ever-present economic imperatives and material desires that drive commercial relations and race relations whether in the past (the interdependence of French textiles and the slave trade) or in the present (the import and export of popular black music) appears in her work as a shifting and changing set of paradigms that sets people apart in unequal power relations but that can also draw them together. For Green, race discourse is a visual technology that can be found in taxonomies of color and regimes of spectatorship. It is also a technique of history, an analytic framework that appears in the structure of the archive; race discourse determines the shape of the archive and defines the limits of archival erasure or oblivion, and it affects whose stories are recorded and whose stories are made public. Race discourse is what underlies territorial geographies and movements of bodies, but it does not have a fixed location.

If Green's art practice is based on citation, it is also part of a more general accretive method for the artist who accumulates images, documents, and artifacts into layers of sedimented evidence. Using carefully selected recorded sound, books, videos, and objects, Green invites her audiences to imaginatively travel in time or across continents not for the sake of voyeurism, but for the purpose of better grasping their own position as historically situated subjects. Race is only one in a multitude of factors

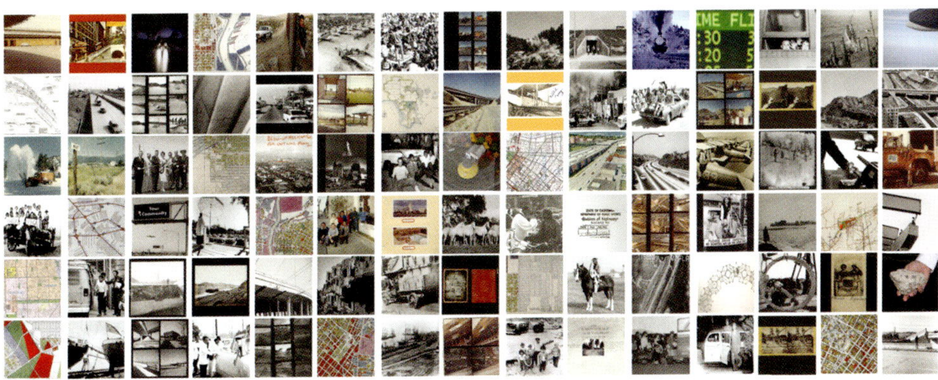

5.29 Renée Green, *Code: Survey,* 2006. Installation detail. Courtesy of the artist and Free Agent Media.

for Green that define the subject as *subject to* history, but it nevertheless plays a significant role for the artist in terms of the stories she recalls, the histories she recounts, and the archives she explores.

For a recent public work *Code: Survey* (2006) at the Caltrans Headquarters in Los Angeles, the artist installed 160 photographic panels on an interior hallway. Each panel displays an archival image related in some way to the history of transportation in the city of Los Angeles or California and is etched with a code number corresponding to a website where browsers can follow out a series of citations that provide historical commentary on each image (figure 5.29).[59] It is also possible to search through key terms such as "riots 1960s," "riots 1990s," "Southern Pacific," or "immigration" and be shown related images on the visual grid. Among views of road construction, freeway maps, and planned transportation routes, Green also inserted images of Japanese Americans boarding trains to internment camps during World War II, Native American members of the YWCA out for a ride, Salvadorian refugees being deported by the Immigration and Naturalization Services (INS), and many other images that attest to the racial diversity and political complexity imbedded in the history of roads, buses, trains, and ships that come under Caltrans's jurisdiction. Each image is accompanied by several key words that lead to quotes from books, recorded comments by Caltrans employees, or other archival information. Sometimes the citation is directly related to the image, but frequently it opens up a series of associative meanings. For example, the word *Exodus* is indexed with an image of an African American motorcycle rider being blessed by a minister (figure 5.30); clicking on Exodus brings up a text by historian Robin Kelly who writes, "After all, the history of black people has been a history of movement—real and imagined. Repatriation to Liberia and Sierra Leone. Flight to Canada. Escape to Haiti. The great Kansas Exodus. The back-to-Africa movements of Bishop Henry McNeil Turner and Marcus Garvey."

Instead of searching for origins, the artist traces the ways in which definitions of culture and race discourse are made to appear, the pathways

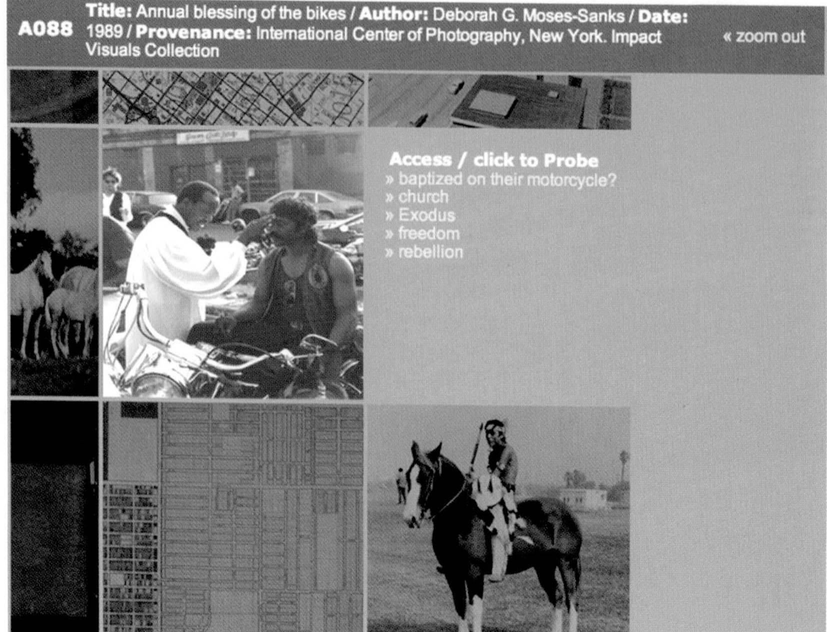

5.30 Renée Green,
Code: Survey, 2006.
Website, image section
(permanently hosted at
the Caltrans District VII
website: http://www
.dot.ca.gov/dist07/
code_survey/intro.htm).
Courtesy of the artist
and Free Agent Media.

that this information takes, and the forms and textures of its archival presence. She delves into the static archives to render them more fluid, more dynamic. Art becomes the process of carefully sampling a system of already circulating signs that are part of a larger geography.[60] In the process, it charts the intersection of what Foucault identifies as the "two great mythic spaces" of the Western imagination. He writes,

> Thus are constructed and criss-crossed the mechanical figures of the two great mythic spaces so often explored by Western imagination: space that is rigid and forbidden, surrounding the quest, the return and the treasure (that's the geography of the Argonauts and of the labyrinth); and the other space—communicating, polymorphous, continuous and irreversible—of the metamorphosis, that is to say, of the visible transformation of instantly crossed distances, of strange affinities, of symbolic replacements.[61]

Spatially, Green's installations explore precisely the intersection of these mythic spaces that are on the one hand about rigidity and power, and on the other about communication and metamorphosis, attending to the ways that human subjects have historically been invested in the imaginary fantasy of distant lands and other people at the same time that they are always already imbedded in a local flow of changing social and cultural affinities.

NOTES

Introduction: Subject to Display

1. Lisa Corrin, "Mining the Museum: Artists Look at Museums, Museums Look at Themselves," in *Mining the Museum*, ed. Lisa Corrin (New York: The Contemporary, Baltimore, in cooperation with The New Press, 1994), 9–10.

2. See Néstor García Canclini, "Remaking Passports: Visual Thought in the Debate on Multiculturalism," *Third Text* 28/29 (Autumn/Winter 1994): 139–146.

3. Stuart Hall, "Subjects in History: Making Diasporic Identities," in *The House that Race Built*, ed. Wahneema Lubiano (New York: Vintage, 1998), 289–299.

4. Michael Omi and Howard Winant, *Racial Formation in the United States: From the 1960s to the 1990s* (New York: Routledge, 1994), 60.

5. Judith Butler, "Subjection, Resistance, Resignification: Between Freud and Foucault," in *The Identity in Question*, ed. John Rajchman (New York: Routledge, 1995), 230.

6. Paul Gilroy, *Against Race* (Cambridge, MA: Harvard University Press, 2000), 252.

7. See, for example, Stephen Jay Gould, *The Mismeasure of Man;* Cornel West, *Race Matters;* K. Anthony Appiah and Amy Gutmann, *Color Conscious: The Political Morality of Race;* Wahneema Lubiano, ed., *The House that Race Built;* Gary A. Olson and Lynn Worsham, eds., *Race, Rhetoric, and the Postcolonial;* and Paul Gilroy, *Against Race.*

8. See, for example, Brian Wallis, "Black Bodies, White Science: Louis Agassiz's Slave Daguerreotypes" *American Art* 9 (Summer 1995): 38–61, or Maria Concepcion Garcia Saiz, *Las Castas Mexicanas: Un Género Pictórico Americano* (Milan: Olivetti, 1989) and Magali M. Carrera, "Locating Race in Late Colonial Mexico," *Art Journal* 57, no. 3 (Fall 1998): 36–45.

9. Coco Fusco, *English Is Broken Here: Notes on Cultural Fusion in the Americas* (New York: The New Press, 1995); bell hooks, *Black Looks: Race and Representation* (Boston, MA : South End Press, 1992); Darby English, *How to See a Work of Art in Total Darkness* (Cambridge, MA: The MIT Press, 2007); Ella Shohat and Robert Stam, eds., *Unthinking Eurocentrism: Multiculturalism and the Media* (London and New York: Routledge, 1994); Kymberly N. Pinder, ed., *Race-ing Art History: Critical Readings in Race and Art History* (New York: Routledge, 2002); David A. Bailey, Ian Baucom, and Sonia Boyce, eds., *Shades of Black: Assembling Black Arts in 1980s Britain* (Durham, NC: Duke University Press, in collaboration with Institute of International Visual Arts and African and Asian Visual Artists' Archive, 2005).

10. Michelle Cliff offers an eloquent account of the struggle of women artists to resist the activities of objectification that race discourse produces in her essay "Object into Subject: Some Thoughts on the Work of Black Women Artists," in *Making Face, Making Soul/Haciendo Caras*, ed. Gloria Anzaldúa (San Francisco: Aunt Lute, 1990).

11. Stuart Hall, "The After-Life of Frantz Fanon: Why Fanon? Why Now? Why Black Skin/White Masks?" in *The Fact of Blackness: Frantz Fanon and Visual Representation,* ed. Alan Read (London: Institute of Contemporary Art and Seattle: Bay Press, 1996), 20.

12. Gilroy, *Against Race,* 35.

13. Annie E. Coombes, *Reinventing Africa: Museums, Material Culture and Popular Imagination* (New Haven: Yale University Press, 1994), 160.

14. For one of the few recent efforts to explore the links between material culture and racial discourse, see Bill Brown, "Reification, Reanimation and the American Uncanny *Critical Inquiry* 32 (Winter 2006): 175–207. Some excellent earlier studies of material culture include George W. Stocking Jr., ed., *Objects and Others: Essays on Museums and Material Culture* (1985); Daniel Miller, *Material Culture and Mass Consumption* (1987); Ian Hodder, ed., The *Meanings of Things* edited (1989); Thomas Schlereth, *Cultural History and Material Culture* (1990); Christopher Tilley, ed., *Reading Material Culture* (1990); Susan Pearce, ed., *Museum Studies in Material Culture* edited by Susan Pearce (1991); Susan Pearce, ed., *Museums, Objects and Collections* (1992); Steven Lubar and W. David Kingery, eds., *History from Things: Essays on Material Culture* (1993); and Neil Cummings, ed., *Reading Things* (1993).

15. Beth Coleman, "Race as Technology," unpublished essay 2002, cited by permission of the author.

16. Irit Rogoff, *Terra Infirma: Geography's Visual Culture* (London: Routledge, 2000), 27.

17. Jennifer González, "Installation Art," in *Encyclopedia of Aesthetics,* ed. Michael Kelly (Oxford: UK: Oxford University Press, 1998), 503–508.

18. For excellent overviews, see also Erica Suderberg, *Space, Site, Intervention: Situating Installation Art* (Minneapolis: University of Minnesota Press, 2000), and Julie H. Reiss, *From Margin to Center: The Spaces of Installation Art* (Cambridge, MA: The MIT Press, 1999).

19. Jennifer Licht, "Spaces," quoted in *From Margin to Center: The Spaces of Installation Art,* Julie H. Reiss (Cambridge, MA: The MIT Press, 1999), 96.

20. Allan Kaprow, *Assemblage, Environments and Happenings* (New York: H. N. Abrams, 1965).

21. Ken Knabb, *Situationist International Anthology,* (Berkeley, CA: Bureau of Public Secrets, 1981).

22. Victor Burgin, "Situational Aesthetics," *Studio International* 178, no. 915 (October 1969): 118–121.

23. Victor Burgin, *The End of Art Theory: Criticism and Post-Modernity* (Atlantic Highlands, NJ: Humanities Press International, 1986).

24. Claude Gintz, "Michael Asher: On the Transformation of Situational Aesthetics," *October* 66 (Fall 1993): 113–131.

25. Claire Bishop, *Installation Art: A Critical History* (New York: Routledge, 2005), 8.

26. Ibid., 10.

27. Ibid., 13.

28. Butler, "Subjection, Resistance, Resignification," 242.

29. For a useful recent analysis of the concepts of *identity* and *identity politics,* see Linda Martin Alcoff, ed., *Identity Politics Reconsidered* (New York: Palgrave Macmillan, 2006).

30. Stuart Hall, "Old and New Identities, Old and New Ethnicities," in *Culture, Globalization and the World System,* ed. A. King (Basingstoke: Macmillan, 1991), 41–68.

31. Ibid., 57.

32. Kobena Mercer, "Black Art and the Burden of Representation," *Third Text* (Spring 1990): 68.

33. Craig Owens, *Beyond Recognition: Representation, Power and Culture* (Berkeley: University of California Press, 1992), 262.

34. Hal Foster, *The Return of the Real* (Cambridge, MA: The MIT Press, 1996), 182.

35. Ibid., 180–181.

36. Ibid., 203.

37. Ludmilla Jordanova, "History, 'Otherness' and Display," in *Cultural Encounters: Representing 'Otherness,'* ed. Elizabeth Hallam and Brian V. Street (London: Routledge, 2000), 249–250.

38. Foster writes, "A parody of primitivisms, a reversal of ethnographic roles, a preemptive playing-dead, a plurality of practices, or a mobility of positions—are all ways to disturb a dominant culture that relies on strict stereotypes, stable lines of authority, and humanist reanimations and museological resurrections of many sorts." Foster, *The Return of the Real,* 199.

39. Ibid., 197.

40. I myself applied the label "visual ethnography" to the work of Amalia Mesa-Bains in 1993, though I argued that her work was as much a confrontation with this discipline as a parallel discourse. See Jennifer González, "Rhetoric of the Object: Material Memory and the Artwork of Amalia Mesa-Bains," *Visual Anthropology Review,* no. 9 (1993): 82–91. I write, "It is therefore possible to see the work of artists such as Mesa-Bains as itself a visual ethnography; one that works in parallel, and in confrontation, with orthodox ethnographic discourse."

41. Foster, *The Return of the Real,* 199–202.

42. It is not possible to summarize here the complex dance that constituted the confluence of a conservative notion of multiculturalism that motivated large institutions to solicit the works of underrepresented artists with the progressive politics of artists working on critiques of race discourse at the same time. The much-maligned Whitney Biennial of 1993 showed how this confluence could backfire in eyes of the critical art establishment, despite the fact that many of the works in that show are now considered classic works of the period.

43. For example, Beyte Saar, David Hammonds, Glen Ligon, Lorna Simpson, Daniel Martinez, Coco Fuco, Guillermo Gomez Peña, Kara Walker, Danny Tisdale, Keith Piper, Los Cybrids, and so forth.

44. For a more detailed analysis, see Jennifer González, "Autotopographies," in *Prosthetic Territories: Politics and Hypertechnology,* ed. Gabe Brahm and Mark Driscoll (Boulder, CO: Westview Press, 1995), 133–150.

45. Walter Benjamin, "N [Re the Theory of Knowledge, Theory of Progress]," in *Benjamin: Philosophy, History, Aesthetics* (Chicago: University of Chicago Press, 1983) 67.

46. This observation first appeared in Jennifer Gonzalez, "Against the Grain: The Artist as Conceptual Materialist," in *Fred Wilson: Objects and Installations 1979–2000* (Baltimore: Center for Art and Visual Culture, University of Maryland Baltimore County, 2001), 22–32.

47. See, for example, Roberta Smith, "Art in Review; Kori Newkirk," *New York Times,* March 17, 2006.

48. Mercer, "Black Art and the Burden of Representation," 78.

49. See Angela Y. Davis, *Abolition Democracy: Beyond Prisons, Torture, Empire* (New York: Seven Stories Press, 2005), see also Avery Gordon, *Keeping Good Time: Reflections on Knowledge, Power, and People* (Boulder, CO: Paradigm Publishers, 2004).

Chapter 1: James Luna: Artifacts and Fictions

1. "I don't want to be an Indian anymore." Performed at The Centro Cultural de la Raza in Balboa Park, San Diego, August 28–29, 1992.

2. There are still differing opinions on the best way to identify members of indigenous cultures of the Americas. In this chapter, I use the word *Indian* to indicate the mythological figure that is the subject of stereotype and legend, and I use the term *Native American* to indicate the human subjects who are of indigenous origin. It should be noted, however, that many indigenous tribe members prefer to be called American Indians.

3. The artist has argued that "performance and installation offers an opportunity like no other for Indian people to express themselves without compromise in traditional art forms of ceremony, dance, oral traditions, and contemporary thought. Within these [nontraditional] spaces one can use a variety of media such as objects, sounds, video, slides." James Luna, "Allow Me to Introduce Myself: The performance art of James Luna," *Candian Theater Review* 68 (Fall 1991): 46–47.

4. Fred Wilson's *My Life as a Dog* (chapter 2) makes for an interesting comparison.

5. For some, black represents the west, where the sun sets in darkness, a place that represents finality; white represents the north, a cleansing power of winter that teaches courage, endurance, and wisdom; red represents the east as a place where peace, light, and new life rise up each day, blood and birth are from the east; yellow represents the south with its strong sun that stands for the peak of life, warmth, understanding, and ability. For the Lakota, for example, the color red signifies the north, yellow the east, white the south, and black the west. William Marder, *Indians in the Americas* (San Diego, CA: The Book Tree, 2005), 111.

6. "From the earth the Creating Power formed the shapes of men and women. He used red earth and white earth, black earth and yellow earth, and made as many as the thought would do for a start. He stamped on the earth and the shapes came alive, each taking the color of the earth out of which it was made. The Creating Power gave all of them understanding and speech and told them what tribes they belonged to." Richard Erdoes and Alfonso Ortiz, *American Indian Myths and Legends* (New York: Pantheon Books, 1984), 498.

7. James Luna, *The Sacred Colors,* exhibition catalog (Sacramento, CA: Galeria Posada, 1992), not paginated.

8. Judith McWillie, "James Luna: Two Worlds/Two Rooms," *Two Worlds,* exhibition catalog (New York: INTAR Gallery, 1989), 4.

9. Homi Bhabha, *The Location of Culture* (London: Routledge, 1994), 114.

10. Ibid., 7.

11. Rasheed Araeen, "A New Beginning: Beyond Postcolonial Cultural Theory and Identity Politics," in *The Third Text Reader on Art, Culture and Theory,* ed. Rasheed Araeen, Sean Cubitt, and Ziauddin Sardar (London: Continuum, 2002), 338.

12. Luna, *The Sacred Colors*.

13. Roger Boyce, "James Luna 'Makes Do' at the ICA Theater," *Art New England* (June/July 1999): 14.

14. Ibid.

15. Miwon Kwon, "One Place after Another: Notes on Site Specificity," *October* 80 (Spring 1997): 85–110; Alice Ming Wai Jim, "Urban Mediations in Hong Kong Contemporary Art: Notes on A Very Good City and Local Orientation," *Positions: East Asia Cultures Critique* 12, no. 3 (Winter 2004): 733–775; C. Ondine Chavoya, "Customized Hybrids: The Art of Ruben Ortiz Torres and Lowriding in Southern California," CR: *The New Centennial Review* 4, no. 2 (Fall 2004): 141–184.

16. Deleuze and Guattari offer the example of the orchid and the wasp: "The orchid deterritorializes by forming an image, a tracing of a wasp; but the wasp reterritorializes on that image. The wasp is nevertheless deterritorialized, becoming a piece in the orchid's reproductive apparatus. But it reterritorializes the orchid by transporting its pollen.... At the same time, something else entirely is going on: not an imitation at all but a capture of code, surplus value of code, an increase in valence, a veritable becoming, a becoming-wasp of the orchid and a becoming-orchid of the wasp. Each of these becomings brings about the deterritorialization of one term and the reterritorialization of the other; the two becoming interlink and form relays in a circulation of intensities pushing the deterritorialization every further." Gilles Deluze and Félix Guattari, *A Thousand Plateaus: Capitalism and Schizophrenia,* trans. Brian Massumi (Minneapolis: University of Minnesota Press, 1987), 10.

17. Luna lists other faculty including Craig Kauffman, John Paul Jones, James Turrell, Lloyd Hamrol, Ed Beral, Robert Irwin, Tony Delap, Barbara Rose and John Coplans as influences on his website, http://www.jamesluna.com/jamesLUNA1 .html (accessed September 2006).

18. The Luiseño name is inherited from the San Luis Rey Mission, established by the colonizing Spanish in 1798. Before the region was called Quechla, and the people were called Quechnajuichom. Lisbeth Haas, *Conquests and Historical Identities in California, 1769–1936* (Berkeley: University of California Press, 1995, 2–3.

19. McWillie, "James Luna," 3.

20. For more on the history of European and U.S. displays of indigenous peoples, see "The Other History of Intercultural Performances," in Coco Fusco, *English Is Broken Here: Notes on Cultural Fusion in the Americas* (New York: The New Press, 1995), 37–63.

21. Calvin Reid, "Inside/Outside," *Art in America* (January 1991): 61.

22. Jean Fisher, "In Search of the 'Inauthentic': Disturbing Signs in Contemporary Native American Art," *Art Journal* (Fall 1992): 46.

23. Miwon Kwon, "Postmortem Strategies," *Documents* 3 (Summer 1993): 127.

24. Barbara Kirshenblatt-Gimblett, *Destination Culture: Tourism, Museums, and Heritage* (Berkeley: University of California Press, 1998), 162.

25. James Clifford, *The Predicament of Culture: Twentieth-Century Ethnography, Literature, and Art* (Cambridge, MA: Harvard University Press, 1988), 224.

26. Olivier Asselin and Johanne Lamoureux, "Autofictions, or Elective Identities," *Parachute* 105, no. 3 (2002): 13.

27. Pratt's concept of autoethnography is preceded by a different use of the term by Francoise Lionnet in her book *Autobiographical Voices* (1989), in which she suggests that Zora Neale Hurston's autobiography *Dust Tracks on a Road* can be considered autoethnographic to the degree that it produces a "figural anthropology" of the self. Hurston, who trained as an anthropologist, situates herself as the subject of a text that is also a vehicle for recounting the story of her life as a participant in, and observer of, her culture. This double position of "inside" and "outside" that attends the two genres of autobiography and ethnography create for Lionnet a productive tension in the reading of Hurston's own ambivalent relation to the telling of her life story.

28. Mary Louise Pratt, *Imperial Eyes: Travel Writing and Transculturation* (New York: Routledge, 1992), 7.

29. Ibid.

30. Ibid.

31. See, among others, Roland Barthes, "Rhetoric of the Image," in *Image/Music/Text* (New York: Hill and Wang, 1977).

32. For a further discussion of this in relation to contemporary digital art and photography, see Jennifer González, "Morphologies: Race as Visual Technology," in *Only Skin Deep: Changing Visions of the American Self,* ed. Brian Wallis and Coco Fusco (New York: International Center of Photography, 2003).

33. See Brian Wallis, "Black Bodies, White Science," *American Art* 9, no. 2 (Summer 1995): 39–61.

34. See John Tagg, "Evidence, Truth and Order: Photographic Records and the Growth of the State," in *The Burden of Representation: Essays on Photographies and Histories* (Minneapolis: University of Minnesota Press, 1988), 60–65.

35. See, for example, J. C. Boileau Grant, "Anthropometry of the Beaver, Sekani, and Carrier Indians," Anthropological Series No. 18 (Washington, DC: Government Printing Bureau, 1936); W. W. Howells, *Anthropometry of the Natives of Arnhem Land and the Australian Race Problem* (Cambridge, MA: Harvard University Press, 1937); or M. J. Herskovits, *The Anthropometry of the American Negro* (New York: Columbia University Press, 1930).

36. This perspective on Native Americans as a "vanishing" race is of course still the dominant one, as the following text from the Library of Congress website reveals: "From 1906 to 1927 Curtis traversed the western United States and British Columbia, studying and photographing the vanishing native American peoples and their many cultures." http://www.loc.gov/rr/print/guide/port-1.html (accessed September 30, 2006).

37. Alan Trachtenberg, *Shades of Hiawatha: Staging Indians, Making Americans 1880–1930* (New York: Hill and Wang, 2004), 195.

38. See Christopher Lyman, *The Vanishing Race and Other Illusions: Photographs of Indians by Edward S. Curtis* (New York: Pantheon Books, 1982).

39. Trachtenberg, *Shades of Hiawatha,* 206.

40. Teresa Harlan, "Creating a Visual History: A Question of Ownership," *Aperture,* no. 139 (Summer 1995): 26.

41. For a more detailed history of this period of image making, see Trachtenberg, *Shades of Hiawatha.*

42. We can see that people at the time also saw Fraser's image as one of *racial* vanishing: "One of the strongest works of the Exposition in its intense pathos is this conception of the end of the Indian race. Over the country the Indian has ridden for many a weary day, following the long trail that leads across a continent. A blizzard is on. He has peered to the right and left, but alas! The trail is gone and only despair is his. So it has been with the Indian. His trail is now lost and on the edge of the continent he finds himself almost annihilated." Juliet Helena Lumbard James, *Sculpture of the Exposition Palaces and Courts* (San Francisco: H. S. Crocker Company, 1915), reproduced at http://www.books-about-california.com (accessed September 2006).

43. Including the Detroit Institute for the Arts, the Fine Arts Museums of San Francisco, and the Reading Public Museum of Pennsylvania, among others.

44. See "Marcus Amerman," in *Staging the Indian: The Politics of Representation,* ed. Jill Sweet and Ian Berry (Saratoga Springs, NY: The Tang Teaching Museum and Art Gallery, 2001), 46–58. For an excellent discussion of the production and significance of photographs of and by American Indian photographers, see Gerald Vizenor, "Imagic Moments: Native Identities and Literary Modernity," *Third Text* 46 (Spring 1999): 25–37.

45. For recent research, see Carter Jones Meyer and Diana Royer, eds., *Selling the Indian: Commercializing and Appropriating American Indian Cultures* (Tucson: University of Arizona Press, 2001).

46. James Luna and David Merritt, *Take a Picture with a Real Indian,* video (Toronto: V Tape, 2001).

47. Ibid.

48. For a short history of this practice, see Fusco, "The Other History of Intercultural Performance," 37–63.

49. Ibid., 48.

50. Stephen Durland, "Call Me in '93: An Interview with James Luna," *High Performance* 56 (Winter 1991): 39.

51. James Luna, *Take a Picture with a Real Indian,* 2001. Transcribed from video.

52. Ann Marie Acklam, "The Body as Spectacle in the Performance and Installation Art of James Luna," M.A. thesis, University of Essex, 1998, 29.

53. Durland, "Call Me in '93," 39.

54. For a discussion of Joseph Beuys's self-identification with shamanism, see John F. Moffitt, *Occultism in Avant-Garde Art: The Case of Joseph Beuys* (Ann Arbor: UMI Research Press, 1988), 105.

55. Ellen Fernandez-Sacco, "Check Your Baggage: Resisting 'Whiteness' in Art History," *Art Journal* 60, no. 4 (Winter 2001): 59–61.

56. For an excellent discussion of the spatial politics of indigenous habitation and virtual museum exhibitions that raises many issues pertinent to the work of James Luna, see Julia Emberly, "(un)Housing Aboriginal Possessions in the

Virtual Museum: Cultural Practices and Decolonization in civilization.ca and Reservation X," *Journal of Visual Culture* 5, no. 3 (December 2006): 387–410.

57. Andrea Liss, "The Art of James Luna: Postmodernism with Pathos," in *James Luna: Actions and Reactions, An Eleven Year Survey of Installation/Performance Work 1981–1992* (Santa Cruz: The Regents of the University of California, 1992), 15.

58. Gay Morris, "James Luna at Pro Arts," *Art in America* 82, no. 7 (1994): 102–103.

59. Pablo Tac, "Indian Life and Customs at Mission San Luis Rey," trans. Minna Hewes and Gordon Hewes, *The Americas* 9, no. 1 (July 1952): 87–106.

Chapter 2: Fred Wilson: Material Museology

1. The exhibition *Rooms with a View* was on view at Bronx Council on the Arts' Longwood Arts Gallery from December 12, 1987, to February 6, 1988. This exhibition was organized by Fred Wilson and included the following artists: Barton Benes, Willi Birch, Serena Bocchino, Marina Cappeletto, Paul Cappelli, Sunjoon Choh, Albert Chong, Pawel Cortes-Wodtasik, Jimmie Durham, Robert Hawkins, Noah Jemison, Alexander Kosolapov, Nina Kuo, Paul Laster, Larry List, Manuel Macarrulla, James McCoy, Tyrone Mitchell, Sana Musasama, Gloria Nixon, Lorenzo Pace, Linda Peer, Lise Prown, Jewel Ross, Robin Ryder, Elena Sisto, Eva Stettner, Ken Tisa, Alvin Toda, and Peggie Yunque. In the publicity poster for this exhibition, a subtitle or descriptive line read: "The Struggle Between Culture, Context and the Context of Art" and "An exhibition of contemporary work in three settings: the Ethnographic Museum, the turn of the century Salon, and the White Box." Room designers included Curt Belshe and Lise Brown. A seminar titled "The Role of the Critic in the Art World" with guest speaker John Yau was organized in conjunction with the exhibition. Thanks to Edwin Ramoran, current director of the Longwood Arts Project for providing this information.

2. Leslie King-Hammond, "A Conversation with Fred Wilson," in *Mining the Museum*, ed. Lisa Corrin (Baltimore: The Contemporary, Baltimore, in cooperation with The New Press, 1994), 31.

3. Susan Vogel, "Always True to the Object, in Our Fashion," in *Exhibiting Cultures: The Poetics and Politics of Museum Display*, ed. Ivan Karp and Steven Levine (Washington, DC: The Smithsonian Institution Press, 1991), 195.

4. Vogel, "Always True to the Object, in Our Fashion," 198.

5. George W. Stocking, Jr., ed., *Objects and Others: Essays on Museums and Material Culture* (Madison: University of Wisconsin Press, 1985), 11.

6. Some of his most famous exhibitions are those that were originally canceled such as his 1971 exhibition at the Guggenhiem Museum that contained works of art revealing the business and personal connections of the museum's board of trustees. Haacke's exhibition at the Wallraf-Richartz museum that included his work *Manet '74* traced the history of class privilege in the provenance of a single Manet painting and tied the funding of the museum to the cultural politics of the cold war. Other works emphasize the function of museums as public relations firms for oil corporations such as Exxon or Mobil; Haacke's "MetroMobiltan" (1985) brings into focus the partnership of the Metropolitan

Museum of Art, the Mobil Corporation, and the South African military forces that Mobil supplied with fuel during apartheid.

7. Another of Lawler's photographs, depicting a statue of Sappho and a patrician bust, highlights the gendered differences at play in the displays of male and female bodies in the museum. The title of the image asks rhetorically: *Is it the work, the location, or the stereotype that is the institution?* In a more recent work, Lawler pictures the circulation of art beyond the art museum—in packing crates for transit, at art fairs, and in temporary exhibitions—but she continues to share with Haacke an interest in demystifying or exposing the unseen and overlooked aspects of the museum as an institution, as well as the economic manipulation of the art object as a circulating commodity. See Hal Foster, "Subverisve Signs," in *Recodings: Art, Spectacle, Cultural Politics* (Seattle: Bay Press, 1986), 99–115. One of Foster's concerns, here as in his later essay "The Artist as Ethnographer," is that the artists who focus on the system of arts display and circulation may ultimately be engaged in its self-conscious perpetuation more than its ironic critique.

8. Douglas Crimp, *On the Museum's Ruins* (Cambridge, MA: The MIT Press, 1995), 47.

9. Julie Marcus takes this "postmodern" critique further. She writes, "In one sense, we know very well that it is only a place in an order of things which confers values on an object, and that unplaced things are nothing. . . . Of greater concern are the relations of power through which the fictions of the museum operate." Julie Marcus, "Postmodernity and the Museum," *Social Analysis* 3 (December 1991): 11. Her comments echo George Stocking's insistence that in studying the three-dimensional space of museums and material culture, one must take into account the fourth dimension of time, the fifth dimension of power, and the sixth dimension of ownership.

10. See John C. Welchman, ed., *Institutional Critique and After* (Zurich: JRP/Ringier, 2006).

11. Andrea Fraser, "From the Critique of Institutions to an Institution of Critique," in *Institutional Critique and After,* ed. John C. Welchman (Zurich: JRP/Ringier, 2006), 130.

12. Renée Green, "Beyond," in *Institutional Critique and After,* ed. John C. Welchman (Zurich: JRP/Ringier, 2006), 160–161.

13. Although it performed admirably for a number of progressive scholars as an abstract concept, "otherness" also came to stand for a generic categorical difference that obscured real relations of power and cultural exchange. One of Renée Green's early works titled *I Won't Play "Other" to Your Same* drew attention to the underlying segregationist logic of the concept while simultaneously referencing Barbara Kruger's feminist work titled *I Won't Play Nature to Your Culture.*

14. Fred Wilson, statement for the Whitney Biennial, Whitney Museum of American Art, New York, 1993.

15. James Clifford comments, "The fact that rather abruptly, in the space of a few decades, a large class of non-Western artifacts came to be redefined as art is a taxonomic shift that requires critical historical discussion, not celebration. That this construction of a generous category of art pitched at a global scale occurred just as the planet's tribal people came massively under European political, economic, and evangelical domination cannot be irrelevant." See James Clifford, "Histories of the Tribal and Modern," in *Discourses: Conversations in Postmodern Art and Culture,* ed. Russell Ferguson, William Olander, Marcia Tucker, and Karen Fiss (Cambridge, MA: The MIT Press, 1990), 412.

16. bell hooks, *Black Looks: Race and Representation* (Boston: South End Press, 1992), 23–24.

17. Homi Bhabha, "The Third Space: Interview with Jonathan Rutherford," in *Identity: Community, Culture, Difference,* ed. Jonathan Rutherford (London: Lawrence and Wishart, 1990), 208.

18. See Abigail Solomon-Godeau, "Photography at the Dock" in *The Art of Memory/The Loss of History* (New York: The New Museum of Contemporary Art, 1985), 48–52.

19. Victor Burgin, *The End of Art Theory* (Atlantic Highlands, NJ: Humanities Press International, 1986), 184–186.

20. James Clifford, "Museums in the Borderlands," in *Different Voices,* ed. Michaelyn Mitchell (New York: Association of Art Museum Directors, 1992), 128.

21. Homi Bhabha, "The Other Question: Difference, Discrimination, and the Discourse of Colonialism," in *Literature, Politics and Theory,* ed. F. Barker et al. (New York: Methuen, 1986), 156.

22. For a discussion of the ways that objects become identified by museums as either art or artifact, see James Clifford, *The Predicament of Culture* (Cambridge, MA: Harvard University Press, 1988).

23. See *The Poetics and Politics of Museum Display,* ed. Ivan Karp and Steven D. Levine (Washington, DC: The Smithsonian Institution Press, 1991).

24. Jose Muñoz, *Disidentifications: Queers of Color and the Performance of Politics* (Minneapolis: University of Minnesota Press, 1999), 146.

25. See Daniel J. Sherman and Irit Rogoff, "Introduction," in *Museum Culture: Histories, Discourses, Spectacles* (Minneapolis: University of Minnesota Press, 1994), 6.

26. See *"Primitivism" in Twentieth Century Art: Affinity of the Tribal and Modern* (New York: Museum of Modern Art; distributed by New York Graphic Society Books, 1984), and Kirk Varnedoe, *High and Low: Modern Art, Popular Culture* (New York: Museum of Modern Art, Distributed by H. N. Abrams, 1990).

27. James Clifford, "Histories of the Tribal and Modern," in *The Predicament of Culture* (Cambridge, MA: Harvard University Press, 1988), 189–214.

28. Clifford, "Histories of the Tribal and Modern," 200.

29. Mary Ann Staniszewski, *The Power of Display: A History of Exhibition Installations at the Museum of Modern Art* (Cambridge, MA: The MIT Press, 1998), 112.

30. Scholar Maurice Berger comments that this work provoked "anxiety and guilt" in the viewer because the skeletons "represent the body as a neutral commodity that is often subject to the whims of the institutions of capitalism." Maurice Berger, "Displacements," in *Ciphers of Identity* (Cantonsville: Fine Arts Gallery, University of Maryland Baltimore County, 1993), 26.

31. Anthony Alan Shelton writes, "Models and dioramas miniaturized the Empire's subjects to a more comprehensive surveillance by the colonial eye." "Museum Ethnography: An Imperial Science," in *Cultural Encounters: Represent-*

ing 'Otherness,' ed. Elizabeth Hallam and Brian V. Street (New York and London: Routledge, 2000), 179.

32. See Anna C. Chave, "New Encounters with *Les Demoiselles d'Avignon*: Gender, Race, and the Origins of Cubism," in *Race-ing Art History: Critical Readings in Race and Art History,* ed. Kymberly N. Pinder (New York: Routledge, 2002), 261–287.

33. Olu Oguibe, "Appropriation as Nationalism in Modern African Art," *Third Text* 16, no. 3 (2002): 243.

34. According to the artist, these were the words apparently uttered by explorer and Egyptologist Lord Carter and his companion when they glimpsed the contents of the Pharaoh Tutankhamen's tomb for the first time. Here, obviously, the words have an ironic function. The museum of art, like the tomb of a pharaoh, houses the sacred and precious objects of a given community. Yet, many of these precious objects have been stolen from sacred sites, the tombs of other cultures that were also meant to be left untouched. The museum reinstitutionalizes these objects as art, thereby repeating the cultural prohibition—again, they cannot be touched. Picasso's painting demonstrates the transformation of a devalued object—the "primitive" African mask—into a precious icon of modernity.

35. A significant majority of museum guards in New York museums are African American, leading to claims by those institutions that they have a racially diverse staff. But, as Maurice Berger writes, "The boards of art museums, publishers of art magazines and books and owners of galleries rarely hire people of color in policy-making positions." Maurice Berger, *How Art Becomes History* (New York: Harper Collins, 1992), 150.

36. Carol Duncan, *Civilizing Rituals: Inside Public Art Museums* (New York: Routledge, 1995), 116–117.

37. For an excellent analysis of the ethnic stereotype as a racist fetish that protects the colonizer from the fear of difference, see Homi Bhabha, "The Other Question," 148–172.

38. Walter Benjamin, *Reflections,* ed. Peter Demetz, trans. Edmund Jephcott (New York: Schocken, 1978), 25–26.

39. Indeed, Wilson in an interview claims to have been directly influenced by the book *Black Athena.* See David Kelleran, "Fred Wilson," *Flash Art* (November 1992), 98. For a critical response to *Black Athena,* see *Black Athena Revisited,* ed. Mary R. Lefkowitz and Guy MacLean Rogers (Chapel Hill: University of North Carolina, 1996).

40. Maurice Berger, "Viewing the Invisible: Fred Wilson's Allegories of Absence and Loss," in *Fred Wilson: Objects and Installations 1979–2000* (New York: Distributed Art Publishers with Center for Art and Visual Culture, University of Maryland Baltimore County, 2001), 17.

41. Judith E. Stein, "Sins of Omission," *Art in America* (October 1993), 110.

42. Corrin, "Mining the Museum," 8.

43. Stein, "Sins of Omission," 112.

44. Corrin, "Mining the Museum," 58.

45. Ibid.

46. Gaston Bachelard, *The Poetics of Space,* trans. Maria Jolas (Boston: Beacon Press, 1969), 89.

47. See Lyle Ashton Harris's discussion of "redemptive narcissism" in *Inside Out: Psychological Self-Portraiture* (Ridgefield, CT: Aldrich Museum of Contemporary Art, 1995).

48. Judy Van Dyke, "Mining the Project Experiences," in *Mining the Museum,* ed. Lisa Corrin (New York: The Contemporary, Baltimore, in cooperation with The New Press, 1994), 55.

49. Ira Berlin, "Mining the Museum and the Rethinking of Maryland's History," in *Mining the Museum,* ed. Lisa Corrin (New York: The Contemporary, Baltimore, in cooperation with The New Press, 1994), 45.

50. Ibid., 41.

51. Interview with the author, September 1, 1995.

52. Corrin, "Mining the Museum," 49.

53. Ibid., 68.

54. Ibid., 61.

55. Ibid., 69.

56. Ibid., 73.

57. Fred Wilson, written statement for the Whitney Museum Biennial 1993, cited in Patterson Sims, "Metamorphosing Art/Mixing the Museum," in *The Museum: Mixed Metaphors* (Seattle: Seattle Art Museum, 1993), 8.

58. Viewer's comments, cited in Patterson Sims, "Metamorphosing Art/Mixing the Museum," in *The Museum: Mixed Metaphors* (Seattle: Seattle Art Museum, 1993), 5.

59. Caption, cited in Patterson Sims, "Metamorphosing Art/Mixing the Museum," in *The Museum: Mixed Metaphors* (Seattle: Seattle Art Museum, 1993), 29.

60. Bruce Barcot, cited in Patterson Sims, "Metamorphosing Art/Mixing the Museum," in *The Museum: Mixed Metaphors* (Seattle: Seattle Art Museum, 1993), 37.

61. Fred Wilson, cited in Patterson Sims, "Metamorphosing Art/Mixing the Museum," in *The Museum: Mixed Metaphors* (Seattle: Seattle Art Museum, 1993), 9.

62. Fred Wilson, quoted in Hilarie M. Sheets, "America's Artist, 2003 Edition," *New York Times,* sec. 2, June 1, 2003, 35.

63. Maurice Berger, "Art in Context," in *Fred Wilson: Objects and Installations 1979–2000* (New York: Distributed Art Publishers with Center for Art and Visual Culture, University of Maryland Baltimore County, 2001), 162.

64. Ibid.

65. Hal Foster, "The Artist as Ethnographer," in *The Return of the Real* (Cambridge, MA: 1996), 196.

66. Ibid., 198.

67. Miwon Kwon, *One Place after Another: Site-Specific Art and Locational Identity* (Cambridge, MA: The MIT Press, 2002), 47.

68. Ibid.

69. Frazer Ward, "The Haunted Museum: Institutional Critique and Publicity," *October* 73 (1995): 84.

70. Ibid., 88.

71. See Irene Winter's essay "Exhibit/Inhibit: Archeology, Value, History in the Work of Fred Wilson," in *New Histories* (Boston: Institute of Contemporary Art, 1996), 182–191. See also Foster, "The Artist as Ethnographer," 191.

72. Michel Foucault, *The Archaeology of Knowledge,* trans. A. M. Sheridan Smith (New York: Pantheon Books, 1972), 49.

73. An archeology "does not imply the search for a beginning; it does not relate analysis to geological excavation. It designates the general theme of a description that questions the already-said at the level of its existence: of the enunciative function that operates within it, of the discursive formation, and the general archive system to which it belongs. Archeology describes discourses as practices specified in the element of the archive." Foucault, *The Archaeology of Knowledge,* 131. Hayden White comments, "Any given mode of discourse is identifiable, then, not by what it permits consciousness to say about the world, but by what it prohibits it from saying, the area of experience that the linguistic act itself cuts off from representation in language." Hayden White, *Tropics of Discourse* (Baltimore, MD: The Johns Hopkins University Press, 1978), 239.

74. White, *Tropics of Discourse,* 239–240.

75. Jacques Derrida, *Archive Fever: A Freudian Impression* (Chicago: University of Chicago Press, 1995), 3.

76. Interview with the author, October 2002.

77. "Fred Wilson: Art in Context," exhibition brochure (New York: Metro Pictures 1995).

78. See the discussion of *autofiction* and *autotopography* in the introduction and in chapter 2.

79. Ralph Ellison, *Invisible Man* (New York: Vintage International, 1995), xvi.

80. Bill Brown, "Reification, Reanimation and the American Uncanny," *Critical Inquiry* 32 (Winter 2006): 175–207, 199.

81. Ibid., 207.

82. Blake Gopnik, "At Venice Biennale, Fred Wilson Colors in the City's History," *Washington Post,* June 18, 2003, C1.

83. Ellison, *Invisible Man,* 200.

84. Peter Erickson, "Respeaking Othello in Fred Wilsons's *Speak of Me As I Am,*" *Art Journal* 64, no. 2 (Summer 2005): 7.

85. Ibid., 8.

Chapter 3: Amalia Mesa-Bains: Divine Allegories

1. Rubén Salazar, "Who Is a Chicano? And What Is It the Chicanos Want?" *Los Angeles Times,* February 6, 1970, B7.

2. Shifra M. Goldman and Tomás Ybarra-Frausto, "The Political and Social Contexts of Chicano Art," in CARA /*Chicano Art: Resistence and Affirmation* (Los Angeles: Wright Art Gallery, University of California, 1991), 83–95.

3. Ibid.

4. Tomás Ybarra-Frausto, "Sanctums of the Spirit: The Altares of Amalia Mesa-Bains," in *Grotto of the Virgins* (New York: Intar Latin American Gallery, 1987), 2–9.

5. See Sybil Venegas, "The Day of the Dead in Aztlán: Chicano Variations on the Theme of Life, Death and Self Preservation" (M.A. thesis, University of California, Los Angeles, 1993).

6. See Lara Median and Gilbert R. Cadena, "Día de los Muertos: Public Ritual, Community Renewal, and Popular Religion in Los Angeles," in *Horizons of the Sacred,* ed. Timothy Matovina and Gary Riebe-Estrealla (Ithaca, NY: Cornell University Press, 2002), 69–94.

7. Tomás Ybarra-Frausto notes, "Creating *altares* as gallery installations was one example among innumerable efforts to validate and reinterpret Chicano vernacular traditions adapting them to vital new social contexts." Ybarra-Frausto, "Sanctums of the Spirit," 4.

8. Anne Barclay Morgan, "Amalia Mesa-Bains" *Art Papers* 19, no. 2 (March/April 1995): 29.

9. Ibid.

10. See also a similar practice described by Karen Mary Davalos as *"ofrenda/installation"* in *Exhibiting Mestizaje: Mexican (American) Museums in the Diaspora* (Albuquerque: University of New Mexico Press, 2001).

11. Ybarra-Frausto, "Sanctums of the Spirit," 6.

12. Julia Kristeva, "Women's Time," in *The Kristeva Reader* (New York: Columbia University Press, 1986), 193–194.

13. Ybarra-Frausto, "Sanctums of the Spirit," 9.

14. The artist has stated that the "installations serve as devices of intimate storytelling through an aesthetic of accumulation; accumulation of experience, reference, memory and transfiguration. Historical works such as the Dolores Del Rio altar contextualize a domestic icon of the cinema within the Hollywood/*Mexicana* dual worlds and act as well for my personal narrative of life events. Amalia Mesa-Bains, "Domesticana: The Sensibility of a Chicana Rasquache," *Aztlán* 24, no. 2 (1999): 165.

15. "The home altar has been built on the boundaries of patriarchal alienation. Deep within the interior of her home the woman's private altar has been a separate space dedicated to the fulfillment of her own ideology, an ideology given to the fruition of social relationships and opposed to alienation." Kay Turner, "Mexican-American Women's Home Altars: The Art of Relationship" (Ph.D. diss., University of Texas at Austin, 1990), 50.

16. Yvonne Yarbro-Bejarano, "The Lesbian Body in Latina Cultural Production," in *Entiendes: Queer Readings, Hispanic Writings* (Durham, NC: Duke University Press, 1995), 185.

17. See Amalia Mesa-Bains, "El Mundo Feminino: Chicana Artists of the Movement—A Commentary on Development and Production," in *CARA /Chicano Art: Resistance and Affirmation* (Los Angeles: Wright Art Gallery, University of California, 1991), 131–140.

18. For an interesting discussion of recent art using the Virgin of Guadalupe, see Catherine Ramirez, "Deus ex machina: Tradition, Technology, and the Chicanafuturist Art of Marion C. Martinez," *Aztlán* 29, no. 2 (Spring 2002): 55–92.

19. Nestór García Canclini, "Memory and Innovation in the Theory of Art," *South Atlantic Quarterly* 92, no. 3 (Summer 1993): 443.

20. Scholar Paula Findlen writes, "Given the passion for constructing grottoes in the gardens of Renaissance Europe, it is obvious that nature's potential to be perceived as a museum expanded in the intricate interplay between art and nature that unfolded in the famous gardens… of the sixteenth and seventeenth centuries." Paula Findlen, "The Museum: Its Classical Etymology and Renaissance Genealogy," *Journal of the History of Collections* 1, no. 1 (1989): 60–61.

21. The artist might also have been inspired by Judy Baca's comment "My grandmother made grottos in her house and altars." See Amalia Mesa-Bains, "Art of the Other Mexico: Sources and Meanings," *Art of the Other Mexico: Sources and Meanings* (Chicago: Mexican Fine Arts Center Museum, 1993), 42.

22. As Ybarra-Frausto observes, the static form of the traditional altar is here "discarded for new spatial patterning derived from random processes like layering, scattering, and piling." Ybarra-Frausto, "Sanctums of the Spirit," 9.

23. See, for example, Robert Morris, *Untitled* (Corner Piece), 1964; Walter de Maria, *The New York Earth Room,* 1977; and Robert Smithson, *Non-Site* (Essen Soil and Mirrors).

24. Alicia Gaspar de Alba notes that "in Kahlo, Chicana artists… found a model of their own struggles within Anglo racism and Chicano patriarchy." Alicia Gaspar de Alba, *Chicano Art: Inside/Outside the Master's House* (Austin: University of Texas Press, 1998), 155.

25. Ybarra-Frausto, "Chicano Movement/Chicano Art," in *Exhibiting Cultures: The Poetics and Politics of Museum Display,* ed. Ivan Karp and Steven Levine (Washington, DC: The Smithsonian Institution Press, 1991), 134. See also Yvonne Yrbro-Bejarano, "The Female Subject in Chicano Theatre: Sexuality, 'Race', and Class," *Theatre Journal* 38, no. 4 (December 1986): 389–407.

26. Ybarra-Frausto, "Chicano Movement/Chicano Art," 133.

27. Turner, "Mexican American Women's Home Altars," 75.

28. Ibid., 262.

29. Amalia Mesa-Bains, "*Domesticana*: The Sensibility of a Chicana Rasquache," *Atzlan* 24, no. 2 (Fall 1999): 161.

30. Celeste Olalquiaga, *Megalopolis: Contemporary Cultural Sensibilities* (Minneapolis: University of Minnesota Press, 1992), 43.

31. Ibid., 45.

32. Ibid., 47.

33. Olalquiaga observes, "In postmodern culture, Mesa-Bains's work would seem to contend, old patriarchal deities are no longer satisfactory. What she has done is to profit from an established tradition in order to convey new values. Beyond mere formal changes her *altares* replace the transcendental with the political. In them the affirmation of feminist and Chicano experiences is more relevant than a pious communication with the celestial sphere." Ibid., 48.

34. The artist has commented, "My worldview is not formed as an educated installation artist, but as a young girl walking the archards where my family worked; the disposition to the altar is not a recuperation or appropriation but the expression of earlier moments of meaning with my grandmother, mother and godmother. It is precisely that working-class upbringing that roots the work in a continuous relationship between tradition and innovation." Email correspondence with the author, December 26, 2004.

35. Laura Laurencich-Minelli writes, "The exceptional nature of several American items may be noted here, particularly a pre-Columbian map, two parts of a pre-Columbian codex, two feather head-dresses from Florida, and nine stone idols from the New World; the collection also included a 'stone knife with a wooden handle with which they sacrificed,' a stone axe, a series of bows and arrows and an obsidian razor, as well as a few items from colonial Mexico, including a small feather mosaic picture and a miter." Laura Laurencich-Minelli, "Museography and Ethnographical Collections in Bolonga during the Sixteenth and Seventeenth Centuries," in *The Origins of Museums,* ed. Oliver Impey and Arthur Macgregor (Oxford: Clarendon Press, 1985), 18.

36. "Of special attraction for a prince of the House of Hapsburg must have been the exotica from overseas territories in North America, Asia and the New World. The most famous items were the pre-Columbian feather works, testaments of the subjection of the New World. From one of these head-decorations the Archduke appropriated some feathers for his own helmet on the occasion of his second marriage in Innsbruck." Elisabeth Scheicher, "The Collection of Archduke Ferdinand II at Schloss Ambras," in *The Origins of Museums,* ed. Oliver Impey and Arthur Macgregor (Oxford: Clarendon Press, 1985), 34.

37. Lorenz Seelig, "The Munich *Kunstkammer,* 1565–1807," in *The Origins of Museums,* ed. Oliver Impey and Arthur Macgregor (Oxford: Clarendon Press, 1985), 83.

38. Gerard Turner, "The Cabinet of Experimental Philosophy," in *The Origins of Museums,* ed. Oliver Impey and Arthur Macgregor (Oxford: Clarendon Press, 1985), 215.

39. "Curiosity, therefore, is a term that indicates a historically and culturally specific attitude to the collection and display of objects, and would have had no meaning before 1550.... Attachment to objects—we might reasonably say, the cult of objects—was an inseparable feature of curiosity, and so was a particular style of display.... Through the work of mourning, according to Freud, the libido will slowly release its hold on the objects that are lost, and fix on new ones in turn. The curiosity, and the museological activity associated with it, is among other things a work of mourning." Stephen Bann, "Shrines, Curiosities, and the Rhetoric of Display," in *Visual Display: Culture Beyond Appearances,* ed. Lynne Cooke and Peter Wollen (Seattle, WA: Bay Press, 1995), 23–24.

40. Ibid.

41. Amalia Mesa-Bains, interview with the author, July 17, 1996.

42. Amalia Mesa-Bains, "The Real Multiculturalism: A Struggle for Authority and Power," in *Different Voices,* ed. Michaelyn Mitchell (New York: Association of Art Museum Directors, 1992), 89.

43. Anthony Alan Shelton, "Cabinets of Transgression: Renaissance Collections and the Incorporation of the New World," in *The Cultures of Collecting,* ed. John Elsner and Roger Cardinal (Cambridge, MA: Harvard University Press, 1994), 184, 193.

44. Barbara Kirshenblatt-Gimblett, "Objects of Ethnography," in *Exhibiting Cultures: The Poetics and Politics of Museum Display,* ed. Ivan Karp and Steven D. Levine (Washington, DC: The Smithsonian Institution Press, 1991), 410.

45. Victor Zamudio-Taylor, "Emblems of the Decade: Body+Time=Life/Death," in *The Interrupted Life*, ed. France Morin and Massimo Vignelli (New York: New Museum of Contemporary Art, 1991), 176–177.

46. As critic Julia P. Herzberg observed, "*Borders* refers to the cultural, regional, linguistic, and psychological meaning of the Chicano border experience (by extension anyone's border experience)." Julia P. Herzberg, "Re-membering Identity: Vision of Connections," in *The Decade Show: Frameworks of Identity in the 1980s* (New York: The New Museum of Contemporary Art, 1990), 55–56.

47. Homi Bhabha, "Double Visions," *Artforum* (January 1992): 88.

48. The kind of domestic collection to which the installation refers is ubiquitous in many communities. Observing a similar practice by African Americans, bell hooks writes that "In many black homes, photographs—especially snapshots— were also central to the creation of 'altars.' These commemorative places paid homage to absent loved ones. Snapshots or professional portraits were placed in specific settings so that a relationship with the dead could be continued…. They provided a necessary narrative, a way for us to enter history without words. When words entered, they did so in order to make the images live. Many older black folks who cherished pictures were not literate. The images were crucial documentation, there to sustain and affirm memory." bell hooks, *Art on My Mind: Visual Politics* (New York: The New Press, 1995), 62–63.

49. Herzberg, "Re-membering Identity: Vision of Connections," 55.

50. Victor Zamudio-Taylor, "Contemporary Commentary," in *Ceremony of Memory* (Santa Fe, NM: Center for Contemporary Art, 1988), 15.

51. Interview with the author, July 17, 1996.

52. Susan Buck-Morss observes, "With the dialectical image, [Benjamin] had consciously placed himself in close proximity not only to the Surrealists, but to the Baroque emblemists as well. The *Passagenwerk*'s pictorial representations of ideas are undeniably modeled after those emblem books of the seventeenth century, which had widespread appeal as perhaps the first genre of mass publication." Susan Buck-Morss, *The Dialectics of Seeing* (Cambridge, MA: The MIT Press, 1989) 228.

53. Craig Owens, "The Allegorical Impulse: Toward a Theory of Postmodernism," in *Beyond Recognition: Representation, Power, and Culture* (Berkeley: University of California Press, 1992), 52–69.

54. Amalia Mesa-Bains, interview with the author, August 2002.

55. Amalia Mesa-Bains, unpublished interview with Chon Noriega, November 1993.

56. Amalia Mesa-Bains has commented, "On the other hand, they did not give me the *image* of pre-Columbian objects. They gave them to me without question. They gave them to me without handling them with gloves. They gave them to me on a hierarchy of two sets of values. These objects were not as valuable to them as the integrity of that European painting. So the institutional experience I am having is precisely what the painting and the pre-Columbian figurines reflect in the history I am examining." Interview with the author, July 17, 1996.

57. In his essay on still-life painting, Hal Foster writes, "A given painting by Jan Davidsz, de Heem, or Willem Kalf may include not only metalware from Nürn-

berg and glass from Venice but also porcelain from China, tobacco from America, shells from the Far East, rugs from the Near East, exotic spices from the
Indian archipelago, and on and on—so many synecdoches, if not of the Dutch
empire, then at least of the Dutch market." Hal Foster, "The Art of Fetishism,"
in *Fetishism as Cultural Discourse,* ed. Emily Apter and William Pietz (Ithaca, NY:
Cornell University Press, 1993), 256.

58. See, for example, Norma Klahn, "Literary (re)Mappings: Autobiographical
(Dis)Placements by Chicana Writers," in *Chicana Feminisms,* ed. Gabriela F. Arre-
dondo et al. (Durham, NC: Duke University Press, 2003), 114–145, and Norma E.
Cantú, "The Writing of Canícula: Breaking Boundaries, Finding Forms," in *Chi-
cana Feminisms,* ed. Gabriela F. Arredondo et al. (Durham, NC: Duke University
Press, 2003), 97–108.

59. Mark Wigley, "Untitled: The Housing of Gender," in *Sexuality and Space,* ed.
Beatriz Colomina (New York: Princeton Architectural Press, 1992), 350.

60. Gallery pamphlet from *Venus Envy* exhibition, 1993.

61. Ibid.

62. For example, see the artworks *Nuestra Señora Coatlicue* (1983) by Yolanda
Lopez and *Expresion Chicana* (1976) by Linda Lucero, among many others.

63. Gloria Anzaldúa, *Borderlands/La Frontera* (San Francisco: Spinsters/aunte
lute, 1987), 42.

64. Davíd Carrasco and Eduardo Matos Moctezuma, *Moctezuma's Mexico: Visions
of the Aztec World,* rev. ed. (Boulder: University Press of Colorado, 2003), 181.

65. See Constance Cortez, "The New Aztlan: Nepantla (and Other Sites of
Transmogrification)," in *The Road to Aztlan: Art from a Mythic Homeland,* ed. Vir-
ginia M. Fields and Victor Zamudio-Taylor (Los Angeles: Los Angeles County
Museum of Art, 2001), 358–373.

66. Incidentally, 1538 was the year the Viceroyalty of New Spain, having subdued the Aztecs and the Incas, was established in Mexico and Central America.

67. James of Vitry describing the piety of Mary of Oignies in Caroline Walker
Bynum, *Fragmentation and Redemption: Essays on Gender and the Human Body in
Medieval Religion* (New York: Zone Books, 1991), 119.

68. As Susan Stewart observes about private collections more generally, "Each
sign is placed in relation to a chain of signifiers whose ultimate referent is not
the interior of the room—in itself an empty essence—but the interior of the
self…the materiality of the body is simply one more position within the seri-
ality and diversity of objects. Private space is marked by an exterior material
boundary and an interior surplus of signification." Susan Stewart, *On Longing:
Narratives of the Miniature, the Gigantic, the Souvenir, the Collection* (Baltimore,
MD: Johns Hopkins University Press, 1984), 158–159.

69. Gaston Bachelard writes, "Wardrobes with their shelves, desks with their
drawers, and chests with their false bottoms are veritable organs of the secret
psychological life. Indeed without these objects and a few others in equally high
favor, our intimate life would lack a model of intimacy. They are hybrid objects,
subject objects." Gaston Bachelard, *The Poetics of Space,* trans. Maria Jolas (Boston: Beacon Press, 1969), 78–79.

70. Juan Eduardo Cirlot, *A Dictionary of Symbols,* trans. Jack Sage (New York:
Barnes and Noble, 1971), 261.

71. In writing about cinematic fantasies of the harem, Ella Shoat and Robert Stam suggest, counter to European views, "Memoirs written by harem women depict a complex familial life and a strong network of female communality across class lines. Despite their subordination, harem women often owned and ran their property, and at times exercised political power. The harem, although fundamentally patriarchal in nature, was clearly a site of contradictions." Ella Shohat and Robert Stam, *Unthinking Eurocentrism* (London: Routledge, 1994), 163.

72. Amalia Mesa-Bains, interview with the author, July 17, 1996.

73. Octavio Paz, *Sor Juana*, trans. Margaret Sayers Peden (Cambridge, MA: The Belknap Press of Harvard University Press, 1988), 83.

74. Orest Ranum, "The Refuges of Intimacy," in *A History of Private Life*, ed. Roger Chartier (Cambridge, MA: The Belknap Press of Harvard University Press, 1989), 231.

75. Kent C. Bloomer and Charles W. Moore, *Body, Memory, and Architecture* (New Haven, CT: Yale University Press, 1977), 48.

76. *A Sor Juana Anthology*, trans. Alan S. Trueblood (Cambridge, MA: Harvard University Press, 1988), 232–233.

77. Shohat and Stam, *Unthinking Eurocentrism*, 180.

78. Emma Pérez, *The Decolonial Imaginary: Writing Chicanas into History* (Bloomington: Indiana University Press, 1999), 6.

Chapter 4: Pepón Osorio: No Limits

1. For a discussion of the relationship between cultural difference and spatial politics, see, for example, J. Macgregor Wise, "Home: Territory and Identity," *Cultural Studies* 14, no. 2 (2000): 295–310, and Rob Kitchin, "Creating an Awareness of Others: Highlighting the Role of Space and Place," *Geography* 84, no. 1 (January 1999): 45–54.

2. As with the Chicano movement, the reclamation of Puerto Rican traditions was considered an anti-assimilation act of cultural rescue. Brenda Alejandro writes that this *rescate de la cultura* was a key defining trope in the Puerto Rican cultural movements of the 1960s and 1970s, not only on the island but also in New York City. This general activity led to the creation of the Taller Boricua, El Museo del Barrio, and El Centro de Estudios Puertorriqueōs. Moreover, the Center for Puerto Rican Studies organized cultural workshops and conferences in New York in the spring of 1974 that had broad popular appeal. Osorio's arrival in 1975 meant that he was quickly exposed to this expanding network of arts and cultural organizations. See Brenda Alejandro, *Living in the Inquiry: Memoirs of a Caribbean Mulatto Woman* (New York: Columbia University Teachers College, 1993), 54.

3. David R. White, "*Rescatar y Descargar*: Unmelting the Pot," in *Con To' Los Hierros: A Retrospective of the Work of Pepón Osorio* (New York: El Museo del Barrio, 1991), 23.

4. Luis Aponte-Parés, "Casitas, Place and Culture: Appropriating Place in Puerto Rican Barrios," *Places* 1 (1997): 54.

5. Aponte-Parés, "Casitas, Place and Culture," 55.

6. White, "*Rescatar y Descargar*," 26.

7. Interview with the author, August 30, 1995.

8. Pepón Osorio, in "The Scene of the Crime" by Michael von Glahn in LIVE (August 1993): 10. Susana Leval writes, "Although definitions of *emblequero* in official Spanish dictionaries convey the negative connotations associated with the words "fraud" and "delusion," Puerto Ricans often use this word with positive implications. Pepón himself defines an *embelequero* as someone who "'can make a temple out of nothing'" (*alguien con la capacidad de hacerte un templo de la nada*)." Susana Leval, "Con To' Los Hierros," in *Con To' Los Hierros: A Retrospective of the Work of Pepón Osorio* (New York: El Mueso del Barrio, 1991), 22.

9. Leval, "Con To' Los Hierros," 13. Osorio recounts that, years after the dream he was told that the African words translated into the phrase "pray Ochun," making reference to the Santería deity. This also influenced Osorio's expanded references to the *orishas* discussed in later works.

10. Interview with the author, August 30, 1995.

11. Osorio has stated, "The cigar, for example, I have always used as way of connecting to the divine. With the smoke you transcend from this existence into the above. So I play a lot with cigar toys. And they were surrounding me on the back of the bed providing me support along with the men's shoes symbolizing the men who have been in my life who have also provided support to move into my marriage and my relationships as a man and a future father. So there were all these things. And garlic, I used to use a lot of garlic—plastic garlic—as a way of protecting. Interview with the author, August 30, 1995.

12. Interview with the author, August 30, 1995.

13. Joan Ross Acocella, "Plastic Heaven," *Artforum* 30 (1992): 65.

14. Coco Fusco, "Vernacular Memories," *Art in America* 79 (1991): 99–100. For a thoughtful exception that reads Osorio's use of kitsch as a gesture of ethnic and class resistance, see Anna Indych, "Nuyorican Baroque: Pepón Osorio's *Chucherías*," *Art Journal* 60 (2001): 72–83.

15. Félix Joaquín Rivera, "Why More Is Better," in *Con To' Los Hierros: A Retrospective of the Work of Pepón Osorio* (New York: El Museo del Barrio, 1991), 35.

16. Leval, "Con To' Los Hierros," 12.

17. Kellie Jones, "Domestic Prayer," in *Con To' Los Hierros: A Retrospective of the Work of Pepón Osorio* (New York: El Museo del Barrio, 1991), 32.

18. Interview with the author, August 30, 1995.

19. Rivera, "Why More Is Better," 37.

20. As Coco Fusco observes, "The domestic sphere of the Puerto Rican household in exile serves multiple functions; it is a kind of liberated space for self-expression. Individually decorated domestic objects become receptacles of personal and collective histories, invocations of community, and marks of personal achievement in the face of adversity." Fusco, *English Is Broken Here*, 92.

21. Interview with the author, August 30, 1995.

22. This "turning around" is the kind of "antidisciplinary" operation Michel de Certeau discusses in his analysis of consumption in *The Practice of Everyday Life*. Understood as active rather than passive, consumption is seen by de Certeau as offering the opportunity to repurpose commodity culture in a way that escapes or challenges social expectations. For de Certeau, consumption retains the possibility of transforming otherwise imposed products or lifestyles. Michel de

Certeau, *The Practice of Everyday Life,* trans. Steven F. Rendall (Berkeley: University of California Press, 1984), 31.

23. The 1993 biennial was controversial for the kinds of work it exhibited, particularly overtly "political" work by artists who were interested in exploring questions of racism and sexism in their work. The show had mixed reviews, and many accused the curators of simply showing "bad" art. The hostility of the reaction revealed the degree to which the work in fact struck a nerve in the art community, which is often as politically conservative as it is fiscally conservative.

24. Interview with the author, August 30, 1995.

25. Santería evolved out of an effort by Africans, displaced by the international slave trade, to practice their own religious traditions under the guise of an imposed Catholicism. Arturo Lindsay credits the endurance of Yoruba traditions in the Americas, the cultural pride in an African heritage, and the shift from a modern to a postmodern form of art practice for the efflorescence of what he calls "*Santería* aesthethics" in contemporary Latin American art. The situational aesthetics and transitory qualities of conceptual and installation art of the 1970s, linked with a desire to revive a lost cultural heritage, offered ideal conditions for the installation of temporary, ritual-based Santería altars in the context of galleries and community-based art centers. Many artists working within a Santería paradigm saw their works as part of an ongoing healing practice linking the human with the divine, the past with the present. See Robert Farris Thompson, *Face of the Gods: Art and Altars of Africa and the African Americas* (New York: The Museum of African Art, 1993), and Arturo Lindsay, *Santería Aesthetics in Contemporary Latin American Art* (Washington, DC: Smithsonian Institution Press, 1996).

26. For a contemporary analysis of Santería influence in the United States, see Erwan Dianteill, "Deterritorialization and Reterritorialization of the Orisha Religion in Africa and the New World (Nigeria, Cuba and the United States)," *International Journal of Urban and Regional Research* 26, no. 1: 121–137.

27. Thompson, *Face of the Gods,* 218.

28. Eduardo Galeano, *Memory of Fire: Genesis* (New York: Pantheon, 1985), 193.

29. In *Collectibles* (1995), Fred Wilson constructed such a patterned "club" out of fragments from the "Mammy" figurines that were smashed in one of the videos—as a reclamation and transformation of racist material culture. Similar bats can be bought in many *botánicas* (Yoruba herbal stores), richly decorated with red and white beads. Thompson, *Face of the Gods,* 241.

30. Thompson, *Face of the Gods,* 192.

31. Ibid.

32. Tiffany Ana López, "Imaging Community: Video in the Installation Work of Pepón Osorio," *Art Journal* 54, no. 4 (Winter 1995): 59. López also observes, "Osorio establishes a direct connection between the wounded body of the crime scene and the imag(in)ing of Latino bodies in dominant cultural production, most especially in Hollywood film, by using video to underscore the relationship between representation and the real" (ibid., 59).

33. See Adrian Piper, *Out of Order, Out of Sight* (Cambridge, MA: The MIT Press, 1996).

34. Victor Burgin, *The End of Art Theory* (Atlantic Highlands: Humanities Press International, 1986), 204.

35. Interview with the author, August 30, 1995.

36. White, "*Rescatar y Descargar,*" 24.

37. Will K. Wilkins, in *Pepón Osorio: En La Barberia No Se Llora,* exhibition catalog (Hartford, CT: Real Art Ways, 1994), n.p.

38. López, "Imaging Community," 64.

39. Wilkins, *Pepón Osorio:* n.p.

40. Coco Fusco, *Pepón Osorio: En La Barberia No Se Llora,* exhibition catalog (Hartford: Real Art Ways, 1994), n.p.

41. Hans-Ulrich Obrist, "An Interview with Pepón Osorio," in *Pepón Osorio: Door to Door* (San Juan, PR: EAP Press, 2000), 6.

42. Interview with the author, August 30, 1995.

43. Fusco, in *Pepón Osorio,* n.p.

44. López provides an excellent account of Osorio's use of video in her essay "Imaging Community"(see note 32). López links Osorio's earlier use of performance and dance to his later inclusion of video monitors, suggesting that the video images are the primary source for the presentation of the corporeal ground around which the rest of the installation's artifacts congregate. While less the case with *Scene of the Crime (Whose Crime?)* or his earlier works, I do think that this is a correct reading of *La Barbería.* See López, "Imaging Community," 61.

45. Henri Lefebvre, *The Production of Space* (Oxford: Blackwell, 1991), 38.

46. Joseph Jacobs, "Pepón Osorio: Badge of Honor," in *Project 5: Pepón Osorio, Badge of Honor/Insignia de Honor,* exhibition catalog (Newark, NJ: The Newark Museum, 1996), 6.

47. Interview with the author, April 1996.

48. Jacobs, "Pepón Osorio," 4.

49. Quotes taken by the author at the time of the discussion.

50. Despite recent declines, the pregnancy rate of Hispanic teenagers is still double that of white teenagers: "The pregnancy rate among Hispanic teenagers, who may be of any race, increased from 162 to 170 per 1,000 women aged 15–19 between 1990 and 1992, but then fell to 138 per 1,000 by 2000—15% below the 1990 rate." *U.S. Teenage Pregnancy Statistics Overall Trends, Trends by Race and Ethnicity and State-by-State Information* (New York: The Alan Guttmacher Institute, 2004), 2.

51. Mervyn C. Alleyne, *The Construction and Representation of Race and Ethnicity in the Carribbean and the World* (Kingston, Jamaica: University of the West Indies Press, 2002), 121.

52. Clara E. Rogriguez, "Puerto Ricans: Between Black and White," in *Historical Perspectives on Puerto Rican Survival in the United States,* ed. Clara E. Rodriquez and Virginia Sanchez Korrol (Princeton, NJ: Markus Wiener Publishers, 1996), 25.

53. The first census undertaken in Puerto Rico in 1530 showed 369 whites, 473 free "protected" Indians, 675 Indian slaves, 1,168 black African male slaves, and 355 black African female slaves. It was not until 1873 that slavery was abolished in Puerto Rico. Manuelo Maldonado-Denis, *Puerto Rico: A Socio Historic Interpretation,* trans. Elena Vialo (New York: Random House, 1972), 16–17.

54. Interview with the author, June 2006.

55. Interview with the author, June 2006.

56. Interview with the author, June 2006.

57. The Honorable Fredrica A. Massiah-Jackson, whose brother also happens to be MacArthur Fellow, was sympathetic to Osorio's request.

58. Francisco Valdes, Jerome McCristal Culp, and Angela P. Harris, "Battles Waged, Won and Lost: Critical Race Theory at the Turn of the Millennium," in *Crossroads, Directions and a New Critical Race Theory,* ed. Francisco Valdes, Jerome McCristal Culp, and Angela P. Harris (Philadelphia, PA: Temple University Press, 2002), 1–2.

59. Ibid.

60. Rosalind Deutsche, *Evictions: Art and Spatial Politics* (Cambridge, MA: The MIT Press, 1996), 59.

61. See, for example, Jean Yves Toussaint and Monique Zimmermann, *User, Observer, Programmer et Fabriquet l'Eespace Public* (Lausanne, France: Presses Polytechnique et Universitaires Romandes, 2001).

62. See Suzanne Lacy, *Mapping the Terrain: New Genre Public Art* (Seattle, WA: Bay Press, 1995).

63. Kwon writes, "Collective artistic practice is a projective enterprise. It involves a provisional group, produced as a function of specific circumstances instigated by an artist and/or a cultural institution, aware of the effects of these circumstances on the very conditions of the interaction, performing its own coming together and coming apart as a necessarily incomplete modeling or working-out of a collective social process.... Such a praxis also involves a questioning of the exclusions that fortify yet threaten the group's own identity." Kwon, *One Place after Another,* 154.

64. Grant Kester, *Conversation Pieces: Community + Communication in Modern Art* (Berkeley: University of California Press, 2004), 122.

65. Ibid., 112, 114.

66. Obrist, "An Interview with Pepón Osorio," 14. See also Laura Roulet, *Contemporary Puerto Rican Installation Art: the Guagua Aérea, the Trojan Horse, and the Termite* (San Juan, PR: Editorial de la Universidad de Puerto Rico, 2000) where she discusses Osorio's work in relation to the idea of the Trojan horse. This comparison addresses the artist's strategy to move into potentially hostile territory, but it misses the fact that Osorio's tactics are not a form of surreptitious "infiltration" but are rather very visible interventions that transform the "host" space in obvious ways from the outset.

Chapter 5: Renée Green: Genealogies of Contact

1. Michel Foucault, "What Is Enlightenment?" in *The Foucault Reader,* ed. Paul Rabinow (New York: Pantheon Books, 1984), 46. Foucault's use of genealogy follows from that defined by Friedrich Nietzsche who rejects any historical search for origins (*Ursprung*) in favor of an analysis that marks paths of descent (*Herkunft*) or emergence (*Entstehung*).

2. Foucault, "What Is Enlightenment?" 83.

3. Alex Alberro, "The Fragment and the Flow: Sampling the Work of Renée Green," in *Shadows and Signals,* exhibition catalog (Barcelona: Fondació Antoni Tapies, 2000), 20.

4. To some degree this topological approach is comparable to the work of Pierre Huyghe and Philip Parreno who seek to *translate* events without directly representing them, to push the limits of a given set of practices to see how they can be deformed, yet retain their original structure. See George Baker, "An interview with Pierre Huyghe," *October* 110 (Fall 2004): 91.

5. Pauli Murray, ed., *States' Laws on Race and Color* (Athens: University of Georgia Press, 1997).

6. See Sander Gilman, *Difference and Pathology: Stereotypes of Sexuality, Race and Madness* (Ithaca, NY: Cornell University Press, 1985), and Yvette Abrahams, "Images of Sara Bartman: Sexuality, Race, and Gender in Early-Nineteenth-Century Britain," in *Nation, Empire, Colony: Historicizing Gender and Race,* ed. Ruth Roach Pierson and Nupur Chaudhuri (Bloomington: Indiana University Press, 1998), 220–236.

7. According to Walter Benn Michaels in his book *Our America,* the original book to which Tom refers was called *The Rising Tide of Color against White World-Supremacy* by Lothrop Stoddard. Walter Benn Michaels, *Our America* (Durham, NC: Duke University Press, 1995), 23.

8. Francis Ellen Watkins Harper, *Lola Leroy: Or Shadows Uplifted* (Oxford: Oxford University Press, 1988). First published in 1892.

9. For *One and Three Chairs,* Joseph Kosuth installed a wooden chair, next to a life-size photograph of the same chair and a large-scale typed dictionary definition of the word "chair." Each time the chair was reinstalled a new photograph of it was taken, in situ, and printed for the installation. In this way, the work was both a conceptual engagement with systems of representation (language, photography, construction), and also a site-specific installation that existed largely as a set of instructions for others to carry out.

10. Roland Barthes, "From *the Neutral*: Session of March 11, 1978," trans. Rosalind Krauss, *October 112* (Spring 2005): 8–9.

11. Ibid., 12.

12. See Stuart Hall, "The After-Life of Franz Fanon: Why Fanon? Why Now? Why *Black Skin, White Masks*?" in *The Fact of Blackness: Franz Fanon and Visual Representation,* ed. Alan Read (London: Institute of Contemporary Art and Seattle: Bay Press, 1996), 20. A comparison might be made with James Luna's *Chapel of the Sacred Colors* as well.

13. Renée Green, quoted in Donna Harkavy, "Insights: Renée Green," *Bequest,* exhibition brochure (Worcester: Worcester Art Museum, 1991), 4.

14. Edgar Allen Poe, *The Raven*; Herman Melville, *Moby Dick*; and W. E. B. DuBois, *Strivings of the Negro People.*

15. For more information, see Waldo Lincoln, "Stephen Salisbury," *New England Historical and Genealogical Register* 60 (October 1906): 326–329. Also see the American Antiquarian Society website: www.americanantiquarian.org/Exhibitions/Portraits/stephensalisbury3.htm.

16. The artist has commented, "Determining how to communicate to a viewer involves setting up spatial relationships between the viewer and the work. This comes partly from my own predilection for thinking in spatial terms and partly from an effort to have the viewer move through the work in a particular way. The architectural, or site-specific, aspects of the work relate to, among other things, notions of travel or movement." Harkavy, "Insights," 1.

17. Cornel West, "Race and Social Theory," in *The Cornel West Reader* (New York: Basic Books, 1999), 262.

18. West, "Race and Social Theory," 263.

19. "Between and Including," exhibition brochure (Wien: Secession und die Künstlerin, 1999), n.p.

20. Arthur C. Danto, *Encounters and Reflections: Art in the Historical Present* (New York: Farrar, Straus & Giroux, 1990), 139.

21. http://visit-bretagne.com/villages/clisson/ (2003).

22. Renée Green, *Certain Miscellanies: Some Documents* (Amsterdam: De Appel Foundation, 1996), 131.

23. Harkavy, "Insights," 2.

24. "Textiles to pay for slaves became so important … that in 1780 Nantes had more than 10 textile mills, employing 4,500 workers. One ship of slaves could yield up to three or four shiploads of coffee, sugar, indigo, cacao, cotton—produced by slave labor. Back in Nantes, as elsewhere in Europe, this cargo spawned sugar, chocolate, and textile mills. Because of this economic web, Nantes kept trading slaves clandestinely for almost 20 years after France banned it in 1817." Marlise Simon, cited in Green, *Certain Miscellanies,* 135.

25. Alberro, "The Fragment and the Flow," 32.

26. Giorgio Agamben, *Remnants of Auschwitz: The Witness and the Archive* (New York: Zone Books, 1999), 158.

27. Adrian Piper, "Notes on Funk I–IV," in *Adrian Piper: Out of Order, Out of Sight* (Cambridge, MA: The MIT Press, 1996), 198.

28. Green, *Certain Miscellanies,* 71–72.

29. Green comments, "I don't think didacticism is wrong; it's just not my particular desire. I'm more interested in sparking the viewer to ponder something, especially the very blurry divisions between fiction and history. My work serves a more heuristic purpose: it functions just as a hint." Harkavy, "Insights," 6.

30. Although the original installation was acquired by the Los Angeles Museum of Contemporary Art in 1996, Green has also produced a digital version of the project in the form of a compact disk that can be regularly updated, providing users the opportunity to access the tapes and interviews through an electronic interface.

31. Kwon, *One Place after Another,* 52.

32. Mary Louise Pratt, cited in Renée Green, "Slippages" in *Radiotemporaire* (Grenoble, France: Magasin Grenoble, 2000), 350.

33. See Andrea Fraser, "What's Intangible, Transitory, Mediating, Participatory, and Rendered in the Public Sphere?" *October* 80 (Spring 1997): 111–116.

34. For a good description of this, see Kwon, *One Place after Another,* 140–141.

35. Renée Green, "Scenes From a Group Show: Project Unité," in *Site Specificity: The Ethnographic Turn,* vol. 4, *de-,dis-,ex-.,* ed. Alex Coles (London: Black Dog Publishing Limited, 1999), 114–134.

36. Piper, "In Support of Meta-Art," in *Conceptual Art: A Critical Anthology,* ed. Alexander Alberro and Blake Stimson (Cambridge, MA: The MIT Press, 1999), 298–301.

37. Green, "Scenes from a Group Show," 134.

38. Renée Green, *After the Ten Thousand Things/Na de tien duizend dingen* (Den Haag: Stroom haags centrum voor beeldende kunst, 1994), 1.

39. Renée Green, "Doris Berger Speaks with Renée Green," *Küstlerbücher/Artist's Books* (Wien: Universität für angewandte Kunst, 2001), 43.

40. Green, *After the Ten Thousand Things,* 13.

41. Ibid., 15.

42. Ibid., 87.

43. Ibid., 9.

44. This is evident in the intertextual references between the books, as well as in terms of the works that are referenced and the critical concerns that are addressed. As collections of words and images at the intersection of two languages, the books map the artist's circuit through cultural contact zones. Several of the books were published by Free Agent Media (FAM), the artist's own publishing venture. "'Free Agent Media,'" the artist writes, "was a kind of imaginary company, a dream company, actually. I was using it as a kind of platform for producing things in different formats, from books to films and videos to cd-roms and so on." In a short manifesto for FAM, Green writes, "In the past we have seen artists imitate museums and factories, as well as publishing endeavors. Artists have often mimicked official institutions and functions, sometimes as ironic yet metaphorical gestures and sometimes as functioning operations which allow artistic play and business sense. Just remember the Bureau de Recherches Surréalistes, Broodthaers's Museum, Warhol's Factory. Artists are always making up mirror institutions reflecting dominant society.... While stemming from a related desire to collect as well as function in a position of strength in relationship to society, to bring into the world things which we want to exist, FAM seeks to maneuver between irony and sincerity." By setting up her own publishing venue, the artist is also able to work around the constraints of mainstream book publishing and to further develop the critique of systems of representation inherent in the rest of her work. Green, *Certain Miscellanies,* 93.

45. Renée Green, "Survival: Ruminations on Archival Lacunae, Adaptations, Re-readings, and New Readings. Introduction to the Following Ongoing Accretive Process," in *Interarchive* (Köln: Verlag der Buchhandlung Walther König, 2002), 149.

46. Ibid.

47. James Meyer, "The Return of the Sixties in Contemporary Art and Criticism," delivered at "Modernity and Contemporaneity: Anatomies of Art and Culture after the Twentieth Century," Carnegie International, November 2004. Paper printed from www.millikengallery.com/web_main/downloads/fg_meyertext.rtf (accessed September 2006), n.p.

48. See Kwame Anthony Appiah, "Cosmopolitan Patriots," *Critical Inquiry* 23 (Spring 1997): 617–639.

49. Samir Alschausky in *Übertragen/Transfer I* (1996), reprinted in *Shadows and Signals,* exhibition catalog (Barcelona: Fondació Antoni Tapies, 2000), 90.

50. The artist's father, quoted in *Partially Buried II* (1997), reprinted in *Shadows and Signals,* exhibition catalog (Barcelona: Fondació Antoni Tapies, 2000), 78.

51. Renée Green, quoted in *Shadows and Signals,* exhibition catalog (Barcelona: Fondació Antoni Tapies, 2000), 84.

52. Robert Smithson, "A Provisional Theory of Non-Sites," in *Robert Smithson: The Collected Writings,* ed. Jack Flam (Berkeley: University of California Press, 1996), 364.

53. Foucault, *The Foucault Reader,* 95.

54. Henri Bergson, *Matter and Memory* (New York: Zone Books, 1991), 133.

55. Bergson, *Matter and Memory,* 134.

56. Elizabeth Grosz notes that Freud's early models of the unconscious are topographical, representing in spatial terms what happens, in fact, temporally. Like Bergson, Freud also uses the metaphor of the camera for this topography—which is not so surprising given that he and Bergson are writing during an era (late eighteenth, early nineteenth century) when photography and the cinema are a new technological paradigm—but Freud's use is significantly different. Freud "asks us to look at the psyche as a 'compound instrument', a series of components within a machine, like a camera, where the components are spatially related in real or virtual space." Elizabeth Grosz, *Jacques Lacan, A Feminist Introduction* (London: Routledge, 1990), 83.

57. Sigmund Freud, *The Standard Edition of the Complete Psychological Works of Sigmund Freud* (London: The Hogarth Press, 1960), 320.

58. Ibid., 308.

59 Renée Green's *Code: Survey,* http://www.dot.ca.gov/dist07/code_survey/intro.htm.

60. See Nikos Papastergiadis, "Restless Hybrids," in *The Third Text Reader,* ed. Rasheed Araeen, Sean Cubitt, and Ziauddin Sardar (New York: Continuum, 2002), 166–176. Papastergiadis cites Yuri Lotman's notion of "semiosphere" that consists of the totality of the cultural system and the semiotic condition for the development of culture.

61. Michel Foucault, "Of Other Places," trans. Jay Miskowiec, *Diacritics* (Spring 1986): 22–27.

INDEX